WOMEN MADE VISIBLE

WOMEN MADE VISIBLE

Feminist Art and Media in Post-1968 Mexico City

GABRIELA ACEVES SEPÚLVEDA

University of Nebraska Press | Lincoln & London

Acknowledgments for the use of copyrighted
material appear on pages xvi–xvii, which constitute an extension of the copyright page.

Library of Congress
Cataloging-in-Publication Data
Names: Aceves Sepúlveda, Gabriela,
1973– author.
Title: Women made visible: feminist art and
media in post-1968 Mexico City / Gabriela
Aceves Sepúlveda.
Description: Lincoln: University of Nebraska
Press, 2019. | Series: The Mexican experience |
Includes bibliographical references and index.
Identifiers: LCCN 2018023889
ISBN 9781496202031 (cloth: alk. paper)
ISBN 9781496213242 (pbk.: alk. paper)
ISBN 9781496213839 (epub)
ISBN 9781496213846 (mobi)
ISBN 9781496213853 (pdf)
Subjects: LCSH: Feminism and the arts—
Mexico—Mexico City—History—20th cen-
tury. | Women in art. | Women in mass
media. | Women—Social conditions—
Mexico—Mexico City—History—20th
century. | Mexico City (Mexico)—
Social conditions—20th century.
Classification: LCC NX180.F4 A29 2018 |
DDC 701/.03—dc23 LC record available at
https://lccn.loc.gov/2018023889

Set in Minion Pro by Mikala R. Kolander.
Designed by L. Auten.

For Sofía

CONTENTS

ILLUSTRATIONS

The seeds of this book were planted in Guadalajara, Mexico, in the early 1990s when, as a young aspiring artist, I began to notice the workings of the male-dominated art system and the lack of women artists mentioned in art history books. It took a copious amount of time and many detours, including moving to another country, starting a family, and making several career adjustments, to have the opportunity finally to explore the issue at length.

Throughout the years that led to the completion of this book, I had the privilege of having the intellectual guidance and friendship of truly amazing people who inspired me and without whom this project would not have been possible. In some ways, this project is as much theirs as it is mine. The most necessary expressions of gratitude go to the archivists, curators, artists, and scholars in Mexico City who kindly guided me toward the materials without which this work would not exist. I am deeply grateful to Mónica Mayer, Ana Victoria Jiménez, Rosa Martha Fernández, Eli Bartra, Magali Lara, Maris Bustamante, Carla Rippey, Sarah Minter, Karen Cordero Reiman, and Cristina Híjar for allowing me to consult their archives and for taking the time to share with me their amazing life experiences and work, which became the inspiration and key sources for this project. Also providing valuable information and intellectual encouragement were Guillermina Guadarrama, Cynthia Pech, Emma Cecilia García, Ana Garduño, Alberto Híjar, Álvaro Vázquez Mantecón, Araceli Zuñiga, Cesar Espinoza, David Arriaga, Felipe Ehrenberg, Edna Torres, Renato González Mello, and Victor Muñoz. I am grateful to all those who assisted me at the Archivo General de la Nación, Galería 2 and 3; Biblioteca Central, UNAM; Biblioteca Daniel Cosío Villegas, COLMEX; Biblioteca de las Artes, Fondos Documentales; Biblioteca Justino Fernández, Instituto de Investigaciones Estéticas, UNAM; Centro Nacional de Investigación, Documentación e Información de Artes Plásticas, CENIDIAP; Filmoteca, UNAM; Fondo de la Secretaría de Educación Pública del Instituto de Bellas Artes, INBA; Hemeroteca Nacional, UNAM; Museo de Arte Carillo Gil; Museo de Arte Moderno; and Promotora Fernando Gamboa. Many thanks to Pilar García de Germenos, curator of collections at ARKEHIA (MUAC-UNAM), for providing access to important material and offering institutional support and lots of encouragement. I am also thankful to Ariel Rodríguez Kuri and Guillermo Palacios y Olivares from El Colegio de México for supporting the early stages of research in Mexico City. Outside Mexico, I am grateful to all those at the Special Collections at Stanford University Libraries.

I especially owe an enormous debt to William E. French and Alejandra Bronfman, who continuously provided intellectual guidance, friendship, and encouragement. Bill was always kind and generous in his determination to make me think like a historian and, in particular, enormously patient in his efforts to make me a better writer. Alejandra always found time and encouragement for me. Whether it was to clarify a concept or to discuss my most pressing personal and academic doubts, Alejandra constantly provided intellectual challenges and guidance that have crucially shaped me as a scholar and teacher. Both Bill and Alejandra have been vitally important in every stage of this book and have truly inspired me to be a historian.

Others have been equally generous with their feedback and encouragement. I am particularly grateful to Jessica Stites-Mor from the University of British Colombia, Okanagan, for her trust in and fundamental support for this project. In the Department of History at the University of British Colombia, I am thankful to Robert Brain for being incredibly generous with his intellect and time; to Michel Ducharme for providing enormous amounts of support; and to Carla Nappi for inspiring me to bring excitement and politics to the history classroom and to think about media more broadly. In Guadalajara, Arturo Camacho from El Colegio de Jalisco and María Teresa Fernández-Aceves from CIESAS Occidente were generous with their time and advice.

The list of friends and colleagues with whom I have shared this time and who, whether explicitly or inadvertently, have played a part in this project is very long. I am particularly grateful to Oralia Gomez-Ramírez, Noa Grass, Laura Madokoro, Ruth Mandujano, Alessandra Santos, and Tucker Sharon for their friendship, courage, and intellect. May Chazan and Melissa Baldwin introduced me to aging studies and encouraged me to think about archives and activism from a new perspective. Thanks are also due to Benjamin Bryce, who organized the monthly meetings of the BC Latin American History Group, which helped develop a community of scholars from which my manuscript also benefited greatly. Kathryn White offered great suggestions and the close reading that my manuscript needed. My colleagues at the School of Interactive Arts and Technology at Simon Fraser University provided a stimulating place to work and the much-needed support to finalize this book.

In Mexico, during the early stages of this project, Natalia Armienta Oikawa came to the rescue with her camera and, along with Lucy Maldonado, provided the best childcare services across Mexico (from Mexico City to Guadalajara to Queretaro and back). I am always in debt to Alex for providing a home for all the family in Mexico City. I thank mis compañeras de vida del Instituto de Ciencias de Guadalajara, and Alejandra Gómez for virtually being with me all the time and keeping things real.

At University of Nebraska Press I would like to thank Bridget Barry for her guidance and support. The two reviewers, of which Mary Coffey was one, offered enormous encouragement and insightful comments that pushed my arguments further, and they deserve a great deal of thanks.

From the time I began research for this book to the time it got published, Latin American women artists have gained more visibility thanks to the organization of numerous conferences, workshops, panels, and exhibitions across the world. At times when other projects and life seem to get in the way, many of these efforts inspired the culmination of this project.

I am thankful to all of those who are working in the field and whose work continues to inspire me.

Special thanks go to my mother, Gabriela, for her unconditional support and for teaching me how to be an artist and how to *agarrar el toro por los cuernos*, and to my father, Félix, and brother, Félix, for inspiring me to work as hard as they do and for their loving attempts to understand why I do what I do. Finally, and most of all, my thanks go to my partner, Roberto, for his love, patience, and endless support, and to Sofía for making the last eight years of my life the most exciting. I dedicate this work to her with the hope that she will be as inspired as I am by the life histories of the remarkable women mentioned in this book.

The book would not have been possible without the funding of the Department of History and the Faculty of Graduate Studies at the University of British Columbia, the Social Sciences and Humanities Research Council (SSHRC), the Consejo Nacional para la Ciencia y la Tecnología (CONACYT), the Canada–Latin American and the Caribbean Research Exchange Grants (LACREG), and the Simon Fraser University Publication Fund.

Parts of chapter 3 were published in "*¡Estamos Hartas!* Feminist Performances, Photography, and the Meanings of Political Solidarity in 1970s' Mexico," in *The Art of Solidarity: Visual Poetics of Empathy*, edited by Jessica Stites-Mor and Maria del Carmen Suescun Pozas (University of Texas Press, 2018), 149–92. Parts of chapters 4 and 6 were published in "Feminism as Counter-Archive: The Collections of Ana Victoria Jiménez, Mexico City, 1970–1990," *Views from the Edge*, 18, no. 1 (2010): 56–71; and in "Being Remembered: Activist Archiving and the Feminist Movement in Mexico," in *Activist Aging: Older, Bolder, and Changing the World*, edited by May Chazan, Pat Evans, and Melissa Baldwin (Women's Press, 2018), 194–207. A version of chapter 8 was published in "*¿Cosas de Mujeres?*: Film, Performance and Feminist Networks of Collaboration Enunciated from Mexico in the 1970s," *Artelogie Recherches sur les arts, le patrimoine et la littérature de l'Amérique latine, No. 5*: "Art et genre: Femmes créatrices en Amérique Latine" (September 2013). Parts of chapter 9 were published in "Imagining the Cyborg in Náhuatl: Reading the Videos of Pola Weiss through Haraway's Manifesto for Cyborgs," *Platform: Journal of Media and Communication* 6, no. 2 (2015): 46–60; and "The Utopian Impulse in the Videos of Pola Weiss," in *Performing Utopias in the Contemporary Americas*, edited by Alessandra Santos and Kim Beauchesne (New York: Palgrave Macmillan, 2017), 283–300.

ABBREVIATIONS

AGN	Archivo General de la Nación
ARKEHIA	Centro de Documentación, Museo Universitario de Arte Contemporáneo
CAMVAC	Centro de Apoyo a Mujeres Violadas
CCC	Centro de Capacitación Cinematográfica
CENIDIAP	Centro Nacional de Investigación, Documentación e Información de Artes Plásticas
CIESAS	Centro Investigación y Estudios Superiores en Antropología
COLMEX	Colegio de México
CONACULTA	Consejo Nacional para la Cultura y las Artes
CONACITE I	Corporacion Nacional Cinematográfica de Trabajadores y Estado I
CONACITE II	Corporacion Nacional Cinematográfica de Trabajadores y Estado II
CONACINE	Corporación Nacional Cinematográfica
CM	Colectivo de Mujeres
CMF	Consejo Mexicano de Fotografía
CMF	Coalición de Mujeres Feministas
CUEC	Centro Universitario de Estudios Cinematográficos
DFS	Dirección Federal de Seguridad
DGIPS	Dirección General de Investigaciones Políticas y Sociales

FNALIDM	Frente Nacional por la Liberación y Los Derechos de las Mujeres
IBERO	Universidad Iberoamericana de la Ciudad de México
INAH	Instituto Nacional de Antropología e Historia
INBA	Instituto Nacional de Bellas Artes
INI	Instituto Nacional Indigenista
ISI	Import Substitution Industrialization
IWY	International Women's Year celebration
LF	Lucha Feminista
MAM	Museo de Arte Moderno
MAS	Mujeres en Acción Solidaria
MFM	Movimiento Feminista Mexicano
MLM	Movimiento de Liberación de la Mujer
MNM	Movimiento Nacional de Mujeres
MUAC	Museo Universitario de Arte Contemporáneo
MUCA	Museo Universitario de Ciencias y Artes
PAN	Partido de Acción Nacional
PCM	Partido Comunista Mexicano
PGN	Polvo de Gallina Negra
PRI	Partido de la Revolución Institucional
PRT	Partido Revolucionario Troskista
SINAFO	Sistema Nacional de Fototecas
STUNAM	Sindicato de Trabajadores de la UNAM
TGP	Taller de Gráfica Popular
UNAM	Universidad Autónoma de México
UNMM	Unión Nacional de Mujeres Mexicanas

WOMEN MADE VISIBLE

Introduction

WOMEN MADE VISIBLE

Como mujer lo que más me disgusta de la ciudad es . . .
(as a woman, what I most dislike of the city is . . .)
—Mónica Mayer

In the spring of 1978 visitors to the New Tendencies exhibition in the Museum of Modern Art in Mexico City encountered a wooden frame structure that resembled a clothesline, a place where women traditionally hung clothes to dry, among the other fifty-nine artworks that were part of the exhibition. *El tendedero* (The Clothesline), a participatory art installation by Mónica Mayer, consisted of more than eight hundred small pieces of pink paper hung at somewhat regular intervals, fastened by clothespins to lines of yarn that were tied to the wooden frame (fig. 1). On each piece of paper Mayer wrote the phrase, "as a woman, what I most dislike about the city is . . . (*Como mujer lo que más me disgusta de la ciudad es . . .*), and she distributed these around Mexico City to more than eight hundred women of different ages, social classes, and professions and asked them to write a response. Then she attached the papers to the clothesline to create *El tendedero*. During its exhibition at Mexico City's Museum of Modern Art many other women also wrote their thoughts on the pink pieces of paper. The written responses ranged from feeling threatened to being called names such as *mamacita* (hot momma) or getting a *nalgada* (spank on the bum). The answers articulated how the

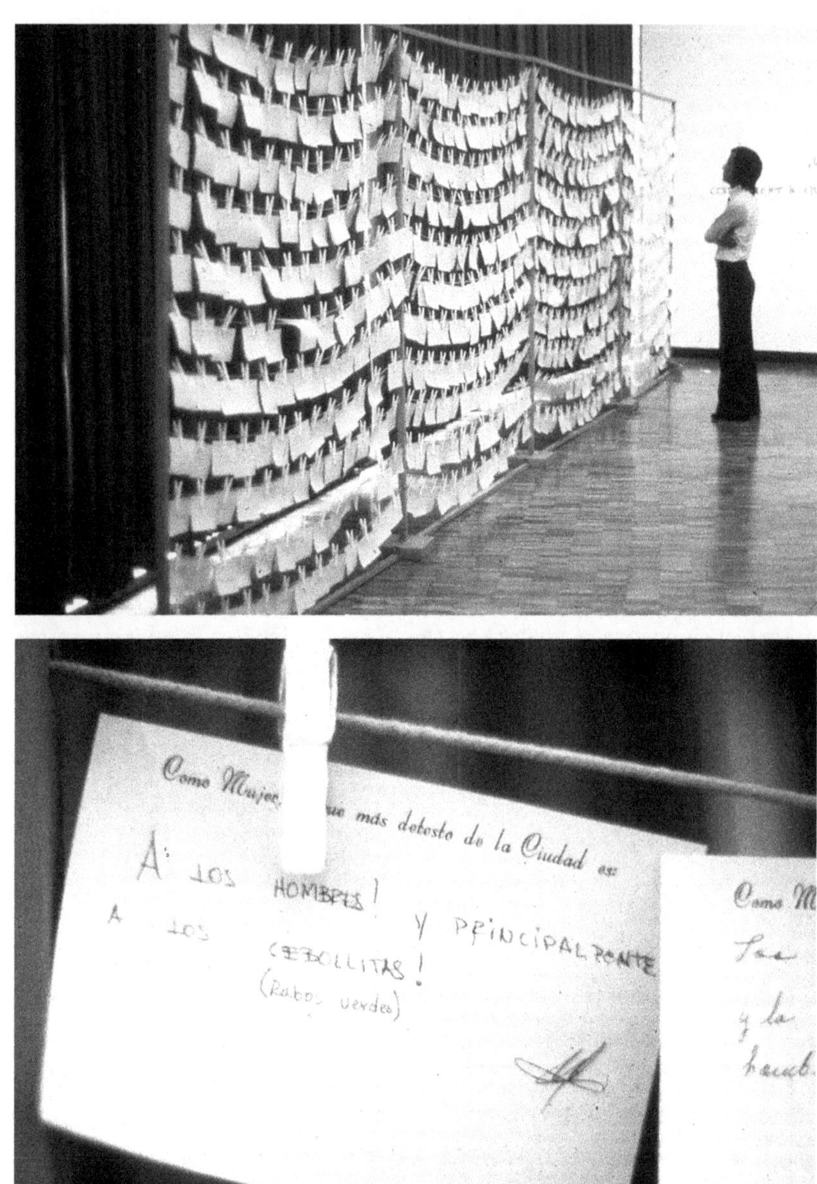

FIG. 1. *El tendedero.* © 1978 by Mónica Mayer. Photo courtesy of the artist.

participants' experience of the city was mediated by the sexualization of their female bodies.

By the 1970s Mexico City was already considered one of the world's largest urban settlements. The push for urbanization and industrialization in the prior two decades had not only offered a concrete face-lift but had also attracted numerous migrants to the capital city. Many of its residents were adjusting to new urban spatial dynamics brought about by rapid growth and development (busy expressways, shady underpasses, dimly lit subway tunnels, and isolating concrete high-rises). In response to these urban changes Sebastián and Mathias Goeritz, the organizers of the exhibition, adopted the city as a theme to bring together fifty-nine young artists (thirty-three Mexican and twenty-six international) whose practice involved the newest trends in the arts.[1] While all the fifty-nine pieces in the show addressed the effects of urban development on people's lives, the work of Mayer stood out due to its focus on the ways the female body was sexualized throughout Mexico City streets. In recording what women detested most about the city, *El tendedero* mapped out a series of encounters between bodies as they were experienced through urban space, and through these encounters, the female body emerged as one that was threatened and was only ascribed value in sexual terms.

By installing a clothesline in an art museum to exhibit the ways in which women's experience of urban space was mediated through their bodies in highly gendered and sexualized terms, Mayer was also transgressing the divide between the public and the private, a key issue at the time for feminist artists and activists like Mayer. In Spanish, the word *tendedero* refers not only to a place of female domestic labor (where women gather to hang clothes after washing them); the term is also used pejoratively to signal a place where women gather to talk, gossip, and reveal things to one another. Alluding to the double meaning of the term, *El tendedero* transformed a traditionally private female sphere into a public one by making women's everyday experiences, which do not normally belong in an art museum, visible to the public. In so doing, Mayer's *El tendedero* elevated female domestic labor to the stature of art and thus momentarily transformed the art museum into a public forum where women's everyday experiences could be discussed and made visible.

Bringing together practices of sociological and participatory art to record and store information, *El tendedero* also resembles one of the most ancient practices of filing important things. As Sven Spieker recalls, "hanging or stringing up objects to a rope was one of the first forms of filing." Even nowadays, many agree with Spieker that archives come into being "when several documents that share a common subject are combined by either physically tying them together in a binder of some sort or grouping them as a loose collection."[2] I am interested in *El tendedero* not only because it resembles an archive of sorts due to its form but also because it interrogates and furthers the notion of the archive through the kind of information it seeks to record, how it does so, and to what ends. In *El tendedero* Mayer turned to the archive to point to its absences by recording women's everyday experiences and making them visible in a museum of modern art. The installation also disrupts the institutional order of the archive by using a domestic format to file and store data. At the same time, the participatory aspect of the installation produced new records that not only made evident the ways in which sexual difference was constructed and experienced through the streets of Mexico City but, most important, prioritized women as the agents of the archive.[3]

This book is about a group of women who, like Mayer, produced visual and material records of female bodies by taking on the task of creating and keeping visual representations and statistical information about how gendered, classed, racialized, and sexed bodies were produced in relation to the urban landscape. It traces a shift in the ways women would represent, conceptualize, and politicize their bodies in response to the particular context of Mexico City, with both national and transnational ramifications and connections, and particularly framed within the reemergence of new wave feminisms around the world, the hosting of the first United Nations Women's Year Conference (Mexico City, 1975), and important reforms granting Mexican women equality (on paper, 1974).[4] These transformations also included key shifts in the Mexican intellectual sector and the increased influence of broadcast media and participation of women in such industries. Equally important, however, was the increased public visibility of gay and lesbian urban activists and of diverse generations of political actors who were radicalized by the events of 1968 and the reverberations of the Cuban, Guatemalan, Nicaraguan, and Salvadorean revolutions along with the many transnational networks they fostered.

More specifically, this book explores how the visual and embodied manifestations of feminist activists and media artists—Ana Victoria Jiménez (b. Mexico City, 1941), Rosa Martha Fernández (b. Mexico City, 1942), Pola Weiss (b. Mexico City, 1947), and Mónica Mayer (b. Mexico City, 1954)—challenged established structures of power and knowledge and the ways in which their practices opened up avenues of expression to different forms of political subjectivity. In doing so, I contend that their works constructed a different range of archives (both in content and in form) from which alternative histories could emerge and spoke to changing and emerging regimes of media and visuality in which normative representations of the female body—both aesthetically and in formal politics—were being contested.

I use the term *regimes of media and visuality* to point to the ways in which politics has to do not only with institutions but also with the complex and constitutive field of power relations in everyday life and, most important, with how media (understood broadly) and the way we see, how we see, and what is allowed to be seen (visuality) strategically intervene in the production and deployment of such power relations and in the production of knowledge.[5] The films, photographs, videos, exhibitions, and performances that these women created were developing both new discourses and visual representations of the female body and also new ways of seeing and looking at the female body across different media, including the built environment. In so doing, they actively participated in the production, distribution, and circulation of regimes of media and visuality that would be mobilized to make claims for women's sexual reproduction rights and to denounce and criminalize violence against women.

The development of these new regimes was influenced by, even as it helped shape, three important shifts within the Mexican intellectual sector of the second half of the twentieth century. First was the broad shift away from an exclusive emphasis on literate-print culture and toward an embrace of audiovisual communications; second was the increased participation of women in the public sphere; and third was the reemergence of the feminist movement that gave rise to diverse political sensibilities. These three changes were indicative of larger transformations in historically constituted fields of power and knowledge.[6] In Latin America these fields of power and knowledge have been theorized by Angel Rama as being constituted by lettered urban men (the *letrados*) who held power over written discourse and by the central role of the city in deploying and reproducing that power.[7]

This book draws from Rama's attention to written media and discourse, urban living, and power to trace the development of what I call the *visual letradas*—self-identified women who, by the second half of the twentieth century, became more openly concerned with performing and recording audiovisual information about how their bodies were visually construed and politicized. I use the term to point to an increased participation of women in intellectual spheres of influence previously conceptualized as privileged masculine territory, the space of the letrados. While women in Mexico have fought for women's rights and Mexican women artists have portrayed and interrogated normative gender roles at least since early twentieth century, the role of Mexican women was radically altered following World War II. After gaining their right to vote and be elected to office in 1955, Mexican women held posts as ambassadors, magistrates, and high-level bureaucrats. By the time new wave feminists began demonstrating in the streets of Mexico City, the government had already set out a family planning media campaign to promote the use of birth control methods. In combination with the advent of new audiovisual technologies and advances in the broadcasting industry, these events unleashed a sexual revolution that granted independence for some women but also altered the ways female bodies were construed and represented in public discourse. New avenues of expression were opened up for women to express diverse and competing political subjectivities, including conflicting visual representations of female bodies. In this context, visual letradas took on the task of producing and keeping visual representations of their bodies in order to construct a different range of visual and performative archives that made women's rights a central issue of public debate.

In this book I explore how the practices of the visual letradas speak to a shift in the letrado tradition as audiovisual media (mostly television broadcasting and video) began to take more prominence over written discourse, and women began to have a more visible role in the public sphere. Using recently opened archives of the Mexican secret services (Dirección Federal de Seguridad and Dirección General de Investigaciones Políticas y Sociales) as well as photographic documentation on feminist demonstrations, oral testimonies, interviews, videos, performances, and films, this book maps out how the increased participation of women in Mexico's mediascapes shaped the emergence of competing political subjectivities that posited the female body, gender difference, and sexual violence at the forefront of public debates during the last decades of the twentieth century. In contrast to the closed disciplinary focus and national parameters that have characterized the twentieth-century Mexican historiography of feminisms, media, art, and women's history, in this investigation I use the archive, the city, and the media as the main categories of analysis to show the interconnections between disciplines. By bringing an interdisciplinary, local, and transnational lens to bear on these categories and by showing how visual letradas appropriated them as key spheres of action, this project narrates how normative representations of the female body (visually and in formal politics) were contested throughout Mexico City and how, in turn, such challenges affected and effected politics.

Feminizing the Space of the Letrado: The Archive, the Media, and the City

In Mexico, as in the rest of Latin America, keeping files, creating archives, and writing history have all been conceptualized as masculine territory. As Angel Rama has argued, the letrados have wielded power in Latin America since the colonial period. Letrados were magistrates, notaries, scribes and state-appointed *cronistas* (historians) who generated, wrote, and filed legal and historical documents that powerfully influenced the writing of history. For Roberto González Echevarría, the connections between Latin America, the writing of history, the archive, and letrados are fundamental. He argues that since Latin America "existed as a legal document before it was physically discovered," its origins are in the archive.[8] For Carlos Monsiváis, the gendered and exclusionary aspects that bind the writing of history and the archive in Mexico are evidenced, for example, in historical narratives of the 1910 Mexican Revolution. Most dominant narratives of the revolution, argues Monsiváis, are written according to a patriarchal doctrine positioning history as an exclusive masculine territory in which "neither power nor violence nor indubitable valor nor historic lucidity are women's issues."[9]

Nonetheless, despite the letrados' power, one cannot assume their reach or authority was all encompassing. As Kathy Burns argues, the documents they produced, and the practices through which these were produced, were highly mediated events wherein a multitude of desires, values, and power relations converged.[10] Moreover, their sphere of influence was not limited to the writing of documents but also included image-makers.[11] However, the identities and practices of the letrados as well as most public spheres of influence—formal politics and definitions of citizenship—were conceptualized in gendered terms as principally masculine.

In tracing the development of the visual letrada through the practices and different political subjectivities of Fernández, Jiménez, Weiss, and Mayer, I am not suggesting that women did not participate or engage in the letrados' sphere before the 1970s or that they refrained from attempts to destabilize the exclusively masculine nature of the overall patriarchal structures that drove Mexican political, social, and cultural structures up to that time. On the contrary, this project builds on the histories of women and feminisms of twentieth-century Mexico. I trace the continuities and ruptures of a process that began in the post-revolutionary period—or even earlier—and that feminized the spheres of influence of the letrados. By feminizing the sphere of influence of the letrado I do not point to a practice that corresponds to those who define themselves as women or as feminine, as if such an identity existed in the singular. Drawing from Nelly Richard's understanding of *feminization* as a process that breaks down the barriers of biological determinism and symbolic roles, I use feminizing to describe a process whereby the geographies of Mexico City (both symbolic and physical) became stages of contestation for many countercultural movements that sought justice and a change in the patriarchal structures of power.[12]

Writing in the 1960s, in the midst of worldwide urban unrest, to which the residents of Mexico City were no strangers, Henri Lefebvre defined cities as spatial and social products of human relations, and works of appropriation on the part of their residents, rather than as static entities produced by urban plans imposed upon them from above.[13] Lefevbre's productive and processual understanding of cities is crucial to the process that I refer to as feminizing the space of the letrado (in this case urban space), however I understand this process through the work of feminist scholars who have argued for the gendered, racialized, embodied, and performative dimensions of social relations that are crucial to understanding the production of space and the sense of self, place, and Other.[14] Hence, I conceptualize the multiple human and material interactions that shape the urban space of Mexico City—and in turn are shaped by it—as gendered and embodied experiences. These interactions (including those mediated by and through audiovisual communications) shape a sense of place, self, and Other that are always in flux and not limited to national or geographic boundaries. The city, while located in a particular topography, exists and is simultaneously produced outside its physical dimension through the movement of peoples, objects, and ideas. The city is thus conceived as an urban space that organizes and distributes social practices, but one that can never be fully comprehended. As García Canclini argues, it is only understood in fragments or imaginaries that exist simultaneously and at different levels.[15] Therefore the process of feminization of Mexico City that I map out takes place on multiple levels or spatial geographies; it flows through different mediascapes and across diverse local, national, and transnational networks. Here I extend the use of Arjun Appadurai's term *mediascapes* to refer to the messages that flow through all kinds of media (not only imaged based) and that elicit embodied responses from the audience, shaping in turn their sense of self and place as a crucial element that constitutes one of the cultural geographies of Mexico City.[16] As I discuss later in this introduction, in the 1970s Mexico City was increasingly experienced and imagined through broadcast media. Reforms in the film and television industry not only increased the participation of the private sector but also opened up professional opportunities for women. In spite of the growing importance of audiovisual media, media here are understood broadly to signal all the other intellectual fields of production—including written discourse (writing and publishing) and radio broadcasting—that were important avenues in the development of a feminist cultural critique and, most important, the visual arts, including street demonstrations and street theater, which were equally important spheres of action for the visual letradas. Hence I map how the increased participation of women in private, public, and independent media transformed Mexico City mediascapes.

Crucial to the transformation of the geographies of Mexico City was the widespread critique of the dominant patriarchal structures of power that ruled Mexican society. This critique was not only performed by feminist activists or those who defined themselves as women; it was also the product of a widespread dissatisfaction expressed by the mobilization of students, artists, intellectuals, and worker organizations that had become politicized by worldwide events such as the Cuban Revolution (1953–59), revolutions in Central America (1960s–90s), and the Vietnam War (1955–75). In Mexico the implementation of an economic model benefiting only a minority of the population and of a hardline style of government that violently repressed or co-opted any kind of opposition fed a sense of dissatisfaction among many youths, propelling a countercultural movement and a series of student-led demonstrations culminating in the massacre of students in 1968. Consequently, the feminization of urban space consists of a process whereby the geographies of Mexico City became stages of contestation for many oppositional movements that sought social justice amid a widespread social and political crisis. These movements sought to effect social change and contest hegemonic structures and institutions; that is, systems of knowledge and power considered to be masculine practices and discourses that both women and men were equally implicated in sustaining and reproducing. These movements included the emergence of gay and lesbian activism, workers' and urban popular movements, and student and countercultural movements that took to the streets of Mexico City to challenge its symbolic and physical order.

In locating the practices of Fernández, Jiménez, Weiss, and Mayer as meaningful expressions in this ongoing process of feminization, my aim is to discuss how the space in which these women enacted their interventions was feminized through diverse practices that were equally implicated in developing a space where gender and sexual difference could be enunciated. These spaces were not, however, without symbolic or physical violence.

The Outline of Visual Letradas

The first time I saw Mayer's *El tendedero* was as part of WACK! Art and the Feminist Revolution, at the Vancouver Art Gallery in 2009. At that time I didn't read it as an archive, but I did notice that it was the only artwork by a Mexican artist included in this worldwide survey of feminist art.[17] When I saw it, I was just beginning research on 1970s Mexico, a narrowly studied period in modern Mexican history. It is a decade that has, until recently, been overshadowed by the histories of 1968 and Mexico's economic transformation in the 1980s, or has been conceived either in laudatory or disparaging terms, due mostly to interpretations of President Luis Echeverría Álvarez's government (1970–76).[18] I was particularly interested in exploring the conjunctures that were unraveled by Echeverría's reforms in the cultural sector, beyond the feuds between intellectuals and artists who opposed or supported his policies.

At the time, I was researching Los Grupos, a diverse assemblage of artist collectives that attempted to rearticulate the relationship between visual arts and politics by taking art to the streets, establishing art collectives, and experimenting with non-traditional aesthetic languages (performances, installations, street happenings, graffiti, everyday objects, video, and super-8 film). In recent years Los Grupos' work has come to the attention of some scholars who are revising assessments of the rise of collectivism after 1945 and others who argue for including Latin American art in the international histories of conceptual art practices and who, as a result, are revising and recuperating post-1968 Mexican visual culture.[19] As part of my research, I interviewed Mónica Mayer for the first time in the summer of 2009. Through our conversations something that I was beginning to suspect became apparent: even in the context of the recent academic interest in revising post-1960 Mexican visual culture and Los Grupos' work, the legacies of Mexican feminism in the visual arts have been mostly ignored, not only by art historians but by feminist scholars, who were more interested in narrating the political successes and failures of the movement.[20] Besides her commenting on this issue and discussing her work and that of Los Grupos, what really caught my attention was Mayer's interest in and commitment to protecting artists' archives and archival practices, a growing concern of various artists and academics whom I was also interviewing at the time.[21]

Mayer introduced me to Ana Victoria Jiménez's archive, a photographic and ephemera collection of 1970s feminist activism and art in Mexico City. While studying Jiménez's archive, I couldn't help but notice the role that 1970s feminist collectives had in giving rise to distinct networks of women artists and creative practices that explored and politicized conceptions of the female body. Their practices and collaborations constituted experiments with different media and aesthetic languages (music, publications, street theater and demonstrations, film, photography, and television broadcasting). I realized that these experimentations were political not only because of the feminist demands that drove them but also because they entailed explorations across disciplines and through networks that challenged the parameters of the nation, Latin American solidarity, and artistic collectives as they were defined at the time. Rather than taking a narrow anti-Western stance or Third World vs. First World framework, characteristic of many attempts at collectivism at the time, these feminists built relations with non-Latin American feminists, and through those relations they affected and effected local politics. Their practices produced creative cross-fertilizations and interconnections between various fields, and in doing so, they questioned disciplinary boundaries and genres and, perhaps most important, historical metanarratives that defined the production of knowledge in the fields of feminism, media, and art.

Among the early participants in feminist collectives were Ana Victoria Jiménez, then a member and militant of the Unión Nacional de Mujeres Mexicanas (UNMM), and Rosa Martha Fernández, an emerging film director who had founded the feminist film collective Colectivo Cine-Mujer (1975–85).[22] Jiménez began participating in feminist demonstrations as early as 1971, when Mujeres en Acción Solidaria (MAS) organized a march toward the *Mother's Monument* on March 9 to demand a change in the ways mass media manipulated Mother's Day celebrations and objectified women.[23] From that moment onward, she took her camera and began documenting these demonstrations. She also preserved pamphlets, graphics, and posters that, along with her photographs and documentation of her artwork, now constitute a valuable—if only recently recognized—visual archive of the history of the feminist movement and of post-1968 Mexico.[24]

In 1975 Mayer and Jiménez found themselves collaborating in Fernández's Colectivo Cine-Mujer. From 1975 to 1985, Colectivo Cine-Mujer produced a series of films on issues affecting women, including abortion, rape, and prostitution. To raise consciousness about these issues, the early films of Cine-Mujer produced under Fernández's direction combined conventions of documentary film (interviews, testimonials, and archival footage, including Jiménez's photographs) with a fictional narrative. By fusing documentary and fictional cinematic strategies to address the ways in which the female body was the site of political, sexual, and cultural violence, these films also work as records of a potential archive of feminist demands, women's living conditions, and alternative modes of representing them.

Fernández decided to study film after her experience with Cooperativa de Cine Marginal (1971–75), an earlier film collective that produced super-8 films serving as communication tools between different workers' unions across the country.[25] Super-8 offered these collectives the ability to produce films independently (without a crew and with almost no budget)—a flexibility that would also be afforded by video later on. By then Fernández was already a university professor of psychology at Universidad Autónoma Nacional de México (UNAM). She had become politically active a few years earlier after witnessing the 1968 movement in Paris as a psychology student. She was then introduced to feminist activism while studying television production in Japan in 1972. Upon her return to Mexico, and parallel to her participation with Cooperativa de Cine Marginal, she participated in various feminist collectives, including Cine-Mujer, as well as small feminist consciousness-raising groups. In 1980 Fernández left Cine-Mujer and volunteered with the Sandinistas in Nicaragua, where she produced television programs for women and children and directed movies until her return to Mexico in 1984. Years later, as director of TV UNAM (1989–94), she negotiated the establishment of an archive of Pola Weiss's videos at TV UNAM.[26]

By the mid-seventies Pola Weiss (1947–90) was beginning to produce her first videos. Weiss graduated with degrees in political science and communications from UNAM in 1975, with the first thesis produced in video in Mexico.[27] In it, she proposed the use of video in the production of television programming outside the commercial parameters that defined Mexican television at the time. As a student and later an instructor in the Department of Social and Political Sciences at UNAM, Weiss wrote scripts and directed documentaries for television. While she championed television as an artistic medium, by 1977 she had complemented her work in television with a search for alternative and artistic uses of video. From 1977 until she took her own life in 1990, she produced more than thirty-eight videos through her own production company, artTV.[28]

Pola Weiss's videos *Somos mujeres* and *Ciudad-mujer-ciudad* were also shown at the February Biennial, and like Mayer's *El tendedero* also addressed the production of gendered, classed, and racialized corporealities in relation to an urban space. More important, her videos work as an archive of sorts that consists of keeping audiovisual records on how daily experiences are inscribed onto the female body.

In *Somos mujeres* the camera moves between psychedelic dissolves, modern buildings such as La Torre Latino Americana, and poor indigenous women begging on the streets with children in their arms (fig. 2). The soundtrack mixes dialogues in indigenous languages with the weeping sounds of women and children crying. At some point in the video we see the indigenous women throw things at Weiss's camera. Weiss's incorporation of feedback (the women's responses) speaks to her overall interest in exploring the alternative uses of video and television broadcasting as media that could reactivate the viewer through different visual strategies. It also, quite literally, reflects on class differences and competing perceptions of public and private space. In contrast to the gendered encounters mapped in Mayer's *El tendedero*, in *Somos mujeres* the encounters take place between differently classed and racialized female bodies. Weiss and her camera make visible how the intersections of class and race are produced and reproduced through the urban environment.

In *Ciudad-mujer-ciudad* Weiss weaves together two narratives by intermixing images of a naked female body with urban scenes using post-production techniques such as solarization effects and Chroma key to produce composite images (fig. 3). The first narrative represents the changing rhythms of a day in the city, from eve to dawn. The second narrative uses the female body as an allegory for urban decay, reinforced by the irruption of Weiss's voice stating, "*No hay agua porque tengo seca la boca . . . no, no hay agua, agua no fluye no corre, ciudad te hundes y nos hundimos contigo*" (There is no water because I have a dry mouth . . . there is no water, the water is not running, city you are drowning, and we are all drowning with you).[29] At the time, water shortages and rationing were commonplace for Mexico City residents, and media reports warned of imminent droughts to come.[30] In using post-production techniques and experimenting with the audiovisual medium, Weiss searched for a new language to express how everyday urban experiences were inscribed on the body and how, in turn, both natural and material ecologies and infrastructures were affected by urban changes and increasingly mediated through audiovisual means.

Unlike Fernández, Jiménez, and Mayer, Weiss was never a militant in any feminist collective. However, her work can be read as an expression of feminist concerns due to her approach to videomaking and her interest in

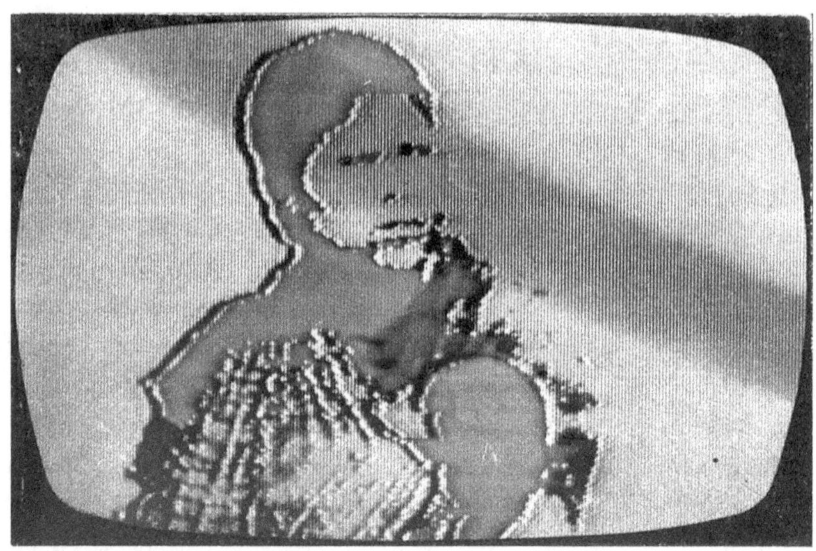

FIG. 2. *Somos mujeres.* © 1978 by Pola Weiss. Fondo Pola Weiss, Catalogación Edna Torres-Ramos, Centro de Documentación ARKEHIA, Museo Universitario Arte Contemporáneo, UNAM.

exploring alternative ways of representing the female body. Her practice was in meaningful dialogue with the work of other feminist-minded artists who, like her, experimented with video technologies in other places around the world. In the Mexican context, however, Weiss's experiments with video technology and performance were not only novel but, like the work of Fernández, Jiménez, and Mayer, showed an interest in archival technologies. As I will explain, Weiss, like Mayer, expanded the notion of an archive by using video as a medium to keep a record of her life but also as documentation of her performance—a use that was already prevalent within art circles all over the world.

Mónica Mayer's life trajectory, feminist activism, and interest in the archive shapes and delineates the interconnections and practices of the visual letradas discussed in this book. At the time of the 1978 New Tendencies exhibition at the Museum of Modern Art, Mayer was about to begin her studies at the Feminist Studio Workshop of the Women's Building in

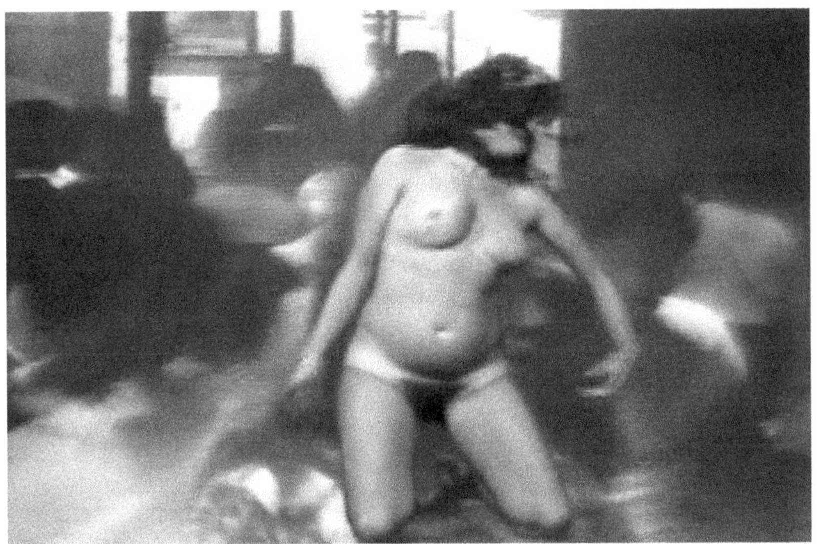

FIG. 3. *Ciudad-mujer-ciudad.* © 1978 by Pola Weiss. Fondo Pola Weiss, Catalogación Edna Torres-Ramos, Centro de Documentación ARKEHIA, Museo Universitario Arte Contemporáneo, UNAM.

Los Angeles, California.[31] Before going to LA, Mayer had participated in various feminist demonstrations in Mexico City organized by Movimiento Feminista Mexicano and had collaborated with Cine-Mujer, a feminist film collective established by Rosa Martha Fernández in 1975. Upon her return to Mexico in 1981 Mayer began to promote the development of feminist art in Mexico. She taught feminist art courses; established Polvo de Gallina Negra, a feminist art collective, with fellow artist Maris Bustamante; and she also promoted the establishment of other feminist artist groups. Parallel to all these activities Mayer developed a twin interest in the archive—a concern for keeping and recording information and for exploring the limits of what could be considered an archive—a concern that was already present in *El tendedero.*

Beginning in 2009, in the midst of a growing concern for recuperating the memory and practices of activists and artists active in the 1960s and 1970s, Mayer convened a group of scholars and artists to classify and digitize

Jiménez's archive, and in March 2011 Jiménez's archive was donated to the library of the Universidad Iberoamericana in Mexico City, a private academic institution.[32] It was through the reading of this archive that I began to map out the relations among these four women and the importance of 1970s feminism as an influence on their work.

The Archive at Two Distinct Moments

The practices of Fernández, Jiménez, Weiss, and Mayer developed at two distinct but interconnected moments that transformed the ways in which archives were conceived in Mexico. First, they emerged at a momentous time for international women's rights battles and in the midst of a violent decade in which the Latin American region wrestled with the devastating consequences of the Cold War. Second, attention to their archival practices resurfaced approximately three decades later, when the adoption of neoliberal economics and democratization treatises in Mexico, as elsewhere in Latin America, began to transform the state's role in managing valuable cultural and historical property, including archives. This second moment also coincided with worldwide transformations in patrimonial and archival discourses that challenged the power dominant social structures and institutions had in determining and controlling what is considered patrimony and what counts as an archive. From unearthing the remains and records of the victims of military dictatorships and state repression to feminists' demands over the inclusion of women in narratives of the era, the consequences of the Cold War and new wave feminisms continue to challenge the ways Latin American historians think about the post-1968 period. These two events continue to trouble discussions and explorations of what counts as an archive, what is considered the patrimony of the nation, and who has the right to determine which events are worth commemorating and how.

In Mexico the first moment was initially swayed by the populist policies of President Luis Echeverría Álvarez (1970–76). Echeverría's administration began with a nationwide campaign for democratization known as *apertura democrática*, a strategy aimed at siding with disenfranchised and defiant sectors of the population in order to redeem his popularity and that of the ruling party, both severely damaged after the massacre of students in Mexico City in 1968. In order to do so he implemented a series of wide-ranging reforms that targeted economic, political, and cultural sectors, including crafting an image of himself as an international Third World ambassador.[33] The hosting of the first United Nations International Women's Year Celebration in Mexico City in 1975 played an important role in supporting such goals. Equally important was the campaign to extend full rights of citizenship and social equality to the female population in 1974. However, at the same time, he continued to support a system of surveillance to spy on activists and leaders of diverse left-wing organizations. He continued to use violence to dispel demonstrations on the streets of Mexico City and brutally suppressed rural and urban radical activity in the rest of the country. As in previous years, agents working for the Mexican bureaus of secret intelligence (Dirección Federal de Seguridad, DFS, and Dirección General de Investigaciones Políticas y Sociales, DGIPS) infiltrated social movements and kidnapped and tortured several people.[34] Records of these activities, along with daily reports on all kinds of suspicious gatherings, were dutifully kept as part of the activities of these two organizations. It is not surprising, then, that a group of government agents and infiltrators followed several feminist activists, keeping detailed records and photographs of their daily activities.

A high point in the second moment began in 2002 as a result of the promises of Mexico's democratic transition. This moment was driven by debates regarding the protection of cultural patrimony brought about by the privatization of culture beginning in 1989 and the granting of public access to post-1968 archives as part of Mexico's transition to democracy during the latter decades of the twentieth century. After a long civic battle, public access to documentation of Mexico's 1968 student movement and 1970s Dirty War was tacitly granted as some DFS and DGIPS files were declassified and transferred to Mexico's National Archives (Archivo General de la Nación, AGN).[35] The records documenting feminist activism were filed in the same boxes in the AGN and possibly were included in the transfer.[36] These files were accessible to the public from 2002 to 2015, a time that coincided with the donation of Jiménez's archive to Universidad Iberoamericana de la Ciudad de México (IBERO), which represents a major undertaking for the recovery of the historical memory of the feminist movement and for the recent quest to preserve artists' archives and photographic archives, which, unlike Jiménez's archives, have not found a host institution or private funds for their conservation.

Equally significant, the institutionalization of Jiménez's archive through a private institution points to a shift in the management of cultural patrimony from an exclusively state endeavor to a private or mixed one, a transformation that took place in Mexico during the last three decades of the twentieth century. In regard to Mexico's photographic patrimony, a greater emphasis on its conservation, classification, and storage has been taking place since the establishment of Sistema Nacional de Fototecas (SINAFO) in 1993.[37] SINAFO coordinates approximately twenty photographic archives across the country from the central branch of the Fototeca Nacional in Pachuca, established in 1976 with the institutionalization of Casasola's archive. The content of these photographic archives is mainly focused on visual records that have a relation to national interests, such as the Mexican Revolution or previously consecrated artists. In contrast to the attention to certain photographic archives, the archives of artists working in the 1960s and 1970s have received little attention from the government.

Federal archives, like the ones managed by SINAFO, are considered patrimony of the nation and are protected under the federal law of Monumentos y Zonas Arqueológicos, Artísticos e Históricos (1972). In general, the president has the exclusive power to make patrimonial designations; however, everyone invokes patrimonial language to defend and negotiate the protection of their wealth and histories at the local, regional, national, and transnational levels. The shift toward privatization has also opened the possibility of transferring archives outside the country. Although this was a practice already in place, the sentiments, remuneration, and legality surrounding it have changed in the last three decades. Despite what many see as a neocolonial strategy on the part of the private sector (national and transnational) to embezzle valuable cultural property, several artists interviewed told me that given the state of disrepair of some archives, and the lack of interest from national authorities, they wouldn't think twice about selling their archives to a foreign institution.[38]

The shift in the management of cultural patrimony developed in tandem with a worldwide transformation in patrimonial discourses that has expanded their range of focus to include the conservation of intangible patrimonies. Such intangible patrimonies or practices have raised questions regarding methods of preservation and practices of knowledge transfer from generation to generation.[39] New ways of thinking and defining intangible patrimonies tend to be mostly directed to indigenous and popular oral and performative practices. In Mexico such patrimonies include, for example, indigenous dances and celebrations like the Day of the Dead and musical traditions such as mariachi. Until recently, the work of many conceptual and performance artists working from the 1960s to the 1980s, or their personal archives, have not been considered a part of these intangible patrimonies despite their ephemeral qualities, and they are just beginning to be recognized as part of the artistic patrimony of the nation. By ephemeral qualities I mean that the artwork that these artists produced was not easily preserved. It included performances, street happenings, self-made books, zines, or ideas and discussions printed on napkins or sent via post to a colleague. Even though some of these works were recorded using tape recorders, photographic or film cameras, or filed away in personal archives (documents that now constitute artist archives), their ephemerality also resides in the lack of interest and mechanisms for preserving such works, in contrast to conservation measures for more traditional works of art, such as sculpture or paintings, for which a system of collecting, classification, restoration, and preservation is mostly in place.

The struggles for the preservation of their artistic archives, as well as artists' engagement with the notion of the archive, have added another line of inquiry to patrimonial discussions, one that relates not only to methods of documentation and preservation but also to the creation and conceptualization of archives. While arguably artists have always been in dialogue with the archive in the modernist sense that their work is either a break with the previous record or a continuation, in recent years visual artists have more consciously questioned the archive as a way to probe questions of identity, memory, and the power structures that underpin historical narratives.[40]

The Politics of the Archive

Parallel to the challenges that the expansion of patrimonial discourses and the work of conceptual and performance artists brought to notions of the archive, scholars and critics have also questioned and reexamined the definition and constitution of the archive, a process that Ana Laura Stoler and others have labeled as the "archival turn."[41] Through different modes of reading—against or along the grain—feminist and postcolonial scholars have uncovered silenced voices, untangled hierarchies of historical production, scrutinized gender biases, and made visible how certain sexual identities are condemned in traditional archival practices.[42] Others have scrutinized the exclusionary mechanisms of the archive by expanding its limits to include oral traditions and reenactments as powerful and valid archival mechanisms in the process of knowledge transfer from generation to generation.[43] These diverse configurations of the archive have played a critical role in questioning the authority of those who determine what is historically valuable and in dismantling dominant structures that have erased diverse ways of being and oral traditions. Nonetheless, as Anjali Arondekar reminds us, as a result of the archival turn, the archive "has become a preapproved allegory for all modes of contestation," and its connection with "minoritized forms of knowledge formations—particularly queer and feminist—has led to simplistic and triumphant modes of empiricism" that annihilate the politics of the archive.[44] How, then, does one recover the politics of the archive?

Following Arondekar, the interest here is not to recover women's voices in the archive but rather to make visible how they increasingly became agents of the archive. That is, to show how they meaningfully engaged in creating and enabling archives at crucial moments of transformation in intellectual, cultural, and political spheres and in making feminist demands a crucial aspect of these transformations. In doing so, the focus here is on making evident how the visual letradas emerged as political subjects and how their practices spilled across disciplinary boundaries, making apparent how power and knowledge are embedded, produced, and deployed in everyday life and inside and outside institutions.

I use the archive as a category, a concept, a practice, a medium, and a collection of varied objects rather than as a site where documents no longer in use are kept. Drawing from Foucault and Rama, the archive as category of analysis determines the parameters of the historical narrative, and as a concept, it disrupts and regulates the terms of historical discourses. The archive as a practice not only emphasizes the process of archiving, as Stoler has theorized; it also points to the gendered and the performative dimensions of the archive and to the ways in which archival practice shapes a sense of self that involves multiple temporalities.[45] In theorizing the performative aspects of the archive, I am also interested in showing how the trace of the performance is always embedded in the archival record, as Rebecca Schneider and José Esteban Muñoz have argued, and how, in turn, it produces embodied archives.[46] Rather than focusing on how the logic of the archive renders the performative and ephemeral absent, and in contrast to Diana Taylor, who differentiates the *archive* (a house of documents and things) from the *repertoire* (as embodied practices), I follow Muñoz and Schneider and conceive the performative as a crucial aspect in the formation of embodied archives whose remains are translated and reinterpreted in different media and practices. By this I mean that the record of a live performance elicits an embodied and intersubjective response that then gets carried into another form of recording or performative act.[47]

As medium, the archive points to the inscriptive qualities of the human body and recording technologies such as film, video, and photography. Traditionally, film and photography have been discussed as archival technologies due to their ability to record time and to create a direct reference to their subject's existence, producing images that could be considered indexes of a past. In the context of the development of technologies such as video and television broadcasting and following more recent ways of conceptualizing archives, I include performance and urban landscape as archival technologies. Like other technologies these media deal with and organize practices, experiences, and things through time and across space. As collections of objects, archives are no longer viewed as something to be stored in vaults exclusively reserved for researchers, but rather as things that circulate and that are exhibited, curated, and in some cases transformed into art works. I propose then to read the work of these four women as archives in relation to other archives and to archival practices that emerged at the same time in order to restore their power, explore the mechanisms that allowed for their exclusion, and most of all, to explore the challenges they pose to one another and the competing claims they make.

Intergenerational and Transnational Networks of Exchange

The book moves back and forth in time between 1971 and 2011 to reconstruct the relations and collaborations between Fernández, Jiménez, Weiss, and Mayer, who represent two generations of visual letradas with a shared but quite distinct feminist sensibility. By tracing the networks of artistic exchange and analyzing the aesthetic interventions of a variegated group of urban middle-class women as meaningful political practices in and of themselves, I also seek to restore their historical importance and make visible the mechanisms of exclusion that have obscured their power in various fields. This book challenges, builds on, and provides an alternative to dominant narratives on the histories of new wave feminisms that focus on the failures and successes of feminist movements.[48] It interrogates why the aesthetic and political legacies of the early 1970s feminist movement have been mostly disregarded in the dominant narratives of twentieth-century Mexican art movements. Through oral interviews and a careful reading of personal archives of many feminist activists and artists, and the reports filed by DFS and DGIPS agents on feminist activities, I trace the diversity of networks and coalitions that 1970s' feminist collectives wove together with many different social and artistic political movements. Moreover, by drawing connecting lines to an earlier and longer tradition of women activists, I question fixed definitions of the category of class that have curtailed the legacies of these groups of women and propose to see 1970s Mexican new wave feminisms as a more porous and open practice than is conventionally understood, as an intergenerational movement of those who, despite their backgrounds, age, and education, were concerned and aware of inequalities within the movement and the different oppressions faced by women of different classes.

I recover the emphasis on developing a feminist cultural critique as advocated by a number of activists in the early 1970s. For instance, parallel to the first feminist demonstration in 1971, many activists were publishing feminist analyses in established cultural magazines such as *Siempre!* [49] In 1975, the same year that Cine-Mujer began to produce films, the collective La Revuelta began publishing a journal that dealt with topics such as abortion, sexuality, and prostitution.[50] In 1976 Margarita García Flores and Alaíde Foppa established *Fem,* a feminist magazine that set out to interrogate women's condition from different perspectives.[51] That same year Foppa, along with Elena Urrutia, began to host *Foro de la mujer,* a radio program to discuss women's issues. By 1977 there were more than twenty self-identified feminists writing for diverse publications with nationwide distribution. I discuss these practices along with debates occurring concurrently in the visual arts and explore the street performances or the interdisciplinary aspects of the movement as politically meaningful acts in and of themselves: as encompassing all the practices of the visual letrada.

At a transnational level, the feminist collectives and Fernández, Jiménez, Weiss, and Mayer were in dialogue with visual and embodied practices that manifested an overall interest in dismantling the dominant structures of visual representation and the international emergence of feminist art.[52] Their practices speak to the inquiries of several scholars who, in the early 1970s, began to study how the production, distribution, and reception of visual images created and reproduced patriarchal power relations. These arguments had a stake in discrediting the disciplinary and hierarchical boundaries of art historical discourses that, until then, were proprietary in the study of how images produced meanings.[53] I posit that through their practices, Fernández, Jiménez, Weiss, and Mayer were meaningful players in these transnational debates.

This book, then, contextualizes the production of these four women within the 1970s global landscape and looks at their practices as interrogations of how the representation of sexual and gender difference was performed through visual, performative, and archival practices. It accounts for the participation of women as crucial actors in the search for new visual languages, embodied practices, networks of exchange inside and outside the national framework, and links with social movements. Rather than imposing theory on their work, I consider their practices as forms of theoretical and political expression, in and of themselves, that are in meaningful dialogue with transnational debates. These four women did not produce work inside a Latin American or Mexican vacuum, as their works have, if at all, mostly been framed. They were in dialogue with and participating in various networks that traversed different geographies as much as they were affected by, and effected, local issues.

The Structure of the Book

The book is divided into three sections, each corresponding to one of the main categories of analysis used: the city, the archive, and the media. Part 1, "Feminizing the City," traces how the urban space of Mexico City was feminized through a series of independent as well as government-led practices and creative expressions that placed women's bodies and rights on the agenda for public debate. These practices transformed the geographies of the city by opening up spaces where competing configurations of gender and sexual difference could exist; however, these changes were not without violence. In order to map out how the process of feminization took place, I discuss the proliferation of various intersecting practices that both produced and interconnected the diverse cultural and spatial geographies that coexisted and shaped Mexico City during the 1970s. This section is divided into three chapters that I conceptualize as three maps of Mexico City. These maps frame the ways in which urban space is crucial to the production of sexualized, gendered, and racialized bodies and, in turn, how bodies shape the urban landscape.

In chapter 1, "The Official City," I discuss a series of reforms targeting women's juridical standing and changing roles, including family planning campaigns, in order to show how these state-led initiatives marginalized feminists' demands but also opened up avenues for discussion of such demands. The official map of the city begins with President Luis Echeverría Álvarez's administration (1970–76). Yet his policies responded to and were a continuation of issues that had begun decades earlier. The contours of the official city, however, do not end with Echeverría's administration; some of its outlines, while faded, continue to have visibility in the present. Others—such as Rosa Martha Fernández, Ana Victoria Jiménez, Mónica Mayer, and Pola Weiss, who actively shaped discourses on women's bodies as they flowed through different media and the urban landscape—have been mostly silenced by the dominant historical narratives of the era. In order to provide a broad context of the situation that visual letradas faced within the field of visual arts, I review a series of discussions regarding the condition of women visual artists in Mexico through state-led initiatives, and I also consider the connections between feminist collectives and the emergence of a supposedly independent movement of art collectives known as Los Grupos. Most of these art collectives denied the inclusion of women's rights in their political aims.

Chapter 2, "The Media City," looks at Echeverría's efforts to reform the television broadcasting and film industries in the face of growing private intervention—particularly in television—and increasing international interest in giving women access to decision-making posts in broadcasting media industries in the context of the International Women's Year celebration. Particular attention is given to the ways in which private and state-owned channels were more receptive to the inclusion of women as news anchors, reporters, and producers. I also discuss the production of feminist films and feminist directors in the context of reforms in the film industry and a movement of independent politically committed film. While neither was receptive to feminist demands, they opened up opportunities for the development of female film directors and all-female film collectives. In these first two maps the state becomes a crucial actor and broker of feminist demands; however, it is the access and control of media industries—particularly film and television—over which visual letradas, the state, and the private sectors would compete. It is through this battle for access and control of diverse media from which alternative representations of female bodies and roles for women would emerge. The televisual performance *Madre por un día* (Mother for a day), by Maris Bustamante and Mónica Mayer, and Pola Weiss's research on the artistic and experimental uses of television are discussed as examples of this battle.

Chapter 3, "The Embodied City," discusses feminist-led initiatives that flowed through alternative means of communication such as demonstrations, street plays, and spontaneous gatherings, flyers, banners, periodicals, and objects constructed for the demonstrations. By reconstructing several feminist demonstrations and street plays using sources from the recently opened archives of the Mexican Secret Service, I show how these demonstrations collaborated in the production of an embodied city. In this embodied city established discourses that wielded control over the meanings and representations of women's bodies and behaviors were contested, leaving important remains throughout Mexico City streets.

Part 2, "The Archival Practices of a Visual Letrada," introduces the archive and archival practices of Ana Victoria Jiménez. Chapter 4, "The Archival and Political Awakenings of Ana Victoria Jiménez," provides an overview of Jiménez's wide-ranging career in order to offer a sense of her relation to her archive and of her feminist militancy. Throughout the chapter I trace Jiménez's self-fashioning as an archival persona, one who is conscious of the importance of documenting her activities as a political practice in and of itself. This persona emerges in two different but interconnected moments: first, at the performative moment of the creation of her collection, and second, at the moment of the self-reflexive understanding of her collections as an archive. In chapter 5, "Secret Documents and Feminist Practices," I read Jiménez's visual archive against and along the intelligence reports filed by state agents on feminist demonstrations to explore the intersections, interruptions, and the challenges they pose to one another.

I discuss how both these archives provide valuable information on the activities of feminist activists that are usually not available (or not read) in the historical records. By reading the visual focus of Jiménez's archive against the textual focus of the secret service's archive, I contend that one of the things surfacing through this comparative reading is the women's demand for the right to see and to be seen—that is, the right of women to return the gaze, even that of state informants. This difference in focus also points to the gendering of the spheres of action of the letrados and visual letradas. Chapter 6, "Performing Feminist Art," focuses on Mónica Mayer's and Ana Victoria Jiménez's engagement in the establishment of a feminist art movement. In particular, I discuss the performance *La fiesta de quince años* by the feminist collective Tlacuilas y Retrateras, established in 1984 by Jiménez along with other artists and academics, to provide yet another perspective on Jiménez's feminist militancy and relation to her archival practice.

The final section, titled "Protesting the Archive," closely examines how the practices of Ana Victoria Jiménez, Rosa Martha Fernández, and Pola Weiss challenged dominant definitions of what constituted politically committed art or a political engagement in the arts. I argue that their practices contested dominant visual regimes and actively participated in the development of alternative regimes of media and visuality. Chapter 7, "Interrupting Photographic Traditions," locates Jiménez's photographic practice and way of seeing as an alternative to two genres of photography that were revitalized in the 1970s: the first, that of ethnographic photography, particularly as it was practiced by photographers such as Graciela Iturbide, and the second, photojournalist and documentary photography as it emerged in Mexico and throughout Latin America. Such a contextualization enables me to analyze how her way of seeing was not considered within these dominant regimes of visuality. In chapter 8, "Feminist Collaborations in 1970s Mexico," I discuss the collaborations of Ana Victoria Jiménez and Mónica Mayer in the films that Rosa Martha Fernández directed as part of Colectivo Cine-Mujer. I trace the ways in which their collaborations with Cine-Mujer shaped their feminist militancy toward a political practice with an interest in questioning women's living conditions through the arts. I also explore how Cine-Mujer's production destabilized normative constructions used to define parameters of politically committed art and how these two films provided an alternative to dominant conventions of representation. And finally, in chapter 9, "*POLArizing* the Archive," I discuss some of the ways in which Weiss's practice altered Mexican regimes of visuality and collaborated in the development of video as a communicative and artistic media. I locate Weiss's practices as part of a transnational network of people—artists, dancers, musicians, and technology aficionados—interested in the potential of video and television broadcasting as a medium of artistic expression rather than as a commercial medium of communication. I suggest that Weiss's video production not only broke with dominant ways of seeing and representing the female body but also championed video production and television broadcasting as media that could develop an awareness for embodied forms of perceptions. Her eccentric and at times idealistic approach represented a political engagement that anticipated relations between self and technology that would become prevalent in the decades to follow.

PART 1

Feminizing the City

1

The Official City

The Battle for the Official City

In the summer of 1975 a tune by urban troubadour Oscar Chávez was heard on radio stations and performed live at *peñas* (live music venues) throughout Mexico City. In a style that mixed the traditional Mexican corrido with the trendy "Nueva Canción de Protesta" (Latin American Protest Song), Chávez popularized the highlights of the first United Nations International Women's Year conference (IWY), celebrated in Mexico City from June 19 to July 2:

> Don't be surprised, in June of 75, a thousand women gathered in Mexico City to speak badly about men.
>
> They came from all over the world to proclaim that it is unfortunate that there are still women without purpose in life who continue to praise the *macho*.
>
> The women told the president of the congress, general solicitor Mr. Pauyada, because you are a man you won't preside over our congress.
>
> (Chorus) Absolute freedom is a woman's goal, but please do not stop doing that which we spoke about . . . even if it is only as a favor or with pain . . . to preserve honor or keep up appearances . . . to satisfy sexual desires or even without will or love . . .
>
> Then, Allende's widow did a very good thing, she asked for the expulsion of the Chilean delegation . . .

The women demanded the legalization of lesbianism, polygamy, abortion, and prostitution . . .

They praised Indira, Golda, and *Isabelita,* all liberated women but also very pushy.

Because they were decent ladies, only they were considered liberated, and the entrance to the congress was denied to my poor fellow countrywomen.

Guerilla fighters, seamstress, farm workers, prostitutes, beggars, and petty thieves were all left out in the cold.[1]

Besides recounting the top events of the conference in various verses, the song described an alteration to the soundscapes of the city brought about by the convergence of hundreds of foreign women who gathered to speak ill of men. But certainly by 1975, the chatter of 1,200 delegates attending the UN's IWY celebration and 4,000 more participating in the parallel nongovernmental forum *La Tribuna de La Mujer* was not the only thing altering Mexico City's mediascapes.[2] In preparation for the UN's IWY celebration the government of president Luis Echeverría Álvarez (1971–76) secured equal rights legislation for women in 1974 through the modification of article 4 of the Mexican Constitution, thus marking an important milestone in the achievement of the yet to be accomplished gender equity. The reforms were put in place after a series of hearings between government officials and representatives of several women's organizations, including members of various feminist collectives. During that time in Mexico, as elsewhere, a renewed feminist movement was burgeoning. As early as 1971 a group of professionals, students, and militants from left-leaning organizations had begun to organize lively street demonstrations throughout Mexico City to demand the end of discrimination against women at all levels of society and their right to self-determination, including sexual freedoms. They established small consciousness-raising groups, joined women workers' movements across the country, organized conferences, hosted radio shows, and published articles discussing the emergence of new wave feminism elsewhere inviting Mexican women to join their cause. The broadcast and live performance of Chávez's song was one of the many creative expressions carried out throughout the decade in response to the attention brought to women's issues by the hosting of un's iwy celebration, the demands of a new generation of feminist activists, and government reforms targeting women's rights.

Echeverría's administration began with a nationwide campaign for democratization known as *apertura democrática* (democratic opening). It aimed at siding with disenfranchised and defiant sectors of the population in order to redeem his popularity and that of the ruling party, as both had been severely damaged after the 1968 student massacre. In order to do so, the president implemented a series of reforms that targeted economic, political, and cultural sectors in hopes of crafting an image of himself as an international Third World ambassador. The hosting of the iwy celebration as well as a campaign to extend full rights of citizenship and social equality to women played an important role in supporting such a goal.

On the economic and political front, Echeverría broke the unstated pact between the private sector and the Partido de la Revolución Institucional (pri) by promoting economic nationalism through supporting the establishment of numerous parastatal industries. By expropriating more than 35,000 hectares of commercial agricultural land and redistributing more than 25,000 hectares in northern Mexico, he earned the belligerency of commercial agricultural leaders. In addition, his 1975 edition of *libros de texto gratuitos* (public text books) enraged the Catholic Church and conservative sectors of the population. Moreover, prominent private art collectors turned to smuggling valuable pieces of art in order to avoid their expropriation due to his campaign to build a registry of valuable material culture and reforms to laws that protected the cultural patrimony of the nation. These actions, along with the kidnappings and assassinations of prominent industry leaders by emerging guerrilla groups, convinced many businessmen to join the opposition.

At the same time, Echeverría tried to appease the Left through different means, such as tacitly allowing the establishment of workers' unions; attempting to start a dialogue with university students; welcoming refugees from Argentina, Chile, Brazil, and Nicaragua; releasing political prisoners; and adopting a foreign diplomacy rhetoric that favored third worldism against the imperialist forces of the United States. Furthermore, by welcoming young functionaries into his cabinet, he attempted to craft a youthful image for the party and for himself—an image more aligned with 1930s Cardenismo than with the immediate generations of PRI presidents, who had turned to the right politically since the mid-1940s. However, at the same time, he continued to support a system of surveillance to spy on activists and leaders of left-wing urban and rural organizations, including feminist activists, thus sustaining the traditional use of violence and repressive tactics to dispel public gatherings and demonstrations on the streets of Mexico City and elsewhere in the country.[3]

These seemingly contradictory strategies would characterize his time in office. His democratic opening functioned as a strategy of co-optation following the hegemonic impulses of the ruling PRI, which played an important role in the development of what many have labeled "a schizoid political culture" throughout the twentieth century.[4] In Echeverría's case, the schizoid nature of his policies became even more pronounced as he aimed to appease all sectors of the population, particularly those on the Left, while covertly engaging in a dirty war to eliminate urban and rural unrest. Nonetheless, some of his reforms—particularly in the cultural sector and women's rights—led to the establishment of governmental institutions and to the opening of discussions that would, to a large degree, establish the terms of debate in the decades to follow.

By the time President Echeverría Álvarez took office, Mexico City was already considered one of the world's mega-cities, with a population estimated at eight million. The city's growth and development had started in the 1940s, as the Mexican government turned to the right of the political spectrum and the capital began to enjoy economic growth due to the adoption of the Import Substitution Industrialization model (ISI). Between the 1940s and 1960s Mexico City more than doubled in size and became the showcase of the country's economic growth. Changes in population were accompanied by a large investment in urban infrastructure—expressways, tunnels, overpasses, subway systems, and concrete housing projects—aimed at turning the nineteenth-century Haussmann urban plan into a city more in tune with an international modernist model.

The spoils of the economic development acquired symbolic recognition as Mexico City was elected to host important international events—the signing of the Tlatelolco Treaty (1968), the Olympic Games (1968), and FIFA's World Cup (1970). The hosting of international events was an opportunity to invest in urban infrastructure while at the same time such infrastructure showcased the modern standards of living of Mexico City residents. However, not all the population benefited from such standards of living. Rather, all these public works altered the social fabric of the city. Many neighborhoods were bulldozed to make way for overpasses, and a network of interlocking freeways made vehicle traffic the priority over the majority of pedestrians, who needed to learn how to navigate the recently inaugurated subway system (1967–69). At the same time, rural to urban migration caused serious overcrowding and a growth in slums and illegal settlements. A lack of employment accelerated male patterns of migration that altered the traditional arrangement of the Mexican family. More and more urban women became the sole providers for their families, many living in poverty and turning to informal work (prostitution, begging, or domestic work).

All these changes prompted adaptations in the ways that Mexicans kept informed and connected. By then, broadcast media—television in particular—had become an important tool for keeping the public informed.[5] Advances in broadcasting technology such as satellite networks (1968) and the use of video (1970) expanded the reach and the velocity with which information could be transmitted via television broadcasting.

In Mexico, as elsewhere, the growth of broadcast media during the second half of the twentieth century was consistent with the development of capitalism in the world but also responded to more local concerns. On the one hand, the growth of consumer culture required the use of broadcasting media to promote products on a massive scale; on the other hand, the Mexican government sought to use these media to incorporate a mostly illiterate society into a national project in crucial need of renovation. According to some reports, between 1950 and 1970 the number of television sets throughout the country soared from 100 receivers to 4.5 million.[6] Even though the majority of viewers lived in Mexico City, television stations had been established in twenty-nine of thirty-two states (*estados*) by the end of the 1960s. A fundamental part of the renovation of the national project was a change in the government's pronatalist polices.[7] In order to align the country with international standards that encouraged population control as a condition for development, by 1974 Echeverría's government launched a media campaign promoting birth control methods. Advances in broadcasting media were crucial to such a campaign. Another important change in broadcast media was the increased participation of women in the industry. One of the outcomes of IWY was to raise public consciousness with respect to the changing roles of women in society and particularly to transform the ways in which the media tended to reinforce traditional attitudes and portrayals of women that were both degrading and humiliating.[8] In tune with this resolution, both private and public television broadcasters began to foster the participation of women as anchors, producers, and reporters.

During the 1970s, reforms in the film and television industries not only supported the Mexican government's needs and aligned with international patterns; they also accelerated transformations within Mexico City's intellectual sectors. In turn, these changes opened up spaces of expression for the kind of emerging visual letradas addressed in this study. By then Mexican intellectual sectors were already marked by a shift from an exclusive emphasis on literate-print culture toward an embrace of the audiovisual communication media of the era (television, video, and film) and the increased participation of women in the public sphere. The growing importance of audiovisual communications would require further adaptations on the part of this sector, which was also confronted with the increased participation of private interests and independent academic institutions in cultural matters. State reforms in the cultural sector and broadcasting industry led to the opening of media spaces from which various visual letradas launched divergent conceptions of women's bodies.

By the time transnational new wave feminism made Mexico City the stage of its demands, the dreams of turning the city into a model of modernity had been seriously shattered. The ISI model began to show signs of exhaustion and so did the city. Reports and studies flooded the media, warning of a series of catastrophes awaiting the city if population growth and construction development were not halted. The dreams of progress and modernization were shattered principally by the violent attack against students unleashed on Mexico City streets.

In effect, on October 2, 1968, just days before the inauguration of the Olympic Games, government forces massacred hundreds of protesting students in the Plaza de las Tres Culturas, located just north of the city's downtown district. The site also happened to host a leading modernist housing complex project, Nonoalco-Tlatelolco, designed by architect Mario Pani and commissioned by President Miguel Alemán. The killings turned the flagship model of modernization into a site of violence and bloodshed. The attacks against students revealed the amount of violence that the ruling party, the PRI, was willing to unleash in order to preserve the status quo and made visible a political and social crisis that had been brewing all over the country in the past decades. The Tlatelolco massacre unleashed a crisis that represented an overall disaffection with the dominant social, political, and cultural structures that ruled Mexican society, which were symbolically embodied and put into practice by the Mexican government. Three years later, on June 10, 1971, a second attack, known as the Corpus Christi massacre, against students by the paramilitary group Los Halcones (the Falcons) sent Mexico City residents a reminder of the continued state of violence in which they were living. The Corpus Christi massacre resulted in the killing of several students near the entrance of a subway station, altering the symbolic meaning of the recently inaugurated line 2 of the transit system (1970) and turning La Normal subway station into a site of remembrance for the killings rather than a signifier of progress. These two events significantly altered the meanings attached to material symbols of modernity and progress. They unveiled the shallowness of the PRI's inclusive revolutionary rhetoric and converted the already contested streets of Mexico City into a battleground, as a growing number of political and civil organizations, grassroots movements, and feminist collectives made it the site from which they would enunciate their demands, in spite of fears of repression. As I discuss throughout part 1, state bureaucracies, government institutions, private media conglomerates, and independent academic departments as well as myriad grassroots and political organizations would become active players within this battle for symbolic presence throughout Mexico City streets.

While information about the killing of students did not flow freely through official media channels, the residents of Mexico City shared information about these events through street theater, graphics, graffiti, and billboards produced by several students and activists. At the time a renewed interest in collectivism was emerging in Mexico, as elsewhere, and many students who had participated in the protests of 1968 or had links with other counterculture movements began to establish art collectives. Filmmakers, writers, visual artists, protest singers, feminists, gay and lesbian activists, and rock musicians established a wide range of different collectives and initiatives seeking aesthetic and political freedom of expression. Confronted with massive urban changes (including overpopulation, bulldozed neighborhoods, and pollution) and the memories of their experiences in the student movement, the majority of these collectives made Mexico City the stage, the media, and the content of many of their expressions. For instance, reflecting on Mexico City's growing population, the art collective Suma (1976) developed a series of visual icons that represented all characters in the city (the bureaucrat, the unemployed, the migrant, the beggar, the construction worker, etc.) and used them to paint urban murals (graffiti) on the streets of Mexico City. Similarly, members of Grupo Mira (1977), after having participated in the production of graphics for the 1968 student movement, began to produce a series of print portfolios entitled Comunicados Gráficos, in which they addressed urban problems faced by rural migrants, such as unemployment and lack of health and sanitary services. Some of these art collectives aimed at building alternative links with existing and emerging oppositional political groups and forces while attacking official cultural institutions and experimenting with different media and aesthetic languages. Performative practices such as street happenings or theatrical plays were renewed as one of the most subversive means to reach wider audiences, build coalitions, and demand civil rights. Yet other artists and intellectuals located themselves within Echeverría's third worldist platform by joining his cabinet or embracing Latin American protest music to counter the imperialistic influence of English rock music.[9] These variegated series of movements sought to effect social change and contest established structures of power and institutions. However, the majority of these collectives did not build meaningful links with the feminist movement, despite the collaboration of many feminists with various art collectives. Feminism in the early 1970s was, and sometimes still is, perceived by many in Mexico and elsewhere in Latin America as an imported imperialist ideology and a distraction from more pressing social injustices afflicting Latin America as a region.

In the context of the geopolitical pressures of the Cold War in the 1970s, the IWY celebration also served as an outlet for the alleged and stated antagonisms between First World and Third World feminists, or as Oscar Chávez puts it, between those decent ladies considered as liberated (*mujeres liberadas*) in contrast to Chávez's compatriots, who were denied entrance to the celebration and were left out in the cold. Certainly the IWY celebration served as a stage for voicing a multitude of interests; these included pitching feminism as an imported imperialist ideology—one that emphasized women's sexual liberation, the legalization of abortion, the open discussion of lesbianism, and the rights of prostitutes—over other concerns like poverty, health, and access to education. The open discussion of sexual rights shocked the mostly conservative Catholic sectors of the Mexican population as well as many on the left of the political spectrum, who preferred that women's issues remain framed under the banner of class struggle rather than through the sexual and self-determination emphasis espoused by some feminists.[10]

Some verses of Chávez's song clearly represent the demeaning and sexist reception that feminist demands encountered in Mexico. According to the chorus, as long as women continued to have sexual relations with men, no matter under what circumstances (as a favor or with pain, to preserve honor or keep up appearances, to satisfy desires, and even without will or love), women could go on organizing and demanding whatever they wanted. The chorus served as a humorous outlet for the threats to Mexican traditions and social mores unleashed by discussions about women's sexual liberation, including lesbianism, in the context of the IWY celebration and the reemergence of the feminist movement in Mexico. The song sarcastically reflects on the value given to women's bodies and self-determination at a time when initiatives, official and non-official, transnational and national, had raised such topics as urgently in need of public debate.

In spite of such reception and antagonisms, the hosting of the IWY conference and the parallel NGO forum provided a political juncture that strengthened competing feminist agendas and political interests in Mexico, as elsewhere.[11] As the city prepared to host these gatherings, members of at least three feminist collectives active at the time decided to organize a counter-congress and boycott the UN conference and the forum because they were in disagreement with the top-down, capitalist approach of such events. The counter-congress took place at the theater Eleuterio Méndez in Coyoacan, a neighborhood located in the southern part of the city.[12] Meanwhile, the main events of the IWY celebration took place in the building of Foreign Affairs, located in Tlatelolco, the site of the 1968 student massacre.

From these two different locations (one unofficial, represented by the counter-congress's location; the other official, represented by the Tlatelolco buildings) and the interstices between them, different approaches to women's rights, feminism, and political solidarity were launched, placing women's issues on the agenda of public debate in the decades to follow. One way that these different approaches was expressed was through the organization of street demonstrations, a practice that new wave feminists had used since 1971 and that intensified in the aftermath of the IWY celebration. Hence, just as the repression of students in the streets of Mexico City began to alter the cultural memory attached to symbols of progress, so too did various feminist activists, who took over important sites in the city as the stage for their protests. Moreover, as diverse art collectives began to critique urban development and state cultural policy by taking art to the streets in order to counter hegemonic discourses and build alliances with other political organizations, so did various feminist collectives. By demanding their right to decide over their bodies and denouncing violence against women, feminist activists proposed another way to engage with politics. They placed the personal at the center of public debates. By doing so, they altered and proposed different ways of experiencing and producing civic engagement in a highly contested urban landscape.

Controlling Women's Bodies: Gender Equity and Family Planning

The renewed interest in woman's issues that took place in Mexico City during the 1970s was due to several factors particular to the country but also consistent with international developments in the field of women's rights, population, and development. Even before the IWY celebration and the reemergence of the feminist movement, the increased enrollment of women in universities and their participation in social protests as well as a state campaign that promoted the use of contraceptives and chastity intensified the development of a critical mass awareness of the gender inequalities in Mexican society. These included the existence of double standards in state discourse with regard to women's bodies and sexuality that, on the one hand, promoted family planning and, on the other hand, criminalized abortion. Hence, within the contours of the official city, competing women's roles began to emerge as the Mexican government aligned itself with international policies regarding population growth and women's rights, forcing a change in the traditional role conferred on women by the state and the Catholic Church—that of the loving mother often represented as the Virgin of Guadalupe, but always as the bearer of fertility in charge of populating and protecting the nation. In turn, family planning media campaigns that promoted the use of contraceptives and a more active role for women as mothers as well as reforms to the Mexican Constitution targeting women's rights constituted an important political juncture for the strengthening of emergent feminist collectives.

The feminist collectives active in Mexico City in the 1970s were roughly divided into two ideological currents: liberal feminists, represented by such organizations as Mujeres en Acción Solidaria (MAS, 1971) and Movimiento Nacional de Mujeres (MNM, 1972); and socialist feminists, represented by La Revuelta (1975), Movimiento de Liberación de la Mujer (MLM, 1976), Lucha Feminista (LF, 1978), Colectivo de Mujeres (1978), and Coalición de Mujeres Feministas (CMF, 1976).[13] Liberal feminists represented the first generation of activists to come together in the 1970s whose focus was on reforming and working with the Constitution (Civil and Labor Code). Those who participated or sympathized, but who increasingly came to realize that the Left was not meeting their demands, represented social-ist feminists. Despite these distinct ideological tendencies, two trends of feminism, what some have labeled as feminism of equity and feminism of difference, influenced the establishment and drove the demands of these collectives. The first trend demanded the equality of women in relation to men under the law in all spheres of economic, sexual, and political life. The second trend emphasized the existence of sexual difference and the ways in which this difference acted as the source of inequality. All these groups identified violence against women and the decriminalization of abortion as their main concerns.[14]

The year prior to the IWY celebration, President Echeverría's government organized a series of hearings to launch a package of reforms to expand the rights of the female portion of the population, who had obtained the right to vote in national elections in 1953.[15] In these meetings members of some of the emerging feminist collectives voiced their opposition to the UN conference and Echeverría's reforms, despite the fact that some gov-ernmental proposals did echo their demands.[16] In general terms, feminist activists were in disagreement with the capitalist orientation of development that the conference espoused and understood the reforms to be symbolic gestures on the part of the government in order to gain legitimacy. Some activists were concerned about the lack of consideration of women's voices and the top-down approach in crafting such reforms. While several activists collaborated with the government, many others distrusted it and sought to be completely autonomous from the state, a strand of feminism that would be labeled *feminismo autónomo* (autonomous feminism).[17]

The series of reforms proposed by Echeverría's government integrated some feminist demands with a more conservative perspective. However, Congress did not pass most of them. The reforms included a plan for free distribution of contraceptives; the decriminalization of abortion; the removal of the term *divorcee* from women's official documents; the elimination of the use of the preposition *de* (from, indicating belonging to) added to the last name of all married Mexican women; and the withdrawal of Melchor Ocampo's epistle from the civil matrimony contract.[18] Ocampo's letter, written in the 1850s, describes women's and men's character and their respective roles in marriage. In the letter a woman is expected to render obedience to her husband as an essential trait of the feminine character.

> A woman, whose principal qualities are obedience, beauty, compassion, good judgment, and tenderness has to give and should be committed to render obedience, kindness, assistance, counsel, and comfort to her husband, the person who vehemently supports and defends her, with the care and sensibility of someone who does not wish to exasperate the brusque, irritable, and harsh part of him, qualities deemed appropriate to his character.[19]

In turn, a man is expected to use his sexual qualities, defined by his strength and bravery, to provide protection, food, and direction to his woman, the most delicate, sensitive, and refined creature.

> A man whose main sexual characteristics are braveness and strength has to give and be committed to protect, feed, and direct his woman, treating her always as the most delicate, sensitive, and refined part of himself, with the magnanimity and generous benevolence with which those who are strong render to the those who are weak, especially if the weak renders her body and soul to him, as entrusted to him by society.[20]

This letter and its performative qualities—that is, its inclusion in the civil matrimony contract and its recitation during the civil ceremony—symbolize and dictate the still current heteronormative roles for males and females sanctioned by Mexican liberal reformists since the nineteenth century. Similarly, the reforms to article 4 (the only reform passed by Congress) granted men and women equality on paper but continued to frame it through the prescriptive gender roles established in Ocampo's letter. Article 4 of the Constitution begins by stating that men and women have equal juridical rights: "*el varón y la mujer son iguales ante la ley*" (women and men are equal before the law). It also gives individuals the right to choose how many children to rear:

> Each individual has the right to choose freely how many children to have and the time difference between pregnancies; this decision should be made in an informed and educated manner.[21]

Despite this discursive freedom of choice, the article does not mention how it should be enacted and still entrusts women to be solely responsible for the family: "*ésta protegerá la organización y el desarrollo de la familia*" (woman shall protect the organization and development of the family).[22] Thus the article effectively excluded men from day-to-day family responsibilities and continued to dictate appropriate masculine and feminine values. The wording of the article expresses the difficulties that aspirations for gender equity posed to the as yet unchanged traditional heteronormative gender roles, which exclude men from any role in rearing children and endow women with all the responsibility. In spite of this, many feminists understood the modification to article 4 as an opportunity to demand the decriminalization of abortion as a way to exercise their right to decide freely how many children to have.[23]

By 1977 the core demands of feminist activists had evolved into three principal issues: (1) voluntary motherhood, signaling the right to sexual education, contraceptives, and legal abortion, (2) the end of sexual violence, and (3) the right to self-determination.[24] In 1979 in the context of President José López Portillo's (1976–82) political reform allowing the legalization of various left-leaning political parties, the Frente Nacional por la Liberación y Los Derechos de las Mujeres (FNALIDM, 1979), an alliance that united feminist collectives with leftist political parties, elaborated a project on voluntary motherhood legislation that revisited the issue and would present it to Congress by the end of the year. However, neither their set of demands nor their legislative proposal was well received by a mostly Catholic and conservative society ruled through patriarchal social, political, and cultural structures.

Between 1971 and 1982, just as feminist collectives demanded the decriminalization of abortion, the government launched a national media campaign (through televised soap operas, radio, ads, short films, and posters) that promoted family planning. This vision was consistent with international policies that considered population growth an impediment to development.[25] The campaigns also responded to a shift in the Mexican government's pronatalist policy to one that supported family planning and contraceptive use. These campaigns effectively transferred the authority to determine how many children a couple could and should have from a religious platform to one governed by the dictates of the state. At this time, family planning was indispensable in the face of soaring population growth, particularly in Mexico City, due to the centralized model of development that attracted migrants from all over the country to the capital. While these campaigns promoted the more active participation of women, for the emergent generation of feminists the population campaigns revealed the government's double standards on sexuality, which promoted both the use of contraceptives and chastity while also criminalizing abortion.[26] Equally, this new power of decision bestowed upon women was not well received by the male population, which, according to reports, complained about the emphasis on women's control over family matters and urged a change toward a couple's choice.[27]

Despite these criticisms, these state-sponsored media campaigns proposed alternatives to previous conceptions of women's bodies and reproductive capacities from a signifier of fertility and a loving and virginal mother to a body that needed to exercise sexual restraint and accept contraceptive methods (the Pill or intrauterine devices) in the face of newly acquired civic responsibilities and national goals.[28] Such responsibilities placed women's bodies at the center of a renewed modernization project that continued to entrust females with an important patriotic role, that of controlling population growth. Moreover, advances in birth control methods opened up the female reproductive system to public scrutiny. This public discussion about female sexuality through audiovisual technology (media campaigns) resonated, as I later discuss, with the explorations of the visual letradas and important changes in archetypical feminine roles portrayed in national films.[29] However, this official discourse on women's reproductive system granted very limited political self-determination (difficult access to birth control methods and forced sterilization) to those who embodied a female body, and when it did so, it became a source of public indignation for the male population. The caveat here is that while family planning should indeed be a couple's choice, at the time (and still), those who defined themselves as women had fewer legal, social, and cultural rights and resources than those who defined themselves as men in matters of reproduction rights.

La mujer en el arte or Feminist Art?

As part of the cultural events of the IWY celebration, three collective art exhibitions to extol women's creativity were organized by Echeverría's government in Mexico City, including *la mujer en la plástica* at the Palacio de Bellas Artes; *La mujer como creadora y tema de arte* at the Museum of Modern Art (MAM); and *Pintoras y escultoras* at the Polyforum de Arte Siqueiros.[30] Many others were organized in different parts of the country.[31] These women-only exhibitions were not well received by many, but they encouraged discussion on the conditions of Mexican women's art and whether feminist art even existed in Mexico. For instance, while these exhibitions appeared to endow women with equal participation in the arts, Mónica Mayer argues that the majority of participants were men; women were mostly the predominant subject matter rather than active participants.[32] Moreover, the works and the curatorial objectives of these exhibitions were not concerned with questioning how images represented women. Consequently, various artists refused to participate. Renowned art critics voiced their disagreement at the objectives of these exhibits, which they perceived as prejudiced, since boosting women's creativity, for many of them, was an act of discrimination in and of itself as creativity is not gender biased.[33] Yet for others, this series of exhibitions, which showcased the work of more than eighty women artists from various generations, gave women great visibility by encouraging recognition of them as protagonists of the Mexican artistic tradition.[34]

Following these events, a year later, in 1976, the most important government-sponsored art magazine in Mexico City, *Artes Visuales*, published an issue titled "Women, Art, and Femininity" and dedicated it to discussing the participation of women in the arts.[35] The issue included a debate between Mexican artists and art critics regarding the relevance of being labeled a woman artist, along with essays by prominent feminists from the United States. On the whole, the magazine introduced contemporary feminist art practices in the United States to a Mexican audience. The publication of this issue prompted Mónica Mayer to pursue feminist art studies in Los Angeles.

Art historians, artists, and critics responded to a series of questions posed by Carla Stellweg, editor of the magazine.[36] The questions revolved around the relative nonexistence of women artists in comparison to the dominance of women as art historians and critics; on whether formal feminine qualities existed in the works of women artists; and on whether a critique of women's conditions was present in works of art made by women.

While the objective of these questions was not to arrive at definite conclusions, but rather to begin a discussion about the conditions of women artists in Mexico, they revealed the positions of leading intellectuals in the field. Most of the respondents agreed that artistic expression and creativity were universal, and as such it was ludicrous to think that artistic expression had gender. Moreover, the development of style or the acknowledgment of the existence of a movement based solely on supposedly feminine qualities was not received with enthusiasm. For art critic Teresa del Conde, feminine and masculine qualities in a work of art were not exclusive to the artist's sex. Masculinity and femininity, she argued, were not fixed notions but rather a matter of degree: "*lo femenino y lo masculino son cosas de grado.*"[37] At the time, gender was not typically employed as a category of analysis and was mostly used interchangeably with sex. Yet an interesting acknowledgment on how gender could be a matter of choice and a social construct seems to be at work in del Conde's statement; however, her article fails to propose a critique of the dominant art system or the role she played as an art critic in maintaining its status quo. By failing to do so, she ignored the ways in which the work of women artists and critics was and is embedded in a social context in which notions of race, gender, and class are questions that affect the value of a work of art or a career.

From a social art perspective, art historian Ida Rodríguez Prampolini placed emphasis on the root of the problem: the patriarchal and capitalist socioeconomic system that had turned art into a commodity.[38] For her, it was no use speaking of a feminine and masculine problem without a change in social structures. With regard to feminine formal qualities in works of art, painters Frida Kahlo, Leonora Carrington, and Remedios Varo were discussed through their affiliation with surrealism, a style that, according to Rita Eder, provided them more expressive freedoms with which to explore their subjectivities.[39]

The difficult conditions that women faced in the art world or the role of art critics and historians in reproducing the patriarchal workings of the system were seldom directly addressed except for two notable contributions (interestingly, these contributions were put forth by artists and not critics). Ángela Gurría (b. 1929), a well-known sculptor, wrote about her fears and insecurities as she began to win prizes with her sculptures. Gurría described how critics and judges were surprised to learn that she was a woman when she showed up to pick up her prizes. Since she signed her sculptures "A. Gurría," it was difficult to know whether she was male or female.[40] Concurrently, fellow sculptor and art promoter Helen Escobedo (1934–2010) shared the ways in which she was able to divide her activities as mother, wife, artist, and art manager in a successful manner, suggesting that sexism existed in the eye of the beholder.[41] The testimonies of Gurría and Escobedo are interesting since, as sculptors, they probably had to deal with the most masculine and closed field of production in the Mexican arts. While both sculptors were firmly against the idea of a feminine aesthetic, they addressed some of the difficulties that they encountered as women working in the arts, which was one of the chief concerns not only of those in Mexico but also of the then-emergent feminist art movement around the world.

An interesting counterpoint to the views by leading Mexican artists and critics was provided by U.S. feminists, artists, and critics, including Judy Chicago, Arlene Raven, Lucy Lippard, and Charlotte Moser, also published in the special issue of *Artes Visuales*. Their articles talked about the importance of developing an alternative corpus of theory and practice to the dominant cultural system and about the role that art critics played in privileging men or women artists; they also presented several feminist art initiatives, such as the establishment of the Women's Art Building in Los Angeles in 1973, a nonprofit public art center focused on showcasing women's art and developing art education programs with a gender focus, and discussed the reception of several controversial feminist works.[42]

This was by no means the first time that U.S. feminist ideas were discussed in the Mexican media. In fact, many feminist scholars agree that the starting point of new wave feminism in Mexico was an article by Marta Acevedo published in the cultural magazine *Siempre!* in 1970 in which Acevedo discussed issues debated by U.S. feminists.[43] According to Ana Lau Jaiven, the article caused such a stir that it resulted in the establishment of the first feminist group informed by U.S. and European feminist ideas, but with a sense of the particular realities of the Mexican context.[44] This group became Mujeres en Acción Solidaria, and it organized its first meeting at the *Mother's Monument* in 1971 in an attempt to challenge the ways mass media represented motherhood.

One of the underlying differences between U.S. and Mexican contributions to the issue of *Artes Visuales* was an awareness of how notions of class and economic access played a crucial role in the Mexican artistic scene. While not all the Mexican contributors discussed it, María Eugenia Vargas de Stavenhagen and Carla Stellweg both made note of it. Stellweg discussed how most recognized women artists up to that point in Mexico had foreign (non-Spanish) last names or came from upper-class families, and how this situation played a crucial role in smoothing the difficulties encountered in gaining access to and reproducing the dominant workings of the art system.[45] For her part, Stavenhagen recounted how in the traditional division of labor the production of crafts had been mostly relegated to *campesinas* or indigenous communities.[46] Despite the crucial role that crafts played in the development of high arts in Mexico, both as an aesthetic language and in the development of artistic personae, the division between high and popular arts played a key part in casting the fields of cultural production in gendered terms, wherein high arts were usually a male activity while crafts were mostly a feminine one.

Most Mexican contributors to this issue of *Artes Visuales* acknowledged their position of privilege but did not recognize their role in reproducing the patriarchal workings of the art world. As many have noted, class-based analysis trumped the adoption of gender-based perspectives in Latin America until the late 1990s.[47] This situation was not different in the art world, where social art history and formalist analysis took precedence until recently.[48]

Reforming the Visual Arts

Besides promoting women's art, during his administration President Echeverría aggressively courted visual artists and intellectuals, provoking enormous tensions in the cultural arena. These tensions would have important repercussions in transforming the role of the state in managing visual arts and material culture. For instance, by enforcing regulation on the ownership of valuable objects and artworks, Echeverría's reforms on cultural patrimony put a strain on the incipient development of a private art market in Mexico. To counter such regulations Echeverría courted visual artists by establishing the prestigious award Premio Nacional de Ciencias y Artes and a program that allowed the payment of taxes with art work.[49] He also rehabilitated the estranged muralist David Alfaro Siqueiros with the inauguration of *Polyforum Cultural Siquerios*. But most importantly, he assured the artistic community that in Mexico official art did not exist and manifested his support for freedom of expression: "Intellectual creation is not a product of state ideology nor of economic pressures. No one is persecuted. Freedom of public expression is authorized to everyone who wishes to express philosophical, scientific, economical, or political opinions."[50]

This message was partially directed to an emergent generation of artists who had been radicalized by the 1968 student movement and who by 1973 had begun to establish art collectives and build links with diverse political organizations.[51] These art collectives, later known as the Los Grupos movement, were varied in their composition (and included visual artists, writers, filmmakers, playwrights, communication experts, photographers) and had different approaches to aesthetic languages, ideas about collective experience, and political militancy. They began to experiment with different technologies and aesthetic languages to contest traditional materials, values, venues, and tactics of art. Many collectives embraced the use of photocopies, text, radio, and television. They also staged street actions and other kinds of ephemeral practices like street poetry.

Something that distinguished them from previous attempts at bringing art to everyday life, and everyday life to art, was their regional and international focus. They were no longer concerned with a national framework or with making art to construct a national identity, as were previous art movements. Some collectives promoted involvement with workers' unions, community-based organizations, and urban neighborhoods, while others abandoned the adherence to left-wing class-struggle radicalism for identity politics; still others assumed a contemptuous approach with a mocking attitude toward overtly political militancy and art institutions. By addressing themes such as migration, police violence, and state repression, many of these collectives aimed at confronting passersby with the violence of urban life and providing alternative means of communication in the face of mainstream media distortions. According to some members, they were no longer interested in becoming famous individual artists. They preferred to be called "cultural workers" and attempted to change the parameters of art making while building links with local and international communities interested in social change.[52] While several women, including some feminist activists, participated in such collectives, the recognition of women's labor and living conditions, their depiction as sexual objects, and their overall discrimination were not at the center of their demands.[53] Because they privileged a political perspective of class struggle, women's issues were seen as secondary problems.

Overall, these self-defined cultural workers sought to position themselves as a block of resistance and change that would ultimately affect the mainstream parameters of art making, even though this meant changing the process from within the system. For instance, they participated in exhibitions sponsored by state institutions or sought economic support from them.[54] In fact, the majority of Los Grupos collectives followed what Alberto Híjar, one of their ideologues, called *afectar todo el proceso*—a constant negotiation and confrontation with the state rather than adopting an oppositional strategy that negated its existence.[55]

This type of collaboration or relationship with state institutions is perhaps not surprising within the Mexican environment. The state has had a pivotal role in supporting the arts since the end of the 1910 Revolution. It is also not surprising that art making and politics should be intertwined. Although most of the time art and politics have been narrated as two separate stories in mainstream art history, in Mexico the legacy of the Syndicate of Technical Workers, Painters, and Sculptors (1922) and the political and aesthetic militancy of David Alfaro Siqueiros (and his contemporaries) has led in the opposite direction.[56] Given this situation, to negate the existence of the state in cultural matters in Mexico, particularly in the visual arts, was almost impossible and also not completely desirable. Effectively cutting links to state institutions and bureaucracies could potentially hinder an artist's rise to fame. Following a post-revolutionary tradition, the state controlled—sometimes tacitly—a great number of art venues in which various artists and intellectuals held positions of power that allowed for significant career opportunities for many members of Los Grupos despite their attempts at being autonomous from state-sponsored institutions and bureaucracies and their denial of any individual career aspirations.

Within the porous boundaries of the official city, competing women's roles and conceptualizations of the female body began to emerge as the Mexican government aligned itself with international policies regarding population growth and women's rights. These policies forced a change in the traditional role conferred on women by the state and the Catholic Church. Family planning media campaigns and reforms to the Mexican Constitution targeting women's rights opened up the female body to public scrutiny as her traditional role as a fertile body was transformed into one that had to perform sexual restraint in order to control population growth. Such transformations in national discourse regarding female bodies and sexuality, as well as women's roles in society, constituted an important political juncture for the strengthening of emergent feminist collectives and competing feminist interests. The visual arts were not immune to these changes. Yet, while established and emerging groups with links to the official city did not open a space for feminist demands, the boundaries of the official city were, nonetheless, becoming increasingly defined by the reach of the media industries. And in this, visual letradas would play a role. Just as Oscar Chávez's song altered the soundscapes of the city, visual letradas would, through television, film, radio, and print, alter the mediascapes of the capital.

2

The Media City

Para nosotras la televisión es hoy el museo de arte moderno
(For us today, television is the museum of modern art)
—Maris Bustamante and Mónica Mayer

The Battle for the Media City

Throughout his administration President Echeverría confronted a public polarized as to the role that the state should play in regulating and managing broadcast media and the arts. Up until then, television and radio broadcasting, since their establishment, had been mostly in private hands whereas state institutions, for example, had mostly managed other cultural sectors, such as the visual arts. Film production, for its part, had been managed through a combination of private and public investment in which the state played a mostly regulatory role.

By the end of the 1970s and as a result of a complicated series of political maneuverings and government reforms, three main actors were consolidated as promoters of broadcast media and the arts in Mexico City. The state intervened in the field through existing government-sponsored cultural institutions like the Institute of Fine Arts (Instituto Nacional de Bellas Artes INBA, 1946) and established state-owned museums and galleries. More significantly, Echeverría increased the state's intervention in film and broadcast media through the establishment of institutions such as television Canal 13 (1972); a series of parastatal companies that financed the production of films (CONACINE, CONACITE and CONACITE II, 1974–75); as well as a film school (Centro de Capacitación Cinematográfica, CCC, 1975) and a national film archive (Cineteca Nacional, 1974). In 1973 the second actor, Televisa S.A de C.V., was consolidated as two private television broadcasting companies (Telesistema Mexicano and Television Independiente de México) merged to establish one of the largest and most influential media conglomerates on the continent. And finally, the third actor was Universidad Autónoma de México (UNAM). Already by the 1970s UNAM was an established center for the production and promotion of culture in the capital city and an important site from which opposition to the government was articulated and student radicalism concocted. UNAM had a radio station (Radio UNAM, 1942); a film school (Centro Universtiario de Estudios Cinematográficos, 1963); several museums, galleries, and theaters, including Museo Universitario de Ciencias y Artes and Casa del Lago; and a closed-network television production station, TV UNAM (1952), which began broadcasting on an open network in association with Televisa in 1976. All these spaces provided venues for aesthetic experimentation for the intellectual community as well as for the emergent generations of visual letradas. As Maris Bustamante and Mónica Mayer express in the preceding epigraph, feminist artists at the time understood the value of television as a new medium for the arts, one that would allow them to reach broader audiences and also open up the art system by moving away from traditional aesthetic languages and their exclusive workings. But most important, it would allow visual letradas like them take charge of the ways in which their bodies and concerns were represented in public media. As in the official city, in the media city the state is a crucial actor and broker of feminist demands; however, it is the access to and control of media industries—particularly film and television—over which visual letradas, the state, and the private sectors would compete. It is through this battle for access and control of diverse media that alternative representations of female bodies and roles for women would emerge.

Television Broadcasting in 1970s Mexico

By the time Echeverría took office, several attempts to develop legislation to regulate the television sector had ended in backroom deals with private broadcasters in order to cover up footage that might prove the government's responsibility in the 1968 student massacre. Echeverría set out to change the situation, and early on in his campaign he declared plans to nationalize television broadcasting.[1] This produced a media battle that polarized public opinion regarding the role of privately owned broadcasting and its mostly foreign, imperialistic, and commercial programming that allegedly degraded the morals of the Mexican public. Cultural critics, government officials, business leaders, and private citizens wrote numerous articles discussing the influence of television programming on children and youth. As elsewhere, debates over television's bad reputation as a technology that promoted laziness and hindered critical thinking (Monsiváis's *la caja idiota*) were not novel, but in the early 1970s the publication of *Para leer el Pato Donald*, by Ariel Dorfman and Armand Mattelart, a book that conceptualized television as a tool of U.S. cultural imperialism, added a harsher tone to this criticism.

This conceptualization of television as an ideological tool of U.S. imperialism became a useful justification to promote state interference in television programming; it also prompted public debates over the role of the state in cultural matters.[2] For instance, an article published in *El Universal* in 1971 accused *Siempre en Domingo,* a contest and live musical show, and its host, Raúl Velasco, of being agents of a bad moral invasion that was penetrating Mexican homes.[3] In December of that same year, Mario Bravo Ahuja, director of the Ministry of Public Education (Secretario de Educación Pública, SEP), asked the government to stop broadcasting *Los Polivoces* and *Los Beverly de Peralvillo,* popular comedy shows that, like *Siempre en Domingo,* were produced by privately owned Telesistema Mexicano (soon to be Televisa, 1973). Government officials supported state intervention in order to produce quality programming with the participation of intellectuals so as to avoid "official ideologies."[4] Cultural critics and *cronistas* such as Paco Ignacio Taibo and Luis Spota criticized Echeverría's double standard since, on the one hand, the government criticized private programming, but on the other hand, it didn't reinforce existing quotas or finance the production of state programming. Instead, it continued to allow the unregulated use of broadcasting technology and the development of political alliances with private broadcasters.[5] Others thought INBA, the Institute of Fine Arts, should be in charge of producing cultural programming for television. In fact, in 1947 when President Miguel Alemán established INBA, Carlos Chávez, its director, declared that one of the purposes of the institution was to produce cultural programming and use television as a broadcasting tool for national cultural productions. In 1947 Chávez, under instructions of President Alemán, sent Salvador Novo and Guillermo González Camarena to study British, French, and U.S. television broadcasting models. It is well-known that President Alemán followed and encouraged the private model of the United States rather than the state model of Britain. By the early 1970s it was clear that television had not fulfilled Chávez's aspirations and that, on the contrary, the Alemán family had been instrumental in sustaining the commercial and private uses of the industry. In 1970 Miguel Alemán Valdés, son of President Alemán, was hired by Telesistema Mexicano to establish and direct its news division after a falling out with the newspaper *Novedades,* up until then the main purveyor of news for the broadcasting company.

The establishment of Telesistema Mexicano's news division was an important event that significantly transformed the mediascapes of the country at many levels. The production of news programming led to the consolidation of the most popular prime-time news program, *24 Horas,* anchored by Jacobo Zabloudosky. It coincided with the transition from film to videotape that cut costs of production while facilitating the archiving— including the erasing—of news programs. Telesistema Mexicano had used video technology to produce soap operas since the 1960s, but it was not until the establishment of its news division that it began to use video more widely. Together with the advent of satellite communications in 1968, the use of video dramatically improved the speed and facilitated the transmission of live reports.[6] In turn, the increased practice of live reporting opened up spaces for the participation of women as news reporters.[7] But most of all, the establishment of a news division, with the potential of becoming a threat to the government, ultimately turned into an important negotiating currency for lucrative arrangements that were beneficial for the government and for Televisa.

In this context and confronted with the looming merger of two independent broadcasting companies that would establish the media giant Televisa S.A. de C.V (1973), Echeverría began proposing reforms to existing broadcasting laws.[8] In 1972 Echeverría ordered the purchase of Canal 13, then owned by Francisco Aguirre. The company was located in downtown Mexico City on Mina Street in an area well-known for its prostitution houses, *cantinas*, and burlesque theaters such as Teatro Blanquita and the King Kong cabaret.[9] The location of Canal 13 in such areas of the city contrasted with that of Televisa's studios on Chapultepec Avenue and San Angel, both prime locations in Mexico City. Televisa's San Angel Studios filmed and produced soap operas, and the Chapultepec venue, destroyed in the 1985 earthquake, was reserved for news programs. From these two different locations, Televisa's channels, with nationwide broadcasting capacities, and Canal 13, with limited broadcasting capacities, launched mostly competing messages about the role of women in broadcasting and what cultural programming should look like. Canal 13 went on to produce a wide range of cultural and educational programming with the participation of renowned cronistas such as Carlos Monsiváis and Juan José Arreola.[10] Soon afterward, Televisa followed suit in order to win some leverage with regard to Echeverría's push for reforming the industry. And as early as 1978 Televisa gained the support of the most respected Mexican intellectual of the time, Octavio Paz, who began to appear regularly as part of its programming by the mid-1980s.[11] However, perhaps one of the initial differences between Televisa and Canal 13 programming concerned the participation of women in broadcasting.

Women and Television Broadcasting in 1970s Mexico

By the 1970s the participation of women in television was mostly welcomed, but it still posed some challenges for many women who aspired to work in the media. In a published memoir of people who worked at Canal 13, Laura Gámiz, also a presenter of *La barra femenina* and an anchor of the first all-women news program, *Las doñas*, on Canal 13, spoke about the resistance she encountered in this mostly male territory and the contradictory messages she received from her male colleagues, who welcomed female participation but also felt threatened by it: "The role of anchoring in television programs had always been a masculine territory on Canal 13. Even though the directors supported the participation of women in broadcasting, something floated in the air, like a sense of intrusion. Our participation caused surprise to many, they considered us pushy, but at the same time they were pleased that we were there."[12]

The contradictory messages that Gámiz received from her male colleagues are also reflected in the title of the news show. *Las doñas* refers to a group of older women whose marital status is unknown but who have a certain social prestige. It is a multivalent and mostly derogatory term that refers to women who spend their time gossiping and preaching social norms. At the time, a study on women and broadcasting indicated that viewers were ambivalent about females anchoring news shows. Viewers seemed to like female anchors because they appeared to be motherly, and this made some news content easier to deliver, but if there was something negative to report, female anchors could also appear to be scolding the audience.[13] The title *Las doñas* played upon this ambivalence regarding the role of women as anchors but also made a sarcastic reference that diminished the professionalism and the content of the news show.

Gámiz recalls the attraction that women felt toward television, as many went to ask for jobs, but most of them had no education and could not speak properly; "They were only pretty looking," Gámiz reports.[14] According to Gámiz, many of those who aspired to a position in Canal 13 had previously had experiences in radio or in performance arts (theater), hence her emphasis on voice and ability to speak. As both Lisa Gitelman and Christine Ehrick have argued, the performative and gender aspects of voice and speech were crucial elements that had shaped early twentieth-century sound recording and radio broadcasting.[15] Moreover, as Gitelman has also pointed out, new media—in this case television broadcasting—emerge according to the practices of older media.[16] However, despite the shared practices between media, in contrast to radio's disembodied qualities that separated the body's aural and visual components, television broadcasts are a fully embodied performance. The question of embodiment in media studies is a broad discussion with a long tradition.[17] I tend to agree that all messages received are embodied in the sense that the receiver comprehends them with her full body regardless of the media used to transmit them. However, in this instance I do distinguish between radio and television due to the latter's ability to disseminate images as well as sound. The overall audiovisual and visible performative qualities of television broadcasting offered women a different platform from which to explore various career options in which their physical looks would indeed play an important role. Within the following decades, as more women were appointed as news anchors or protagonists in *telenovelas*, television surpassed film and radio as the most powerful medium through which female looks and fashion as well heteronormative gender roles were set out and contested, while, in turn, the increased participation of women deeply shaped television broadcasting.

Despite Gámiz's observations and her ambivalent reception on the part of male colleagues, in 1972 more than ten women began working as presenters (anchorwomen) at Canal 13, and this number increased substantially across the industry in the following decades. Soon Canal 13 produced a series of programs devoted to women's issues informed by a feminist perspective, such as *La barra femenina* and *A brazo partido*, hosted by Marta de la Lama. Marta de la Lama, a militant of the feminist collective MNM, went on to produce a series of programs that dealt with issues of gender and sexuality.[18] By the mid-1980s Mónica Mayer, Maris Bustamante, and Ana Victoria Jiménez participated in various editions of *A brazo partido* as well as other television programs produced by de la Lama to promote feminist art.[19] For her part, de la Lama is credited with being the first woman to have appeared pregnant (full body shot) while conducting a program on national television, and in the 1990s, as the representative of the 1st District of Mexico City, she participated in the crafting of the first law against domestic violence in Mexico.

Televisa also opened its doors to women in broadcasting. In fact, many female reporters who joined the ranks of Canal 13 had been trained in private broadcasting media. This was the case for Patricia Berumen, who worked for Telesistema Mexicano and later produced programs that offered a space for discussion to feminist artists like Mónica Mayer.[20] Many female reporters working for the then Telesistema Mexicano are also credited with reporting events organized by new wave feminists in a mocking and defaming manner. Most of Televisa's programming followed the official media discourse of the time that identified feminism as a threat to Mexican women. The majority of feminists agree that the lack of support and the mocking attitude they encountered in mainstream media outlets was one of the factors that led them to open up their own spaces.[21] However, despite its defaming views on feminism, Televisa produced the most popular Mexican female broadcaster. In 1974 Lolita Ayala began to co-anchor the prime-time evening news program *24 Horas* along with Jacobo Zabloudosky on Televisa's channel 2. In 1987 she even hosted her own afternoon news program, *El noticiero con Lolita Ayala.*

Despite Ayala's popularity and her important role in broadcasting, which perhaps inspired many women to reassess their career and life goals, she is also a symbol of Televisa's well-known media distortions and conservative endorsement of women's roles and of social justice through corporate philanthropy. It was Guillermo Ochoa, the anchorman of Televisa's most popular early morning news program, who opened up a space for one of the most humorous and transgressive feminist performances in Mexico's recent broadcasting history.

In 1987 the self-declared feminist art collective Polvo de Gallina Negra (Black Chicken Powder), established by Mónica Mayer and Maris Bustamante, appeared on Televisa's *Nuestro mundo* news set, artificially inseminating Ochoa and transforming him into a *Madre por un día* (Mother for a day, fig. 4). The name of the collective, Polvo de Gallina Negra, refers to a dark powder popularly used to protect oneself against the evil eye, envy, and gossip. Bustamante and Mayer adopted the name knowing that

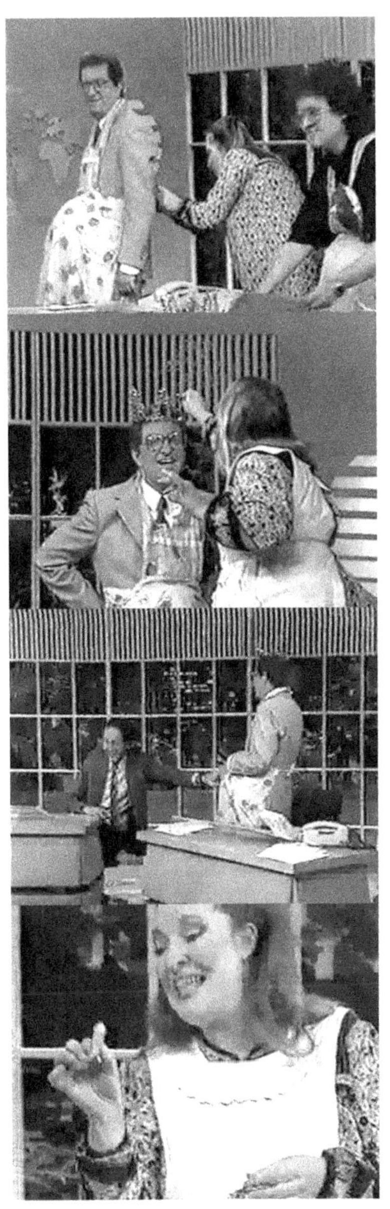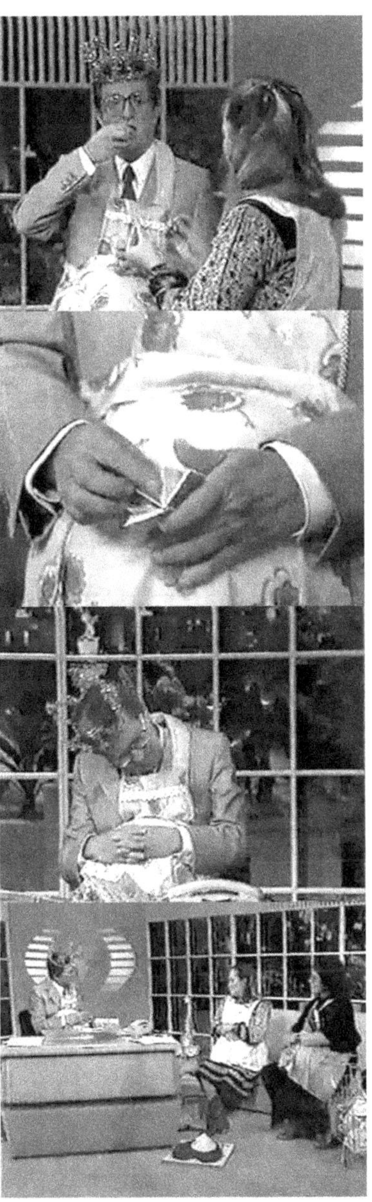

FIG. 4. *Madre por un día.* © 1987 by Polvo de Gallina Negra. Video stills courtesy of Mónica Mayer.

by calling themselves feminist artists they would become easy targets in a male-dominated art system and a mostly conservative society.

During the show, Mayer and Bustamante impregnated Ochoa by making him wear an apron with a prosthetic belly and giving him several pills—*chochitos*—with the purpose of simulating the characteristic ailments of pregnancy (cravings, morning sickness, etc.). They also endowed Ochoa with a golden crown to make him "queen for a day" and gave him a tiny golden book (*El libro de oro*) of home remedies to help him overcome any obstacle during his pregnancy and subsequent journey into motherhood.[22] The tiny golden book was a direct reference to a golden book of children's stories given as a present to first-time mothers, but in this case it was meant to be the first diary for the first male-mother (*El primer diario del primer hombre-madre*) created by PGN. It contained a coin to help provide for the child, because contrary to the popular saying that a child always brings wealth to the home (*el niño trae la torta bajo el brazo*), mothers need money to provide for a child. The tiny book also included a nail as a symbol of good luck, a small hanger in case Ochoa wanted to quit (*colgar los tenis*)—to commit suicide, perhaps, or to have an abortion—and a piece of dry pasta, so he could start learning to cook. With humor and wit, the tiny book covered most fears and anxieties of the experience of pregnancy.

During the show Ochoa, who amusingly played along, pretending to have multiple cravings and aches, interviewed Mayer and Bustamante about their art practice. The pair explained the difficulties they faced not only as women artists but as feminist artists in a male dominated environment. They also assured an incredulous Ochoa that what his more than 200 million viewers were about to see (his transformation into a mother for a day) was considered a work of art, which they defined as *una acción plástica* (later considered a performance). Further, Mayer and Bustamante told Ochoa that their purpose was to offer alternative representations of motherhood and maternity because "men created those currently in circulation." They also emphasized their choice to perform on television because, they said, "today television is the museum of modern art."[23] Then they gave Ochoa a diploma as a record of his participation and officially named him the first male-mother. Immediately after the appearance of PGN, *Nuestro mundo* received a number of calls from viewers who were offended by Ochoa's pregnancy. *Nuestro mundo*'s audiences perceived PGN's performance as an insult to motherhood. In spite of these immediate responses, not all the viewers were offended; nine months later many also called wondering about the sex of Ochoa's offspring.[24]

Madre por un día was part of Mayer and Bustamante's project *¡Madres!*, which lasted almost two years and consisted of a series of events that explored the concept of motherhood. The project began when both artists were pregnant. It included a mail art project among the artistic community, a contest entitled *Una carta a mi madre*, in which the general public (Mexico City area) was invited to write letters to their mothers telling them everything they had ever wished to say but hadn't; a poetry reading; an exhibition by Mayer that explored the feminine archetypes in a romance novel; the birth of Bustamante's second daughter, and finally their appearance on *Nuestro mundo*.[25] *Nuestro mundo* aired on Univision, a network that reached audiences in the United States and some regions of Latin America. The process of making Ochoa pregnant turned the social order upside down and, through humor, invited his more than 200 million viewers to interrogate gender and sexual roles.

The performance *Madre por un día* and the presence of PGN on a television show with audiences all over the continent encapsulate the issues that were at stake for Mexican feminist art collectives in the 1980s, including a critique of the art system and the ways it impeded the full participation of women, along with a conscious desire to create feminist art, both as an act of denunciation and as a search for different aesthetic languages, demonstrated by PGN's amusing transgression of dominant perceptions of motherhood and the use of television broadcasting as a medium of art creation. The appearance of PGN on *Nuestro mundo* also gave continuity to several issues present in Mexican arts since post-revolutionary times and renewed in the 1970s. Although most of the time not fully resolved, these issues included an attempt to make art for the people, to link art with political activism, and, moreover, to open up the art system by moving away from traditional aesthetic languages and their exclusive workings. The variations that PGN and other feminist collectives brought to these questions included a different definition of politics—one that considered the personal political and that did not shy away from discussing in public what are otherwise women's everyday private experiences, such the anxieties caused by pregnancy; a concern with deconstructing and subverting hegemonic gender roles; an interest in exploring everyday life as an aesthetic language; and most of all, a commitment to giving voice to women's concerns. In contrast to Bustamante and Mayer's interventions on television, Lolita Ayala's daily performance on television reinforced a female look and self-fashioning (her whiteness and moral standards) that spoke (and still speaks) to the racialization of beauty and the standards of permitted social behaviors granting access to such coveted positions of power. For instance, every day Ayala's desk was adorned with a fresh flower, a rose, symbolizing her femininity and delicate nature when delivering the daily news.

Echeverría's reforms, alliances, and animosities with Televisa did not appease public opinion; neither did the establishment of Canal 13. Likewise, Canal 13 was not the only space available for women in broadcasting. Still, the state-owned channel did propose an alternative space to commercial television in Mexico. As the de la Lama experience suggests, state interference in television broadcasting opened up alternative spaces for the participation of women, who slowly began to produce programming that discussed gender and sexuality issues in national broadcasting. In comparison, however, the welcoming of Bustamante and Mayer on Guillermo Ochoa's program sheds some light on the creative freedoms allowed inside institutions and corporations that are ultimately composed of, and function through networks of, social relations that, like the state, are not monolithic entities. Bustamante had appeared on Ochoa's programming already in 1979 to announce her recently acquired copyright on the *taco, La patente del taco*. Ochoa invited Bustamante after he read the print coverage of *patente del taco*. Since then, they had kept in contact, and Ochoa was always eager to know what kind of work she was doing. In 1981 Bustamante appeared on another of Guillermo Ochoa's shows entitled *Hoy mismo*, in which she presented the performance *Las amas de casa*. For Bustamente the experience of appearing in Ochoa's programs was an opportunity to put into practice her critique of the art establishment and goals of reaching wider and different audiences. So while Televisa's productions and the corporation itself were one of the main bastions for the reproduction of conservative and mainstream views on gender relations in Mexico, they were also, on some rare occasions, a place of experimentation.[26] Hence by the mid-1980s both state and private television programs had opened up spaces for the discussion of feminist art and gender and sexuality issues and for the presentation of different kinds of visual letradas.

Video: From *la caja idiota* to *la caja mágica*

As debates over the role of television became prominent in the Mexican media, Pola Weiss began to explore both the experimental potential and non-commercial uses of television broadcasting via the arrival of video, a relatively new technology in Mexico. During the 1960s most video equipment was in the hands of private television broadcasting companies and academic departments linked to UNAM. In the 1970s video equipment became available mostly through the black market, but it was only in the 1980s that it was used more widely following developments in technology that made it more accessible and less expensive.[27] In the early seventies Pola Weiss traveled to Europe to research the artistic and experimental uses of television, visiting several broadcasting companies including the BBC in England, VPRO in Holland, OFRATEME in France, and RAI in Italy.[28] In doing so she performed a trip that had already been accomplished in 1947 by writer Salvador Novo and Guillermo González Camarena, credited as the inventor of color television, under the orders of President Alemán to look for the best suitable model for television in Mexico. In 1970 Miguel Alemán Velasco undertook a similar trip under the orders of Emilio Azcarraga, director of Telesistema Mexicano, to search for the best model of television news production. However, this time the research was entrusted to a woman. What Pola Weiss encountered was a model for alternative uses of television broadcasting through the use of video technology. However, the model she would eventually embrace (discussed further in chapter 9) she found in New York in 1976, mostly through her own experimentation.

In 1975, Weiss proposed a project to investigate didactic uses of video in television for non-commercial purposes, a project that led her to obtain a bachelor's degree in political science and communication. She argued: "The visual order that has been mostly used to manipulate and alienate human consciousness can be equally used in the opposite manner, slowly to invert the meaning of the messages by using the same means to eliminate the ideological alienation that such messages produce and by making an efficient use of the marginal spaces that are opened up by mainstream, academic, and state media corporations."[29]

While Weiss criticized the commercial and imperialistic uses of television, she also recognized the experimental and didactic capabilities that video could bring to television programming by working in collaboration with media corporations. A year later, through the establishment of her television production company artTV (1976) and her appointment as professor at the faculty of communication and journalism (1977), she began to champion alternative uses of video technology. For instance, Weiss supported and fought for the production of several video-theses. And, following the theories of Rudolph Arnheim, she argued for the recognition of audiovisual technology as a valid form of intellectual exploration vis-à-vis the predominance of the verbal and written focus of academia. Citing Arnheim, she signed her approval of a thesis submitted in video: "I advocate and affirm that a person who paints, writes, composes, or dances (imagines or televises) thinks with all her senses."[30]

Weiss's conceptualization of the social uses of video and of visual perception as a valid form of intellectual activity were in tune with the emergence of video art and theoretical developments on new technology elsewhere. The development of the hand-held video camera (Sony Portapack) in the early 1960s had prompted the emergence of a network of international artists who had begun experimenting with the subversive potential of video technology and advancing the establishment of radical television collectives. As early as 1973 international video art exhibitions and festivals were being hosted in several Mexico City galleries. In 1973 the exhibition *Video art estética visual*, shown at the Museum of Modern Art and sponsored by the U.S. embassy, introduced the work of various video innovators as well as several experimental television collectives active in the United States.[31] In the essay for the exhibition, Neil Hickey gave an account of the diverse ways in which independent artists, private foundations, universities, and private and state-owned television channels were fostering the experimentation of video and television broadcasting in the United States.[32] In his review of the show, Juan Acha acknowledged the difficulty that video art posed to Latin American artists due to the high cost of the equipment but also noted that perhaps these kinds of experimentations could provide a solution to the commercial abuses of television broadcasting.[33]

In 1974 Televisa hosted a conference to discuss the future of mass media communications with leading media theorists and philosophers, including Marshall McLuhan and Umberto Eco. The conference was widely covered by the media, and besides introducing debates over the uses of television, the encounter also furthered the animosities between President Echeverría and Televisa. Echeverría delivered a speech in which he made television, and in particular private commercial television like Televisa, responsible for distorting the moral values of Mexicans in favor of corporate interests.[34] At the moment when Televisa and Canal 13 were in competition to attract new talent, and discussions over the future of the industry were the subject of public debate, the timing of these events cannot be taken lightly. Rather than reinforcing the perception that due to the costs, Mexican publics and artists were not aware of debates and trends in international video art and media theory, these two events—despite the particular interests that drove their organizers—introduced Mexico City–based artists to several experimental practices in video and broadcasting.

In spite of these antagonisms and competing interests, by the mid-1970s Mexico City was a node within a network of global discussions regarding video and media theories, discussions that were equally sponsored by private and state institutions as well as UNAM. In 1977 Weiss participated in *IX Encuentro internacional de video* hosted at Museo de Arte

Carrillo Gil, a joint privately and state-owned Mexico City venue, with a number of video artists from Canada, the United States, Europe, and South America. On the occasion of the *Encuentro*, Weiss also published an article in *Artes Visuales*. In *La TV TE VE* she argued for the consideration of video as an aesthetic language in and of itself and proposed artTV (experimental video programming broadcast on television) as a way to distribute an alternative aesthetic and audiovisual language to a mass audience, and in so doing, she proposed new parameters for thinking about television. Weiss also urged state cultural institutions to take video production more seriously.[35] Some years later she would propose, as a counter to Monsiváis's *la caja idiota*, the *caja mágica*, a box that had the capacity to create different experiences that put human beings in touch with the "cosmic man," a sensorial being.[36]

Weiss's experiments with video technology, along with the participation of feminist activists at Canal 13, began to shape two areas of action for the visual letrada: television broadcasting and video production. Moreover, Weiss provided a view of televisual media distinct from that espoused by leading Mexican leftist intellectuals such as Carlos Monsiváis. However, at the time, these intellectuals were not the only ones blind to Weiss's views on video. Rather than seeing the potential of video as an art for the masses, many artists saw it, due to its cost, as a *"lujosa bofetada para la mayoría de la población"* (a luxurious slap in the face for the majority).[37] The equipment was large and cumbersome and did not offer the portability or independence of super-8 film, for example. Unlike in France or the United States, where feminist collectives used video technology as early as 1970, in Mexico this was not the case due to the high costs of the equipment and restrictive access to the technology. Weiss was able to pursue the use of video due to her connections with TV UNAM and Canal 13 as well as her middle-class status, which afforded her the means to invest in and have access to such equipment. Some records indicate that while she was able to acquire her video equipment with the income she earned as a professor and her occasional work for the television industry, she always complained about not being able to afford all the equipment she needed.[38] It would not be until the 1980s that video technology would replace film, partly because costs came down and video equipment became easier to manage. But Weiss's early experiments as well as the series of international events organized in Mexico to discuss and exhibit new audiovisual technology located Mexico and Weiss as meaningful actors within an international geography of audiovisual experimentation.

Women Behind the Camera: Competing Approaches to Politically Committed Film

By the mid-1970s a vibrant experimental film movement was under way in Mexico, as elsewhere, that would offer another area of development for the visual letrada.[39] At the same time, the mainstream film industry was in decay. Many saw the Mexican film industry as commercial; that is, "as empty, escapist, and completely apart from the national entrails," a situation that Echeverría used to promote the production of films reflecting the realities of the country.[40] Recognizing the importance of film, President Echeverría, as part of his efforts to protect the cultural patrimony of the nation, established the Cineteca Nacional in 1974, a center for the preservation and exhibition of national films.[41] To promote film production, Echeverría established a new film school, El Centro de Capacitación Cinematográfica (CCC) and reestablished the Banco Cinematográfico, which he had directed in the past, to finance films through the three companies CONACINE, CONACITE, and CONACITE II. He also assigned his brother Rodolfo to be director of the Banco Cinematográfico and established a "package" mode of film production whereby the film workers postponed their salaries until such time as the movies prospered.[42]

During Echeverría's tenure, films that addressed poverty, class inequality, and social repression as well as sagas involving national heroes were encouraged. The production of such films gave the impression that Echeverría's government was open to criticism. For instance, *Canoa* (dir. Felipe Cazals, 1975) tells the story of the massacre of students perpetrated by conservative and Catholic sectors of the population in the town of San Miguel de la Canoa in the state of Puebla on September 14, 1968.[43] At the same time that

Canoa was produced and shown in theaters (in Mexico and the rest of the world), information about the massacre of students in Tlatelolco in 1968 and the recently perpetrated Corpus Christi massacre in 1971 by the paramilitary group Los Halcones, under Echeverría's command, was completely silenced. Disputes over Echeverría's involvement in this event and the still present memory and unresolved disagreements over his responsibility in the student massacre in Tlatelolco in 1968 led to serious hostilities between UNAM students and Echeverría, which peaked with the famous stoning of Echeverría—with bricks and bottles—when he visited UNAM in 1975.

By allowing the production of films that appeared to be critical and establishing a new film school, Echeverría also aimed to construct a platform for many young filmmakers and to silence the growth of independent cinema and super-8 collectives that had strengthened in the aftermath of 1968. The majority of these independent filmmakers came from El Centro Universitario de Estudios Cinemátograficos (CUEC), a film school affiliated with UNAM and established in 1963. As early as 1960 an independent new wave of Mexican cinema known as Nuevo Cine Mexicano had begun to appear.[44] Influenced by French New Wave Cinema, Nuevo Cine films were preoccupied with aesthetic considerations rather than with following the official cinema style, one that portrayed an idyllic version of the social and economic realities of the country and censured issues of sexuality, or the more commercial and populist films of *lucha libre* and *comedias rancheras.* Another major influence for the development of Nuevo Cine was the need to reform the film industry, something that came to fruition with Echeverría's presidency but had begun to take shape during the 1960s. One of the main concerns was the structure of the film industry unions, which denied the participation of young filmmakers.[45] To this end, in 1963 Echeverría, as president of the Banco Cinematográfico, organized the first competition of experimental film.[46] Throughout the 1960s various competitions were organized and a particular emphasis on experimental films shot in super-8 began to emerge.

After experiencing the censorship of many films shot about the 1968 student massacre, many independent and young filmmakers began to counter these government-led competitions, and in 1971 a group of cultural promoters linked to the Committee of Cultural Provocation of the School of Economics at UNAM organized a super-8 experimental film contest. From this contest two main groups emerged: El Taller de Cine Experimental, which declared itself to be independent from the film industry, particularly as Echeverría began to promote films such as *Canoa*, and La Cooperativa de Cine Marginal, which proclaimed itself marginal and against the film industry, which its members saw as an instrument of the state.[47] In tune with the international development of Octavio Getino and Fernando Solana's "third cinema" and Julio García Espinoza's "*cine imperfecto*," members of la cooperativa sought to use film as a communication tool to raise consciousness about social issues rather than to produce works of art.[48]

The resurgence of the labor movement and rural organizations was also an important influence for the emergence of various politically inclined film collectives, such as La Cooperativa.[49] By 1972 this collective had been approached by two unions—Sindicato de Trabajadores Electricistas de la República Mexicana (STERM) and Movimiento Sindical Ferrocarilero (MSF)—and, soon after, they began to produce visual *comunicados* that were used as communication tools between workers' unions and student groups to help raise consciousness of each other's struggles.[50] These films were shown at university and high school gatherings all over the country but also at union facilities. Young filmmakers and members of La Cooperativa attempted to provide an alternative source of information in the face of Televisa's distortions and known alliances with the state. A great number of the members of La Cooperativa studied at CUEC. Others came from various fields in the humanities or had working-class backgrounds and learned filmmaking and political organizing through La Cooperativa.

In 1972 Rosa Martha Fernández worked as a camerawoman with La Cooperativa filming a national workers' demonstration by Medalla de Oro, a mostly female textile-workers union that marched from the city of Monterrey to Mexico City to demand better wages and job security.[51] As the marchers arrived in Mexico City, Fernández was detained and imprisoned while filming the demonstration. Demetrio Vallejo, a labor activist, leader of the railroad workers' union in the 1950s, and founder of the Mexican Workers' Party (PMT) negotiated her release.[52]

Fernández's experience provides an example of the roles available to some women and how such roles intersected with other social factors. While Fernández acknowledges the existence of sexist attitudes toward women and a politics that privileged class struggle over feminist concerns in La Cooperativa, she was empowered by the fact that she was already a university professor, and her salary allowed her to finance some projects and personal needs of other members of La Cooperativa. In a sarcastic tone she told me, "*Mantuve a uno que otro que acabo siendo súper maestro de la universidad*" (I ended up feeding many members who are now well-known UNAM academics).[53] Fernández's self-recognition as a main provider of La Cooperativa both reinforces and inverts some traits of the supposedly masculine and feminine character described in Ocampo's epistle; however, it also aligns Fernández with the experiences of many lower-class working mothers who had to sustain their families, an experience in the rise of professional women such as Fernández herself. According to Rosa Martha Fernández, La Cooperativa was a *semillero*, a group that planted the seeds of political action and commitment in many of its participants who are now leaders in their own fields, such as Paco Ignacio Taibo II, Gabriel Retes, and Armando Bartra, including feminist scholars and artists, as her own career path attests.

Inspired by her experience in La Cooperativa, Fernández enrolled in CUEC in 1974, and a year later she established an all-women film collective, Cine-Mujer, along with the Brazilian-born Beatriz Mira and other CUEC students. Several feminist activists collaborated with Cine-Mujer film productions, including Mónica Mayer and Ana Victoria Jiménez, as did many young filmmakers who went on to establish individual careers in Mexico and abroad.[54] From 1975 to 1985 Cine-Mujer produced more than ten films dealing with such subjects as abortion, domestic work, sexual violence, and rape, issues that were still taboo for the majority of Mexicans. Cine-Mujer was the first collective of its kind in Mexico, and its independent way of working was also meant as a criticism of the film industry itself.

Cine-Mujer developed a team of women who tackled all aspects of the film industry, including production, content, and distribution. Their films were shown through alternative networks of distribution and in marginal spaces such as women's collectives around the country, university and high school forums, and at informal gatherings, but also through established venues. In spite of the scathing reviews of their productions by the film establishment, in 1978 *Cosas de mujeres* (dir. Rosa Martha Fernández, 1975–78) was nominated for an Ariel award.[55] The collective also developed its own mechanisms of distribution in collaboration with UNAM and through the establishment of an independent distributor, ZAFRA.[56] Not only did their films break with taboos in terms of content and production; they also disrupted cinematic and generic conventions through which women had previously been represented. Earlier independent movements had already begun to contest normative gender roles. Movies like *Tajimara* (dir. Juan José Gurrola, 1965) represented sexual roles in a different light. Women appeared as having their own individual will, and they no longer adhered to traditional representations as mothers, matriarchs, or sexual objects. Moreover, an interest in showcasing women working within the state film industry also emerged in the context of the 1975 IWY. A retrospective of the work of Matilde Landeta, one of the first female directors working in Mexico from the 1940s to the 1950s, was organized and initiated her revival. At the same time, the work of director Marcela Fernández Violante became more prominent in the state-sanctioned film industry. In this context Cine-Mujer can be seen as one of the many ways in which some visual and generic conventions of femininity were challenged through film.[57]

During the 1970s women's participation in the film industry had increased substantially. According to Márgara Millán, in 1970 there were around twenty-four women studying film at CUEC, as opposed to two in the 1960s. By the mid-1980s, the majority of students at both film schools, CCC and CUEC, were women. In the early 1980s there were only two women recognized for their work as film directors, Matilde Landeta (1913–99) and Marcela Fernández Violante (b. 1941), a member of the first generation of film students at CUEC (1964).[58] Fernández Violante produced her first feature film *De todos modos Juan te llamas* (1975), a critique of the Cristero War and the coming to power of the PRI, then controversial topics, under the auspices of UNAM and Echeverría's democratic opening. Matilde Landeta's official recognition began in 1975, in the context of the UN's IWY celebration, when the recently opened Cineteca Nacional organized a series of film showings directed by women that included Landeta's movies. Fernández Violante's film practice, and to a lesser extent Landeta's career, represent one of two distinct models opened for the participation of women in cinema and the production of politically committed films during the 1970s. Fernández Violante responded to a practice that, while espousing a political stance sanctioned by the government's interests, managed to offer an alternative narrative on the role of the Catholic Church and the state. By proposing an alternative approach to politically committed film production, Cine-Mujer represents another model that was opened to the participation of women in cinema. Growing out of independent Latin American and Mexican practices of politically committed film, their audio-visual productions politicized the female body and, by doing so, broke with conventional forms of representation to propose an alternative approach to film production.

La mujer liberada

As Cine-Mujer began to film *Cosas de mujeres* and Landeta's work was being shown at Cineteca Nacional, the Mexican media also turned their attention to women's issues. In preparation for UN's IWY celebration the recently established Televisa organized a meeting with European and North American feminists that produced a series of exchanges with Mexican activists.[59] During the IWY, Canal 13, already a state-owned channel, broadcast a synthesis of the discussions that were taking place as part of the IWY every Saturday at 10:30 p.m.

Concurrently, the national press ran extensive coverage of the celebration and of parallel activities that showcased women's issues across the country. While many of the articles praised the event, many others criticized it as a political smokescreen that relegated the resolution of women's demands to a secondary level. One of the main criticisms, as Oscar Chávez's song tells us, centered on the designation of Pedro Ojeda Paullada as the president of the conference, a man who, at the time, also happened to be the procurador general de la República (attorney general) in President Echeverría's cabinet. For Betty Friedan, feminist author and U.S. delegate, his designation was the kind of incongruity to be expected from *"la tierra del machismo."*[60] This criticism, as well as an extensive exposition of women's demands and feminist agendas, was already being addressed months prior to the event through well-established newspaper columns devoted to the discussion of women's issues, written by prominent members of various Mexican feminist collectives, including Rosa Martha Fernández.[61]

In "La Mujer Mexicana y la Conciencia de la Opresión," an article published in the cultural supplement *La Cultura en México* in 1972, Fernández spoke about how the subordinate condition of Mexican women cut across class differences.[62] She argued that Mexico's dominant patriarchal structure—which rendered gender distinctions as biological and natural rather than as cultural constructs—subordinated women to men across social classes. To back up her arguments she analyzed several advertisements that essentialized women's roles as submissive mothers and wives. In the same issue of *La Cultura en México*, Marta Acevedo and Cristina Laurel published an article on the origins of sexism in Mexico, titled "Sobre el Sexismo Mexicano." These articles were framed by an array of advertisements that supported women's liberation, such as one sponsored by the Comisión Federal de Electricidad arguing that modern women owed their existence to electricity, or an advertisement by Latino Americana de Cosméticos, a cosmetic company, which promoted women's liberation by prompting women to join their door-to-door sales team as a way to escape from family chores and responsibilities.[63] According to Rosa Martha Fernández, the emergence of these feminist voices was welcomed by the intellectual elites, who were proud of finally acquiring a feminist discourse in Mexico. However, she also perceived this welcome as a form of co-optation that took the political edge away from the movement: "Most leftist intellectuals were happy to have feminists. It seems that they realized that they needed to have some and suddenly they realized they had them. This situation favored the movement but because we became their "pets," it tamed our struggles and ultimately was a kind of co-optation."[64]

Another example of this mixed reception of feminism is palpable in sarcastic comments and humorous editorials about the IWY conference and women's demands that flooded the media. These responses reveal another layer of tensions provoked by the international event and the activities of feminist activists. In "El día de la invasión: La mujer liberada," Jorge Ibargüengoitia describes speaking with a taxi driver who shockingly recounts a conversation that he overheard between two conference delegates. One of the delegates said to the other that the use of the preposition "*de*" commonly added to the last name of married Mexican women indicated "property of." Surprised by this interpretation, the taxi driver told Ibargüengoitia, "For goodness' sake! We all know that the preposition "of" used in the last name of a married woman is what gives her honor. It means that she has already chosen her life, made a home, and is a devoted mother to her family."[65] In fact, the removal of the preposition was one of the demands made by several of the Mexican feminist collectives and was also part of Echeverría's proposals. Ibargüengoitia's story (whether fictional or not) shows how both the IWY and the activities of feminist collectives, sometimes described as elitist endeavors without much of a popular following, powerfully transgressed the mores of common citizens. Most tellingly, the anecdote points to the important role that honor—always defined in terms of women's proper sexual behavior and a social virtue that only acquires value in relation to masculinity—has had in defining gender relations in Mexico since the colonial period.

In the aftermath of the IWY, the already significant participation of feminist writers in the press increased as various independent feminist publishing initiatives were launched, including *La Revuelta* (1976–78), *Cihuatl* (1977), and *Fem* (1976–2005), the last of which would become one of the most influential feminist publications in Latin America. By 1976 there were more than twenty feminist activists working for established journals and newspapers and at least one radio program devoted to the discussion of women's rights: *Foro de la mujer*, hosted by Alaíde Foppa (also director of *Fem* magazine) through UNAM radio.

State and private media channels provided platforms of experimentation from which competing political female subjectivities emerged throughout the 1970s and into the 1980s. Marta de la Lama, a feminist militant and anchor for feminist-minded television programming working for Canal 13, and Lolita Ayala, an anchor for Televisa's media distortions and manipulations, represent polar opposite examples of the kinds of visual letradas that were fostered throughout these years. In between and outside the models that de la Lama and Ayala represent, interdisciplinary generations of media-savvy visual letradas encountered each other and played a crucial role in feminizing the media city. Complicating the models established by de la Lama and Ayala is Guillermo Ochoa, a male anchor for Televisa who opened up his international newscast show to Mónica Mayer and Maris Bustamante's experimental and transgressive televisual performances. Ochoa provides an example of the important roles that multiple actors and institutions, as well as humor, would play in opening up spaces for visual letradas in the media city. Pola Weiss offered yet another model of the visual letrada. Like Mayer and Bustamante, Weiss also sought to use television as an artistic platform. Weiss proposed a different framework to think about the uses of video and television broadcasting outside the dominant ideological battles that cast them as commercial and imperialistic technologies. In collaborating with both state and private broadcasting institutions, as well as working independently, Weiss forged a new avenue for political and artistic engagement in the media that would be influential in the decades to follow.

The film industry was a crucial stage for feminist-minded visual letradas. Echeverría's reforms to the film industry fostered the participation of women as film directors and, together with significant international and national developments, promoted, in part, the establishment of Cine-Mujer. Cine-Mujer was a vital platform for the experimentation with distinct forms of representation and different parameters of politics in the arts. The politics espoused by the early films of Cine-Mujer directed by

Rosa Martha Fernández's were not in tune with the politically committed film traditions practiced in the Latin American region at the time. Hence Fernández's career path, much like Ana Victoria Jiménez's path (discussed in part 2) is an example of the transformation in the political stands of some visual letradas who, like her, adapted their class-based politics for a perspective that incorporated women's sexual and reproductive rights. In particular, Fernández's career as filmmaker, activist, and writer provides a key and poignant example of the kinds of interdisciplinary practices in which visual letradas engaged.

The media city provided a varied and rich platform from which visual letradas proposed alternative and competing roles for women and visual representations of female bodies. If by the end of the 1950s Mexican women held posts as ambassadors, magistrates, and high-level bureaucrats, during the 1970s women began to have more prominent roles as film directors, news anchors, and television producers. In these roles they powerfully influenced a transformation and development of new and existing regimes of media and visuality. In tune with feminists elsewhere who criticized the ways in which broadcasting media and film objectified women's bodies, feminist activists in Mexico established independent media outlets and collectives. Yet others worked in mainstream media as well as in academic and governmental media outlets.

3

The Embodied City

A la que nos amó antes de conocernos . . .
por que su maternidad fue voluntaria
(To the one who loved us before knowing us . . .
because her maternity was a product of her own will)

—Inscription, *Mother's Monument*, Mexico City

The *Mother's Monument*

On May 9, 1971, a group of fifteen women gathered at the *Mother's Monument* located in Jardín del Arte in Parque Sullivan, at the crossing of Reforma and Insurgentes avenues in Mexico City.[1] They carried banners and distributed flyers and balloons bearing the question: "*Somos madres ¿y qué más?*" (We are mothers and what else?) (fig. 5).

The gathering was inspired by an article written by journalist Marta Acevedo published in *Siempre!* in September 1970. In it Acevedo described the experiences and tactics of the women's movement in San Francisco, California, and rallied Latin American women to analyze their social condition and realize their creative potential: "What's needed is that each woman should become aware of her potential and demonstrate her creative capacity not only in maternity but in every act of her life."[2] After reading the article, Antonieta Rascón and Antonieta Zapiaín, also journalists, joined Acevedo and began to search for other women who, like them, would be interested in exploring the living conditions of Mexican women.[3] They organized small meetings and interviewed various

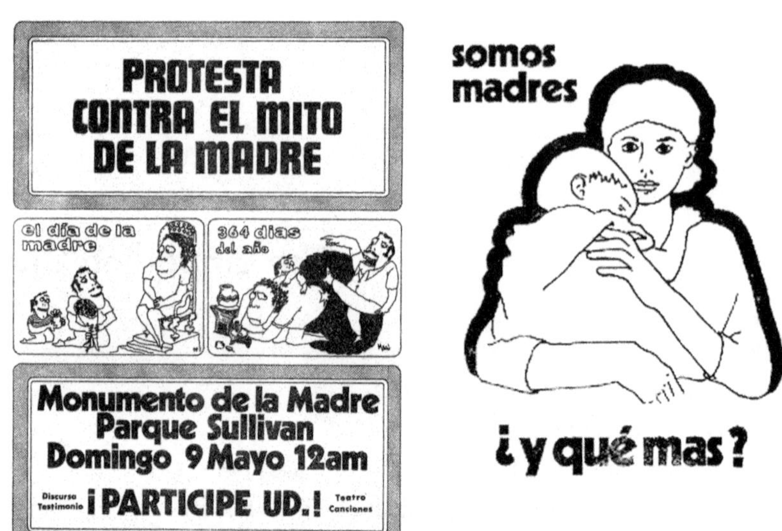

FIG. 5. *Somos madres ¿y qué más?* and *Protesta contra el mito de la madre*. Posters for protest organized by Mujeres en Acción Solidaria (MAS), 1971. Archivo Ana Victoria Jiménez, Biblioteca Francisco Xavier Clavigero, Universidad Ibero-americana, Ciudad de México.

women about their experiences as mothers. They were joined by Nancy Cárdenas, a lesbian activist and theater director, folk singer Amparo Ochoa, and writer and journalist Elena Poniatowska as well as by some militants of the Unión Nacional de Mujeres Mexicanas (UNMM), including Ana Victoria Jiménez.

The idea of meeting at the *Mother's Monument* came about at the small gatherings organized by Acevedo, Zapiaín, and Rascón. Their objective was to question women's social roles and the ways mass media manipulated Mother's Day celebrations and objectified women. These women were aware of the historical relation between the institutionalization of Mother's Day as a national celebration in Mexico, on the one hand, and the fight for women's rights, on the other hand, and sought to rekindle this historical consciousness in the wake of a renewed international feminist movement and President Echeverría's democratic opening.

The history of Mother's Day celebration in Mexico started in 1922, at a time when the recently established government of Alvaro Obregón (1920–24) embarked on major cultural and educational reforms; Mother's Day was established as a national holiday to discredit and silence the feminist movement that had emerged in the southern states of the country.[4] As elsewhere, these early feminists demanded suffrage rights, but they were also discussing birth control and the incorporation of sexual education in public school programs, two highly controversial issues that were not well received by conservative sectors of the population.[5] The outrage caused by these discussions spilled over to the national level, and to counter the assault on proper feminine values posed by them, journalist Rafael Alducín, then head of the newspaper *Excelsior*, launched a nationwide campaign to establish Mother's Day.[6] The revolutionary government and the nation in general warmly received the proposal, and since then Mother's Day has been celebrated on May 10.

Like the institutionalization of Mother's Day, the construction of the *Mother's Monument* several years later coincided with important political events and urban developments that placed women's role as mothers at the forefront of Mexico's modernization project. In 1948, at a time when the Catholic Church and state sought to reconcile with each other after a succession of revolutionary socialist and anti-Catholic administrations, the newspaper *Excelsior*, along with several Mexico City governmental institutions, launched a call for proposals to construct a monument to honor Mexican mothers. The monument, designed by architect José Villagrán and sculptor Luis Ortiz Monasterio, both representatives of the Mexican modernist school in their respective disciplines, was inaugurated in 1949 by President Miguel Alemán. During Alemán's tenure (1946–52), as the PRI began to shed its socialist revolutionary rhetoric for a more conservative tone and to embrace capitalism, Mexico embarked on a modernization program financed in part as a result of the changing economic environment after World War II and the adoption of ISI. Part of this modernization program was visibly reflected in the architecture and urban planning of Mexico City, where a considerable urban transformation took place, led by the modernist urban designs of a new generation of architects. These architects embraced the use of concrete and the construction of high-density *multifamiliares* (housing complexes). The construction of the *Mother's Monument* was part of this modernization program, whereby neighborhoods originally developed under Porfirio Díaz's tenure (1870–1910), which had followed the French style architecture favored during his regime—such as Colonia San Rafael where the *Mother's Monument* is located—were transformed through the international modernist designs of Mario J. Pani, Luis Barragán, and Mathias Goeritz.

The *Mother's Monument* consists of three sculptures carved in stone, of which the central figure is a woman wearing a long dress and a *rebozo* and carrying a baby in her arms. The central figure is meant to embody female values and representations that both the Mexican state and the Catholic Church traditionally conferred on women: *la madre patria*, the working mother and the indigenous virgin, representations that are constantly mobilized and promoted by various sectors of the population and the government in times of social crisis. The two smaller figures that frame the central figure are a sculpture of a man in a writing position and a woman with a cornhusk in her hand, symbolizing education and fertility, two pillars of Mexico's modernization project. Under the central figure a plaque reads: "*A la que nos amó antes de conocernos*" (To the one who loved us before knowing us) (fig. 6).

Soon after its construction, the *Mother's Monument* became part of an official series of monuments located near and along the Reforma Avenue corridor, a place where official ceremonies take place and proper civic values are constantly reinscribed and performed. Parque Sullivan and the *Mother's Monument* became popular gathering sites for all kinds of people. The park became known for its weekend art market, hence its popular name Jardín del Arte (art garden). The *Mother's Monument* became a cherished landmark nationwide due to its popularization through hit movies like *Víctimas del pecado* (dir. Emilio "El Indio" Fernández, 1951). The appearance of the *Mother's Monument* in this and other movies served to propagate sanctioned feminine roles and to popularize the monument as a national site in honor of motherhood and as a shrine of redemption for fallen women, in the case of *Víctimas del pecado*.

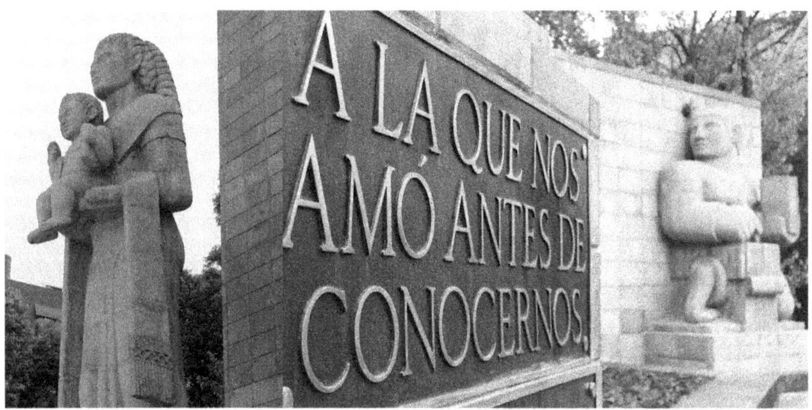

FIG. 6. *Mother's Monument* (detail of main sculpture and plaque), 2011. Courtesy of the author.

The new generation of feminists that emerged in the 1970s contested both the cultural history and the sanctioned conceptions of motherhood embodied by the monument and the Mother's Day celebration. By staging demonstrations at the *Mother's Monument* on Mother's Day, new wave feminists turned both into sites of enunciation enabling a process of change whereby the histories and meanings of the monument and the celebration would be continuously contested. In doing so, feminist activists collaborated in transforming the geographies of the city, coinciding with another wave of urban transformations that took place in the area—the construction of two major transit networks and of high-rises located in Tlatelolco, the latter becoming symbols of state repression rather than progress.

As Acevedo, Rascón, and Zapiaín recruited other women for their meeting, fears of gathering in public spaces in Mexico City were still present after the student massacre in 1968.[7] In order to secure their safety they solicited permission from the authorities to congregate at the monument. Despite the fact that their petition was denied, which only added to the dread of many, fifteen women showed up to distribute flyers and propaganda. As it turned out, the denial of the permit was caused not by a prohibition of public gatherings but because the *Mother's Monument* was already booked for another event. Their meeting coincided with a delegation of candidates from the show *Señorita México*, which had brought an offering to the monument in honor of all Mexican mothers. As a television crew filmed the performance of the *señoritas*, members of what would become the first feminist collective, Mujeres en Acción Solidaria (MAS), took advantage of the situation and also spoke to the cameras. In the gathering the group grew from 15 to 150, and as Marta Acevedo recalls, this was the first time the demands of this new generation of feminists were broadcast on national television.[8]

A year later, in June 1972, another more surreptitious event was organized at the entrance of Metro Insurgentes to protest against the Father's Day celebration.[9] The Insurgentes subway station was inaugurated by President Gustavo Díaz Ordaz in 1969 and is located at the Insurgentes roundabout at the intersection of Chapultepec and Insurgentes avenues The modernist design of the metro station by architect Pedro Ramírez Vázquez represents the bell that Father Miguel Hidalgo rang when he called the Insurgentes army to fight for independence from Spain in 1810.

This time, members of MAS constructed a torso of a man out of papier-mâché and hung it like a piñata at the entrance of the metro station for all passersby to see (fig. 7). The figure was decorated with phrases alluding to fatherhood and its role in sustaining traditional masculine and feminine roles: *Padre: ¡Libérate, liberando a tu mujer!; ¡Vale la pena ser padre, pero no vale ser madre!* (Father: Free yourself, by liberating your woman!; It is worth being a father but not a mother!) (fig. 8). At a time when patriarchal values were being simultaneously attacked and violently reinforced in the streets of Mexico City, this group of women had the audacity to mock how historical symbols of masculinity and patriarchal values had silenced not only women's participation in History but also how normative gendered constructions were rallied around as signifiers of moral and civic behavior. The Insurgentes metro station—in and of itself a symbol of Mexico's path toward modernization and progress—honors symbols of patriotic masculinity (Father Hidalgo, his bell, and his army) that are constantly mobilized to sustain a patriarchal pantheon of historical heroes and civic mores. The papier-mâché man hung at the entrance of the metro station in representation of the Father (Hidalgo, the father of independent Mexico) was also deployed as a reminder of how a violent patriarchal state had turned the symbols of modernization into sites of violence. It accomplished this by serving as a gruesome reminder of the bodies of those students who had been killed during the Corpus Christi (June 10, 1971) and Tlatelolco massacres. However, simultaneously, as a trunk with no limbs, the *piñata* of a man, the Father, was represented as a dismembered body no longer able to mobilize its extremities in the face of an emergent civil society that would take to the streets in greater numbers to criticize the patriarchal order of things and, in doing so, explore new ways of imagining and experiencing an embodied citizenship. By embodied citizenship I mean a broad range of everyday life activities through which diverse communities claim a space in society and eventually their rights. Citizenship is thus conceptualized as a process rather than as a legal category or a government-issued document.[10] Due to the importance that modern cities play in many Latin American countries, urban space is an important site, if not the main site where diverse communities congregate to enunciate distinct and competing claims to citizenship.

The two events organized by MAS, as with many public performances of dissent, formed part of a broad range of everyday life practices through which urban dwellers experienced the city. Such performances leave a mark on their audiences and actively shape a sense of self as embodied: gendered, racialized, sexualized, and differentiated via social class. Embodied citizenship refers to the ways in which public performances of dissent invite passersby and their audiences to imagine change and the terms through which change can be articulated while enabling the negotiation of competing ideas of community. Ultimately, public performances are in and of themselves claims to citizenship.

At stake for Mexican feminist activists during the 1970s was bringing issues of the private sphere into the public sphere in order to articulate political claims that would ultimately redefine their status as citizens. These claims were based on the discursive and material status of their bodies.

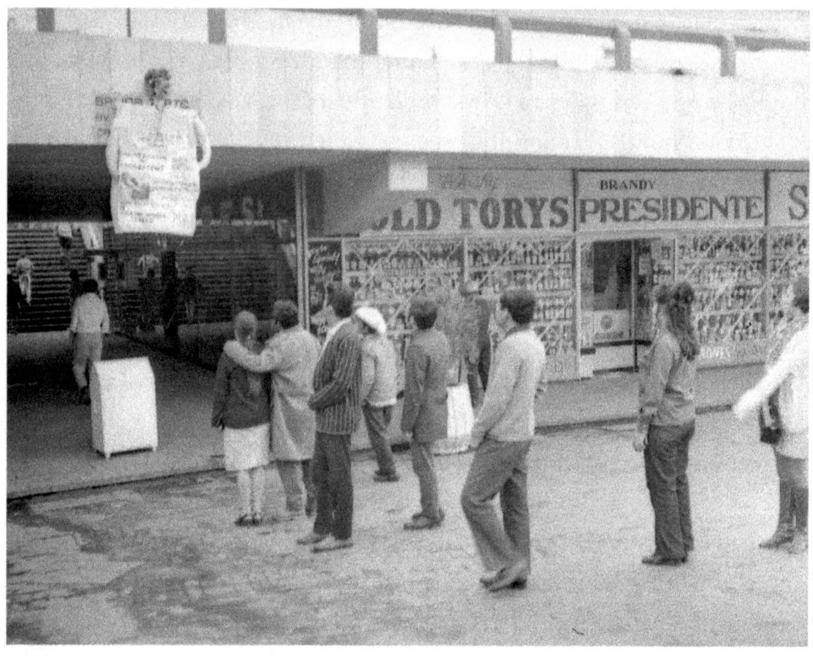

FIG. 7. *Father's Day demonstration.* Insurgentes Metro Station, Mexico City, MAS. Photo © 1972 by Ana Victoria Jiménez. Archivo Ana Victoria Jiménez, Biblioteca Francisco Xavier Clavigero, Universidad Iberoamericana, Ciudad de México.

Their multifaceted practices tackled both embodied encounters and the terms through which their bodies were discursively constructed by laws, social mores, and images. The relation between the discursive and material status of their bodies was conceptualized as interconnected and dialogically produced, not as two separate realms. As Elizabeth Grosz has argued, the body is not only "a concrete, material, animate organization of flesh, organs, nerves, and skeletal structure, which are given a cohesive unity and form through the physical and social inscription of the body's surface," but also "a series of uncoordinated potentialities that require social triggering, ordering, and long term administration." The body becomes a human body when it is defined by "the limits of experience and subjectivity only through the intervention of the (m)other and, ultimately, the Other (the language-

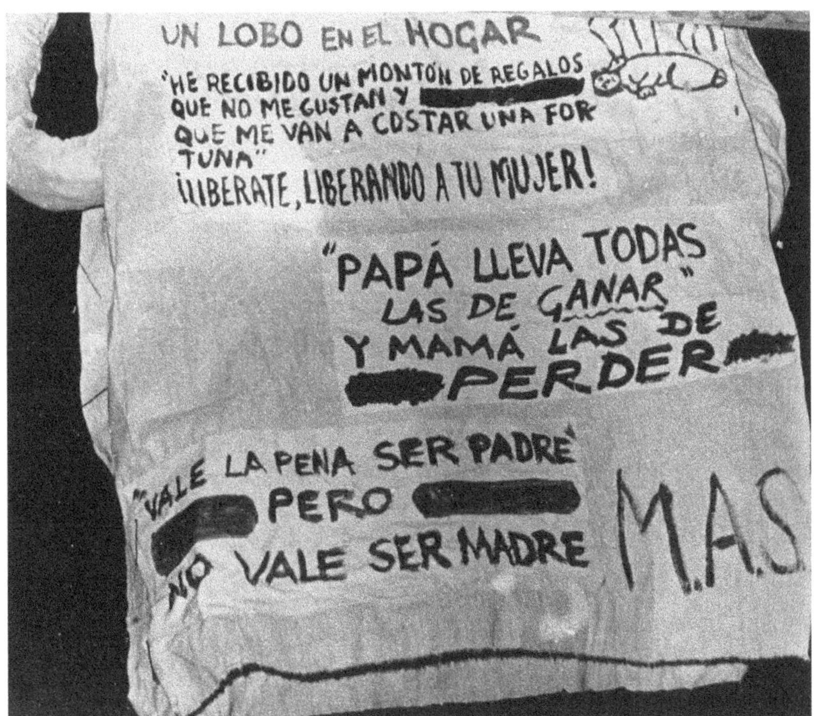

FIG. 8. *Father's Day demonstration* (detail), Insurgentes Metro Station, Mexico City, MAS. Photo © 1972 by Ana Victoria Jiménez. Archivo Ana Victoria Jiménez, Biblioteca Francisco Xavier Clavigero, Universidad Iberoamericana, Ciudad de México.

and rule-governed social order)." Moreover, Grosz's understanding of the dialogical relation between the city and the body helps shed light on the ways that feminists' claims to an embodied citizenship surfaced and were shaped, even as they also helped shape urban space. For Grosz, "the city provides the order and organization"—what she refers to as an interface—"that automatically links otherwise unrelated bodies." The urban landscape, according to Grosz, is "the condition and milieu in which corporeality is socially, sexually, and discursively produced."[11]

These two first meetings organized by MAS, along with Acevedo's article, were the catalysts for the emergence of what some have labeled as second wave feminism or *neofeminismo* in Mexico.[12] In addition, these two events were also key moments in a wider process of transformation that began decades earlier: a process through which patriarchal values and established structures of power began to be questioned and attacked by Mexican civil society. This process responded to generational shifts and political and social transformations that were happening all over the world but were also particular to the Mexican context. Within this local context, the reemergence of feminism, and in particular the presence of feminist militants in the streets of Mexico City, would play a crucial role in proposing alternative models of an embodied and engaged citizen. This engaged citizen followed a long tradition of street performances (protests, strikes, street art, picket lines). By placing emphasis on women's right to their own bodies, this claim to citizenship differentiated itself from this tradition. In doing so, the performative practices of second wave feminists made visible the ways gender and sexuality intersected and served as crucial aspects of any claims to citizenship.

La (re)cámara de diputados: The Personal Turns Political

In the aftermath of these two initial meetings organized by MAS, as Antonieta Rascón recalls, feminists were courted from all sides of the political spectrum.[13] Concurrently, some established media outlets like *Siempre!* opened a space for this new generation of feminists to voice their opinions. By the end of 1972 another collective, the Movimiento Nacional de Mujeres (MNM), was established by Esperanza Brito de Martí along with other women working in broadcasting and print media industries, such as Marta de la Lama. Ana Victoria Jiménez also joined this group.

During the early 1970s MAS was well-known in Mexico City and in other regions of the country. Several members of MAS decided to join women workers' struggles in the textile industry developing in other states (Rivetex and Hilos Cadena in Morelos and Medalla de Oro in Monterrey). Others began to organize conferences in other regions of the country, including Zacatecas, San Luis Potosí, Morelia, Guanajuato, Jalapa, and Chihuahua. Yet other members published articles in national media, organized conferences, and established the project Casa de la Mujer, a short-lived daycare and support group for feminist militants and working women in Mexico City. Soon differences of opinion and strategy emerged among its members (particularly about the kind of relation the collectives should have with governmental institutions), and in 1974 a small group of women who separated from MAS established Movimiento de la Liberación de la Mujer (MLM). As their demands became more centered in the legalization of abortion and the criminalization of sexual and domestic violence, many venues that were initially opened—in particular, political and labor organizations—were not so welcoming to their demands. In contrast to some members of MAS and MLM, members of MNM would work more closely with governmental institutions to promote reforms.[14]

Within the following decades, as differences of opinion between activists led to the establishment of other collectives, the founding members of MAS and MNM became the most well-known feminist activists in Mexico. While some activists participated in both collectives, the main difference between the two resided in their members' willingness to collaborate or not collaborate with the state and over whether or not to integrate other women's movements into their collective efforts. The decision to collaborate with the government or not would become a contentious issue among feminist activists. This difference, to a large extent, would shape the development of the feminist movement and the ways its histories have been written. However, rather than tracing the histories of alliances and antagonisms between activists, I concentrate on their joint efforts and the effects of their practices that led to the feminization of the urban space.

In the context of Echeverría's program of reforms and the looming celebration of IWY, several members of MAS and MNM worked as consultants for government agencies seeking to reform the Civic Code and Labor Laws of the Mexican Constitution; this resulted in further polarization among feminists and between feminists and the government, since most of their demands were not passed by Congress.[15] However, media coverage of the meetings that took place between women's organizations, members of Congress, and Mario Moya Placencia, secretary of the interior, shed light on the ways the presence of women demanding their right to self-representation altered the cityscapes of Mexico City. The media attention to feminist activity called certain publics into being. In conjunction with the increased presence of women in the streets, the media attention to women's issues during this decade developed publics that were both receptive to and critical of feminist demands and created spaces for the emergence of counter publics.[16]

On October 30, 1974, the cover illustration of the magazine *Siempre!* was a mostly monotone cartoon of the façade of the Chamber of Deputies, then located on the corner of Donceles and Allende streets in Mexico City's historic downtown. In the cartoon, the left side of the building's façade depicts a colorful group—including a woman with an Afro hair style (possibly a reference to Irma Serrano), a posh lady, an oversized indigenous woman with no front teeth, a short-haired white intellectual woman with glasses, and a well-endowed female wearing only underwear—taking over the building. The women carry on their shoulders the heavily built woman in her panties and bra, who places a sign with the letters "RE" on top of the entrance sign of the Chamber of Deputies, transforming the *Cámara de diputados* (the chamber of deputies) into the *Recámara de diputados* (the bedroom of deputies). The illustration sarcastically plays off the official media's view of feminist militants as a small group of unattractive, angry women who were a threat to the majority of Mexican women.[17] But the cartoon also anticipated the mass presence of women about to take over the streets of Mexico City during the IWY celebration and its aftermath (fig. 9).

The IWY celebration prompted the establishment of more feminist collectives and their return to the streets, hence the illustration, which rightly, albeit in a sarcastic and demeaning tone, points to a transformation of urban space in Mexico City. Moreover, by turning the sacred temple of the deputies into a bedroom (a *recámara*), the cartoonist depicted an ongoing process of change in the urban space of the capital city—predicting a transformation of the terms of debate regarding women's rights that effectively placed topics previously deemed private at the center of the public agenda. The *cámara* was feminized as it was turned into a *recámara*, and through this process,

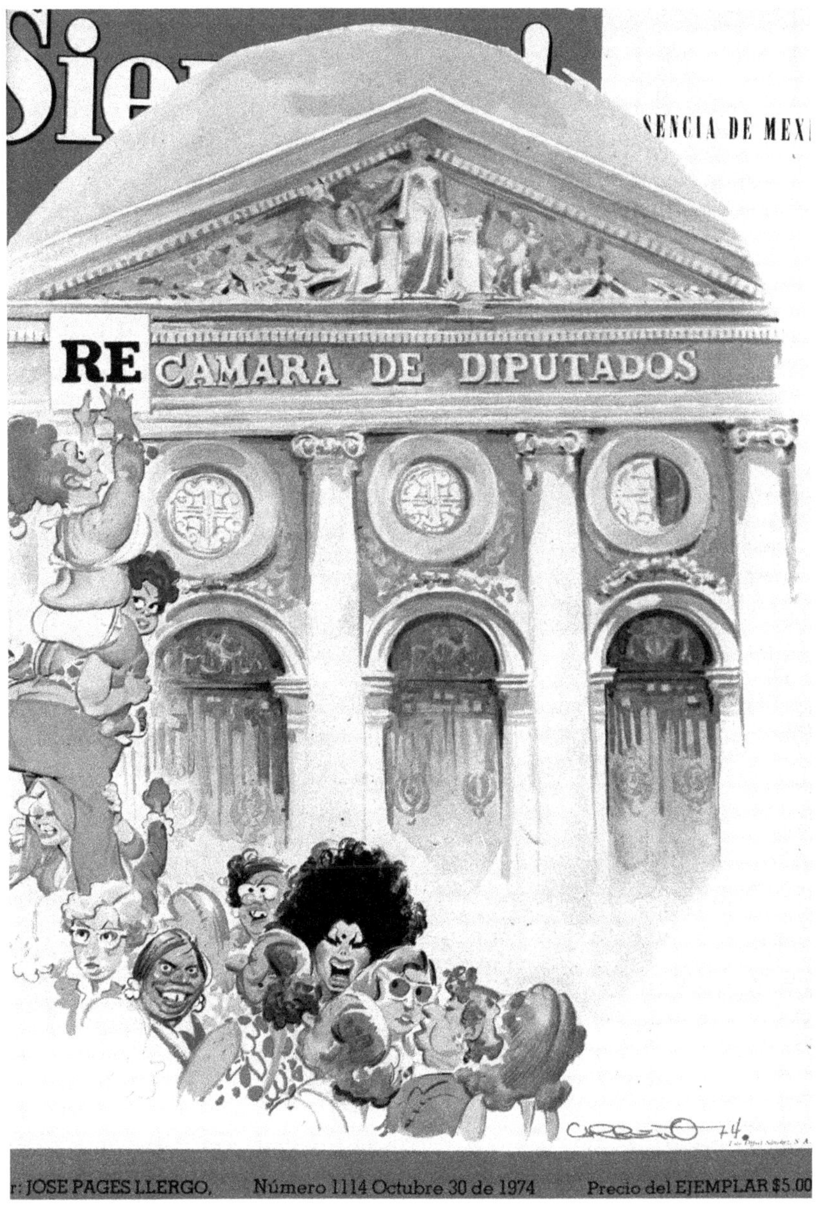

FIG. 9. Cover of *Siempre! Presencia de México*, volume 20, October 30, 1974. Courtesy of Archivos de la *Revista Siempre! Presencia de México*.

the masculine temple of law was opened up to discussions of sexual and domestic violence, gender equity and sexual difference, and other themes that, while still taboo and treated with high doses of sarcasm and violence, would become more openly discussed in the decades that followed.

Fed-Up Women and Beauty Pageants: Unacknowledged Legacies in Mexican Theater and Performance

In the aftermath of the IWY celebration and in spite of the differences among feminists, more collectives, broader coalitions, and exchanges with feminists from other nations were established. In 1975 several members of MLM decided to establish La Revuelta, with the purpose of communicating their demands to wider audiences through different means. In order to do so, members of La Revuelta concentrated their efforts on the publication of a periodical by the same name (1976–78) and on the organization of street theater performances. As a result feminist demonstrations became livelier as many other militants also began to perform songs during their gatherings.[18]

On May 10, 1976, more than fifty women gathered around the *Mother's Monument* in Mexico City singing in chorus verses from Estamos Hartas: "We are fed up with having illegal abortions that put our health at risk; our body is our property and thus together we will fight to defend our rights."[19] At the monument the women staged a theatrical farce entitled *La opresión de la mujer* (Women's Oppression) that ridiculed how the military, the Catholic Church, the government, and the advertising industry oppressed women by dictating supposedly proper feminine values, virtues, and looks.[20] According to a newspaper report the audience included several passersby and members of the Partido Mexicano de Los Trabajadores del Arte (Mexican Party of Art Workers), who joined in the singing and watched the play attentively along with fifty female university students reported to be wearing jeans and shirts without brassieres. Members of La Revuelta carried several large cartoon figures representing a soldier, a priest, a drunk man, an ad man, a politician, an intellectual, and a hippie, while another woman lay on the floor in protest against the male archetypes represented

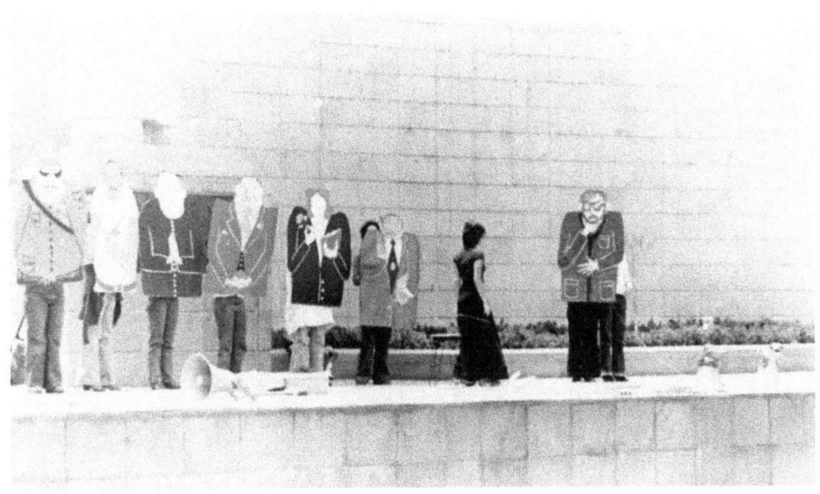

FIG. 10. *Movimiento Nacional de Mujeres y Movimiento de Liberación de la Mujer, Colectivo La Revuelta performing La opresión de la mujer outside Mexico City's National Auditorium* (detail of the military, the woman, and the priest). Photo © 1976 by Ana Victoria Jiménez. Archivo Ana Victoria Jiménez, Biblioteca Francisco Xavier Clavigero, Universidad Iberoamericana, Ciudad de México.

by the cartoon figures (fig. 10). From her prone position, shouting in a high-pitched voice through a loudspeaker, the woman denounced how each male figure oppressed the female portion of the population.[21]

In this performance masculine and feminine roles were essentialized. The use of stereotypical roles was an expedient melodramatic resource that allowed feminist activists to elicit an immediate response from the audience with the least amount of information. By placing those stereotypical icons of masculinity and femininity in an urban public setting, feminist militants invited their audiences to imagine new ways not only of engaging in civic life but also of interrogating established gender roles. While a woman in a prone position represents the feminine role, a role that could potentially reinforce passivity, the act of shouting and denouncing avoids the pitfalls of victimhood. The voice of the woman is the main character in the play. It is a voice that enunciates and articulates forms of oppression in public.

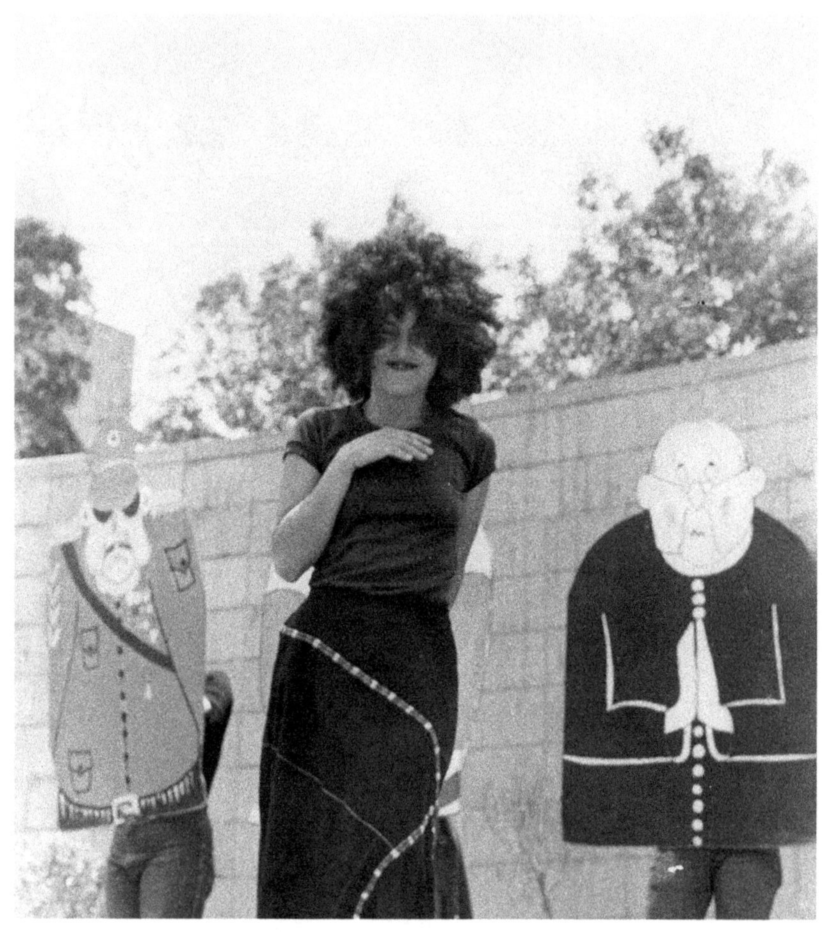

FIG. 11. *Movimiento Nacional de Mujeres y Movimiento de Liberación de la Mujer, Colectivo La Revuelta performing La opresión de la mujer* (detail of the military, the woman, and the priest). Photo © 1976 by Ana Victoria Jiménez. Archivo Ana Victoria Jiménez, Biblioteca Francisco Xavier Clavigero, Universidad Iberoamericana, Ciudad de México.

Moreover, as we can see from the images, the woman is also seen to be standing and even moving in a self-assured manner in between the characters (fig. 11). The play thus encouraged passersby to enact and demand their rights and to interrogate whether they understood traditional gender roles as forms of oppression.

The song "¡Estamos Hartas!" ("Stiamo Stuffi" in Italian) was written by Italian feminists and had arrived in Mexico via exchanges and the travels of several activists.[22] Just as in 1971 the article by Marta Acevedo describing the experiences of U.S. feminists had been an inspiration for the establishment of small conscious-raising groups and feminist collectives, the influx of Italian feminists' experiences and practices injected new energy into the Mexican movement.[23] In Mexico, "¡Estamos Hartas!" (we are fed up, tired, or sick) was performed on several occasions throughout the seventies and, in the process, was adapted to the local context to express feminists' frustrations, becoming a staple phrase in all songs and discourses performed in feminist protests.

Also in 1976 a coalition of more than four collectives including La Revuelta joined forces to establish Coalición de Mujeres Feministas (CMF). CMF organized yearly campaigns to raise awareness on abortion and promote its decriminalization (*Jornadas Nacionales Sobre por el Aborto Libre y Gratuito*, 1976–79).[24] The national campaigns to promote the decriminalization of abortion consisted of a variety of events, including the presentation of books, films, and publications authored by feminist militants who were quite aware of the power of media. Many had careers as journalists or broadcasters and since early 1971 had seized every opportunity to disseminate their demands through various media outlets and were also actively establishing their own platforms of expression.

During its first year of existence, CMF organized a series of events to raise awareness of their national campaign to demand the decriminalization of abortion. They organized gatherings at various venues in the city, including the Auditorio de Recursos Minerales, located at Niños Heroes Avenue, and Casa del Lago, a venue linked to UNAM located in Chapultepec Park. Their events were animated with different kinds of presentations and activities that show the interdisciplinary aspects of both the meetings and the diverse activities in which the members of the collectives were involved. For instance, according to a report by agents of the DGIPS, during a meeting on September 24, 1977, a book written by Rocío Villagarcía, a journalist, and Patricia Berumen, television producer and reporter, was presented. In addition, two movies were shown that dealt with abortion, *Tritste alborada* (dir. Odile Herrenschmidt) and *Aborto clandestino* (dir. Rosa Martha Fernández, possibly *Cosas de mujeres*).[25] Later that year, CMF would begin to publish its own periodical, *Cihuat* (1977), which was distributed freely during their events and demonstrations.[26]

By 1978 CMF's demonstrations had grown considerably. CMF members sought alliances with the gay and lesbian movements and also began seeking more meaningful alliances with workers' unions and integrating open calls for social justice into their demands.[27] Their claims continued to focus on the right to own their female bodies; however, their demands began to denounce other forms of oppression. In doing so, they continued to unveil the workings of social, cultural, and political structures and practices that shaped bodies and dictated appropriate forms of civic conduct. By denouncing other forms of oppression, they forged connections with the plight and demands of other social groups and thus showed how these other demands intersected with those for women's rights.

The activity that attracted the most media coverage and state surveillance throughout 1978 was a series of demonstrations against the hosting of two beauty contests, Señorita México and Miss Universe, both events sponsored by Televisa in collaboration with state and regional governments. At the time, feminist activists all over the world were demonstrating against beauty pageants. Feminist demonstrations against beauty contests are regarded as an important aesthetic milestone in diverse historical narratives of performance and theater. For instance, demonstrations against Miss America and Miss Universe staged by U.S. and UK-based feminist collectives during 1968 to 1971 are considered the first stage in the development of feminist theater in both countries.[28] As in the fields of the visual arts, film, and photography, the legacies of feminist collectives within the disciplines of theater and performance have not been given sufficient attention even though at the time, according to Katherine Nigro, a genre was emerging that could be labeled Mexican feminist theater.[29] Surprisingly, performance scholars who look at the surge of Mexican feminist theater and queer performances in the 1990s, such as Jesúsa Rodríguez or Astrid Hadad, for example, have concentrated on established screenwriters or popular forms of performance such as *carpa* to contextualize their practices.[30] This focus also erases the work of 1970s feminist collectives.

The reasons for this neglect are multiple and intersect many factors, including an apparent lack of sources on these street plays. Most studies of theater rely on the existence of scripts, since plays are mostly studied as a literary genre. Feminist street plays were ephemeral and spontaneous, and to my knowledge there are no records of written scripts. However, as I show, like other social movements that resorted to street plays to voice their demands, this one does have records in the form of photographs, oral testimonies from activists, newspaper articles, and in the recently opened Mexican Secret Service archives containing detailed reports of DGIPS agents who were present at feminist street demonstrations.

Another important factor that has precluded a deep engagement with feminist street plays resides in the ways they contested the definition of political street theater or public expressions of protest that were prevalent throughout the Latin American region at the time. The demands espoused by many feminist militants were perceived as being too closely related to those of "first world" feminists.[31] This closeness makes their street plays less relevant for those who seek to demonstrate a Latin American or Mexican exception. In contrast, what I find interesting is the ways in which ideas, people, and things travel and, in the process, are a response to and actively shape their local contexts. Having said that, while the U.S. women's movement and Italian feminism were crucial influences for Mexican activists, it would be a huge misrepresentation to negate the many ways in which Mexican feminist activists actively located and enunciated their demands in response to and through a meaningful relation with their local context. Likewise, the stage strategies of feminist street plays—including their spontaneity, their use of humor and irony, the lack of a linear narrative, and their use of agitprop strategies—position them in close relation to several traditions of street theater and performance in Mexico as elsewhere in Latin America, such as Augusto Boal's Theater of the Oppressed. In particular, Boal's image-theater is relevant due to its connections with the Italian feminist movement and its emphasis on images created through embodied practices. Boal's image-theater consists of several nonverbal techniques through which participants express feelings, roles, attitudes, relationships, and abstract concepts through physical imagery, such as the cartoon figures used by feminist activists to represent stereotypical male roles. At the time, the famous Brazilian playwright and director spent time in France and Italy working with all-women street theater groups. It is not clear whether Boal influenced Mexican feminists' approach to street plays, but Italian feminists did. Discussing feminist collectives' street plays in the context of these two frameworks—the emergence of feminist theater in Mexico and Boal's image-theater—places these marginal feminist expressions at the intersection of important developments in the histories of performance and theater.

Miss Revolución

Demonstrations against Miss Mexico and Miss Universe were scheduled to take place at various sites in Mexico City as well as in the state of Guerrero during the month of July. On May 28, 1978, more than one hundred feminist militants gathered at the Auditorio Nacional in Mexico City, located on Reforma Avenue, to protest against the two beauty contests scheduled to take place a couple of months later in the town of Acapulco in the state of Guerrero.[32] They demanded that the millions of pesos invested to finance these events, which were sponsored by Televisa in partnership with governmental institutions, could be better used to develop jobs and social programs for women. They also carried banners that read "*Ni objeto decorativo ni sufrida madre abnegada*" (Not a decorative object nor a suffering, self-sacrificing mother) and demanded that sexual violence and the objectification of women be denounced and legally prosecuted.[33]

As elsewhere, their demands were directed against what they perceived as the sexual objectification of the female body performed by such contests. A flyer printed by CMF and distributed during the meeting defined the terms by which this objectification happened: (1) multinational corporations gain financial resources by exploiting female bodies; (2) the government utilizes such contests to distract the population from more urgent matters; and (3) patriarchal society uses such contests to create rivalry among women who have to aspire to be the most beautiful in order to be liked and/or have worth.[34] Mexican feminists did not consider how participation in these contests could grant upward mobility to many of the contestants—a view that was consistent with feminist criticism toward beauty contests elsewhere. Surprisingly, the flyer printed by CMF did not define or attack the beauty standards espoused by such contests, which had been a historical source of contention in previous twentieth-century Mexican beauty pageant traditions.[35] However, a DGIPS report does. In the report, a state informant writes that feminists were protesting against "*un estilo gringo de belleza*," a beauty model that, one suspects, fostered standards of beauty based on light skin and a slim female body.[36] While perhaps not voiced in such terms, the state bureaucrats' report reflected on the views expressed during the demonstration by feminists, many of whom indeed considered the standards of beauty espoused by such contests as a mechanism that promoted aspirations for the majority of Mexican women that could not be fulfilled, not only in racialized terms but in terms of social stratification and privileged access to resources. The profiles of twelve of the thirty-two pageant participants from the organizing committee of Señorita Mexico 1978, found within the DGIPS records, indicate that the young contestants were high school students between seventeen and twenty-one years of age who practiced ballet, tennis, art, or swimming and enjoyed reading. Four of the twelve contestants had green or light eye color and seven had light or white skin tone, although only two, according to the report, had blonde hair.[37]

The demonstrations against beauty pageants marked an important shift in CMF strategies. Besides focusing on the objectification of the *señoritas,* feminist militants also distributed other flyers with information about the violence perpetrated against peasants in the state of Guerrero, including the rape and torture of various women. It was in this information that feminists defined an alternative beauty standard, one that regarded a woman's beauty as a body without traces of violence.

At the time, the region of Guerrero was a site of state violence due to the presence and persecution of members of peasant guerrilla organizations. CMF members distributed flyers providing information about several military attacks and invasions perpetuated during the month of April against fourteen *ejidos* in the state of Guerrero, where women had been tortured and raped.

> On April 15–26, the army abused and killed people in 14 *ejidos* in the state of Guerrero. Men were tortured and women were raped. Until now there has not been any justice. Nonetheless, the port of Acapulco is being prepared to host a masquerade that would serve to showcase an image of this country: during the month of July the contest Miss Universe 1978 will be hosted in Acapulco. Women with slim bodies, with no traces of violence, will be paraded in order to secure profits and to obscure and silence the real conditions that women in the state of Guerrero, in Mexico, and around the world face every day.[38]

CMF's denunciation of state violence in Guerrero brought local relevance to the ways beauty contests objectified female bodies. By making a direct connection between divergent forms of oppression and cultures of violence toward female bodies, CMF reframed their highly politicized demands (decriminalization of abortion and domestic and sexual violence, and media objectification of female bodies) in relation to more recognizable, yet not more visible, forms of violence and oppression. These connections allowed them to reach wider audiences and perhaps incite deeper associations between forms of oppression and the potential disruptions that their acts could represent. They not only demanded that their audiences bear witness to silenced practices of violence but, by making those connections visible, they also demanded some accountability from the structures of power that were invested in obscuring them. Following the work of Elaine Scarry, several performance theorists have argued for the ways in which performing trauma (making visible a personal or communal form of pain) makes visible not only the personal pain but also a mode of citizenship that is resistant to the structures of power and that refuses to see it (the pain inflicted).[39] Scarry argues that the ability to injure others comes from the inability to see them, to witness such injury. Hence performing trauma in urban public spaces makes obscured forms of violence visible and potentially has the power not only of curing trauma but of promoting forms of participatory citizenship and practices of remembrance that are in themselves a powerful means of demanding accountability. While CMF activists did not ground their performance in their personal pain, they used the pain of others to make visible divergent forms of oppression

After several weeks of preparation, CMF planned a demonstration outside the Auditorio Nacional in Mexico City where the Miss Universe swimsuit contest was scheduled to take place.[40] In preparation, CMF members continued to distribute flyers about violence in Guerrero and to show the links between it and the organization of the beauty pageants. They also planned an elaborate series of events including several meetings outside the offices of the Ministry of Tourism, a parade with *carros alegóricos* along Reforma Avenue, and informal gatherings at a venue located in the Coyoacan neighborhood every Friday where several members of CMF performed theater plays for children and families, and on Sundays they hosted a film club.[41]

As it turned out, the swimsuit contest was abruptly canceled; nevertheless, more than 120 people showed up at the demonstration, which took place on June 14, 1978, at the Auditorio Nacional and which was heavily invigilated by security agents. During the demonstrations several women performed a theater farce in which they disguised themselves as Miss Mexico, Miss USA, Miss Italy, and Miss India and performed domestic chores, like washing clothes, in order to show how outside the contest, the beauty pageant contestants continued to be slaves to their domestic lives.[42] They also carried banners that ironically played with the concept of "Revolution," which was particularly resonant in twentieth-century Mexico in reference to the 1910 Revolution and its unfulfilled promises symbolically embodied by the ruling party, the PRI.

CMF members proposed *Miss Revolución*, a new revolutionary standard of female beauty in which sexual pleasure was the main weapon, arguing that feminism was the only route for liberation and change.

> Miss Revolution, a new concept of beauty, equity and justice, and work for all; we are women when we feel the ecstasy of an orgasm, the armed woman will never be raped; Down with the mirror and long live the rifle; Free choice and economic support to perform abortions; Take charge of the word and take over the street; Feminism means freedom and change. Feminism is the fight against sexism in all terrains—the juridical, the cultural, the socio-economic. [43]

With humor and irony, CMF members questioned and subverted established definitions of highly gendered masculine concepts like *Revolución* (revolution) and *Fusil* (gun/firearm) while transforming Emiliano Zapata's famous phrase *Tierra y Libertad* (Land and Freedom) into *Feminismo significa libertad* (Feminism means freedom). Mexican feminist activists inverted Mexico's most recurrent cultural trope and myth of modern nation building—the Mexican Revolution—along with its pantheon of male heroes, tropes that powerfully haunt all narratives of twentieth-century Mexican history. In this way *Miss Revolución* turned the social order upside down by making female sexual pleasure (defined in female terms) the new definition of an engaged and revolutionary citizen. As others have argued, resorting to humor in public performances loosens the reins of the social order, inviting spectators and passersby to step back from the normal rules of everyday life and interrogate their own roles within public civic life.

The use of humor as a transgressive public practice has a long history in Mexican popular performance traditions, but until the 1970s it had yet to be adopted so publicly to demand gender and sexual reproductive rights. Feminist-led street plays and demonstrations, such as the ones enacted by CMF activists, add an alternative and indeed revolutionary lens through which Latin American women might envision parameters of political engagement. In 1966 Mexican philosopher Jorge Portilla wrote *La Fenomenología del relajo* in which he conceptualized the act of *relajo* (goofing off or creating disorder) "as a negation of the required conduct" that "constitutes a position of dissent vis-à-vis the dominant values of the social whole."[44] Yolanda Broyles-González used the concept of *relajo* along with the Mexican *Carpa* tradition and Mikhail Bakhtin's *carnivalesque* to describe how the street performances of Teatro Campesino (1965–80) used high doses of humor to subvert the social order and create a sense of community among their audiences.[45] The multivalent meanings of *relajo* have also been used to understand the forms of cultural resistance that *Madres de la Plaza de Mayo* (Buenos Aires, 1977) enact with their performances aimed at exposing the crimes committed against their sons and daughters during Argentina's Dirty War.[46] Unlike feminist-based demonstrations, the performances of these two groups have become canonical case studies in the field of Latin American performance studies in which the roles of women within Teatro Campesino and the use the archetypical role of motherhood by the *Madres* have been a source of constant debate. Feminist-led street plays and demonstrations neither obscure the participation of women, as in the case of Teatro Campesino, nor excusively resort to the cultural archetype of motherhood, such as *las Madres*. In much the same way, Mexican feminists would begin to use *relajo* more frequently as a way to reimagine what a new participatory (or revolutionary) women's citizenship might look like; that is, as an embodied and engaged citizenship that would place women's rights over their own bodies at the center of the agenda for public debate.

Reading the plays of feminist collectives through the category of *relajo* in the aftermath of the student movement also shows how they transgressed its definition as masculine practice—at least when performed in the public domain. Jaime Pensado's recent study on student revolt in Mexico (1956–71) looks at how *porristas* (male-cheerleaders) used *relajo* (festive disorder) as a boundary marker between youth and adulthood as well as a strategy to shock political groups in search of opportunities to move up the political and social ladder.[47] Particularly relevant for this study is Pensado's discussion of *novatadas* (students' festive parades at the beginning of the school year) along Reforma Avenue. In such events young students cross-dressed as women to ridicule gender roles as part of their overall defiance toward what were considered national appropriate behaviors.[48] In spite of the queer aspect to such performances, such celebrations rendered the use of relajo by young male students as an exclusively masculine sphere of action and a masculine right of passage.[49] In this context, is clear that the use of relajo in feminist performances not only turned the social order upside down in terms of content but also, and equally important, by publicly adopting relajo, a masculine practice, as part of their performances.

On the one hand, the quantity of reports found in DGIPS archives describing the preparation for demonstrations against Miss Universe and Miss Mexico—ranging from accounts of small gatherings for painting banners and crafting bulletins to the biographies of many feminist activists—confirms to some degree that government agents were preoccupied by the possibility of a mass gathering that could place Guerrero's events in an international spotlight. On the other hand, it also points to the bureaucratic workings of the state and its need to produce enemies in order to justify state surveillance and violence. More important, it reveals another front in the battle over women's representation in which feminist activists, media conglomerates, and state institutions were engaged and how these events unfolded in particular sites of the city as well as through diverse performative modalities.

In this battle, four distinct ways of representing the female body were pitched against each other: (1) unattractive feminist bodies, such as the ones that were ridiculed on the cover of *Siempre!*; (2) a transgressive body such as *Miss Revolución* that made sexual pleasure not only a revolutionary weapon but the terms in which feminine citizenship should be defined; (3) the slim and educated bodies of beauty pageants; and (4) the tortured and raped bodies of peasant women from the state of Guerrero. These were by no means the only models of female bodies. In addition, and as mentioned earlier, government institutions and Televisa collaborated in a media campaign promoting family planning. Simultaneously, Canal 13 was in the midst of expanding its broadcasting capabilities to the national level, and programs that dealt with issues of sexuality and women's rights, such as *A brazo partido* and *La barra femenina*, would be aired all over the country. Moreover, after participating in the organization of both events, Televisa introduced a practice whereby the media conglomerate poached beauty pageant contestants in order to transform them into television soap opera (*telenovelas*) stars who set beauty standards and aspirations for many.

As in previous years, competing and divergent images and notions of female bodies circulated, influencing public opinion over the role women played in society. Hence during the 1970s Mexican women were expected to perform sexual restraint in the name of progress rather than be fertile mothers; or they could choose to defend their right to look as they pleased and even parade themselves without bras on the streets while demanding their right to abortion and sexual freedom; or they could be slim, wear high heels, and perhaps dye their hair blonde to aspire to a place in *Señorita Mexico*. Those were the visible bodies. The other bodies—the ones that both mainstream media and the state were not willing to reveal—were those of battered, tortured, and raped women. Through street demonstrations and the distribution of flyers, feminist activists collaborated in breaking with the invisibility of these and other silenced bodies. And, just like their Argentinian contemporaries, Mexican feminists resorted to the cultural archetype of the mourning mother as another performative modality to further their struggle.

Fed-Up Women Take Over the *Mother's Monument*: Fronts and Artistic Coalitions

During the 1970s all kinds of artistic coalitions that sought to place their work at the service of diverse social justice causes were being established all over the city. Many used similar aesthetic strategies to those used by feminist collectives, like street theater, street demonstrations, and other forms of spontaneous improvisation. For instance, in 1978 several art collectives active in Mexico City joined forces and established Frente Mexicano de Trabajadores Culturales (FMTC, 1978–82) to develop relations and facilitate interactions with workers' struggles all over the country and across Latin America with the specific aim of placing multidisciplinary aesthetic practices at their service.[50] To that extent they developed manuals on how to create banners and paint murals; organized conferences, exhibitions, and street theater plays; and participated in street demonstrations. One of the best known events that FMTC organized was "America en la Mira," an international exhibition of print shown in Morelia, Puebla, and Mexico City and a conference on Latin American culture and imperialism.[51] Other coalitions established at the time included Centro Libre de Experimentacion Teatral y Artística (CLETA, 1973–present).[52] CLETA staged plays at Casa del Lago and collaborated with various feminist street plays beginning in 1978 (figs. 12–13).

Resonating with the establishment of other collective fronts, on March 8, 1979, Frente Nacional por La Liberación y Los Derechos de Las Mujeres (FNALIDM) was established with members from several of the initial feminist collectives (CMF, MLN, and Lucha Feminista) and members of the Mexican Communist Party and the Revolutionary Trotskyist Party (PRT), the Union of Workers from UNAM (Sindicato de Trabajadores de la UNAM, STUNAM), the Independent Union of Workers of Colegio de Bachilleres (SINTCB), the teachers' Revolutionary Movement (Movimiento Revolucionario del Magisterio) and UNMM (which later left as some gay and lesbian collectives joined FNALIDM).[53] One of the main objectives of FNALIDM was to elaborate a project on voluntary motherhood legislation that revisited the previous objectives of CMF. By building alliances with various left-leaning organizations they would present their project to Congress by December 1979. In order to raise awareness of the endeavor and their demands, they organized a series of events through which they continued to forge links between different forms of oppression by using *relajo* and, like the Argentinian mothers of La Plaza de Mayo, resorting to the cultural archetype of the mourning mother.

On March 31, 1979, FNALIDM organized its first meeting outside the Chamber of Deputies at which 250 women gathered to demand the right of free and legal abortions in the context of events organized elsewhere as part

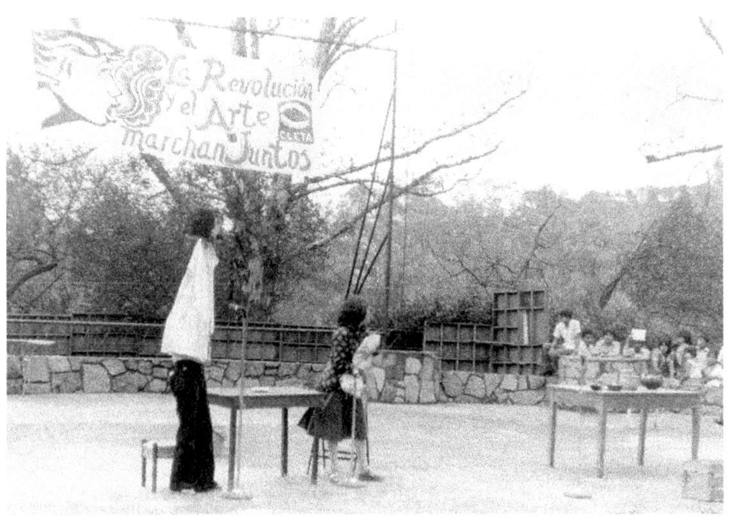

FIG. 12. *Obra sobre el trabajo doméstico, la pareja y el aborto* (close-up view), La Revuelta and CLETA performing at Casa del Lago, Mexico City. Photo © 1978 by Eli Bartra. Photo courtesy of Eli Bartra.

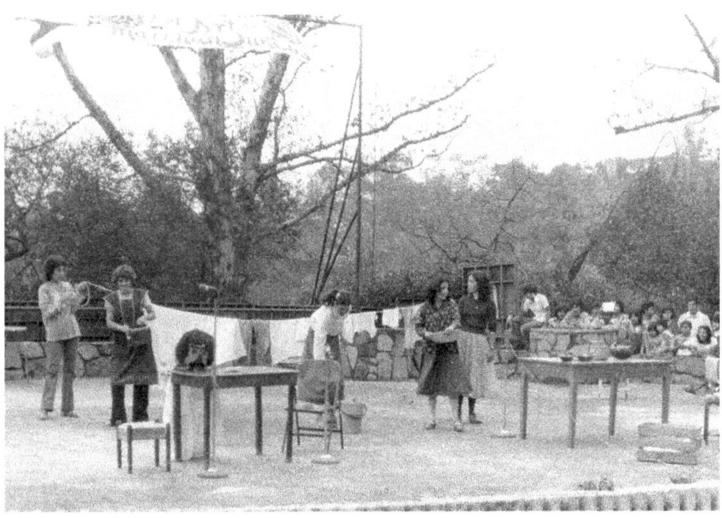

FIG. 13. *Obra sobre el trabajo doméstico, la pareja y el aborto* (wide view of the stage), La Revuelta and CLETA performing at Casa del Lago, Mexico City. Photo © 1978 by Eli Bartra. Photo courtesy of Eli Bartra.

of the International Day of Action.[54] The lyrics of "¡Estamos Hartas!" were printed on a flyer entitled "Estridencias y Desafines" that was handed out to the public. The title of the flyer resonated with earlier Mexican avant-garde art movements, such as Los Estridentistas (1920) and Los Hartos (1960), but the lyrics of the song were transformed to attack Mexico's ruling party.[55] As the demonstrators marched through the streets of downtown Mexico City and toward the Chamber of Deputies they sang "yes, yes, yes, abort the PRI" (*sí sí sí abortemos al PRI*) and "look Hank González the streets are not yours" (*Ya viste Hank González no son tuyas las calles*).[56]

At the time, Carlos Hank González was Mexico City's mayor, and several months prior to this demonstration he had ordered the removal of "Campamento 2 de Octubre," a group of women who demanded justice after state officials had burned their illegal settlement on the outskirts of the city, killing their sons and daughters while they were at work. The banners also made reference to the persecution and battering of gay men. Their banners and chants made further links between different forms of policing and state repression carried out on the streets of Mexico City: "Not only gay (men) are victims of persecution; we demand an end to all forms of policing (*redadas*) and an end to police repression."[57]

In this demonstration feminist activists re-signified their demands by connecting them with other calls for justice: those of destitute mothers over their children's burnt bodies and those of gay men. As mothers from Campamento 2 de Octubre and gay activists demonstrated along with feminist activists, feminist-led demonstrations became the stage on which silenced violence against all kinds of bodies was denounced and made visible. In doing so, the feminist motto "the personal is political" was embodied in the links that formed between private forms of violence and public expressions of state repression.

On May 10, 1979, around 200 women dressed in black walked from *El Angel de La Independencia* and along Reforma Avenue toward the *Mother's Monument* to mourn the women who had died due to abortions performed illegally. They carried a huge funeral wreath made not of flowers but of objects used to induce abortions: knitting needles, coat hangers, turkey feathers, and natural herbs. At the end of the march the funeral wreath was placed at the *Mother's Monument* (figs. 14 and 15). Like the Argentinian *Madres*, feminist militants used the mother archetype to make their opinions heard, but unlike those predecessors, they demanded the right to decide about the number of children to have and demanded safe conditions as well as the infrastructure to ensure such rights. In an interview Carmen Barajas Sandoval, a member of MNM, told a newspaper journalist that 80 percent of women who performed clandestine abortions in Mexico City were married, lower-class women and mothers of more than three children, women who placed their already established families at risk by undergoing abortions in unsafe and illegal circumstances. During the demonstration activists also shared their own experiences with abortion giving passersby an opportunity to become witnesses to a "performance of trauma"; as a result, this performance created alternative spaces for cultural and civic engagement.[58]

The reference to a funeral procession was a powerful performative modality that has a long tradition for Mexico City dwellers and could attract the curiosity of many passersby. This demonstration was also in dialogue with events taking place in the United States. According to Ana Victoria Jiménez, the idea of constructing a funeral wreath was that of Lila Lucido de Mayer, Mónica Mayer's mother and militant of the MNM. Ana Victoria Jiménez and Lila L. de Mayer had met when both were militants of MNM (lead by Esperanza Brito de Marti), and both had participated with the CMF and later with FNALIDM. Mónica Mayer and Ana Victoria Jiménez had also met at several demonstrations organized by CMF and by then had already collaborated with Cine-Mujer. At the time of the funeral-wreath demonstration, Mónica Mayer had already spent a year at the Feminist Studio Workshop at the Women's Building in Los Angeles, California. Mayer had been exposed to the work of Suzanne Lacy and Leslie Labowitz, both U.S.-based feminist artists who had staged street performances and aestheticized media events to demand the end of violence against women. Lacy and Labowitz established Ariadne: A Social Art Network, a feminist group that integrated politics with aesthetics.[59]

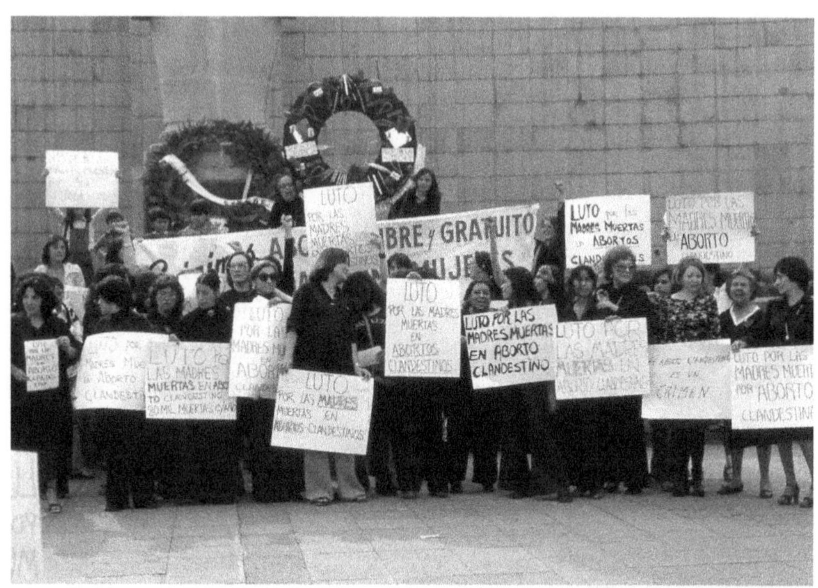

FIG. 14. *Coalición de Mujeres Feministas. Mother's Day demonstration, May 10.* Photo © 1979 by Ana Victoria Jiménez. Archivo Ana Victoria Jiménez, Biblioteca Francisco Xavier Clavigero, Universidad Iberoamericana, Ciudad de México.

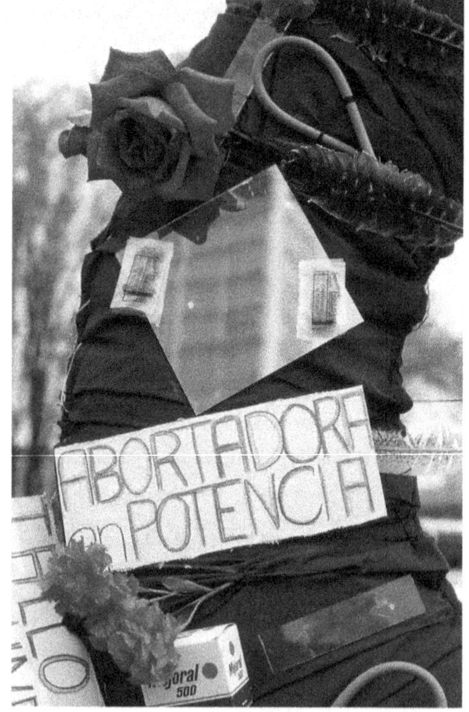

FIG. 15. *Coalición de Mujeres Feministas. Mother's Day demonstration, May 10* (detail of the crown). Photo © 1979 by Ana Victoria Jiménez. Archivo Ana Victoria Jiménez, Biblioteca Francisco Xavier Clavigero, Universidad Iberoamericana, Ciudad de México.

The process of forging connections between U.S.-based feminists and members of MNM had begun earlier that year, when Mexico City was placed on the map in one of the most iconic pieces of worldwide feminist art, of which Ana Victoria Jiménez and Lilia Lucido de Mayer had been the main organizers. On February 14, 1979, Suzanne Lacy began a global project entitled *International Dinner Party* to honor her mentor, Judy Chicago, in the context of the first exhibition of Chicago's *Dinner Party* at the San Francisco Museum of Modern Art.[60] Lacy's international version of the *Dinner Party* consisted of hosting dinners, all on the same evening as Chicago's opening, to honor women in their own regions. At each dinner women collectively wrote a statement that was sent back to Lacy via telegram. At the San Francisco museum Lacy marked each dinner with a red inverted triangle on a twenty-foot black-and-white map of the world.[61] In Mexico City a dinner was hosted at the home of Lilia Lucido de Mayer to honor Adelina Zendejas, Amalia Castillo Ledón, Elvira Trueba, and Concha Michel, all important women in the post-1920 period who had fought for social causes or, as Jiménez would call them, *"nuestras madrinas"* (our godmothers) (figs. 16 and 17). This event passed almost unnoticed in Mexico City's art circles but began to draw connecting lines between different women and conceptions of art and feminism.

Mónica Mayer would continue to foster relations between U.S. feminist artists and a cohort of activists related to her mother and Ana Victoria Jiménez. By the end of the year Mayer returned to Mexico City accompanied by three other American artists, Jo Goodwin, Denise Yarfitz, and Florence Rosen, to develop her project *Traducciones: Un diálogo internacional de mujeres artistas.* The project consisted of generating dialogues and encounters between Mexican and U.S. women artists and feminist collectives. The objective of the encounter was to share the information that she had learned at the Women's Building and promote feminist art in Mexico.[62] Along with Jiménez, Lilia L. de Mayer (Mónica's mother), Ana Victoria Jiménez, Yan Castro, Monical Kubli, Ester Zavala, Marcela Olabarrieta, Ana Cristina Zubillaga, and Magali Lara also collaborated with the organization of the events (fig. 18).

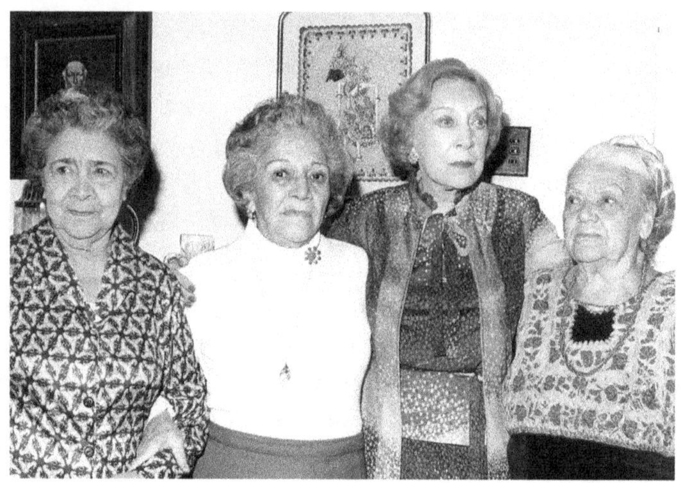

FIG. 16. (*Left to right*) Elvira Trueba, Adelina Zendejas, Amelia de Castillo Ledón, and Concha Michel at *International Dinner Party*, Mexico City. Photo © 1979 by Ana Victoria Jiménez. Archivo Ana Victoria Jiménez, Biblioteca Francisco Xavier Clavigero, Universidad Iberoamericana, Ciudad de México.

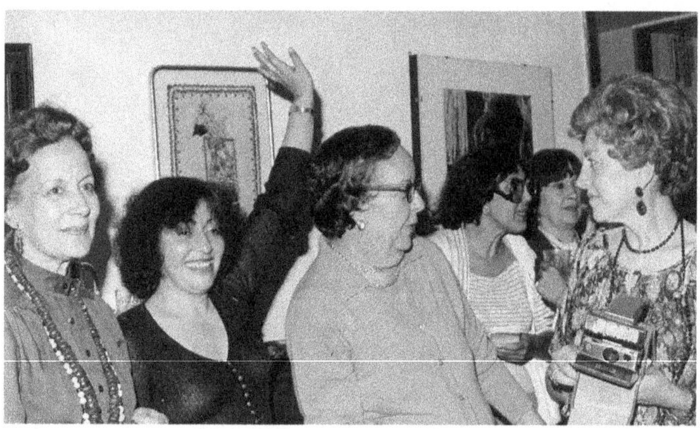

FIG. 17. (*Left to right*) Alaíde Foppa, Ana Victoria Jiménez, and Lilia Lucido de Mayer and other guests at *International Dinner Party*, Mexico City. Photo © 1979 by Ana Victoria Jiménez. Archivo Ana Victoria Jiménez, Biblioteca Francisco Xavier Clavigero, Universidad Iberoamericana, Ciudad de México.

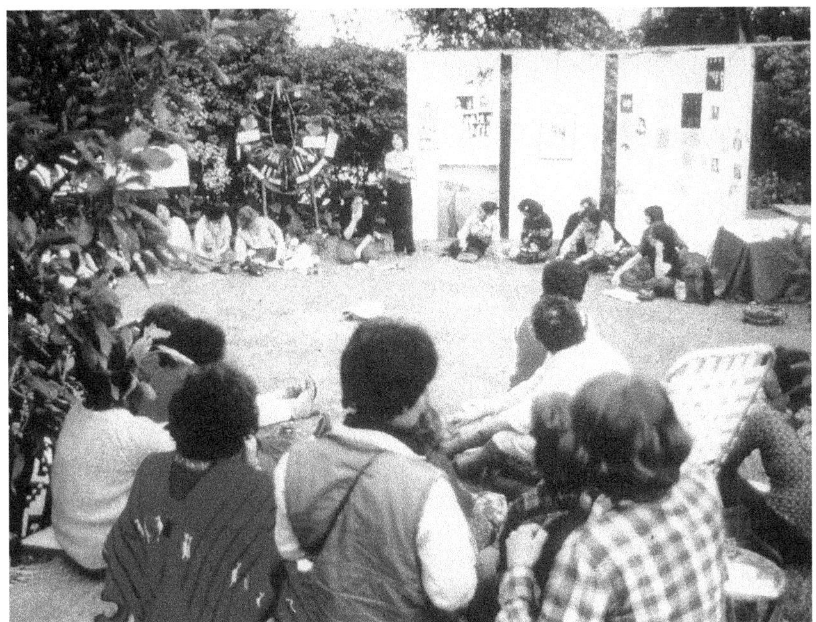

FIG. 18. Encuentro in Cuernavaca, as part of *Traducciones: Un diálogo internacional de mujeres artistas*, Cuernavaca, Mexico. © 1979 Mónica Mayer. Photo courtesy of the artist.

The highlight of the event was a three-day meeting that took place in Cuernavaca at the home of Nancy Cárdenas. Seventy women from all over the country attended the meeting, including artists, feminists, activists, and some women who had never been involved with feminism. The *encuentro*, in Mayer's words, was a very difficult experience.[63] In a report of the *encuentro* that became a work of art authored by Mayer, she explained how Mexican attendees were disappointed and outraged by the format of the meeting. While the Mexican feminists expected a conference setting where different women's committees would present their views, what they encountered was a kind of creative exploratory workshop to investigate the relation between art and politics.[64]

The meeting exposed a crucial obstacle to the recognition of feminist art: that is, the disavowal of art as a political tool by most feminist militants. Art was understood by some militants as a set of traditional practices (mainly painting and sculpture) sanctioned by the art world. Many saw the art world as a bourgeois and patriarchal institution, in spite of the political connections that art had historically had in Mexico during the twentieth century.[65] While in other places feminist critics and artists took a strong stand in dismantling the patriarchal workings of the art world, feminist Mexican academics and militants preferred to dismiss this task altogether. Women artists created work that addressed their feminine condition, but not many criticized the ways in which the art world conditioned their careers as artists based on their gender. Likewise, few established art critics fully adopted a feminist critique of the art world. A few exceptions were in the issue of *Artes Visuales* already discussed, where most of the contributors agreed that a feminine aesthetic per se did not exist, and while there was an acknowledgment of the ways in which dominant sociocultural structures oppressed women, there was not a commitment to developing or differentiating a feminist art movement since art, for many of them, was gender neutral. While the efforts to develop stronger links between established aesthetic practices were not welcomed by the majority of feminists, their practices in and of themselves show how, as in previous years, multidisciplinary aesthetic practices and diverse performative modalities were strongly correlated and in dialogue with social causes. The Mexican feminist demonstrations of the 1970s, which were aesthetically and symbolically charged, are part of this important national tradition and were also in crucial dialogue with transnational practices.

By the end of the decade feminist demonstrations had changed. Their demands expanded as they identified the links between diverse cultures of violence and forms of oppression against all kinds of bodies. Mexican feminist demonstrations asked their publics to imagine what a new participatory (or revolutionary), embodied, and gendered citizenship would look like.

The stage from which they enunciated these alternatives and the people who supported them had also changed, and in the process, they called different publics into being. In the course of a decade they had staged their performances at the most visible landmarks of Mexico City's downtown core. They had met at the Mother's Monument, marched along Reforma Avenue, stopped at the Zócalo (Plaza de la Constitución), the Monumento a la Revolución, and Hemiciclo a Juárez. They had also attempted to build alliances with other social movements. They launched a national campaign to raise awareness about abortion and proposed legal reforms to decriminalize it. Feminist activists had opened a center for victims of rape (Centro de Apoyo a Mujeres Violadas, CAMVAC, 1979). Some activists developed networks outside the parameters of the nation, such as the networks with other feminist artists that Jiménez and Mayer had attempted to forge. Others slowly shed their mistrust toward international organizations and did everything they could to advance their agendas; in order to do so, they celebrated international days in favor of women's reproductive rights and were keenly aware of international developments, using them as platforms for their local demands. In the process, the geographies of Mexico City were transformed as feminist demonstrations were joined by a number of other groups including homosexual and lesbian collectives, worker and university unions, and left-leaning political parties and other coalitions interested in demanding a broad range of civil rights as part of a more democratic political agenda that included sexual liberation and reproductive rights.

Feminist demonstrations left important remains throughout Mexico City's streets, and their practices were inscribed onto the urban landscape. In 1991 a group of women close to Esperanza Brito de Marti, founder of MNM, added a plaque with the phrase *por que su maternidad fue voluntaria* (because her maternity was a product of her own will) to follow the initial phrase *a la que nos amó antes de conocernos* (to the one who loved us before knowing us) (fig. 19).[66] By adding this plaque—which has been an ongoing source of struggle, as it has been removed and replaced several times—feminist activists ensured that their history would have a place in the official pantheon of heroes adorning the streets of Mexico City and that the processes of feminizing the city would be rendered visible.

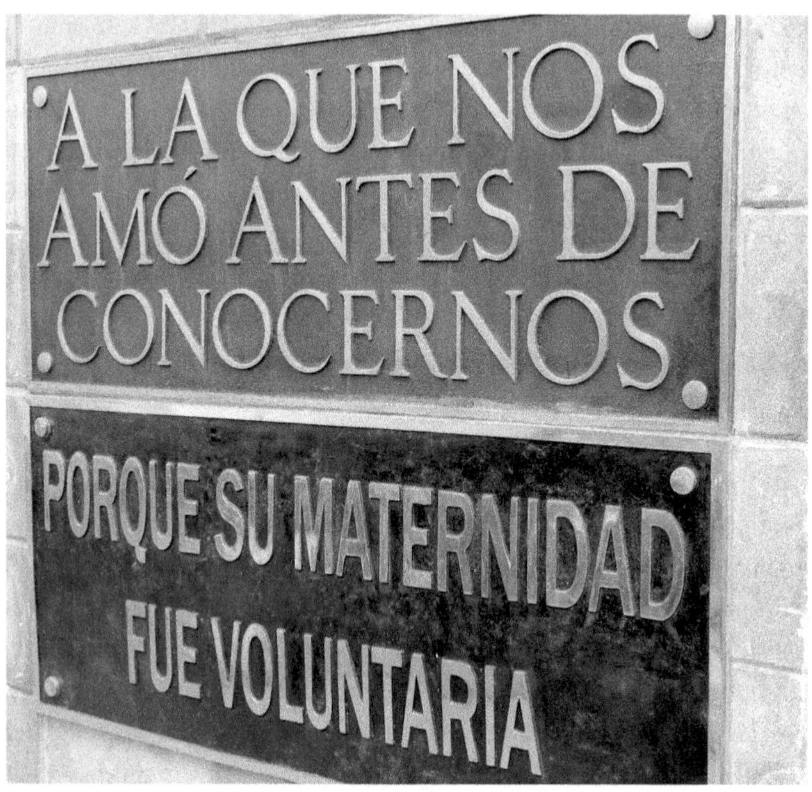

FIG. 19. *Mother's Monument* (detail of the change in the plaque), 2011. Courtesy of the author.

Women's representation (visually and in formal politics) was a central concern of media conglomerates, governmental institutions, international organizations, and feminist activists throughout the 1970s. All these actors played a crucial role in the process of feminizing the cultural geographies of Mexico City. This process entailed a transformation of the urban land-scapes that included a change in its physical aspect—like the change in the *Mother's Monument* plaque. It also required adaptations at various social levels and the adoption of new regimes of media and visuality. New publics that were critical and receptive to feminists' demands were created, as the presence of feminist activists in the streets of Mexico City questioned definitions and conceptions of citizenship and traditional gender roles. Media conglomerates, political parties, and governmental bodies also turned to women's bodies (discursively and visually) as a means of achieving social, commercial, and political standing. The development of new regimes of media and visuality responded to international and national transformations that positioned broadcast media—in particular television—as the most powerful means of communication. Equally important was the development of new modes of subjectivity set in motion by the increased participation of women in the public domain and, in particular, the participation of feminist activists in various social realms. By launching an attack against the juridical system, established art practices, and institutions as well as through the establishment of alternative networks of communication and media practices, feminist activists uncovered the ways in which dominant patriarchal structures worked themselves into embodied regimes of media and visuality. The following sections explore how four visual letradas used different media to construct new modes of subjectivity to counter dominant forms of creative production.

PART 2

The Archival Practices of a Visual Letrada

4

The Archival and Political
Awakenings of Ana Victoria Jiménez

An Encounter with the Archive

When I finally was able to arrange a meeting with Ana Victoria Jiménez, I didn't think anything of it. I thought I would visit, talk, and go over folders of images and documents as I had done while consulting other personal archives. However, upon arriving at Jiménez's place, I realized that her archive and her home were one and the same. Our conversations took place in her office, which seemed to be the living room, full of papers, books, boxes, and filing cabinets. I sat on a chair near a doorway from which I could see her bedroom, also full of documents. During our conversations Jiménez showed me images on her computer monitor, magazine articles, and books as if we were going through a family album.

In the course of our conversations and perhaps driven by Jiménez's performance of a particular sense of self, her archival persona, I discovered myself attempting to classify Jiménez's archive and her archival practice as either a *fama* or a *cronopio*. At first glance, Jiménez seemed to fit Julio Cortázar's description of a *cronopio*, those disordered beings who leave their memories all over the house and, as they wander through their living room, pause to caress them and tell them "don't hurt yourself, walk carefully."[1] I thought Jiménez's interest in collecting and keeping track of her feminist activism was incited by a nostalgic desire and a need to keep track of her daily life as a constant reminder of who she was. I read all the materials that she was showing me as if they were mementos of her life, and they were. But as our conversations progressed, I changed my mind and thought Jiménez's preoccupation with making records and keeping documentation placed her closer to a *fama*.

Cortázar describes *famas* as those who carefully embalm their memories. First, they fix the memory with detail (*pelos y señales*) and then, once it is fixed, they proceed to wrap it from head to toe with a black blanket. Once the embalming procedure is done, they prop the memory against a wall and attach a little white note with details of the memory. As I began to learn of Jiménez's political commitment to feminist causes, I understood that an important part of her self-assigned duty was to keep a detailed record of all the activities in which she participated. Hence, in my mind, her conscious political commitment spoke of an awareness of the value of the documents and images she was keeping and classifying, thus aligning her more closely to a *fama*.

My conversations with Jiménez were framed by my interest in understanding her archival persona as a practice that gave continuity and connected her wide-ranging feminist militancy with her interests in photography and performance art. But they were also framed by Jiménez's interest in making sense of her archive. The potential that her archive and life story could bring for constructing new wave feminisms as being more diverse than they were thought to be was of interest to both of us. Most historical narratives on new wave feminisms in Mexico see the movement as the project of an exclusive group of university-educated women.[2] This argument has been used (even by feminists themselves) as a way of downplaying the influence that feminisms have had on Mexican culture in the past five decades. Defining feminism as an exclusively upper-middle-class movement means that women's popular movements are excluded from being labeled feminist; secondly, it strengthens the myth that feminism had the potential of breaking the tradition of labor and rural movements due to its sexual and gender demands, which were seen as being under the influence of U.S. capitalist and imperialistic interests; and, third, it reinforces the view that feminism's impact and historical relevance was minimal because, as an upper-middle-class movement, it was supposedly elitist. These discourses place the relevance of the feminist movement in a bind where, on the one hand, most of the history of Mexico is written through the lens of elite groups, and on the other, an academic focus on lower-income social movements denies the place that a group of urban middle-class women can play in historical discourses. Tracing the practices and activities of Jiménez shows how new wave feminisms were more diverse than was previously thought.

During the course of our conversations, Jiménez's anecdotes pointed to an ongoing negotiation of sense of self through the deployment of diverse narrative patterns (romantic-epic, comedy-melodrama, tragedy, etc.) and levels of narration (expository and conversational) that allowed her to envision her archival practice as a performance of self in which diverse elements produced tension but also continuity and coherence. As Daniel James points out, in oral testimonies there are different patterns and levels of narration through which the interviewed negotiates a sense of self.[3] James distinguishes two levels of narration that are produced in oral testimonies. The first one consists in the subjects' ability to resort to "a dominant narrative form of professional historical discourse, framing their narrative within the canons of expository narration."[4] Certainly Jiménez's weathered experience as an independent publisher and editor for La Unión Nacional de Mujeres Mexicanas (UNMM), her wide-ranging political militancy, and participation at IWY's NGO forum, along with her relations with activists, artists, and academics, afforded her a deep understanding and awareness of the existence of such canons. The second level, according to James, is composed of "a far more conversational narrative framed as personal experience, anecdotes, and gossip," which was present throughout our conversations.[5] As James goes on, these two levels of narration are, first and foremost, framed by the nature of the relation established between interviewer and interviewee, their personal interests, their distinct social and cultural capitals, and "the power of the interviewee to negotiate the conditions under which communication takes place in the interview situation."[6] This negotiation also includes "the realization that there are things that are not understood due to the fact that one has experienced the event and the other hasn't."[7] Surely in our conversations Jiménez made use of these two levels of narration as well as diverse patterns of narration to negotiate a sense of self and in so doing construct an archival persona in a manner that, to some extent, fulfilled my own expectations.

Ana Victoria Jiménez: Feminist Activist, Archivist, Editor, and Photographer

Jiménez came of political age in the 1960s when she became a member of UNMM, an alliance of women's organizations, activists, and workers' unions, mostly affiliated with the Communist Party established in 1964. Before becoming a member of UNMM she had been a militant in the Communist Youth League and had been marginally involved in the 1968 student movement. As a member of the Communist League she was detained and arrested on April 14, 1965, as part of a crackdown on radical activity undertaken by Mexico City police against members of the Communist Party, Central Campesina Independiente, and Frente Electoral del Pueblo. In 1969–70 Jiménez was the representative of UNMM at the Federación Democrática Internacional de Mujeres in Berlin and for a number of years collaborated in the production of its bulletins.[8] It was at this time that she began collecting graphic ephemera and taking photos of the demonstrations and events organized by the UNMM.

Jiménez's activity as a collector of ephemera and her interest in photography developed in tandem with her militancy in the UNMM; its roots are also found in her career in the graphics industry. In the early 1960s she studied graphic arts at El Sindicato de los Artistas Gráficos, and soon afterward she began to earn a living as a typesetter in a print shop, where her job was to make sure there were no typos in the slugs, the assembled line of metal type used in a linotype press. A couple of years later she went to work for IBM, where she used a portable machine for setting type. Years later still, she established herself as an independent editor and desktop publisher, publishing books on the history of the UNMM, its militants, and a number of artists. At first, graphic material interested Jiménez for purely aesthetic reasons. She told me, "*Guardé los carteles por que me interesaban, porque estaban bonitos*" (I only began to keep the posters that I liked for their aesthetic qualities). She was interested in collecting graphic material as inspiration for projects at her job. And while she also took photos, she explained that she did not keep any of the images she shot in the 1960s because their quality was very poor. In the early 1970s, when she was able to purchase a better camera, she began keeping the photographs, and out of the need to label and keep track of those photographed, she began to develop a system of classification. Photography then, became Jiménez's archival impulse, an urge that Hal Foster defines as a tendency to make historical information—often lost or displaced—visible.[9]

Jiménez did not have a high school diploma (which was not uncommon for women of her generation), and this prevented her from attending university or art school. During our conversations she made a point of clarifying that the Sindicato where she studied, although not related to the famous Taller de Gráfica Popular (TGP), is actually the union of linotype press workers. Jiménez's emphasis on this issue could be read as a mere gesture to avoid confusion between different specializations within the print industry, but it could also be read differently, as a way to distance herself from a visual arts milieu and to assert her position as a working-class woman (a point she also made when asked about her training in photography). While she had been interested in photography since an early age, it was not until 1974 that she was able to study photography at technical college by night in order to complement her career in the graphics industry. As I will discuss, during our conversations, Jiménez distanced herself from established traditions in art, feminism, and women's activism while also claiming a place within some of these traditions. This ongoing negotiation between claiming difference and continuity was a key narrative that Jiménez used to construct her archival persona.

The legacy of TGP, a collective of print artists, founded in 1938 concerned with using art to advance revolutionary causes, is well recognized. Most of its members, including Leopoldo Méndez, Pablo O'Higgins, Luis Arenal, Mariana Yampolsky, and Fanny Rabel, to name a few, are well-established in the annals of art history (albeit more within a history of print culture than "Art"). Jiménez's need to distance herself from the legacy of TGP points to a different career path that led her, like the members of TGP, to an interest in linking art and politics. In this manner, the way that Jiménez constructs her career path offers an interesting counterpoint to the well-known trajectories of other famous Mexican visual artists whose interests also resided in linking art with social causes.[10]

Jiménez's background at the union of linotype workers and her militancy with left-leaning organizations bespeak not only her working-class background (or interest in fashioning herself as such) but also her practice in an industry related to publishing, editing, and journalism. These conditions link her to the life histories of many militants of the UNMM, who built careers as journalists, schoolteachers, and militants of the Communist Party and who, arguably, came from working- and middle-class backgrounds and moved up as they had access to other posts and careers. Particularly during the Lázaro Cárdenas administration (1934–40), a great number of women participated in shaping social change through their work as schoolteachers, their participation in literacy campaigns, and journalism. Many women wrote columns in newspapers, albeit with pseudonyms, and many had to establish their own newspapers and magazines in order to have access to this field. This group of early journalists and activists, many of whom joined the UNMM, included Julia Nava de Ruisánchez, Esther Chapa, María Luisa Ocampo, Concha Michel, Amalia de Castillo Ledón, and Adelina Zendejas.[11]

In the mid-1960s, through her militancy in the UNMM, Jiménez was introduced to the thought and lives of many of these early twentieth-century women activists and militants, those whom she calls "*nuestras madrinas*" (our godmothers). She recalled that she first knew about the UNMM because she was invited to attend a meeting about women's rights (the right to work, pay equity, and upward mobility). At the time she was a militant in the Communist Youth League. While the issues posed by UNMM were very interesting, Jiménez told me that they were all framed within a leftist discourse based on class struggle. For instance, the decriminalization of abortion, the problems brought about by the double shift, unpaid work at home, and paid work outside the home were not considered. Moreover, Jiménez recalled that issues of sexuality did not figure at all. It was not until the 1970s, with the emergence of new wave feminisms, that she began to understand the differences between the objectives of the UNMM and the set of preoccupations of the emergent feminist collectives and new wave feminists around the world. In this instance, Jiménez resorts to constructing her encounter with new wave feminisms through a canon of expository narration following established historical discourses that differentiated between pre-1970s and new wave feminisms in Mexico. Here Jiménez begins to construct her encounter with new wave feminisms through a pattern of narration closely aligned to a romantic-epic. As James notes, the epic pattern of narration allows an individual to identify with the community and its values, leaving little room for personal identity, whereas in the romantic pattern an individual finds her own moral career through her ability to overcome obstacles.[12] Hence the epic sense of this pattern allowed Jiménez to establish identification with a community of new wave feminists and thus to claim membership within this collective identity, while the romantic sense of this narrative placed emphasis on her individual capacity for change and transformation through the adoption of different values.

During the course of our conversations her views about feminism seemed to be informed more by new wave feminisms than historical feminisms (*las madrinas*). However, her constant return to her political awakenings with the Communist Youth League, the UNMM, and her effort to establish links with *las madrinas* speaks of these anecdotes as foundational moments in her life that reinforce a romantic-epic pattern of narration, a story of attaining consciousness and giving coherence and legitimacy to her political commitment as a continuation of the work started by *las madrinas*. This is poignantly represented in the performance of Lacy's *International Dinner Party* (1979, discussed in chapter 3), in which Jiménez pays homage to her *madrinas*: Adelina Zendejas, Amalia de Castillo Ledón, Elvira Trueba, and Concha Michel. This ongoing negotiation with historical feminisms speaks to her interest in documenting her relation with *las madrinas* in order to provide coherence and continuity to her own political commitment to women's movements. By honoring her *madrinas*, Jiménez positions herself as part of this important genealogy of women activists.

Jiménez returned to this narrative pattern on various occasions, and it was one of the key narratives she used to construct her archival persona during our conversations. However, the romantic-epic was not the only narrative pattern available to Jiménez in this regard. As Daniel James points out, "One of the richest interpretative veins that can be mined in studies of life stories lies in probing the relationship between key narrative patterns aimed at creating continuity and other elements that clarify, obscure and make more complex, or simply leave in the tension-laden coexistence of contradictory themes and ambivalent meanings in an account of life."[13] Jiménez resorted to humor, irony, and tragedy on several occasions as she attempted to make sense of her experiences with diverse trends of feminism.

Through our conversations Jiménez's definition of feminism seemed to be more ambivalent, pointing to instances of rupture and contradiction rather than continuity. On the one hand, she recognized the legacy and complexities of pre-1970s feminism and the women's movements, and on the other hand, she seemed to conceptualize this legacy as not so feminist, making a clear division between the early women's suffrage movement and 1970s feminist thought. However, those clear distinctions seemed to be blurred when discussing specific cases. For instance, when I asked her if feminism in Mexico prior to the 1970s could only be characterized as having been defined through a discourse of class struggle, she thought twice and invited me to look at the life of Concha Michel, a post-revolutionary folklore singer and activist, considered by many as the "precursor" of Mexican feminism. Despite her lifelong dedication to improving the lives of women, Michel always denied any association with feminism. However, by the 1970s, as Jocelyn Olcott argues, many named Michel as a "precursor" despite the fact that her ideas were more in tune with gender essentialism and heteronormativity. For Olcott, "Michel's appeal to both cultural nationalists and contemporary feminists stems largely from her simultaneous claims to universality and particularity, to a rootless cosmopolitanism and an assertively autochthonous indigeneity."[14] According to Jiménez, Michel was heavily criticized because, as a militant of the Mexican Communist Party, she stated that women, besides their commitment to social justice, had their own struggle based on the differences between women and men.

At the same time, Jiménez also explained that "new wave feminisms" was an oxymoron since, according to her, feminism in Mexico did not exist before the 1970s. She explained that while a very important women's movement existed in Mexico in the 1930s and 1940s, it was in the 1970s that women became more active and developed a movement that truly differentiated itself from others both aesthetically and politically.

> It was beginning in the seventies when feminism, a movement that many refer to as *new wave*, emerged in Mexico. A very important women's movement did exist prior, in the 1930s and the 1940s, but it dwindled from the 1950s to the 1970s. It is true that women obtained suffrage rights in 1953, but unfortunately this was not a product of women's demands. Women became more socially engaged in the seventies and as a result feminism emerged as a differentiated social movement.[15]

Her views are opposed to some histories of Mexican feminism that trace its genesis to the nineteenth century and, most commonly, establish the emergence of a first wave of feminism in Mexico in 1916 during the first Feminist Congress that took place in the city of Merida.[16] As elsewhere, the main goals of these early Mexican feminists were to obtain citizenship equality and the right to education and suffrage. Mexican women obtained national suffrage rights in 1953; however, despite this achievement, by the early 1950s the feminist movement had almost disappeared. For Jiménez, like for some others, its disappearance coincided with the attainment of important government positions by women and the ways in which suffrage rights were finally obtained through actions that spoke more of political maneuvers than of a gesture toward the empowerment of women or a preoccupation with their rights as citizens.[17]

Two contradictory discourses emerge from Jiménez's perspectives on feminism. On the one hand, Jiménez aligns herself with critical assessments of the women's movement that blame part of its decline on an act of co-optation by a corporatist scheme of the PRI government. On the other hand, she rescues Concha Michel as one of the *madrinas* who, like herself, provide a sense of historical continuity to the narratives of Mexican feminisms. Jiménez's need for distancing pre- and post-1970s feminism also speaks of her archivist persona, one that is consciously aware of classifying, collecting, and periodizing difference. What emerged from our conversations was Jiménez's need to differentiate time periods in feminist history in order to distinguish herself from elite and pre-1970s feminism. This distinction was a key narrative she used to explicate her archival persona. At one level, it worked to negotiate her sense of self as distinct, but at another level, it also pointed to her particular experience with both generations of feminists and her quest to honor *las madrinas*.

Jiménez's perspectives on feminism began to transform in 1971 after she joined the feminist collective Mujeres en Acción Solidaria and later Movimiento Nacional de Mujeres. Through her affiliation with MAS and MNM Jiménez became acquainted with a diverse group of women who were concerned with issues of gender equality and sexual rights. Throughout the 1970s she participated in more than a dozen feminist demonstrations and belonged to various feminist collectives. These demonstrations brought a new set of issues, including abortion, sexual rights, and concerns for the ways women were represented in the media as well as a different way of performing protest and making demands about those issues in public. Unlike union or political party demonstrations, feminist demonstrations, according to Jiménez, were "much more upbeat, with more of a sense of the visual, with a particularly distinct way of expressing demands in their banners and signs."[18]

This difference, she told me, is what inspired her to take photos and collect ephemera more rigorously. Beginning in 1978, influenced by her collaborations in Rosa Martha Fernández's film productions and her participation in various feminist art groups, her militant practice and interest in photography would increasingly be driven by a concern with feminist art, initially as part of a group of militant artists established by Mónica

Mayer, which resulted in an art exhibition entitled "Muestra colectiva feminista" (1978).[19] Next came her involvement in Lacy's *International Dinner Party* (1979) and her participation in the feminist art collective Tlacuilas y Retrateras (1984–85).[20] Soon after she had begun to collaborate with a diverse range of feminist art collectives, she built a dark room at her house, where she developed photolithographs to produce negatives for print production and also began to experiment with this technology to print her own photographs.

Another event that crucially influenced Jiménez's perspectives on feminism was the UN's 1975 International Women's Year celebration in Mexico City. The story of her participation at the NGO forum also speaks to both expository and conversational levels of narration available to Jiménez to construct her archival persona. Unlike many other Mexican feminists who boycotted the intergovernmental event and associated activities, Jiménez attended the parallel three-day NGO forum. For Jiménez, as for others, the official program was nothing more than a political event that reflected the policies of nation-states rather than women's rights and demands. It was at the NGO forum that some of the most interesting discussions and heated debates took place. In particular, Jiménez recalled a number of passionate discussions between participants from developed and under-developed countries that reflected the repertoire of stereotypes cast on feminist activists from these diverse latitudes. Others have argued that these tensions tended to revolve around the views of Third World women, which often focused on structural problems of economic inequality, and Western feminists, who concentrated on sex-specific issues such as reproductive freedom, lesbianism, and abortion. Throughout the conference, Mexican newspapers played a crucial role in casting Western feminism and its alleged emphasis on sexuality as deviant, describing it as an imperialistic form that distracted its advocates from more pressing economic and social issues.

Jiménez told me she was acutely aware of the politics surrounding the event and the ways the media generalized and manipulated the positions of various representatives to accommodate the pressures of the Cold War and show support for anti-imperialistic discourses. She recognized that the differences between Third World and Western feminists was not only the discourse that the media and others used to advance their agendas but also played a crucial role in the display of politics performed at the forum. She particularly recalled the presence of Domitila Chungara de Barrios—a Bolivian tin miner's wife and leader of the Housewives' Committee of the Siglo XX miners—as one of the highlights of the forum and the confrontations between First and Third World feminisms. However, in contrast to the best-known narrative of the encounter, found in Domitila's testimonio *Let Me Speak!*—which focused on Domitila's frustration with the sexual and reproductive rights emphasis she encountered at the tribune—Jiménez recalled how the audience reacted to her participation.[21] She told me: "*Cuando las gringas la oyeron casi les da gripa*" (When the *gringas* listened to what Domitila had to say they almost caught a cold).[22] While Jiménez's recollection of these debates seems to follow the prescription of Western feminists against Third World women, she chose to foreground how the *gringas* (U.S. delegation and in particular Betty Friedan) were outraged by de Chungara's participation and not the opposite version that emphases Chungara's indignation.

The confrontation did not take place, however, between the *gringas* and de Chungara, but between the Bolivian delegate and Esperanza Brito de Marti, leader of MNM, one of the collectives in which Jiménez participated. As Brito de Marti delivered her closing remarks demanding equality for women and unity among feminists, de Chungara interrupted her, exclaiming: "How can we women be equals when we, the wives of laborers, are thrown in jail for organizing to protest their imprisonment? We cannot speak of equality between games of canasta. Women cannot be equals any more than poor and rich countries can be equals."[23]

The encounter between the Bolivian and the Mexican activists has faded in favor of a discourse that pits sexually liberated *gringas* against the Latin American leftist-indigenous-working-class women embodied by Chungara de Barrios. Ironically, as Jocelyn Olcott argues, Betty Friedan's and Chungara's views were more compatible than has been acknowledged. Friedan had previously shunned prostitution and lesbianism as distractions for the feminist movement, precisely the themes that provoked de Chungara's astonishment. Moreover, at the IWY forum, Friedan was more critical and vocal toward transnational corporations than in her support for lesbianism.[24]

Rather than Friedan, Mexican lesbian-feminist activist and theater director Nancy Cárdenas was the protagonist of the media outrage provoked by what many observers perceived as the derailed focus of the forum toward sexual liberation.[25] Cárdenas presented the first Mexican lesbian manifesto, which provoked the publication of numerous newspaper articles and editorials accusing the forum of refusing to deal with the real problems that affected the female portion of the population and of promoting prostitution and lesbianism as a right and not a pathology, as defined by some experts at the time.[26] Cárdenas's session was one of the few that dealt with issues of sexuality, which in turn provoked de Chungara's outrage.[27]

Through her humorous remark (when the *gringas* listened to de Chungara they almost caught a cold), Jiménez obscured the different trends of feminism practiced by Latin American women. Abortion, prostitution, and lesbianism were (and still are) contentious issues among some supporters of new wave feminist militants. The difference of opinion regarding such issues thwarted the establishment of broader political coalitions. For instance, the UNMM decided to abandon the Frente Nacional por la Liberacion y los Derechos de la Mujer (FNALIDM), an alliance of various feminist collectives and left-leaning organizations, shortly after its establishment in 1979, after gay and lesbian collectives joined the alliance.[28]

As a member of UNMM and of MNM, Jiménez actively participated in these two different approaches to women's rights (one that was open to abortion, lesbianism, and prostitution, the other that was not). Throughout our conversations Jiménez continuously negotiated these two facets of her militancy with humor and irony, obscuring her own perspective in the matter. Given her weathered political experience and knowledge of the thorny issues that characterized diverse trends of feminism, our interview and subsequent conversations could be read as a performance in which her ambivalence or particular way of taking sides on controversial issues is crucial to the construction of her own political subjectivity. Equally so, this ambivalence was key to the representation of herself as an archival persona: a persona that possibly tried to encompass as many facets of the movement as possible.

During our conversations Jiménez framed her political militancy and interests on collecting, photography, and feminist art through shifting and sometimes conflicting views on feminism that combined her early affiliations with left-leaning organizations, the legacies of post-1920s feminism, and her involvement with 1970s feminist collectives. However, the last time I asked how her interest in feminism had begun, she shunned all these legacies and described them as innate: "*Estaba interesada en el feminismo desde que estaba chiquita*" (I was interested in feminism since I was a little girl), Jiménez recalled. Similarly, she told me that her interest in collecting was not consciously related to building an archive; rather, she said: "*A mi no me gusta tirar las cosas*" (I don't like to get rid of things). And she added: "*Nunca pensé, voy a archivar algo para el futuro*" (I never thought I would save this or that for the future). Hence Jiménez's quotidian practice of collecting, recording, and documenting feminist demonstrations, more than a conscious act of archiving, could be read as a performative act that was crucial in fashioning her sense of self. Jiménez's collection of things worked as an album of memories but also spoke of a person interested in organizing and classifying information, one "who built information packages of each demonstration" (perhaps anticipating or fully aware of its historical value).

A closer look at Jiménez's career as a writer, publisher, artist, and activist suggests that even though she denies any purpose a priori, her intention behind collecting was driven more by a political stance than by the need to hoard or any nostalgic desires ascribed to amateur collectors. The act of collecting or keeping track of political activities and achievements was not foreign to Mexican women activists, a practice of which Jiménez was quite aware. In our conversations, she mentioned how relatives of previous acquaintances and members of the UNMM had discarded personal papers and books, not realizing the importance of keeping and bequeathing such documents. At the time Jiménez began collecting, feminist activists in Mexico, as elsewhere, were already keenly aware of the importance of documenting and writing women's history as a political intervention itself. Parallel to Jiménez's awareness of the importance of keeping such documentation, a change in the definition and appearance of an archive that had been taking place within academic and artistic circles also influenced the transformation of Jiménez's collection of things into an archive.

Reactivating Jiménez's Archive

In 2009 when the team of scholars, students, and artists led by Mónica Mayer and Karen Cordero began to revise Jiménez's things and look for an institution to which to donate them, academics, scholars, and artists had already been questioning the conception of an archive for quite some time. For instance, influenced by postcolonialist, poststructuralist, and feminist readings, historians now consider archival sources not as transparent collections of documents that tell us how things were in the past but as edited compilations of such things as images, artifacts, letters, sound recordings, documents, clothes, and personal diaries that allow us to ask questions about the moral, affective, and social values of the past and inform us about the present, and equally, as in the case of Jiménez, about the moral, affective, and social values of the collector. At stake in this conception of an archive is the relation between history and memory, a relation that questions the dominant hierarchies in the production of knowledge, how knowledge is transferred from generation to generation through diverse practices, and equally important, how all these practices are gendered. These new understandings of what an archive is have forced academics to rethink who counts as a historian and what counts as history. As Antoinette Burton reminds us, "Memory is always cast (and still is) in gendered terms (as unreliable, dubious [. . .] as female identity)," and "the capacity of women to write history has been considered dubious until quite recently."[29]

In the art world, an engagement with the archive has taken shape in myriad forms throughout the twentieth century. The archive has been the site of critique and the source of inspiration for many artists. Conceived as an institution—that is, as a museum for storing and presenting works in public, and as an art historical discourse—the archive has been criticized for its economic, gendered, racist, and sexist foundations. Envisioned as a source of memory and history, the archive has been interrogated to develop counter-memories or alternative knowledges. In recent years, however, the debate has turned toward the constitution and preservation of artists' archives. At one level of the discussion, there is the work of conceptual and performance artists, whose ephemeral practices only live through documentation; thus the record becomes the artwork. And at another level there are the artists' personal archives, which are turned into works of art through different means, such as their inclusion in art exhibits and sales or through bequests to archival institutions and the acknowledgment of the archive as a work of art in its own right. For instance, Andy Warhol's *Time Capsules*—a work that the artist began in 1974, which consists of 612 cardboard boxes filled with artworks and all kinds of ephemera related to his art practice including photographs, newspapers, magazines articles, fan letters, business and personal correspondence, announcements for poetry readings and dinner invitations—are now part of the Warhol collection and exhibited as works of art.

There has also been an interest in the preservation and institutionalization of both feminist archives (via art exhibitions and bequests) and the archives of Latin American artists working in the 1960s and 1970s. The critical reception of these endeavors has been mixed. For instance, about the interest in the recovery of Latin American artists' archives working under dictatorships and violent populist regimes, art critic Sue Rolnik has argued that, rather than a concern for recovering the memory of that tumultuous period, these efforts respond to a redefinition of the geopolitics of the art world, the aim of which is to neutralize politics through visibility and access.[30] Correspondingly, in terms of the recent proliferation of feminist art exhibits around the world, Griselda Pollock offers a related perspective.[31] In *Encounters in the Virtual Feminist Museum: Time, Space and the Archive*, Pollock worries that the recent attention to feminist art, what she calls "the musealization of the movement," could end up erasing the movement's radical criticality.

While both Rolnik's and Pollock's arguments might be accurate in speaking about some of the perils of turning archives into commodities—that is, their circulation as objects of value within the art market, and their increased value as "marginal objects," and the possible loss of the radical edge of marginal movements—their argumentations disregard the ways that wider accessibility can, at the same time, elicit oppositional responses and nuanced readings. Andreas Huyssen, who has extensively discussed the contemporary desire for memorialization, including the construction of museums and monuments, the institutionalization of archives, and patrimonial declarations, argues that critical assessments of the institutions created by this desire have to consider how "there is always a surplus of meaning [in these practices and institutions] that exceeds ideological set boundaries, opening spaces for reflection and counter hegemonic discourses."[32]

In Mexico, discussions about the condition of Mexican artists' archives of the 1960s–1970s took place in a series of panel discussions as part of the international exhibition entitled *Arte [no es] vida. Acciones por artistas de las Américas, 1960–2000* on view at Museo Carillo Gil in Mexico City from July 3 to August 13, 2009, and revolved around the opposite concern: the lack of interest by state institutions in preserving archives on marginal art movements.[33] The danger of losing the collective memory of this era was discussed as being a consequence of the lack of interest and funding directed to preserving these archives. As the majority of artists and activists from the 1960s to the 1970s worked outside official channels, their work, in the view of the discussants, has not been sufficiently written about or incorporated into historical narratives. Hence the preservation of their work becomes a more pressing issue as they begin to pass away and their documents and work are deemed to be lost. Others also touched on the relation that artists have toward their archives and on the state of disrepair of some archives that have been donated to state institutions. However, the recovery of feminist art was not explicitly discussed as being a matter of concern.

In order to circumvent the state's lack of interest, some artists have managed to sell their archives to foreign universities. For instance, Felipe

Ehrenberg, a self-defined neologist (an inventor of words and concepts) and a pioneer in conceptual art, sold part of his archive to the Special Collections Library at Stanford University in 2000 and has donated another part to the Contemporary Art Museum at UNAM.[34] Others, such as Mónica Mayer and her partner Victor Lerma, have taken matters into their own hands and established independent projects like Pinto Mi Raya. In 1989 the two artists began Pinto Mi Raya as an alternative space to exhibit work that was not shown in galleries or museums. In 1991 it was transformed into a home-based collection of newspaper and magazine publications on Mexican contemporary art. Mayer and Lerma collect and organize this information and sell compilations to libraries, students, and artists. Other projects emerged out of the initial Pinto Mi Raya, such as the online magazine *La Pala*, a series of performances that question the archival and documentation practices in state intuitions and the thorny relations between artist and critics. Mayer and Lerma also sell compilations of these documents to libraries, students, and academics in order to address the lack of information available in academic institutions regarding these practices.

Pinto Mi Raya and Ehrenberg's archive could be considered two of the most successful initiatives emerging from this context in the sense that they have managed to secure greater accessibility and preservation. Both Mayer and Ehrenberg also consider their archives as works of art in their own right. As Vanessa Kam argues, by considering the document to be a work of art, artists like Ehrenberg and Mayer-Lerma go beyond the notion of document as evidence and subscribe to a basic principle of Conceptual Art that, in the words of Paul Wood, "was less a question of rejecting a notion of the aesthetic as of broadening its range of references, outwards from the medium specific, formally achieved harmony of a modernist painting to, potentially, anything, an object, a sound or an action."[35] In doing so, Mayer and Ehrenberg were also in dialogue with an archival impulse in contemporary art that in 2004 Hal Foster described as an interest in making visible forgotten or excluded historical information and presenting it in an unfinished manner. For Foster, archival art is concerned with prompting new beginnings rather than fixed origins, and in the process archival art produces new archives that reveal the Archive's fictional origins.[36]

Particularly relevant for this discussion is that Mayer was crucial in the transformation of Jiménez's collection into an archive, hence Mayer's conceptualization of what constitutes an archive also influenced the conceptualization of Jiménez's collection into an archive. And in turn, and perhaps more important, Mayer's conception of the political importance of documenting is deeply informed by her feminist militancy and awareness of Jiménez's archival activities as political interventions. Mónica Mayer describes the project Pinto Mi Raya as one of "applied Conceptual Art," a concept that Mayer-Lerma coined with the purpose of defining conceptual art projects in which "besides focusing on an idea their purpose is to have a practical application; that is, they need to be functional. And, as we have repeatedly stated, the objective of Pinto Mi Raya has been to lubricate the art world; to detect its problems and propose solutions."[37]

She conceptualizes Pinto Mi Raya's activities as an art practice that is based on ideas but that also has a practical use and proposes solutions to problems. Their definition of applied Conceptual Art is close to an idea of militant art, however, not of modernist utopias or New Left radicalisms but a kind of militancy that actively inserts itself in the production and interpretation of knowledge. It is conceptual in the sense that it broadens the definition of art to an act of collecting and distributing information. Even though, in this sense, it subscribes to Paul Wood's definition of Conceptual Art, within the Mexican context Mayer has had to fight extensively for recognition of her archival practice as art.[38] For instance, Felipe Ehrenberg, who pioneered conceptual practices, confessed in 2008 that it wasn't until the late 1980s that he began to recognize his archive as a work of art.

[I don't] remember when . . . or even how things fell into place. It may well have been shortly after the Great Earthquake of September, in 1985; but at a given moment I began thinking that my files could, in fact, be considered a "work of art," very much akin to other works of mine, of a conceptual nature, an installation perhaps, better yet, a performance, so that by logical extension, it would require special care, the care one gives to an "oeuvre d'art." So I proceeded to give it yet again a new order, not quite knowing how best to frame the idea, how to convince "the powers that be" to perceive it—that ordered mass of papers—as art. It wasn't until a decade after the earthquake that I met Issa Benítez, a young, very intelligent student. . . . Her dissertation was, precisely, on documents as works of art and after discussing her subject matter and aiding her in her research, she confirmed and honed the concept. I'll always be thankful to her for this.[39]

The concept of an archive as a work of art is relatively new and still received with much suspicion in Mexico (at least at the time I was researching this project, from 2009 to 2011). Further, Mayer adds that while she recognizes the paradox and contradiction of making the archive the focus of their activities since it provides durability to their ephemeral practices, she also sees it as an urgent matter. In short, the creation of the archive interests her more for what it can do in the present than for what it can do in the future.[40] In the earliest stages of Mayer-Lerma's project she wrote that "the practice of keeping records in a country that has had to defend its cultural patrimony with all its might (*con la uñas*) is not only a patriotic act but a heroic one."[41]

Beginning in 1989, as part of Mexico's adoption of neoliberal economics, a reform of cultural institutions took place whereby private investment was allowed to intervene more openly in the sponsorship and financing of certain cultural endeavors and in the management of cultural patrimony previously regarded as the sole preserve of state institutions.[42] Private cultural foundations have coexisted with the state structure of cultural management throughout the twentieth century in Mexico; however, in the 1970s there was more open and increased activity in the private sector. Valuable cultural property is designated as such by the president and is protected by the Federal Law of National Wealth and the Federal Law of Archeological, Historical, and Artistic Monuments (1972). This law is still current and does not contain any provisions for the transfer of any property designated or considered cultural patrimony of the nation that is held by private nationals into private foreign hands. Until 2012 there was no law that specifically protected or regulated archives (*archivos documentales*).

These shifts caused major debates in the public sphere, and several artists took prominent roles in protecting cultural patrimony from transnational and national private corporations. One of the artists who engaged most actively in the defense of cultural patrimony from privatization was Francisco Toledo. Among many other activities and initiatives, he organized the *Patronato Pro-Defensa y Conservación del Patrimonio Natural y Cultural de Oaxaca*, in the City of Oaxaca, Mexico. Mónica Mayer has also been a fierce critic of the state of disrepair and the government's lack of interest in protecting the cultural patrimony of the nation. It is in this context that Mayer's earlier statement has to be read. However, more than a decade later, many have changed their views and are more inclined to welcome private and foreign investment in the protection and preservation of cultural patrimony. The emphasis is now placed on obtaining a space and institution that will guarantee maintenance and access to information.

During my conversations with Mayer she confessed that while there is a growing interest in artists' archives in Mexico, there is still a lack of commitment to their preservation: "At this stage in my life and, considering the lack of interest in this kind of work in Mexico, I would prefer if my archives were kept in the United States. I know it sounds horrible and goes against everything I believe in but I prefer it this way rather than having it stay in Mexico, knowing that the next public official, due to a lack of conscience, might throw all my work in the garbage."[43]

Between 2007 and 2011 at least three exhibitions that have the archive as their central focus took place in Mexico City, including one organized around the transfer of Ana Victoria Jiménez's archive to IBERO, *Mujeres ¿y que más?: Reactivando el archivo de Ana Victoria Jiménez* (March 2011).[44] The other two were *Visita al archivo Olivier Debroise: Entre la ficción y el documento* (June 2011), curated by Mónica Mayer, which consists of more than 5,000 documents of the late historian of twentieth-century Mexican art, and *La era de la discrepancia* (March 2008) curated by Olivier Debroise and

Cuauhtémoc Medina. The main idea behind the latter exhibit was to recreate iconic pieces and rebuild an archive of this era. Archives are becoming the central focus of exhibitions, confirming, on the one hand, the commodification of the archive as a work of art and, on the other hand, the blurring of borders between disciplines, practices, objects, and categories (for instance, the difference between a collection and an archive). Moreover, these exhibitions play a crucial role in disseminating the information and collections that are available for consultation. They collaborate in the creation of publics that, in turn, will demand access to such collections or archives.

The Memora Project, the transformation of Jiménez's collection into an archive, has to be read as part of this renewed interest in the recuperation of archives of this era as well as an example of the shift in the management of valuable cultural and historical property. While Ana Victoria Jiménez does not consider her archive as a work of art, she does recognize that it was only through Mayer's and Cordero's initiative to reactivate her archive by organizing an exhibition curated by young art students that the historical importance of her collection has gained visibility. Jiménez's archive not only includes her photographic and performance-based work but documents important practices, until now not fully acknowledged in art historical narratives, elucidating events of relevance that, as Huyssen argues, have the potential to add or interrupt hegemonic narratives in that field. Moreover, the bequest of her archive to a privately owned university exemplifies the shift in the management of cultural patrimony from exclusively a state endeavor to an open acceptance of private and foreign funding.

At first glance, Jiménez's act of daily collecting and visually documenting can be seen as an inextricably feminine act of no historical consequence; however, her awareness of the importance of documenting the activities in which she engaged speaks of a practice with significant political and historical implications. Not only was Jiménez's collection of photographs and ephemera crucial for the construction of her identity as a feminist activist and artist; it also became an important resource for scholars who began to consult her collection when writing the histories of feminism and the women's movement in post-1960 Mexico. Hence Jiménez's archival practice speaks to a more porous understanding of the letrado sphere of influence—one that includes the multifaceted practices of a visual letrada.

By the mid-1980s, as feminist demonstrations gave way to other forms of social activism, Jiménez continued to document these and other important events, such as the devastation of Mexico City during the 1985 earthquake, the garment workers' movement in 1985, and the electoral campaign of 1988, to name a few. After the collective Tlacuilas y Retrateras broke apart, her involvement with artistic initiatives waned, but Jiménez continued to have a prolific role in the publication of memoirs of various activists and in writing the history of the UNMM, using her personal archive as a major source. At present she continues her activism through a project dedicated to helping elderly women achieve a decent quality of life and continues to collaborate with the UNMM as an editor of their publications.[45]

Through our conversations, Jiménez's self-fashioning as an archival persona, one who is conscious of the importance of documenting her activities as a political practice in itself, was envisioned through diverse patterns and levels of narration. By claiming distance from established politically committed artists and from diverse trends of feminisms (while at the same time claiming alliance), she constructed a sense of self that was able to move from a background in communist militancy to new wave feminisms, editor, writer, photographer, and performance artist through networks that, while similar to those of many other artist and activists, operated most of the time outside already established channels of party politics, sanctioned art movements, or upper-class relations. This distancing speaks of an archival interest for classifying, collecting, and periodizing difference. Equally, it speaks of Jiménez's archival persona as one that possibly tried to encompass as many facets of the new wave feminist movement as possible. Ultimately Jiménez's construction as an archival persona serves to position her as continuing the work of her *madrinas* and as a legitimate member of a newly recognized pantheon of new wave feminists and women activists.

Jiménez's archive and archival practice are central nodes in which all her activities connect, find meaning, and are accorded historical relevance. Her collection of photographs and ephemera was crucial for the ongoing construction of her identity as a feminist activist and artist but also became an important resource for scholars. In this sense, as Appadurai reminds us, Jiménez's intentions are not as crucial as looking at how objects circulate and acquire different meanings and relevance, for things, like anything else, have a social life.[46] Hence what began as a personal collection of ephemera and photographs, more in tune with the activities of a *cronopio*, was turned into an archive, in the sense of *fama*, as Jiménez and others began to understand the value of her archive as a historical and political document and began using it to write histories that have, for the most part, been ignored in official historical narratives of the era. What her archive proposes is a different narrative of the histories of new wave feminisms, a narrative that casts it as not an exclusive movement of middle-class, university-educated women but rather of those who, despite their backgrounds and education, were concerned with how the oppression of women encompassed economic ailments as well as social and cultural conditions that were gendered and sexualized.

5

Secret Documents and Feminist Practices

A Story of Two Archives

The streets of Mexico City during the 1970s were contested and dangerous territory. The killings that occurred on the day of the Corpus Christi festival in June 10, 1971, confirmed early on that President Echeverría's democratic opening was not democratic at all, forcing many to take radical actions that would plant the seeds for the emergence of urban and rural guerrilla movements. Agents working for the Mexican bureaus of secret intelligence (Dirección Federal de Seguridad, DFS, and Dirección General de Investigaciones Políticas y Sociales, DGIPS) infiltrated social movements and kidnapped and tortured hundreds of people, with estimates of 532 having disappeared between 1970 and 1980.[1] Records of these activities, along with daily reports on all kinds of suspicious gatherings, were dutifully kept as part of the activities of these two agencies.

As Ana Victoria Jiménez collected ephemera and documented feminist demonstrations, a group of government agents and infiltrators followed in her footsteps, keeping detailed records and photographs of the women's daily activities. The documentation is not surprising considering the state of turmoil in Mexico City's streets, the government's paranoid interest in keeping suspicious activity in check, and the interest in being informed on women's activism in the context of the UN's IWY celebration. However, until recently, not many were aware that spy reports documenting the activities of new wave feminists were kept at Mexico's National Archives (Archivo General de la Nación, AGN).

In 2002, as part of the promises of Mexico's democratic transition and after a long civic battle, public access to documentation of Mexico's Dirty War and the repression of the student movement was tacitly granted as some DFS and DGIPS files were transferred to Mexico's National Archives.[2] The records documenting feminist activism were included in the transfer. Documents, transcripts, and photographs describing the activities of women who participated in feminist and women-led demonstrations from the 1960s to the 1980s are held within the DGIPS files alongside intelligence reports on workers, students, guerillas, and indigenous organizations.[3]

In these documents I found detailed written transcripts of many demonstrations photographed by Jiménez as well as evidence that many of these women were followed. For instance, a document dated October 16, 1972, describes how art critic and UNMM militant Raquel Tibol along with Marta López Portillo de Tamayo and Estela Carreto, president and member of the UNMM, boarded a plane bound for Havana and Santiago de Chile.[4] Another document contains black-and-white photographs of UNMM meetings. The photos are glued to paper with blue pen marks identifying the women in them.[5] The series of photographs were filed alongside mugshot-style images of members of La Liga 23 de Septiembre, one of the many urban guerrilla groups active in Mexico in the 1970s. Another document, dated September 24, 1977, describes a meeting conducted by Rosa Martha Fernández and organized by the Coalición de Mujeres Feministas (CMF) to discuss the decriminalization of abortion.[6] The reports also contain biographical profiles and lists of names of the members of various feminist collectives, speculations as to their political affiliations and relations with other organizations, and detailed descriptions of the demonstrations they organized, including the banners they carried, the songs they sang, the plays they staged, the routes they followed in their demonstrations, and copies of the flyers and posters they distributed.

All these records are typed using a computer or typewriter. They all include the date, and most are signed with cryptic initials such as "P.L.L." or "P.D.H." Most likely these reports were directed to the Ministry of Interior (Secretario de Gobernación).[7] The reports also include documents and newspaper clippings about meetings and demonstrations of women's groups that did not sympathize with the politics of the UNMM or the feminist collectives and organizations—that is, groups that were supportive of Echeverría's policies.[8]

At one level, the finding of spy reports tracking the activities of women's groups as well countless articles supporting Echeverria's reforms is not surprising, considering the celebration of IWY (1975) and the debates that were caused by the reforms to Article 4 of the Mexican Constitution (1974). At another level, one cannot disregard the way in which the amount of documents filed also reflects the bureaucratic and paranoid workings of the Mexican government. Scholars have explained the excess of documents as a mechanism to justify the existence of secret service organizations and to maintain networks of corruption and extortion developed by its agents.[9] According to Sergio Aguayo, between 1958 and 1985, state intelligence operations, and thus the production of reports, increased exponentially.[10] Louise Walker's study of spy reports on middle-class gossip that took place in diverse venues including supermarkets, gas stations, and dry cleaning shops during Echeverría's administration provides a sense of the reach and paranoid workings of these practices of infiltration.[11] Jacques Derrida's psychoanalytical reading of the obsessive need for collecting information, a process he refers to as archive fever, is perhaps useful in trying to understand the Mexican state's obsessive tracking of information at a time when its legitimacy was under attack.[12] Yet at another level, the finding of these documents fulfills my excitement for classified documents, a process that Stoler concludes serves as a "signal to direct attention and cue for one's repeated return to what knowledge should be valued."[13]

Regardless of my excitement and insights on Mexican intelligence workings and the PRI's paranoia, the finding of the DGIPS documents has the potential to change the terms in which the histories of new wave feminisms can be conceptualized. In broad terms, the existence of information about these women in the national archives counters preconceptions about the general exclusion of women from the archives. It also tells us about the increasing importance of visuality in transforming the terms of political engagement of feminist activists and emerging visual letradas. Equally, it speaks to the gendering of spheres of action for letrados and visual letradas. Moreover, it contributes to the development of alternative kinds of histories about the porosity and function of spy reports.

The discussion regarding the exclusion or inclusion of women in the archives is a complex issue. As is well known, the presence of women's voices in the archives depends on modes of reading (against or along the grain) and, moreover, on academic interest and willingness to find female voices.[14] In the context of the recent opening of these files and studies discussing the ways they might change the historiography of post-revolutionary Mexico, the inclusion of reports of state informants spying on the activities of a small group of middle-class women could change persistent forms of academic discrimination toward Mexican new wave feminisms.[15] The importance of this finding is that, to my knowledge, most histories of post-1970s feminism have yet to use these documents as sources. At present, most histories are based on testimonials, writings by activists, or newspaper articles.

Several of the women I interviewed thought very few interested parties attended their activities and recalled that they had to fight for coverage in the press (or provoke it themselves). They believed no one paid attention to their demonstrations. When I shared my findings with some of them, they were not surprised to learn that members of the UNMM were under surveillance. The UNMM was closely related to the Communist Party, and it was known that the government kept their activities in check. They were surprised, however, that documents regarding feminist collectives were also included.[16] Ana Victoria Jiménez was not surprised at all. Years earlier she had experienced the workings of state infiltration when she was detained in the offices of the PCM. When I shared my findings with her, she told me that everyone in UNMM knew that they were being followed: "Yes we knew. There were several women who attended UNMM meetings once or twice. They came with small notebooks and they spent the whole meeting taking notes. It was pretty easy to identify them. But really, I don't understand what agents of the Ministry of Interior gained with such activity."[17]

The fact that the feminist collectives have a place in the national archives can change the way we think about their histories while also confirming the surveillance practices that were a staple of the government at the time. For instance, following the narrative of state informants who filed descriptive reports on any women's organization they encountered, a story could emerge of continuity of women's movements that would crucially link UNMM activism with feminist collectives, despite their well-known political differences.

Reading Two Archives Side by Side and in Opposition to Each Other

The existence of the two archives gives authority to the feminist movement, notwithstanding the differences in the terms with which they record events. Most of the time the DGIPS reports construct feminist activism as a menace in need of surveillance through text-based reports, while Jiménez's images frame the movement as records of a personal experience. The two archives coincide in changing the value of the artifacts saved. For example, in both I found pamphlets and posters of the movement. The act of saving these documents instills in them an aura of importance and permanence that they did not have in the first place. However, the ways these documents are kept speaks of different values ascribed to them. Whereas Jiménez's documents are nicely kept and even photographed as works of art, in the AGN most of the documents are perforated and kept in a dusty binder or as loose pages inside yellowed folders. The faded ink on the reports, causing an erasure of the text, serves as a reminder of the possibility that next time you look for them, these documents may not be around (that, and the countless rumors of their misfilings and mysterious vanishings).

Reading the two archives side by side completes the memories and recollections of many participants who have written testimonies of their militancy in the 1970s, or enacts what Michel-Rolph Trouillot has called "the interplay between historicity 1 and historicity 2, between what happened and what is said to have happened."[18] The documents provide information that supplements oral testimonies, including dates, places, names (often misspelled), and estimates of the number of people in attendance. Jiménez's photos of feminist demonstrations and the DGIPS descriptive reports read in conjunction with oral testimonies and newspaper articles work in a complementary manner to provide a more complete sense of the activities that these women carried out.

A document dated May 28, 1978, reports that a meeting held outside the National Auditorium where the Señorita México contest was under way was attended by more than a hundred activists and was organized by five different women's collectives to protest the beauty contest:

> From 16:30 to 17:45 five feminist organizations held a meeting to protest against the organization of Miss Mexico at the entrance of the National Auditorium. There were approximately 100 people in attendance. The leaders of the meeting were Sonia Riquer, Jan Merin (sic), Esperanza Brito de Martinez among other militants of Comité Mexicano Feminista, Moviemiento Pro Liberacion Feminista, Colectivo de Mujeres, Movimiento Nacional Feminista Mexicano y Comite Revueltos (sic).[19]

Besides stating the names of the participants and affiliations of some attendees, the reports include transcriptions of the banners they carried and a description of theater plays staged by La Revuelta collective, for which scripts, to my knowledge, are nonexistent. These documents are valuable for their descriptions and also because they give us a sense of the reception and the kinds of publics these demonstrations called into being. As Michael Warner argues, publics come into being in relation to a text and its circulation—that is, a particular public does not exist prior to the text.[20]

In Jiménez's archive, black-and-white images of members of La Revuelta wearing masks and performing for an audience while others hold signs reading "We are fed up with all the machista manipulation . . ." provide visual evidence to accompany the text descriptions in the DGIPS reports (figs. 20 and 21).

A particular image from Jiménez reveals how these two archives were perhaps more conscious of each other's existence than I and others initially imagined. The image is a snapshot of La Revuelta's theatrical play (fig. 22).

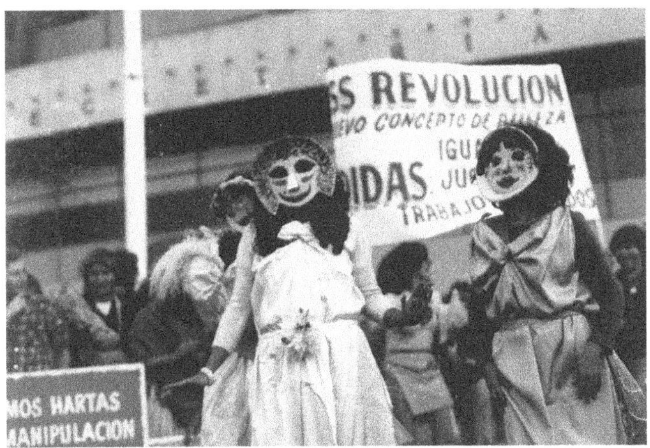

FIG. 20. Two women wearing masks, *La Revuelta performing outside Mexico City's National Auditorium*, Coalición de Mujeres Feministas (CMF). Photo © 1978 by Ana Victoria Jiménez. Archivo Ana Victoria Jiménez, Biblioteca Francisco Xavier Clavigero, Universidad Iberoamericana, Ciudad de México.

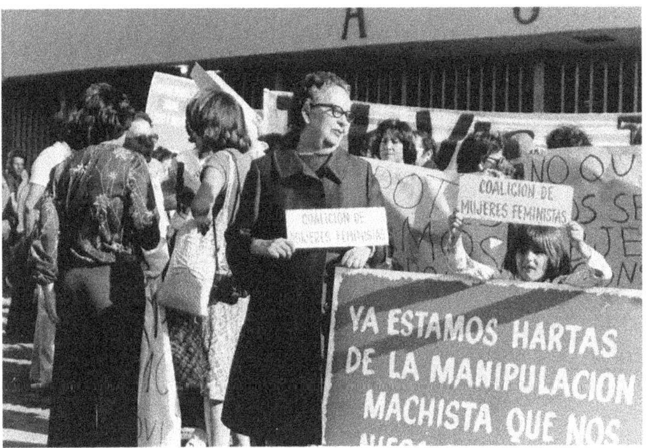

FIG. 21. In the center, Lila Lucido de Mayer, *La Revuelta performing outside Mexico City's National Auditorium*, CMF. Photo © 1978 Ana Victoria Jiménez. Archivo Ana Victoria Jiménez, Biblioteca Francisco Xavier Clavigero, Universidad Iberoamericana, Ciudad de México.

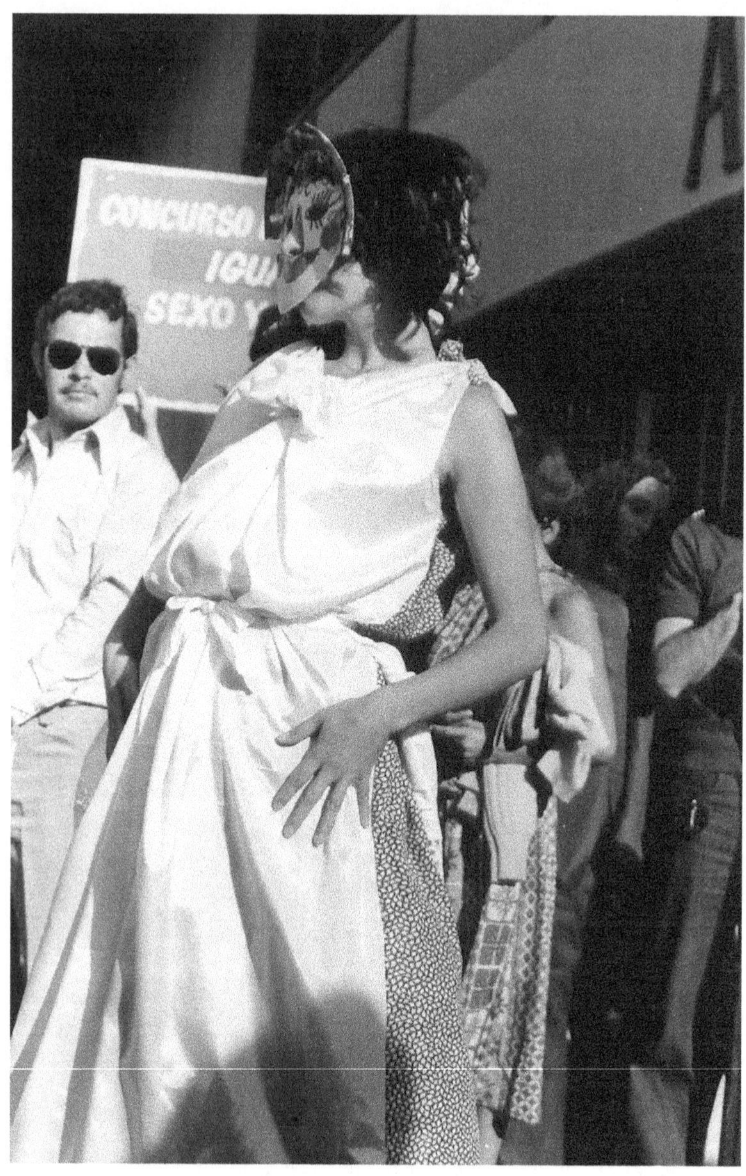

FIG. 22. Masked woman with man in sunglasses, *La Revuelta performing outside Mexico City's National Auditorium*, CMF. Photo © 1978 by Ana Victoria Jiménez. Archivo Ana Victoria Jiménez, Biblioteca Francisco Xavier Clavigero, Universidad Iberoamericana, Ciudad de México.

According to a DGIPS report, the play represented "a critique in which they highlight the masquerade the contestants have to go through and who they exploit indiscriminately. The actors represented Miss Mexico, Miss USA, Miss India, and Miss Italy. They wore a double disguise to show how outside the contests, in their daily lives, these women were enslaved by housework and were submissive to the willpower of their husbands or lovers."[21]

Jiménez's image foregrounds a side view of a member of La Revuelta wearing a disguise that portrays a beauty pageant contestant on the front and a shabbily dressed housewife on the back. However, the focal point of the image is a man standing almost out of the frame in the left corner of the image. The man looks directly at the camera, his piercing gaze trespasses the polarized lenses of his Ray Ban glasses. His upright pose indicates he is aware Jiménez is taking a photo. Arguably, this man could be part of the audience; however, his outfit and self-assured pose suggest his identity as a *guarura*, a bodyguard or an informant of the DGIPS. Was Jiménez as aware of his presence as he seems to be aware of Jiménez's camera?

In our conversations, Jiménez and Mayer described the feminist demonstrations in which they participated as small affairs of no more than twenty to fifty female participants. In this scenario, it might have been easy to detect a mole. But the demonstration at the auditorium was of a different magnitude. It was a heavily invigilated event with a larger-than-normal audience since the beauty contest was under way inside the auditorium at the same time as the feminists demonstrated outside.[22] My desire to find the infiltrator in Jiménez's photo is sustained by my indexical reading of the image, a reading concerned with pointing out the existence of the spy and demonstrating that each acknowledged the other's presence.

Extracting women's agency solely from a straightforward reading of women's presence in photographs is problematic. For instance, Andrea Noble has acknowledged how "photographic images are much more complex than their apparent transparency would have us believe."[23] Noble proposes we focus on the multiple looks in a photograph's production, dissemination, and reception to look differently at the historical narratives in which they are embedded.[24] Following Noble, another reading emerges from this image, one that points to the contested environment of Mexico City's public spaces and the role of women in them. The particular conditions of Jiménez's image pose certain constraints to this kind of reading, since it has not circulated widely; however, multiple looks are indeed embedded in the image.

First is the look of the suspected spy, who adopts a challenging pose toward the camera (or toward the viewers of this image). His demeanor leaves no question about his masculinity. He is there to look at women, to assert his sexual power as a spectator of a beauty contest. But what he encounters is a second look, that of women looking at him. Jiménez is pointing the camera at him. Then there are the looks of La Revuelta's members, who while enacting their play also engage the audience to see the responses. Looking at other Jiménez's images reveals the presence of women in the audience, who also scrutinize the responses of other men in the audience (figs. 23–26). Arguably, by reinforcing how women use their beauty as facades for their submission at home, the play was not challenging masculine desires but actually reinforcing them. However, what emerges from these images and their context is that what was at stake was the right to gaze as women and at women, something deeply related to the objectives of the feminist collectives and that is perhaps more critically brought to bear through this image as a powerful contestation of daily modes of looking.

Jiménez's images also provide important evidence of embodied encounters. The poses and facial expressions of the audience witnessing La Revuelta's play give us a sense of how their performances were interpreted. In figure 23 the young girls seem to laugh and be amused by a close encounter between the protagonist of the play, the Janus-faced housewife/beauty-pageant contestant, and a man standing in the audience. Holding a role of papers in one hand and folding his arm across his chest in a protective demeanor, the man stares at the protagonist's housewife side as she approaches and inadvertently gets closer and closer to him. One reading of the man's protective demeanor and the surrogate weapon in his arm (the roll of documents) could reinforce an interpretation of the intent

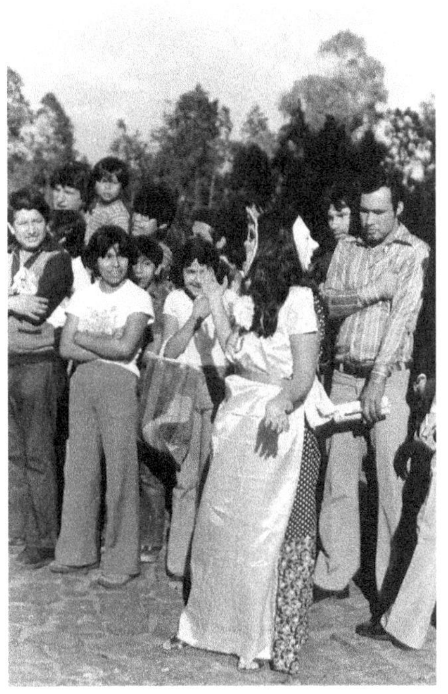

FIG. 23. Masked woman with audience, *La Revuelta performing outside Mexico City's National Auditorium*, CMF. Photo © 1978 by Ana Victoria Jiménez. Archivo Ana Victoria Jiménez, Biblioteca Francisco Xavier Clavigero, Universidad Iberoamericana, Ciudad de México.

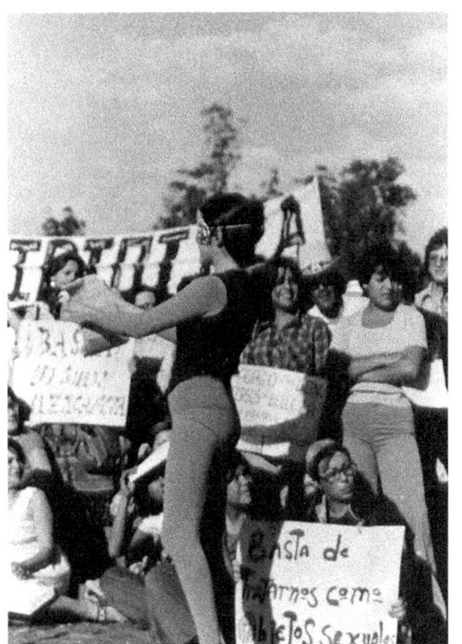

FIG. 24. Masked woman reading, *La Revuelta performing outside Mexico City's National Auditorium*, CMF. Photo © 1978 by Ana Victoria Jiménez. Archivo Ana Victoria Jiménez, Biblioteca Francisco Xavier Clavigero, Universidad Iberoamericana, Ciudad de México.

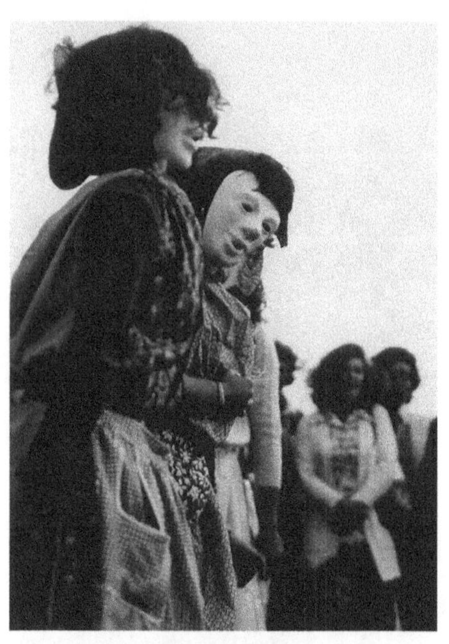

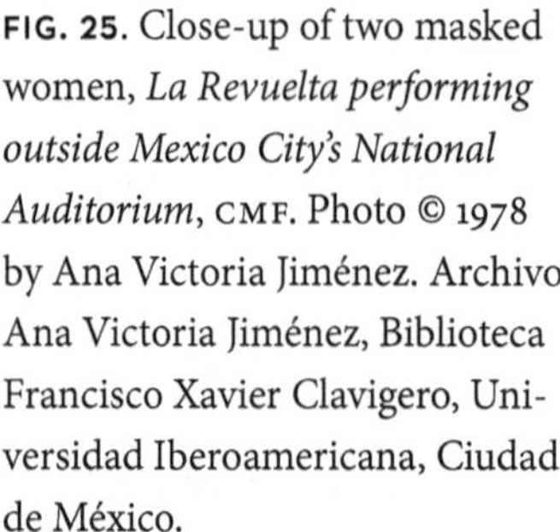

FIG. 25. Close-up of two masked women, *La Revuelta performing outside Mexico City's National Auditorium*, CMF. Photo © 1978 by Ana Victoria Jiménez. Archivo Ana Victoria Jiménez, Biblioteca Francisco Xavier Clavigero, Universidad Iberoamericana, Ciudad de México.

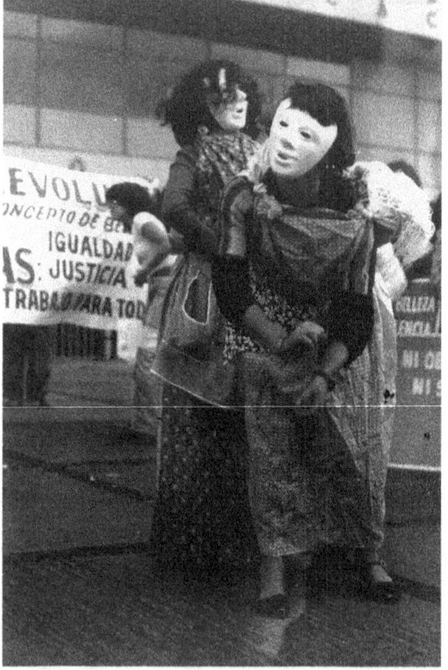

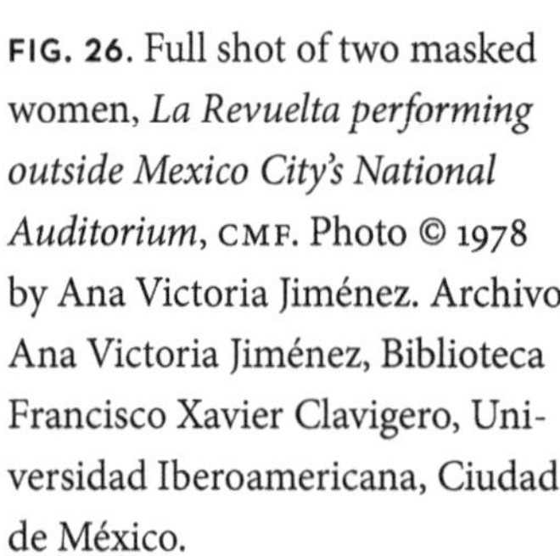

FIG. 26. Full shot of two masked women, *La Revuelta performing outside Mexico City's National Auditorium*, CMF. Photo © 1978 by Ana Victoria Jiménez. Archivo Ana Victoria Jiménez, Biblioteca Francisco Xavier Clavigero, Universidad Iberoamericana, Ciudad de México.

of the play: the way beauty pageant contestants hid their submissive and enslaved lives behind their beauty. The man in the image is ready to pound the protagonist with the roll of documents if she gets too close or if she steps out of line, while the other side of the protagonist's disguise shows the beautiful beauty-pageant contestant to the public. Yet another reading might see the downward look and protective stance of the man as hiding from the ridicule and laughter of the young girls who look at the scene. And most important, here the gender of the letrado is made evident as he holds the documents in his hand, in contrast to the visuality of the visual letrada (Jiménez's camera and the interplay of looks from the public).

Reading the textual focus of DGIPS documents alongside the visual focus of Jiménez's archive allows us to reconstruct different aspects of the cultural practices and legacies of feminist demonstrations. We get a sense of the publics they called into being, the ways in which their plays were interpreted (both by their publics and by state informants), and, moreover, they provide important snapshots of embodied encounters that are usually not available (or not read) in the historical records.

A close reading of some of the language used by state informants also reveals the workings of state surveillance and possibly how the reports could serve as a means of communication between activists and informants; it also raises questions as to the identity of the informants and where their allegiances stood. As Pablo Picatto has noted, the allegiances of informants are as difficult to ascertain and as convoluted as the Mexican intelligence system itself.[25] Famous journalists, intellectuals, and activists are said to have been both informants and victims of state surveillance and violence. Given this situation it is not surprising that many used the system to pursue their own agendas. Here I would like to call attention to two documents that describe the establishment of Coalición de Mujeres Feministas in the context of demonstrations against Miss Universe and Señorita Mexico pageants to show how spy reports were also a means of communication and assertion for feminist activists. The first report, titled "La Coalición de Mujeres en una reunión de temas que les atañen," dated May 31, 1978, describes a meeting with more than seventy women to discuss sexual and domestic violence against women and the decriminalization of abortion. At the end, the informant reports: "Those who spoke at the meeting indicated that their meetings have a social intent and by no means seek any political purpose—that they only seek to improve the quality of life of the female portion of the population. They also indicated that they had a meeting place located at Yucatan Street no. 132–3 in the Roma neighborhood and that they meet on Mondays and Fridays."[26]

The wording of this last paragraph could be read both as an invitation to attend more meetings and as quite an ironic assurance that the intent of CMF in discussing violence against women and the decriminalization of abortion did not seek any political end. At the time, the coalition was working on a legislative proposal on volunteer motherhood that would be presented to Congress by the end of the following year in alliance with several left-wing political organizations, including the Mexican Communist Party, which had recently been legalized in the context of President López Portillo's political reform. The second report, dated June 5, 1978, sends a completely different message: "It is worth noting that we are not aware if this Coalition has an office. We do not know this information because of the hermetic and secretive way in which they conduct their business."[27]

This second report adheres to Sergio Aguayo's assessment as to the purpose of Mexican intelligence, in which the need to create enemies and secret plots fed a whole system of informants and government agents. And yet, despite the surprise of some of the activists about the existence of these documents, these reports, along with Jiménez's images, attest to the ways in which feminist activists were consciously aware of being the object of the state informants' gaze and sought many ways to look back at them (and perhaps protect themselves at the same time).

Read side by side, Jiménez's visual archive and the AGN archive restore the role that women and their activities played in public debates of the time. Read in opposition, the DGIPS reports and Jiménez's images produce different narratives of numerous events. Jiménez's tone is celebratory, while the AGN archive is dry and descriptive. In the DGIPS documents, emphasis is placed on the number and identification of those attending each event along with a detailed transcription of discourses. In contrast, Jiménez's archive could be seen as a snapshot taken in the heat of the moment—images that mostly show a group of women enjoying themselves and engaging with an audience, making the public space their own. But, as I hope I have shown, reading her photos according to a framework that considers embodied encounters and the multiple looks implicated in a photograph, Jiménez's photos can also be brought to bear on other narratives.

In its organization, the AGN archive is linear (despite the questionable order and content of the boxes and documents that can change), and it follows a chronological sequence of events. In contrast, Jiménez's archive (at the time I was able to consult it) was not organized or classified; despite this disorganization, its focus is a bit different than that of the papers in the AGN. It grants political and historical value to some activities, such as Lacy's *International Dinner Party* (1979), that as far as I know were unnoticed by the government bureaucrats who kept track of feminist activities and by the media. The nature of these two archives is essentially different; one is a personal archive and the other is part of the collections of the National Archive. Despite these differences, the two archives share common moments, both of origin and of reappearance as public archives, at a crucial time of interest in the archive. They both pose limits to what can be said about the PRI's rule and, more important, about the practices of new wave feminists and visual letradas and about the state of the archives in Mexico.

While both archives have promising potential in terms of granting public access, they equally share the perils of inaccessibility. On the one hand, the transfer of Jiménez's archive into the special collections of a privately funded university has the potential of ensuring its future preservation, due perhaps to better access to funding and human and technical infrastructure and resources. On the other hand, the location of the IBERO on the outskirts of Mexico City—with no easy access by public transportation and, more importantly, the lack of proper legislation regarding the protection of archives in Mexico—can curtail the promises of accessibility. While the central location of the Mexican National Archives provides easy access to the DGIPS, the lack of proper legislation places similar constraints on them as those posed to Jiménez archive.

On January 24, 2012, after a long debate, a Federal Law of Archives was promulgated. The law is supposed to streamline access to federal archives and regulate the preservation of documents deemed important to the nation, both in private and public hands. Until then, there was no law that protected archival documentation as patrimony of the nation, in contrast, for example, to the still limited *Ley Federal sobre Monumentos y Zonas Arqueológicas, Artisticos e Historicos* (1972) that protects monuments, archeological sites, and works of art that are of historical importance. The Federal Law of Archives doesn't have jurisdiction in the states and, critics argue, its wording is vague, granting a lot of room for maneuvering.[28] Moreover, Article 7 of the law could be read as corroboration that the countless rumors of disappearances and misfilings are, in fact, more than rumors.

> Article 7. Public servants, under no circumstances or exceptions, are allowed to remove archival documents when their job comes to an end.[29]

When this book was written, Jiménez's archive was beginning to be classified and digitized and was available for consultation at the special collections of La Biblioteca Xavier Clavijero at La Universidad Iberoamericana in Mexico City. I was able to consult it between 2010 and 2011, before it was transferred to the IBERO special collections. I consulted the DGIPS files in 2009 and 2010. I found the spy reports on feminist demonstrations by accident while doing a broad search on Echeverría's administration and the IWY. At present, DGIPS and DFS files continue to be accessible, and recently some reports became available online, while others are available by request in digital format for researchers with an address in Mexico City.[30] However, in 2012, access to files of the 1970s Dirty War, which are part of the DFS collection, was restricted with the establishment of a thirty-year embargo on confidential records and a seventy-year embargo on sensitive records—that is, documents containing personal data that could affect the private life of an individual.[31] These changes were part of an ongoing public debate regarding a new General Law of Archives (Ley General de Archivos) established by the outgoing administration of President Felipe Calderón, as Enrique Peña Nieto prepared for the return to power of the PRI after more than a decade of rule by the Partido de Acción Nacional. Debates regarding the General Law of Archives and access to files of the 1970s Dirty War point to the importance of this era for those in power, but more important, they signal the reality that access to certain archives is always uncertain.

Returning to the potential of having access to these two archives (of the AGN and of Ana Victoria Jiménez), each archive promises to advance our understandings of the ways in which visual letradas conceived of their right to see and to be seen (not only in visual terms, in this particular case). As with any other archive, both collections are fraught, and it is only by reading them alongside and against other sources that a more complete sense of the activities of these women can emerge, even if as incomplete representations, such as this one. Through a reading of these two archives, the visual letrada emerges not solely defined by the visual nature of its sources—like Jiménez's photographs. Rather, the visual letrada develops through a willingness to contest and return the gaze through images, ephemera, street performances, archival practices, and embodied encounters as seen through the interplay of looks between publics and performers.

6

Performing Feminist Art

Toward a Feminist Art Movement in Mexico

In comparison to other areas of the humanities that adopted feminist theory and gender studies as crucial frameworks of analysis beginning in the 1980s, the emergence of a differentiated feminist art movement in Mexico and, more important, an awareness of how feminisms could collaborate in dismantling the structures of the art establishment encountered several obstacles. According to Karen Cordero and Inda Sáenz, one of the reasons why art critics and historians have been late in adopting feminist frameworks in Mexico rests with the traditional function that both art and art historiography played as symbolic supports for the hegemonic discursive practices of the groups in power.[1] As in other societies, additional factors at play included the gendered division of labor that deemed the high arts as an exclusively masculine territory while the lower arts or crafts were deemed feminine ones. In Mexico this division became more paradigmatic as popular culture and the pre-Hispanic past became the foundations for the development of a highly masculine school of art, Mexican Muralism, that would not only play an important role in the creation of a national imaginary but would dictate the parameters of art criticism and historiography for most of the twentieth century.

The conception of feminism as an imported ideology also influenced the lack of interest that Mexican artists showed in labeling themselves feminist. During the 1970s, feminism in Mexico was (and sometimes still is) mostly understood as an imported imperialist dogma that prioritized issues of sexual liberation over more pressing class-based and social justice agendas. According to artist and scholar Maris Bustamante, many young female artists in the 1970s feared the consequences of being labeled feminist in an already male-oriented art world. They worried that the label indicated self-indulgence rather than political commitment.[2]

In spite of this, several efforts that explored the role of women in the arts—such as the special edition of *Artes Visuales* magazine (1976) and the First Mexican and Central American Symposium on Women's Research (1977) and its parallel exhibition at the Carillo Gil Museum, *Pintoras/Escultoras/Grabadoras/Fotógrafas/Tejedoras y Cermaistas* (Painters/Sculptors/Printmakers/Photographers/Textile Artists and Ceramists)—were organized during the 1970s. Outside the established circles of art, a limited number of emergent young artists, some of whom were also militants of the feminist movement, began to describe themselves as feminist artists during the 1970s, including Mónica Mayer, Ana Victoria Jiménez, Magali Lara, Rosalba Huerta, and Lucila Santiago.[3] Some of these artists participated in and organized feminist art exhibitions such as *Collage intímo* at Casa del Lago (1977), *Muestra colectiva feminista* at La Galería Contraste (1978), and *Lo normal* (1977) at La Casa de La Juventud. Through drawing, photocopies, etching, and photographs, these artists sought to highlight the personal and social dimensions of the female experience. These approaches to art making distanced themselves from the state-inspired "women in the arts" exhibitions. For instance, in *A veces me espantan mis fantasías* (Sometimes my fantasies frighten me, 1977) from her series *Collage intímo*, exhibited in Casa del Lago, Mayer explores her sexual desires by showcasing frontal images of a female vagina and a male penis as the fantasies of a newlywed (fig. 27). The two images are positioned on the top of the paper and partially covered by a curtain. On the lower part of the paper, a cut-out face of a woman wearing a wedding gown looks up to the images. The use of the curtain to cover this scene signals how female sexuality and desire were still taboo and deemed a private matter, something reserved for after marriage. But the fact that the curtain is not covering the image completely reveals Mayer's interest in making female sexuality and desire a matter of public debate. It also positions the viewer as voyeur of Mayer's sexual fantasies, and in doing so, she playfully puts into question which sexual organ is the object of the viewer's desire (and her fantasy). A year afterward, in 1978, Mayer continued to explore what "normal" sexual desire is (fig. 28). In *Lo normal*, she used the tactics of sociological art that she had explored in *El tendedero* but this time through a test in which she printed the phrase "I want to make love" on a postcard, and below the phrase she printed responses that ranged from: "with my lover, with a woman, with myself, before marriage, with my father, with an animal, and get paid." The postcards also showed a series of numbered photo-portraits of Mayer playfully gesturing, and a series of instructions asking viewers to circle the photo-portrait that most closely resembled their response. The tests were distributed at the opening of the exhibition *Lo normal*. In both *Lo normal* and *A veces me espantan mis fantasías*, Mayer asks the viewer to reflect on what constitutes female sexual desire.

Other independent events included *Traducciones: Un diálogo internacional de mujeres artistas* (1979), which brought together Mexican and U.S. feminist artists, and as mentioned earlier, several feminist militants engaged in interdisciplinary and transdisciplinary practices, such as the street plays of La Revuelta or the films of Colectivo Cine-Mujer. All these endeavors, I argue, constitute valid engagements with feminist artistic frameworks and practices regardless of the apparent disciplinary boundaries and political affiliations that have curtailed their being understood as such. The practices of the visual letradas worked to change dominant perceptions about the lack of existence of a feminist critique and a feminist art movement. In doing so, rather than conceptualizing a feminist art movement in the singular or as a product of a charismatic personality or as a closed disciplinary field, I subscribe to Cornelia Butler's proposal to think of feminism "as a relatively open-ended system that has throughout its history of engagement with visual art sustained an unprecedented degree of internal critique and contained widely divergent political ideologies and practices."[4]

The Golden Era of Feminist Art in Mexico

It was only in the 1980s that the concept of feminist art gained a significant presence in Mexico City's art circles. According to Mónica Mayer, the

FIG. 27. *A veces me espantan mis fantasias.* © 1977 by Mónica Mayer. Courtesy of the artist.

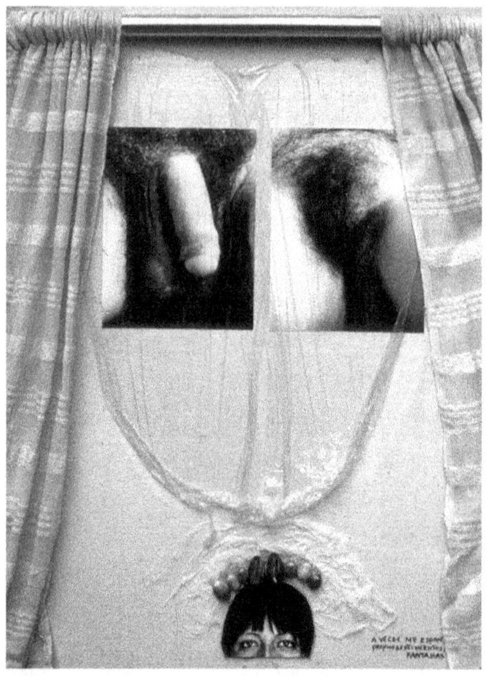

FIG. 28. *Lo normal.* © 1977 by Mónica Mayer. Courtesy of the artist.

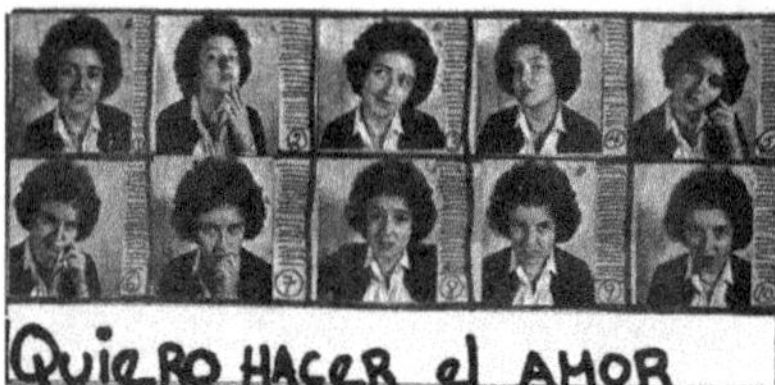

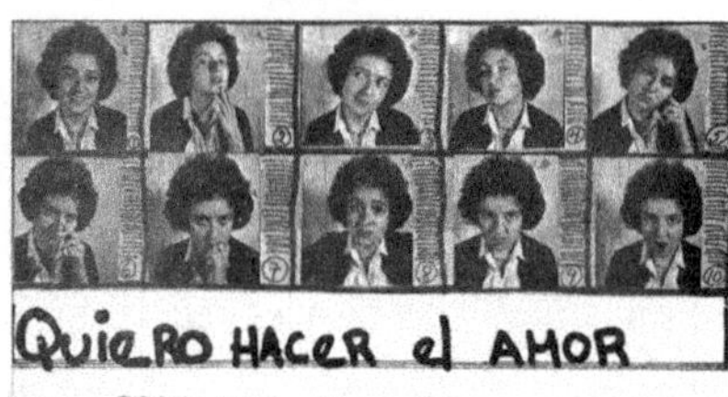

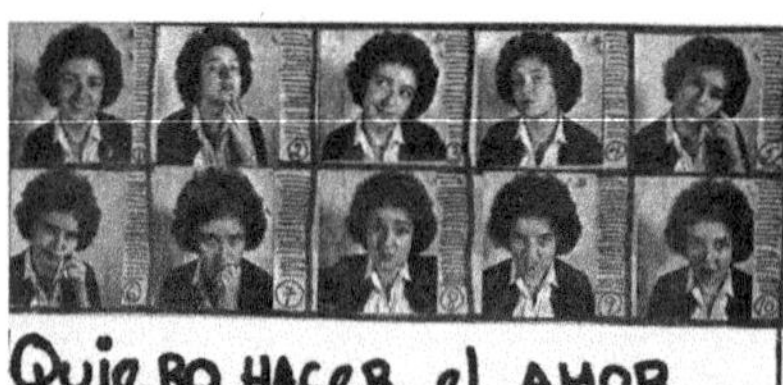

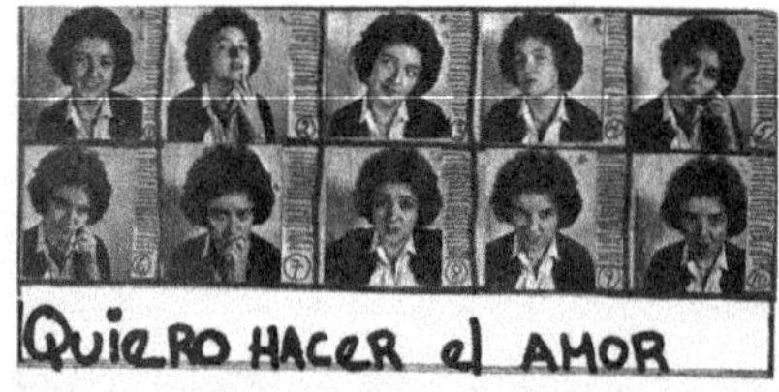

golden era of Mexican feminist art took place in the early 1980s.[5] Various feminist art collectives emerged during this time, and the specialized feminist magazine *Fem* dedicated issue number 33 to women's art (*La mujer en el arte*).[6] In the editorial note the editors, with an ironic tone, however, apologize to *Fem* readers for also including in the issue a discussion about the economic crisis that at the time was devastating Mexico's economy: "It will surprise our readers that in this issue dedicated to the arts we discuss prosaic problems such as the rise in the price of beef and the scarcity of milk. We certainly do not want to offend those who expect to find in these pages solace for the spirit, but it seems difficult for us to escape—even for a few moments—the harsh realities that Mexican women/*las mexicanas* experience nowadays."[7]

The conception of art as a bourgeois practice or an experience differentiated from the troubles of daily life continued to haunt feminists. As discussed earlier, Mayer and Jiménez had witnessed how many feminist militants perceived art as part of a bourgeois practice and the art world as a patriarchal institution with no interest in change. The editorial also reflected the harsh economic realities experienced by the Mexican population in the mid-1980s. It sent a reassuring message to women activists, from all social spheres, who were beginning to come together to form a wider women's movement and who, arguably, were the magazine's intended audience.

Established in 1976 by Alaíde Foppa and Margarita García Flores, *Fem* magazine by 1984 was the best-known independent feminist magazine in Mexico (and perhaps Latin America). Since its establishment it had been a significant media outlet for many new wave feminist militants as well as an alternative to established cultural magazines. Articles published in *Fem* included economic and political analyses that affected the female portion of the population as well as critical essays on theater, visual arts, film, and literature produced by women.

During the 1980s many militants from the early 1970s collectives turned their efforts toward developing links with popular urban and rural women's organizations as well as grassroots organizations, which would grow into a trend of feminism labeled *feminismo popular* (popular feminism).[8]

This transformation was motivated by a number of factors that produced important changes in the geographies of Mexico City during this decade. One of these factors was the economic crisis beginning in 1982 that produced massive unemployment and consequently displaced large numbers of women into the informal sector. Many of these women became responsible for the survival of their families, and along with increasing numbers of rural migrants to the city, they would reveal the feminization of poverty, a situation that many activists would begin to address. Equally important was the influence of crucial measures implemented by international organizations via the UN in the context of the UN's declaration of the Women's Decade after the IWY conference (1975–85). The following year wider forms of collective and solidarity actions among women would emerge as a result of the 1985 earthquake, including the mobilization of the Union of Seamstresses, Sindicato de Costureras 19 de Septiembre.[9] Hence the editorial's justificatory tone in the special issue on women's art (mostly perceived as a bourgeois practice) needs also to be read in the context of this crucial moment in the establishment of wider coalitions among women's groups—an objective pursued by many feminist activists (many of whom collaborated in *Fem*).

Eight years after the special issue of *Artes Visuales* (1976) dedicated to the discussion of women in the arts, several things changed within the established circles of art. The articles in *Fem* recognized the work of many women artists and showed interest in the potential that feminism offered to developing a critical methodology in the arts as well as to recovering the role of women within Mexican art history. Art historian Raquel Tibol, who had already begun publishing work to recover the place of women artists within the narratives of art history, criticized scholars who were beginning to write the histories of women artists; specifically, she criticized those placing emphasis on twentieth-century women and disregarding the importance of various nineteenth-century women artists.[10] Rita Eder, an art historian who had also participated in the discussion in *Artes Visuales*, introduced feminism as part of a shift in academic discourses that placed emphasis on minorities as a way to destabilize the white-male, Western-centric focus of academia.[11] Indeed, this was a response to changing academic discourses but also a response to the greater number of women taking part in visual art practices who were adopting a critical stance about the ways femininity had been visually represented, whether they declared themselves as feminists or not.[12] Other articles published in the special edition of *Fem* included Leticia Ocharán's genealogy of the participation of women in the graphic arts since the mid-nineteenth century and Bertha Hiriart's discussion of films made by women in the 1980s.[13]

This special issue of *Fem* also included articles by Mónica Mayer and Ana Victoria Jiménez. Each of these articles revealed the author's intention of establishing a feminist art movement that endorsed a critique of the patriarchal workings of the art establishment and that would offer an intervention in art education. Mayer published her proposal for what feminist art in Mexico could look like. She defined feminist art as not only "the objects produced by artists but the critical influence of feminist culture in the arts," and she traced the existence of four genres of feminist art that were active in Mexico City at the time.[14] First, she pointed to an individual approach taken by artists whose work dealt with feminine content, and second, to the then recent organization of women-only exhibitions. These exhibitions, she said, although rescuing the work of women from oblivion, at the same time worked against the objective of analyzing the patriarchal structures of the art world. Consequently, presenting these exhibitions as a solution to achieving women's representation in the arts missed an important critical opportunity. Then Mayer mentioned the practice of feminist militant art, citing the pieces that Ana Victoria Jiménez, Lila Lucido de Mayer, and Rosalba Huerta designed for the 1979 campaign against abortion, along with many other graphics and ephemera produced for some feminist demonstrations. And lastly, Mayer discussed the work of several art collectives. The participation of Jiménez in the special issue of *Fem* consisted of a bibliography featuring relevant works on the topic of feminism and the arts, including national and foreign articles, and her collaboration in the article published by the feminist art collective Tlacuilas y Retrateras.

In 1984, inspired by a feminist art workshop directed by Mayer in 1983–84 at the National School of Visual Arts (La Escuela Nacional de Artes

Plásticas, ENAP), at least three feminist art collectives were established in Mexico City.[15] Along with Maris Bustamante, Mayer established the two-woman collective Polvo de Gallina Negra with the purpose of analyzing the representation of women in the arts, promoting the participation of women in the arts, and creating alternatives to traditional representations of femininity from a feminist perspective.[16] Artists Nunik Sauret, Roselle Faure, Rose van Langen, Guadalupe García, and Laita established Colectivo Bio-Arte with the objective of addressing the biological transformations of women through visual means.[17] The third collective, Tlacuilas y Retrateras, was established by Ana Victoria Jiménez, Consuelo Almeida, Karen Cordero, Lorena Loaiza, Patricia Torres, and Elizabeth Valenzuela (fig. 29).

Taking their name from the Náhuatl word *Tlacuilos*, meaning a group of men in charge of painting pictograms, and *Retrateras*, a neologism related to the pictorial tradition of portraiture (*retrato*), these women set out to analyze the working conditions of Mexican artists and propose theoretical and practical alternatives. Among the objectives of Tlacuilas y Retrateras were (1) to promote discussion about the state of affairs of Mexican women artists, (2) to demand that artists have access to the same basic rights as other workers (childcare, medical insurance), (3) to promote the study of Mexican visual artists, (4) to develop feminist art workshops, and (5) to endorse the potential of the arts as tools for political consciousness.[18]

Tlacuilas and Retrateras published a collective article in issue number 33 of *Fem*. The article outlined the results of the first part of a research project regarding the working conditions of women artists in Mexico—focusing exclusively on women's participation in the visual arts.[19] The second part of the project aimed to focus on women's participation in other creative practices, including crafts (to my knowledge this part was not completed). The project consisted of interviews that centered on the following questions: Under what conditions do women intervene in this field? What kind of social constraints do women face (family, work peers, teachers)? The results showed that at the time, fewer than 20 percent of recognized artists were female; that their work was valued at a lesser price than that of their male counterparts; that it was not distributed equally; and that they had

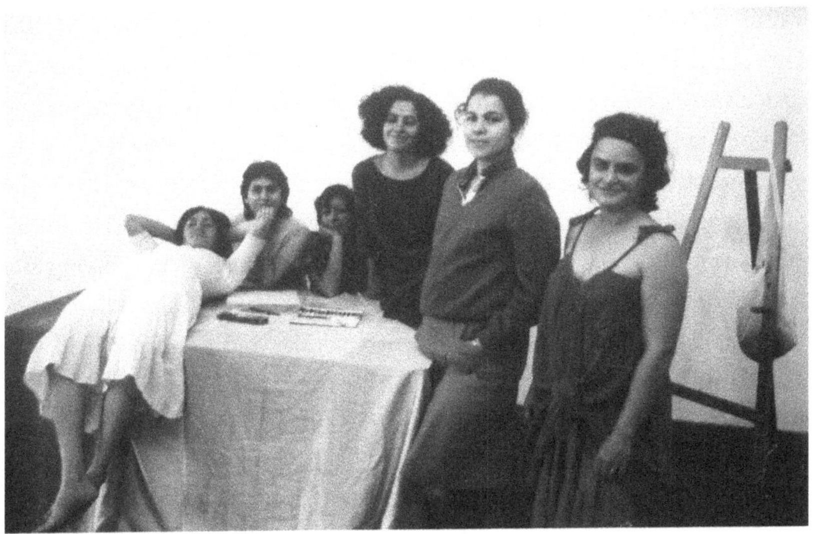

FIG. 29. (*Right to left*) Karen Cordero, Consuelo Almeida, Lorena Loaiza, Ana Victoria Jiménez, Patricia Torres, and Elizabeth Valenzuela, *Todas las Tlacuilas y Retrateras*. Photo © 1984 by Ana Victoria Jiménez. Archivo Ana Victoria Jiménez, Biblioteca Francisco Xavier Clavigero, Universidad Iberoamericana, Ciudad de México.

to deal with a lot of family and social preconceptions in order to pursue a career in the arts. For instance, in terms of the art school environment, many female students spoke about how neither the art professors nor their male counterparts would take their work seriously. And in terms of the family environment, a number of testimonies discussed how some families accepted that women studied painting only because it would endow the female student with some cultural capital and make her a more interesting housewife. Other testimonies spoke about how families would equate art school with a libertarian and sexually promiscuous environment and had trouble accepting that their daughters would study art. Still other families did not consider art to be a real profession through which a decent living could be earned.

This kind of sociological approach to art was in close dialogue with the projects and practices of other feminist artists and activists around the world, including Mónica Mayer, Teresa Burga, Suzanne Lacy, the Guerrilla Girls, and also the French sociologist Hervé Fisher.[20] Fisher coined the term *sociological art* in 1971 with the purpose of bringing art back to the society that created it. In 1983 Fisher organized the exhibition "Where does the street reach?" which took place at the Museum of Modern Art in Mexico City. In addition to the exposé quality of these kinds of practices, this project also points to the widening sphere of action of visual artists. Taking into consideration the context in which the issue of *Fem* was published gives us an idea of the publics that the work of Tlacuilas and Retrateras and *Fem* called into being. Just as the publication of *Artes Visuales* on women's art in 1976 was an inspiration for Mónica Mayer's career as a feminist visual artist, the publication of *Fem* responded to increased and widening interests in feminist practices. At the time, a process of institutionalization and professionalization was in place, one that would mark the entrance of 1970s activists into formal politics and the establishment of women's studies and gender studies in academia. Regardless of these advances, the activities of this group of women were still not welcomed within the established circles of art.

A few months after the publication of *Fem*, in August 1984, Tlacuilas and Retrateras organized the public performance entitled *La fiesta de quince años* at the San Carlos Academy in downtown Mexico City.[21] The objective was to analyze the traditional celebration that marked the sexual rite of passage from girlhood to womanhood, a topic already addressed by Jiménez in the context of the meeting with U.S. artists and Mexican feminists held in Cuernavaca in 1979. Three other collectives participated in the Tlacuilas' performance along with several artists, writers, musicians, and critics. It consisted of five *acciones plásticas*, or performances, an exhibition of more than thirty artists, and a public reading of poetry.

The performance by Tlacuilas y Retrateras was the central piece of the event. It consisted of staging the traditional celebration by enacting the dance usually performed by fifteen-year-old girls accompanied by their male *chambelanes* (chaperones) and the eating of a cake in the shape of a woman's high-heeled shoe, donated by Sanborn's restaurant (fig. 30). Also part of the celebration was the presence of art critic Raquel Tibol as *la madrina* (godmother), artist Fanny Rabel and Nahum B. Zenil as godfathers, and the father of the fifteen-year-old played by José Luis Cuevas.[22] Four other performances followed the staging of Tlacuilas and Retrateras, including a performance by Mónica Mayer and Maris Bustamante along with their respective partners Victor Lerma and Ruben Valencia. They represented the romantic and sexualized nature of heteronormative relations. Mayer and Lerma romantically kissed with a huge red heart as a backdrop, while Valencia sprayed the public with a liquid representing semen, which came out of a small bottle that he had ripped from a prosthetic sexual organ that Bustamante was wearing.[23] The event concluded as two young women appeared with their bodies covered with pieces of meat, pointing to the sexual availability of the fifteen-year-old that underlines the purpose of these celebrations.[24]

As Jiménez explained to me, the passage between girlhood and womanhood, which locates women as fertile beings, is brought to bear in this celebration. This passage is constrained by social discourses that stress the values of chastity and virginity, while at the same time announcing to the world that *la quinceañera* is sexually available.

By this time Jiménez defined feminism as a way of looking at the world that makes us aware and questions the roles imposed on women by society, allowing us to see how these roles define and constrain women's sexuality. The invitation to *La fiesta de quince años* included a series of questions that probed this celebration from a feminist point of view (fig. 31):

Why does the fiesta de Quince Años continue to be practiced? Is it a pre-Hispanic rite-of-passage ritual or is it a practice imported from developed countries? Why is this celebration so engrained in our society? Is it a patriarchal tradition that offers a daughter in marriage or is it a commercial enterprise aimed at maintaining a social status? What is it and what is the significance of the iconography that is used in this celebration? Is this celebration relevant for contemporary 15-year-olds? How would we want girls to initiate their lives and toward what aim? Is there something still valuable from this celebration? What alternatives could we propose?[25]

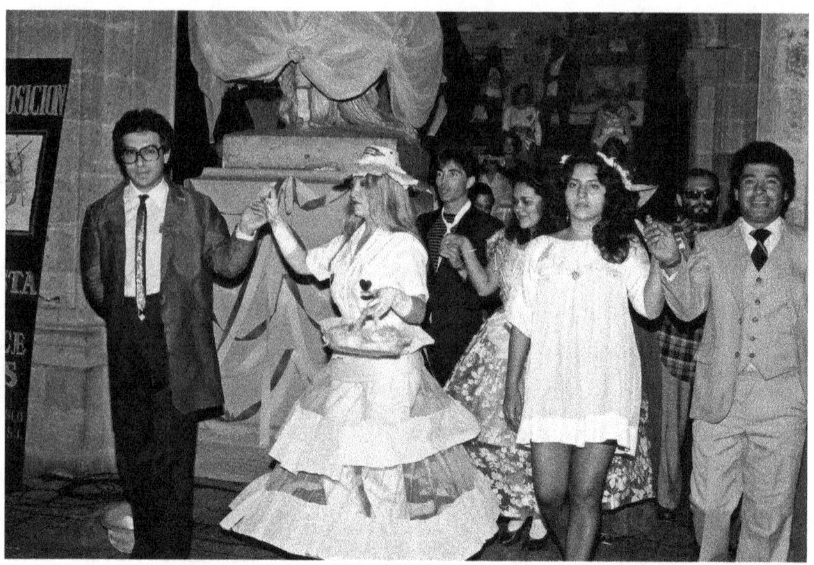

FIG. 30. *Fiesta de quince años* at the San Carlos Academy, downtown Mexico City. Photo © 1984 by Yolanda Andrade. Courtesy of Mónica Mayer.

Besides organizing and participating in the event, Jiménez constructed a board game based on the game El Juego de la Oca (snakes and ladders), titled *El juego de la sirena tratando de romper el circulo sin fin.*[26] Jiménez reconstructed the game using found illustrations and her photos, mostly taken in the *novias* (brides) district in downtown Mexico City. The piece reconstructed the life of Mexican women as a game dictated by celebrations, traditional myths, and female archetypes including the mermaid, Sor Juana Inés de la Cruz, the cult to San Antonio (which states that if you put a statue of the saint upside down it ensures you will get married), as well as bodily functions and social issues such as menstruation, violence against women, and prostitution. While the instructional text has a prescriptive tone, the fact that it was intended as a participatory piece—that is, a game of losers and winners—adds a sense of possibility and agency to Jiménez's views on such topics.[27] Moreover, the fact that both men and women could play the game, which referenced both female archetypes and

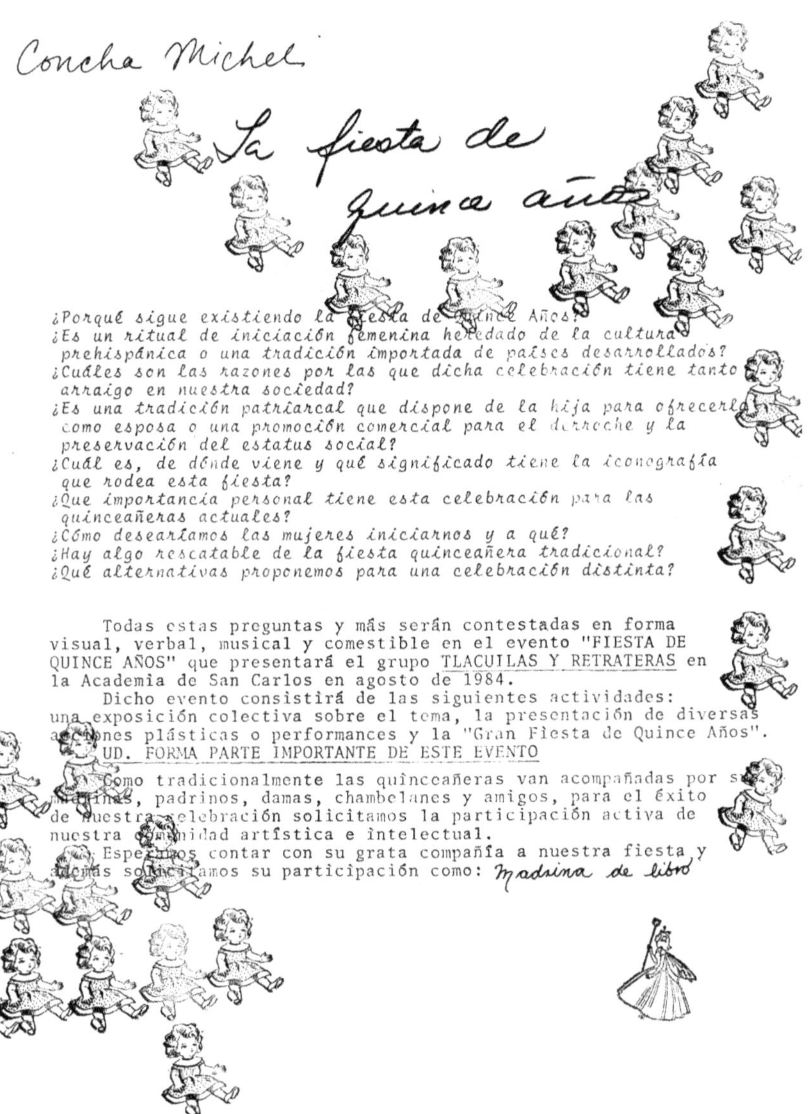

Concha Michel

La fiesta de quince años

¿Porqué sigue existiendo la fiesta de Quince Años?
¿Es un ritual de iniciación femenina heredado de la cultura
prehispánica o una tradición importada de países desarrollados?
¿Cuáles son las razones por las que dicha celebración tiene tanto
arraigo en nuestra sociedad?
¿Es una tradición patriarcal que dispone de la hija para ofrecerla
como esposa o una promoción comercial para el derroche y la
preservación del estatus social?
¿Cuál es, de dónde viene y qué significado tiene la iconografía
que rodea esta fiesta?
¿Que importancia personal tiene esta celebración para las
quinceañeras actuales?
¿Cómo deseariamos las mujeres iniciarnos y a qué?
¿Hay algo rescatable de la fiesta quinceañera tradicional?
¿Qué alternativas proponemos para una celebración distinta?

Todas estas preguntas y más serán contestadas en forma
visual, verbal, musical y comestible en el evento "FIESTA DE
QUINCE AÑOS" que presentará el grupo TLACUILAS Y RETRATERAS en
la Academia de San Carlos en agosto de 1984.
Dicho evento consistirá de las siguientes actividades:
una exposición colectiva sobre el tema, la presentación de diversas
acciones plásticas o performances y la "Gran Fiesta de Quince Años".
UD. FORMA PARTE IMPORTANTE DE ESTE EVENTO

Como tradicionalmente las quinceañeras van acompañadas por sus
madrinas, padrinos, damas, chambelanes y amigos, para el éxito
de nuestra celebración solicitamos la participación activa de
nuestra comunidad artística e intelectual.
Esperamos contar con su grata compañía a nuestra fiesta y
además solicitamos su participación como: madrina de libro

social issues that victimized women, created a queer space of engagement in which normative roles could potentially be transgressed by the players as they played the game (fig. 32):

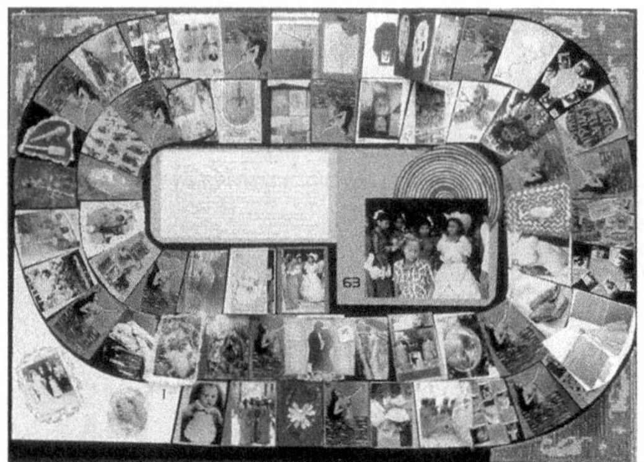 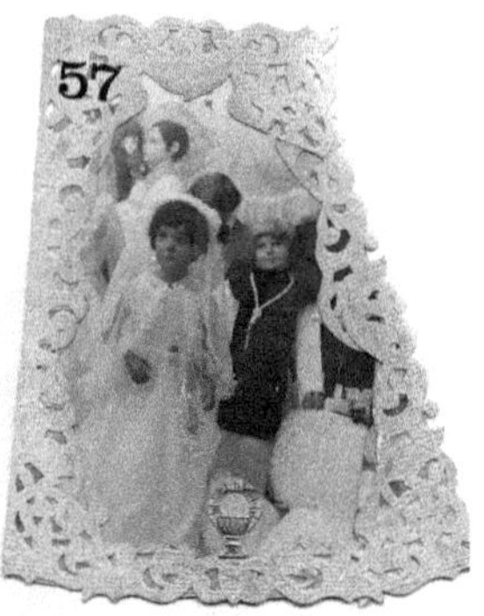

FIG. 32. Board game *El juego de la sirena tratando de romper el circulo sin fin* (*left*), detail of the board, and translation of game instructions (below). © 1984 by Ana Victoria Jiménez. Archivo Ana Victoria Jiménez, Biblioteca Francisco Xavier Clavigero, Universidad Iberoamericana, Ciudad de México.

Game of the Mermaid or attempting to break the unending vicious circle—a version by Ana Victoria Jiménez.
You need a couple of dice to play. The game is played by an unlimited number of players. If in the first roll of dice the player gets a **5** and **3**, the player should move to case number **28**. If the dice rolls **6** and **4** the player should move to case number **12**. If the player stops on the **mermaid case** (a fabulous half woman and half fish being that, according to mythology, was supposed to sink ships when sailors listened to her singing and because she is capable of breathing air and living underwater, she represents women trying to escape myths without fear of shipwrecks) the player should continue to advance. The player who lands in case number **12** should continue to advance. When a player reaches case number **21**, her or she loses two turns.

When a player arrives at case number **29, Rape** (sexual abuse inflicted on a woman by one or several men. It can be performed using force or psychological violence and will have lifelong psychological repercussions on the victim), the player should stay there until another player falls on the same case. Whoever arrives first to case number **39, To Dress Saints or to See if San Antonio Can Grant Us a Miracle,** continue to case number **44. The Labyrinth, case 44,** is the place where women find themselves since childhood even though they desire to escape. The player will remain there until someone else falls on case **44. The Butterfly,** case number **47,** represents the metamorphosis of a silk worm, as beautiful and as ephemeral as dreams. Like all the fairytales that we've been told, whoever falls in this case shall return to the beginning of the game. Whoever gets to case number **49, Sor Juana Inés de la Cruz** (1651–1695), Mexican poet and writer who dedicated her life to study, not to know more but rather to be less ignorant, shall return to case **39.** Whoever falls in case number **52, The Jail,** shall remain there until another player gets to it. The player who falls on case number **58** shall begin the game again. If a player falls on case number **60, Prostitution,** a patriarchal institution that designates a number of women to please the masculine community, shall move to case number **52.** If a player falls on case number **53, illusions,** a mistaken sense perception that makes us confuse appearances for reality, [the player] shall return to case number **31.** Whoever gets to case number **55** shall recite stories about princes and shoes and shall return to case number **42.** When a player gets to case **56, Menstruations,** a physical process that marks the ability to conceive children, move to case number **31.** Whoever gets to a case that is occupied by another player shall remain in that place and the first player shall switch places with the second player. The player who earns more than the necessary points to reach case number **63** shall back up the surplus number of points. The player who arrives to case number **63** is the winner!

Acknowledgments: Maria Salud Ramírez, Ana Álvarez, Ramon Tirado, and Pablo Jiménez. Some definitions are based on Victoria Sau. The illustrations of the Mermaid and the Jail are taken from original board games.

In spite of the fact that at the time, the art establishment seemed to be more open to exploring feminist issues in art, *La fiesta de quince años* stirred up the art community of Mexico City. Raquel Tibol, the famous art critic, feminist, and militant of the UNMM, who was designated a *madrina*, wrote scathing reviews of the event. Other reports captured the views of the audience, who felt insulted by the ridicule inflicted on the *quinceañera* tradition. Further, a neighbor of San Carlos commented: "These rich girls do not understand the significance of this celebration in popular terms. This is not only the only but also the most important celebration for a marginal girl. It is her party and no one else's. They [the rich girls] should acknowledge what it means to be poor and what the significance of this celebration is."[28]

Jiménez felt that the event was misunderstood by the art community and by the audience. This misunderstanding points to the constraints within the art community of accepting a multidisciplinary event as such *La fiesta de quince años* as art. In fact, many famous artists who had agreed to participate did not show up.[29] On the other hand, and perhaps more significant, the responses of the audience and the passersby, as the statement of the neighbor of San Carlos attests, exposed the celebration as a space of contestation, where not only feminist criticisms but also those of broader publics had a stake in celebrations and representations of feminine gender and sexuality. According to one newspaper report, more than two thousand people were in attendance.[30]

Indeed, the meaning of this event could become more complex if different voices were allowed into the discussion. While this was one of the intentions of Tlacuilas y Retrateras, the discussions in the following days revolved around the attacks of Tibol and the defensive responses by Mayer and others that were aimed at the ways in which the art world discriminated against these kinds of performative practices.[31] The discussion was framed as one pertaining only to the arts community. Even though the media covered the event, there was no engagement with other audiences. Overcoming this inability has been, and still is, the quest of many avant-garde movements that attempt to break with the constraints of their cultural fields, only to be pulled back into them in order to defend themselves and take a stand, as in this case, or to gain recognition, paradoxically sustaining their fields of production.

In part due to the public reception of *La fiesta de quince años*, the collective Tlacuilas y Retrateras disbanded—some members seeking to develop careers as visual artists preferred not to stir up the art establishment. Jiménez told me, however, that ultimately, she felt the event was a success. More than thirty artists participated, representing what *La fiesta de quince años* meant to them. There were romantic, ironic, insulting, and critical interpretations with an audience of more than two thousand people. For Jiménez the event was about exposing and provoking, not about coming to closure. It was yet another avenue in which visual *letradas* exercised their right to self-representation.

The reception of *La fiesta de quince años* summarized the constraints that the establishment of a differentiated feminist art movement in Mexico faced. Not only did feminist scholars show limited interest in linking art with feminism; the art community also completely shunned their efforts.[32] Critics disqualified the activities of the feminist collectives on the grounds of the poor aesthetic quality of their events, arguing that they were a copy of the U.S. feminist model.[33] Others also argued that a feminist critique was evident in the work of previous artists who didn't need to proclaim their militancy so literally and through such public events. Clearly the public aspect of the performance transgressed, even then, the elitist nature of the art gallery. *La fiesta de quince años* brought together several practices that had been introduced by feminist collectives in the 1970s and the practices of art collectives such as *Los Grupos*. *La fiesta* was a collective experimentation with performative languages in a public space that engaged with a particular kind of politics: the ways in which normative femininity and masculinity were constructed through cultural traditions. It was an event that questioned traditional art formats and conceptions of how the relation between art and politics had been conceived in Mexico for most of the twentieth century. These actions by a women's art collective provoked the art establishment into publicly taking a stand on where they thought the direction of women in the visual arts should go. Art critics were not ready to discuss the interdisciplinary nature and the different aesthetics espoused by feminist collectives as art. Therefore, even though many were interested in researching the working conditions of women in the arts and critiquing the representations of femininity, the majority of artists ultimately opted for more subtle and personal tactics for disturbing the patriarchal workings of the art world and its visual conventions.[34]

The Twilight of a Golden Era

Like other art collectives, by the early 1990s the feminist collectives established in the 1980s had disbanded.[35] Visual artists were not immune to the economic crisis, and many collectives dissolved as artists sought to establish individual careers. By the mid-1990s a new generation of artists would begin to establish collectives and alternative spaces at the same time that Mexican art rose to popularity in international markets. The politics that drove 1970s and early 1980s collectives—including feminism—were shed for an interest in participating in the global languages of contemporary art, effectively erasing the legacies of this earlier period.

The short-lived establishment of feminist collectives, or for that matter, the attempt to develop a militant feminist art movement seen through the perspective of Mayer and Jiménez, casts it as the failed project of a small group of women. However, tracing its connections with 1970s feminist militancy and collective practices, as well as with *Los Grupos*, locates their efforts at a crucial time when many sought to redefine the links between militant politics and art practices, and at the crossroads of an increased participation of women in the public sphere due to social and political developments at both local and international levels. Moreover, as I have shown, tracing Jiménez's activism through the lens of her archival practice proposes a more nuanced narrative of the histories of Mexican new wave feminisms, one that casts it not as an exclusive movement of middle-class, university-educated women but rather as an intergenerational movement of those who, across their different backgrounds, ages, practices, and forms of education, were concerned about inequalities within the movement and about how different oppressions implicated women of different classes.

Jiménez's archive is thus a valuable resource allowing us to look at the ways several women sought to challenge structures that oppressed women within the art world, including feminist discourses that conceived of art practices and the art world (traditionally defined) as bourgeois practices and not a priority for feminist struggle. Equally, they regarded the creation of a feminist art movement as a foreign and imperialistic imposition. Jiménez's documentations read alongside oral testimonies and media reports show how these discourses were not rigid but, rather, were constantly produced and contested through interconnections between distinct and sometimes competing feminist interests. Moreover, Jiménez's practice as a visual artist shows another facet of her militancy that speaks of her shifting stance toward feminism and her archival persona. In light of her earlier political experiences, her engagement in Tlacuilas and Retrateras provides a more nuanced account of the histories of new wave feminisms pointing to a narrative of both rupture and continuity with other women's movements and the crucial role that aesthetic practices played in such endeavors.

PART 3

Protesting the Archive

7

Interrupting Photographic Traditions

Society is concerned to tame the Photograph, to temper the
madness which keeps threatening to explode in the face of
whoever looks at it. To do this, it possesses two means. The first
consists of making Photography into an art, for art is not mad. . . .
The other means of taming the Photograph is to generalize, to
gregarize, to banalize it until it is no longer confronted by any
image in relation to which it can mark itself, assert its special
character, its scandal, its madness.

—Roland Barthes, *Camera Lucida*

Between the 1970s and the 1980s the practice of photography in Mexico, as
elsewhere, underwent various transformations. Encouraged by influential
meditations on how we make sense of photographic images, such as the
preceding observation by Barthes, a critique that addressed the power
relations implicit in the act of taking a photograph began to unfold. At the
same time photography was being elevated as an artistic discipline in its
own right. Around the world, exhibitions on photography were organized,
giving material weight to an already developed photographic canon as the
work of some photojournalists and amateurs was elevated to the category
of auteur photography. In Latin America photographers began searching
for a distinct way of seeing to characterize the image production that was
concerned with promoting social change through the representation of
the political and social hardships experienced in the region. Influenced

by the militant practice of many photographers and the excitement over the triumphant revolutions of Cuba (1958) and Nicaragua (1979), Latin American photographers foregrounded photography as a weapon that could transform the social and economic realities of the region, *una arma de transformación social* (a weapon for social transformation).[1] Such a weapon, however, was often wielded in highly gendered ways. Whereas the vast majority of the images of the photographers who attended these meetings either glorified the masculinity and heroism of revolutionary fighters or portrayed the miseries and precariousness of Latin American realities, women were mostly represented as companions of revolutionary leaders, as sexualized ethnic beauties, or as victims of class and racial disparities.

In Mexico, events such as the establishment of Agustín Víctor Casasola's archive in 1976 not only stressed the importance that photographic images had in the construction of national imaginaries and official historical narratives but pointed to the significance that visual archives would continue to play in such constructions. Moreover, echoing developments around the world, the Mexican state began to legitimize photography as an independent artistic practice by including photography as a discipline in state-sponsored art exhibitions. At the same time, it financed the exploration of diverse indigenous communities and the publication of photo-essays, thus renewing the practice of ethnographic photography (*fotografía etnográfica de autor*). Likewise, the practice of photojournalism in Mexico would gain some legitimacy as photographers were granted more credit for their images and were able to work more freely due to the establishment of independent media outlets. Within this context of crucial transformations and debates in the field of photography, Ana Victoria Jiménez began to photograph street protests by feminists in Mexico City.

For the most part, Jiménez's repertoire of images, until recently, has eluded any form of genre or stylistic classification. This lack of recognition is mostly due to the exclusion of her practice from historical narratives—the result of a lack of awareness about her work—and, most notably, the marginalization that her kind of practice has been subjected to by the structures that legitimize the field of photography. Jiménez herself, over the course of several interviews with me, emphatically denied that her photographic work could be considered either art or photojournalism, in spite of the fact that her images had circulated, although marginally, in art galleries as well as having been published in some newspapers. Perhaps Jiménez's somewhat modest assertions echo Barthes' concerns about what drives us to frame photographic images as art or as any genre for that matter, thus offering a strategy for tempering or taming them, as he notes in the epigraph to this chapter. In other words, it is conceivable that Jiménez was worried that her images would have their madness tamed by means of categorizing them within disciplines or styles. By denying their categorization as art or photojournalism, she ensured that her images had no referent, and in this condition, their meanings were loose and lost and, arguably, carried their madness within themselves for a longer period of time. Madness could be understood as the polysemic capacities of photographic images, which Barthes has theorized extensively, or as a radical political impulse, which is ascribed to things that have been kept at the margins.

Photographic images do produce visual discourses and circulate in certain economies that influence our understandings of self; in turn, they are influenced by these understandings, despite the fact that their meanings are never fixed. Moreover, the act of taking a photograph, as many have argued, is an encounter of uneven power relations.[2] Taking this into consideration and following the work of Deborah Poole and Michelle Shawn Smith, both of whom read photographic images as they relate to other archives, I read Jiménez's photographic practice against and alongside other visual archives that emerged within this landscape of debate over photography.[3] Reading the emergence of distinct visual archives concurrently at the moment of their conception enables the possibility of finding photographic meaning in the interstices between them in "the challenges they pose to one another," as Michele Smith puts it, "and in the competing claims they make."[4] In addition, this reading situates Jiménez's repertoire of photographs as part of a network of images and visual discourses, as distributed within a system of production, circulation, and consumption. This approach allows me to investigate more fully the economies that drive the production of knowledge; those economies that decide what should be tamed and what should be left in a state of madness.

Cross-Dressing as Indigenous and the Gendering of Photographic Practice

Photography arrived in Mexico in 1839 and has played a crucial role in imaging and constructing the nation since that time. In Mexico, as elsewhere, photography has been entangled with modern fantasies and fears, as much as it has defined artistic, scientific, and political projects. In the early twentieth century greater access to cameras and the widespread reproduction of all kinds of photographs sealed its association with modernity. And as Esther Gabara argues, "photographs captured the circulation of products, objects, and people that contributed to the development of an epistemology that related seeing with knowing and represented the subjects of modernity marked by race and gender."[5] For Walter Benjamin, photography and cinema revolutionized our conception of the arts by shifting their conventional association with ritual and tradition into a relation with politics.[6] Photography was able to dismantle the "aura" (authenticity and value) attached to the work of art as a unique representation because it was able to reproduce images serially and mechanically. Images could be more readily used to elicit particular affiliations and experiences and could potentially collaborate in the emergence of a more democratic visual economy—the distribution of images in a system of production, circulation, and consumption.

In Mexico, as if to confirm Benjamin's observations, photographic images became primordial resources to advance state cultural programs.[7] One of the ways this was done was through the use of the photograph as historical evidence—a practice that was institutionalized with the Mexican Revolution. Out of the armed conflict, photojournalism and the photoessay emerged as genres that would support and represent the histories of twentieth-century Mexico, both nationally and internationally. As John Mraz argues, since the 1920s the story of Mexico's past has often been told through illustrated histories where Great Men are celebrated as the makers of Mexico.[8]

Photography has also played a crucial role in the state's policies of *indigenismo*, a set of reforms and practices that attempted to integrate indigenous cultures in the development of a national narrative in order to construct a modern sense of Mexicanness (*mexicanidad*). Indigenismo was a process of internal colonization and expropriation whereby the image of the Indian emerged as the source of mythical originality and the basis of national identity.[9] The emergence of anthropology as an academic discipline and as an amateur practice of many local and foreign intellectuals and artists furthered the agenda of the post-revolutionary government to civilize indigenous communities and teach elite sectors of society to revalue their Indian heritage. To this end, the government organized anthropological expeditions to all regions of the country in order to photograph, study, and educate indigenous communities. Anthropology became the scientific discourse that legitimized and underwrote the post-revolutionary project of national construction through shifting discourses of indigenismo.[10] Photography (along with cinema) visualized and gave material weight to this anthropological discourse, and it was also the most effective means through which this discourse was popularized. Photographs (and films) circulated widely, and in so doing they reproduced anthropological discourse and actively participated in the construction of a sense of *mexicanidad*.

This inextricable relationship between anthropology and photography that emerged in the post-revolutionary era renovated two already established image-making traditions that gendered ethnicity as female. The first consisted of romantically depicting indigenous women as exotic beauties engaged in their daily practices as they traversed ravished landscapes. This tradition was shaped by an orientalist way of seeing that had its roots in colonial conventions and the visual desires of many nineteenth-century travelers, as Carlos Monsiváis and others have extensively argued.[11]

The second tradition emerged out of a sanctioned repertoire of images of *tipos mexicanos* produced as a catalogue of regional traits in order to promote a unified sense of Mexican culture that had its origins in colonial depictions of *castas* and nineteenth-century *costumbrismo*. From this new collection of sanctioned cultural attributes, two dressing styles became symbols of Mexican femininity—the Tehuana and China Poblana.[12] Throughout the twentieth century images of women dressed as Tehuanas or as Chinas Poblanas became popular signifiers of Mexican femaleness and the standard for Mexican beauty.[13] Concurrently, urban women, including famous artists and intellectuals, cross-dressed as indigenous and in so doing also collaborated in the establishment of a national fashion style. The performance of urban women dressed as indigenous both inscribed and contested a normative gendered view of indigenous as female. As Erica Segre argues, for many this cross-dressing performance was a strategy to criticize the feminization of ethnicity or a form of empowerment and transgression of middle-class mores.[14]

These two visual traditions of gendering ethnicity as female were renewed at a time of great anxiety regarding the performance of femininity in public spaces. As anthropologists were sent out into the regions to study, photograph, and educate indigenous communities, the female portion of the emergent middle classes was demanding a place in the new national landscape. In the aftermath of the first feminist congress in Mexico, held in Merida in 1916, several feminist magazines were established, and after the First Congress of the Pan American League for the Elevation of Women celebrated in Mexico City in 1923, a letter demanding equal political rights was crafted and sent to Mexico's president, Alvaro Obregón.[15] Women in urban centers were not only demanding suffrage rights but were out on the street having *vidas públicas*, as Esther Gabara put it.[16] They had joined the workforce. They had emerged as consumers in their own right. They had adapted their looks to the latest trends of transnational fashion and beauty, smoking cigarettes, and listening to jazz music.

These unruly performances were the subject of many discussions about women's proper behavior in all kinds of media, particularly in printed matter (comic books, newspapers, and magazines).[17] The attention given to the images of these feminine performances reveals the centrality that feminine virtues had for the state's national project and the important role that images played within this project. On the pages of newspapers and in magazines, a "war of images" directed at women took place. Advertisements of Clavel Cigarettes, Hinds Cream, Tequila Victoria, Oliver Typewriters, Electric Irons, and Kodak cameras along with images of women dressed as *pelonas* (flappers) or Tehuanas proposed contradictory virtues and looks of the Mexican *chica moderna*.[18] As Anne Rubenstein argues, contrasting ideas of invented pasts and imagined futures were played out through competing representations of *chicas modernas* and traditional women.[19] However, by the 1940s the modernity espoused by *chicas modernas* began losing ground as government leaders upheld conservative social values. The virtues and images of *chicas modernas* became unattractive in comparison to the virtues of the submissive and long-suffering Mexican mother who never left home as the state shifted its rhetoric from an emphasis on progress to a language that combined tradition and progress.[20] This shift would give preference to motherhood as the primordial signifier of feminine values shaped by the virtues of the Virgin of Guadalupe and the beautiful traits of mestizo women dressed in *traje nacional* (Tehuana, China Poblana, or a mixture of both). Nonetheless, as the modernizing project gained momentum due to economic and coerced political stability, indigenismo was reproduced and internalized through commercial films and photographs.[21]

As printed photographs in the media visualized and contested the proper virtues of Mexican women in the early decades of the twentieth century, many intellectuals conceived of photography as an effeminate medium. In the early 1930s Salvador Novo described photography as the daughter of the fine arts because she followed in the footsteps of her mother, painting, without yet being able to develop her own aesthetic language.[22] Following Walter Benjamin, others have argued that the process of legitimizing photography as an art form was complicated by various technological, political, and cultural factors.[23] For feminist art historians, photography represented a frontal attack on the male-dominated art world, a world was based on constructions or assumptions of originality and exclusivity represented by the signature of the male artist and by the ability of the connoisseur to recognize an artist's style.[24] Moreover, the invention of the handheld camera that brought photography to the masses also carried with it the potential for stripping the (male) photographer of his exclusive status as an art producer. Photography, as a technology and a mass practice, represented a threat and a revolutionary means of accessing many fronts (the art establishment, national projects, and consumer practices).

These tensions also played out in the pages of Mexican illustrated magazines, where Kodak advertisements depicted women as both the object and subject of photography.[25] Ads directed at middle-class women labeled photography as "the best job for women."[26] Hence, in the context of the early twentieth century, characterized by a male-dominated Mexican muralist art scene in tandem with photography's arbitrary status as an art form due to its use in the advertising industry, it comes as no surprise that Novo conceived of photography as "effeminate."[27]

In the aftermath of the revolutionary conflict, photography emerged as a tool for reproducing and popularizing the project of national construction through its links with anthropological practices and discourses of indigenismo. However, the widespread development of print communications (press, comic books, magazines) and the advancements of industrial and consumer capitalism developed competing practices and image repertoires, providing some alternative perspectives on how female looks and virtues were envisioned and intersected by a variety of desires other than those promoted by post-revolutionary projects.[28]

By the mid-1970s the inextricable relation between photography, indigenismo, and a concern over women's bodies in public spaces was reconfigured through various events. President Echeverría's reforms in the fields of folklore, craft, and indigenous rights inaugurated the renewal of discourses of indigenismo. In 1975 his government convened the First National Congress of Indigenous Peoples of Mexico, "giving Indians an opportunity to claim a role in the complex political process of formulating a new version of national Indian policy while demanding self-determination."[29] He complemented his support by promoting folklore and the production of *artesanías* through the creation of the National Fund for the Promotion of Craft (FONART). And most symbolically, the presidential couple adopted, as official attire, a dressing style from *los tipos mexicanos*—for the president a *guayabera*, a southern-Mexican-Caribbean linen shirt; and for María Esther Zuno de Echeverría, the president's wife, a Tehuana or China Poblana dress.

Another important event in this renewal of indigenismo was orchestrated in 1976 by the National Institute for Indigenous Affairs (Instituto Nacional Indigenista, INI), a governmental institution established in 1948 to deal with indigenous communities, when it commissioned several photographers, including Nacho López, Pablo Ortiz Monasterio, Mariana Yampolsky, and Graciela Iturbide, to go and explore regions of the country accompanied by an anthropologist (or an intellectual) in order to produce photographic books of an indigenous community of their choice.[30] In these books, discussed in the following sections, the work of these photographers followed, for the most part, an anthropological way of seeing established by their predecessors in the 1920s.

In the midst of the 1970s official revival of indigenismo and in the context of debates over Latin American photographic practice, hundreds of new wave feminists began to demand a broad range of rights. They were out on the street claiming their sexual and reproductive rights and asserting their right to represent their own bodies in the media. Groups of women wearing skirts and blouses, bell-bottom jeans, and platform shoes, or dressed in *jipiteca* style (an indigenous blouse with jeans, signaling the adoption of 1960s U.S. hippie fashion with an Aztec twist) began to organize protests in Mexico City. As in the early 1920s, the performance of urban women dressed as indigenous both inscribed and contested a normative gendered view of indigenous as female. In the context of the Cold War, the legacies of the Cuban Revolution, the emergence of military dictatorships, and the United States' penetration in the Latin American region, indigenismo became not only an integral part of Mexican folklore and identity but also a symbol of Latin American and Chicano protest and pride. Images of women dressed as Tehuanas were a contested sign of subversion entangled in the geopolitics of the Latin American Cold War. While government officials and artists continued to exploit these images as lures of the exotic via art exhibitions and economic and cultural exchanges, all over Mexico urban women dressed as Tehuanas flocked to the *peñas* to sing protest songs (*canciones de protesta*) against Anglo-American imperialism and Latin American dictators.

As in the 1920s, by the 1970s images of women cross-dressing as indigenous were part of a fashion style that overtook Mexican urban centers, as elsewhere. This fashion practice signaled a new configuration of gendered and political subjectivities that merged transnational fashions, rock music, protest songs, feminist demands, and anti-imperialistic discourses with more fluid and contested claims over indigenous roots.

Women Wielding the Camera: Images and Genealogies of Photographic Practices

The emergence of new wave feminism and the hosting of the UN's first International Women's Year conference in Mexico City also coincided with a shift in the gendering of photographic practice—from one considered a dubious feminine practice to a full-fledged masculine revolutionary practice—thus renewing the war of images over the representation of Mexican femininity. In the context of the reconfigurations of gender and political subjectivities that took place in the 1970s, and following the dictates of state institutions, some women photographers sought a still more "authentic" feminine essence, traveling to rural communities in search of mythical examples of matriarchal indigenous organizations, while others pointed their viewfinders toward women on the street, and thus fought the war of images on another front. I would like to highlight two images that visually represent these distinct image-making traditions.

The first image, taken by Jiménez in 1982, depicts a group of women from the Coalición de Mujeres Feministas performing what looks like line-dance choreography celebrating the establishment of the first Red Nacional de Mujeres (RNM), a national network of women's groups that fought for women's rights from different ideological perspectives (fig. 33).

It belongs to a series of images that document a performance on the occasion of the celebration of the II Encuentro Nacional de Mujeres (II National Encounter of Women). In the foreground four women holding hands and dressed in jeans, shirts, sweaters, and tennis shoes appear to

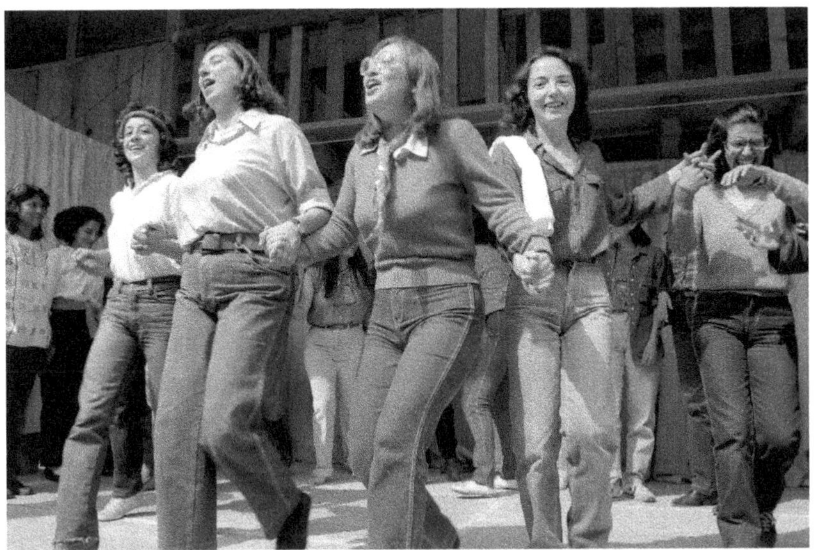

be singing (shouting or laughing in chorus) as they walk toward Jiménez's camera. More women performing similar actions fill up the background of the image. In the left corner of the photograph a woman wearing a kind of *huipil* (an embroidered indigenous blouse) and jeans holds the hands of another woman in preparation for some movement. The woman wearing the embroidered blouse seems to have a darker skin tone than the women who occupy the foreground.

Despite running the risk of arriving at facile conclusions about the class and racial backgrounds of the members of Coalición de Mujeres based only on this image, I would nevertheless like to call attention to this image as a signpost of the diversity of women who are depicted in Jiménez's visual archive and the range of audiences and perusals these women were attempting to reach. This emphasis on diversity not only points to the ways in which urban femininity was lived and experienced on the streets of Mexico City but, most important, it also speaks to the contested attempts of a wide range of women's groups (unionized groups, grassroots, urban, and indigenous movements as well as feminists and lesbians) that came together in the 1980s with the purpose of constituting broader coalitions from diverse ideological perspectives to demand women's rights throughout Mexico.

As noted earlier, the Coalición de Mujeres Feministas was established in 1976 by various feminist collectives to demand three basic rights: (1) the decriminalization of abortion, (2) penalization of rape, and (3) protection for battered women. In 1982 they joined another ensemble of feminist and lesbian collectives to establish RNM. This network was an inclusive attempt to construct and promote dialogue among women's groups across Mexico without demanding their adherence to any common goals, ideology, or lines of work.[31] More than twenty-one groups joined the network, including eight from different regions in the country.[32] The network disbanded in 1985, but many of its members continued to work toward legislation on a broad range of women's rights, and many consider these failed attempts at building coalitions as crucial stepping-stones that helped open spaces for the discussion of women's rights from different perspectives throughout the country.[33]

The other image I wish to highlight was taken three years earlier, in 1979, by Graciela Iturbide (b. 1942), one of the most renowned among Mexican photographers (fig. 34). The image, entitled *Our Lady of the Iguanas*, is a portrait of an indigenous woman with iguanas on her head. The woman, Iturbide tells us, arrived at the market of Juchitán to sell the iguanas. As she was putting them on the ground, Iturbide asked to photograph her; the woman agreed and put the iguanas back on her head.[34] To take this shot, the woman and Iturbide rehearsed various positions.[35] Finally, Iturbide chose to position her camera below the eye-line, producing a pronounced visual angle that magnifies the woman's size, giving her an aura of empowerment. This visual composition breaks with the traditional framing of portraits taken from an eye level angle and with aesthetic conventions of traditional ethnographic photography.

In contrast to Jiménez's photograph, *Our Lady of the Iguanas* has circulated widely in different venues and belongs to Iturbide's famous pho-

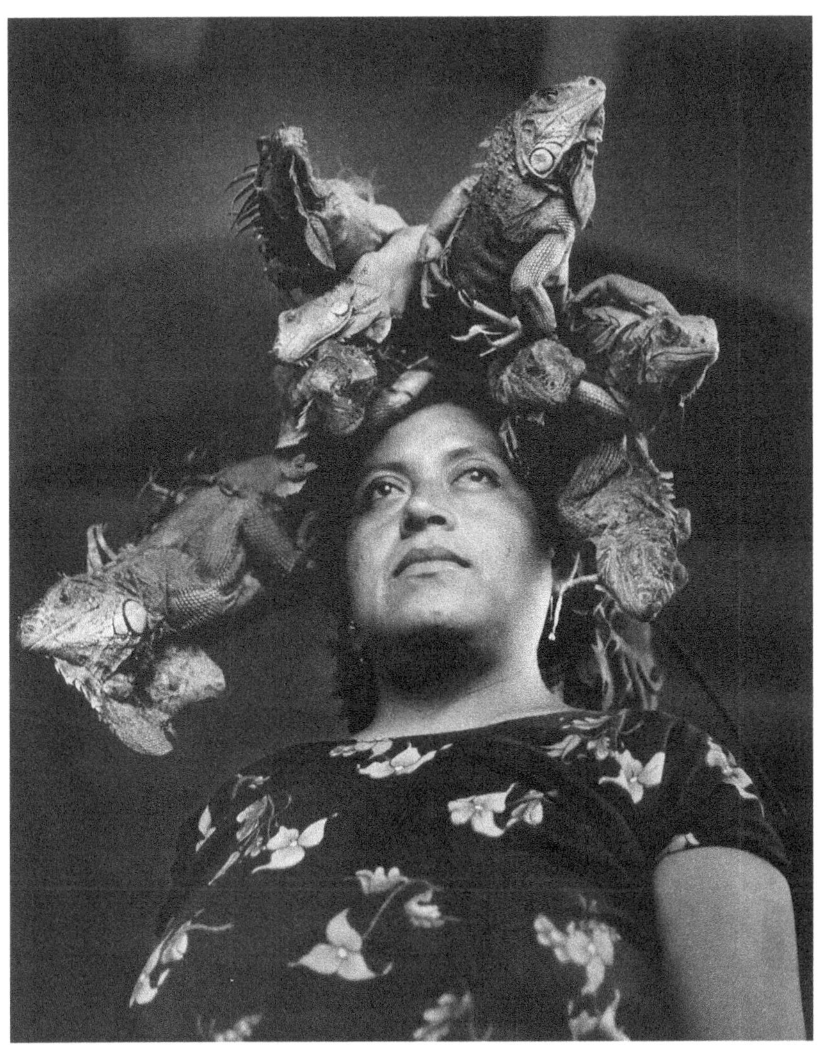

FIG. 34. *Nuestra señora de las iguanas (Our Lady of the Iguanas)*, Juchitán, Oaxaca, Mexico. Photo © 1979 by Graciela Iturbide. Courtesy of the artist.

tographic study of the women from the region of Tehuantepec, *Juchitán of Women* (1989). In 1979 Francisco Toledo invited Iturbide to Juchitán, a Zapotec town in the Isthmus of Tehuantepec, to witness the turmoil in the region.[36] The emergence of the Coalition of Workers, Peasants and Students of the Isthmus (COCEI, 1973) during Echeverría's *apertura democrática* set in motion a grassroots movement that sought autonomy and self-governance.[37] The result of this invitation was the publication of the photo book *Juchitán of Women* with text by Elena Poniatowska.

This work established Iturbide as an internationally renowned photographer. In 2007 the Getty Museum in Los Angeles organized the exhibition *The Ghost Dance: Photographs by Graciela Iturbide* on the occasion of the museum's tenth anniversary.[38] The focus of this exhibition was Iturbide's images "on the powerful matriarchal aspects of Juchitán culture," which, according to the curator, are "now considered central to Iturbide's oeuvre."[39]

About this body of work that gave her international recognition, Iturbide states that over a ten-year period she lived in the region in order to develop a better understanding of the lives of these women. These sojourns allowed her to develop collaborative and participatory relationships: "In Juchitán I spent a lot of time at the public market, hanging out with the women there, these big, strong, politicized, emancipated, wonderful women. I discovered this world of women and I made it my business to spend time with them and they gave me access to their daily world and their traditions."[40]

Iturbide's images were romantically framed by Poniatowska's text that accompanied them:

> Juchitán is not like any other town. It has the density of its Indian wisdom. Everything is different; women like to walk embracing each other, and here they come to the marches, overpowering, with their iron calves. Man is a kitten between their legs, a puppy they have to admonish, "Stay there." They trade roles; they grab men who watch them from behind the fence, pulling at them, fondling them as they curse the government and, sometimes, men themselves.[41]

Poniatowska's text, which serves to anchor the meaning of Iturbide's images, showcases Juchiteco women as sexually and politically independent. Produced at a time when issues of indigenous forms of governance were being fought for in the region, Iturbide's images and Poniatowska's text emphasized their overt sexual nature and the prominent role they played in the political life of the region. Not only was the book an important accomplishment in Iturbide's career; it also exalted the myth of the matriarchal organization of the region's Zapotec communities. While the participation of Juchiteco women was crucial for the organization of COCEI, Lynn Stephen has argued that a very small number of women achieved leadership positions.[42] Echoing the concerns of others who have studied the COCEI movement, Stephens has also noted that "the myth of Juchitán as a matriarchy is far from true."[43]

If one considers that these images were also produced at the height of the new wave feminist movement, one has to wonder about their intended audience. Indeed, Iturbide's images have been adopted as symbols of a kind of feminism that exalts the alleged matriarchal structure and political organization practiced by these women. For Iturbide herself, this experience made her a strong supporter of feminism.[44] However, at precisely a time when many women took to the streets to reclaim their right to represent themselves, Graciela Iturbide's feminist search turned to a tradition that romanticized the myth of matriarchal politics that was supposedly practiced by the women of Juchitán. Following this tradition not only continued to exoticize Mexican femininity; it also relegated female political participation to a kind of matriarchal structure that only works in opposition to patriarchy in a secluded and mythical setting. Moreover, by framing and justifying traditional feminine virtues through the tropes of indigenismo, Iturbide's image took visual prominence as a symbol of "Mexican feminism," nationally and internationally. Meanwhile, images such as that of Jiménez depicting the struggle of Mexican women who were out on the streets demanding a change in the structures that undermined their rights were relegated to oblivion.

Iturbide's iconic *Our Lady of the Iguanas* has been appropriated and re-signified in numerous ways by different communities. In 1996 it was featured as a symbol of women's independence in the feminist film *Female Perversions* (dir. Streitfield and Hebert, 1996) and was adopted as powerful sign of women's emancipation by other communities who refer to the image as "la medusa de Juchitán."[45] These reappropriations do speak to the impossibility of linking a particular ideology to an image, given the instability of photographic meaning and, in a broader setting, to the social lives of things. However, Iturbide's images also participate in a transnational visual economy that was supported by the Mexican regime in order to broadcast its pride in "ethnic pluralism." As such, her practice is in dialogue with, and plays a part in, various structures of knowledge production sustaining the different ways that the Mexican regime dealt with the question of the Indian—from an ethnographic search to support a national project and induce pride in the nation's Indian heritage to a discourse that was aimed at taming unruly bodies as well as critical attempts at deconstructing this project.

Iturbide belongs to a genealogy of internationally known women photographers including Tina Modotti (1896–1942), Lola Álvarez Bravo (1903–93), and Mariana Yampolsky (1925–2002), whose best-known work contributes to the repertoire of romantic depictions of indigenous women. Like Iturbide, all these photographers traveled to the region of Tehuantepec and other rural communities to produce images of indigenous women, and arguably, they all proposed different and critical ways of seeing them.[46] This genealogy helps legitimize and frame Iturbide's photographic career within a tradition of women photographers who chose to tread a dangerous path; that is, they attempted to criticize a photographic tradition that continues to be consumed and circulated in a manner that idealistically fixes and feminizes ethnicity.

Similar to Iturbide's *Our Lady of the Iguanas*, Tina Modotti's famous image *Woman of Tehuantepec* (ca. 1929), which depicts a woman of the region of Tehuantepec carrying a painted gourd on her head, is also shot from below rather than frontally, helping, in my reading, to capture the dignity and pride of these women while avoiding the picturesque qualities of a frontal portrait taken at eye level (fig. 35). Moreover, like Iturbide's,

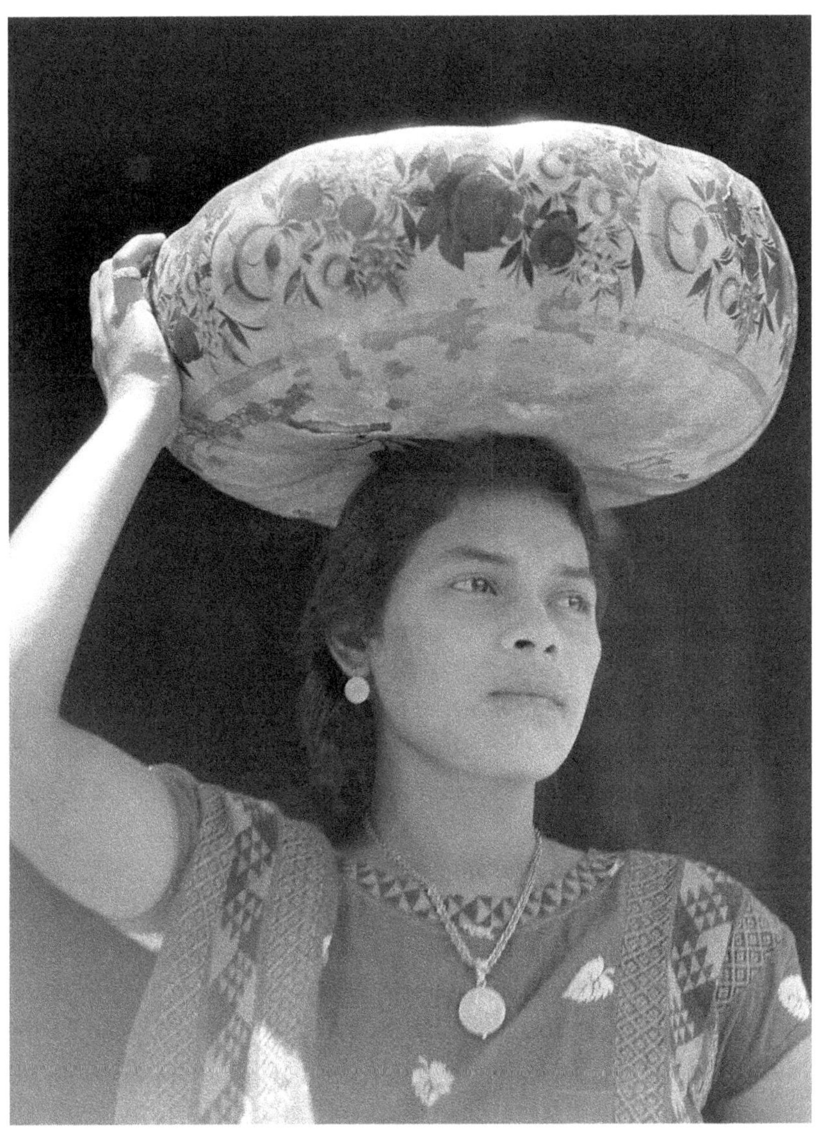

FIG. 35. *Mujer con jícaras (Woman of Tehuantepec)*. Photo © ca. 1929 by Tina Modotti. 35277 CONCACULTA-INAH-SINAFO-Fototeca Nacional.

Modotti's interest in the women from this region has been explained as an interest in their political organization.[47] During Modotti's time in Mexico (1923–29), the women of Tehuantepec were highly regarded for their sensual beauty and sexual freedoms, a conception developed through the imaginaries of nineteenth-century travelers but reified by the images of Sergei Eisenstein and Diego Rivera, among others. At the time it was also widely believed that the women from the isthmus possessed unusual political power since many thought that they managed their societies according to the rules of matriarchy.[48]

Like Modotti, Lola Álvarez Bravo was an active participant in a transnational network of artists and intellectuals that defined Mexico's 1920 artistic milieu. They participated in the intellectual effervescence set in motion by José Vasconcelos's cultural program and the emergent international modern photography movement, and they are part of a generation of creative females who broke with traditional mores that defined women's roles in their time (Frida Kahlo, María Izquierdo, Concha Michel, Antonieta Riva Palacio, Nahui Olin, Guadalupe Marín, and Rosa Casanova, among others). All these women were lured by the powerful myth of the women of the Isthmus of Tehuantepec, and many have discussed their performance of cross-dressing as Tehuanas as an ironic critique of the spectacle of gendering ethnicity as female.[49]

In contrast to Modotti's fleeting and turbulent career as a photographer, Lola Álvarez Bravo, who also spent time in Oaxaca in the 1920s, was able to establish herself as a photographer and educator. Between the late 1930s and the 1950s she visited the region of Oaxaca on various occasions and took her most memorable images there.[50] At the time she worked for the National Institute of Fine Arts (Instituto Nacional de Bellas Artes, INBA) and, as part her work, was sent to study and gather information on popular dances and traditions to be used for urban artistic productions, yet another strategy to integrate indigenous cultures into the national culture. Most notably her photos were used by Anna Sokolow, at the time director of INBA's Dance Company. One of her best-known images, *Entierro en Yalalag* (*Burial in Yalalag*, 1946), was taken in the Zapotec region as part

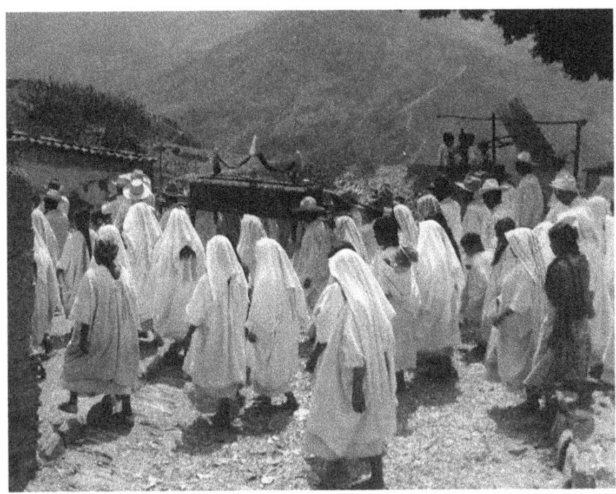

FIG. 36. *Entierro en Yalalag (Burial in Yalalag)*. Photo by Lola Alvarez Bravo, 1946. Lola Alvarez Bravo Archive, © 1995 by the Center for Creative Photography, the University of Arizona Foundation.

of an INBA project (fig. 36). The image depicts a group of women covered in white *rebozos* walking behind a coffin. None of the women are facing the camera; they represent an amorphous mass of sorrowful mourners. The image is taken from a distance that allows the photographer to depict the mass of mourners as they walk through the mountainous landscape.

Lola Álvarez Bravo was well aware of how photography had collaborated with the mystification and commodification of the Indian into a discourse of national identity. In spite of the fact that her images were used to develop national dance choreographies that, in turn, collaborated with this mystification, she developed a theory of photography to counter it. According to Erica Segre, Lola Álvarez Bravo's photographic investigations had to do with an interest in going deeper into the image, to provide an antidote to a superficial kind of seeing that had allowed for the commodification of the image of the Indian, mostly manifested through embodiments of feminized ethnicity.[51] To this end, Lola Álvarez Bravo posited *"lo popular profundo"* as a corrective to *"la mirada engañosa"* (the deceiving gaze) that had turned national identity into a commodity. She proposed the "third eye," which combined the pleasure of the search and the finding: an eye that allowed the photographer to see all and then select the best image.[52]

As we can see, Lola Álvarez Bravo's third eye was only concerned with the ethics of composition and framing that would provoke in the spectator a more ethical awareness about the Other (the indigenous communities and their authentic traditions). Clearly, she was not concerned with the complex set of encounters and relations set in motion by the photographic act. Her strategy to break away from dominant nationalist stereotypes was to provide the spectator with a more profound and complex image—what she believed to be a more "authentic" representation of Otherness posited by "*lo popular profundo*." Nonetheless, Lola's search, like that of many others, ended in another form of essentialism that failed to do away with the distancing effect between the subject and the object.[53]

Like Lola Álvarez Bravo, Mariana Yampolsky made photographic images at a time when the 1920s Cultural Revolution was being institutionalized. Between the late 1940s and 1960s, anthropologists turned to photography with the intent of deconstructing the homogenizing tendencies of ethnographic archetypes established by the institutionalization of the revolution's cultural program.[54] These anthropologists' efforts were not devoid of essentialist views. Like Lola Álvarez Bravo, Yampolsky directed her attention to the Indian and the rural as part of an interest in undoing these homogenizing myths. As Erica Segre notes, Yampolsky and Álvarez Bravo "were aware of the mystifications of the ethnographic gaze, the discursive aesthetics of cultural nationalism in art and film in the 1930s and 1940s and the compelling archive produced by foreign photographers."[55]

Younger than Álvarez Bravo, Yampolsky approached her subject influenced by a concern with collaboration and participatory observation, a strategy that Iturbide would follow in her work on Juchitán women. Yampolsky encouraged her subjects to take responsibility for the ways in which they were represented, welcoming collaboration in the construction of her shots. This emphasis on collaboration became a powerful seduction for postmodern ethnographic practices in the 1980s. As Stephen A. Tyler argues, "Because postmodern ethnography privileges 'discourse' over 'text,' it foregrounds dialogue as opposed to monologue, and emphasizes the cooperative and collaborative nature of the ethnographic situation in contrast to the ideology of the transcendental observer."[56] For instance, in Yampolsky's series of portraits of women from the Mazahua region in central Mexico, the women portrayed were largely responsible for constructing the ways in which they wanted to be represented.[57]

Like Yampolsky, Iturbide emphasizes the idea of collaboration and dialogue, which includes everything from asking permission to take a photograph to letting the subjects chose they way they want to be photographed to the more committed ethnographical move of going and living within the chosen community in order to learn from another culture or expiate the guilt of the transcendental observer. These strategies that serve to justify the less objectivizing ways of seeing of these photographers are enmeshed in debates over the politics of representation, and as I discuss in the next section, are in dialogue with a more "ethical way of seeing" that many Latin American photographers were searching for at the time.

The images of these four photographers (Modotti, Álvarez Bravo, Yampolsky, and Iturbide) belong to many private collections and specialized archives; they are often published in photo books and are commonly included in surveys of Mexican photography. Many factors have contributed to the international recognition of these photographers. One would like to think that the reason is first and foremost the aesthetic quality of their images. However, the fact that they are women working in the highly masculine art environment of Mexico City has also played an important role in how their lives and careers have been excavated and have become symbols of diverse feminist-oriented projects. Moreover, all these women forged relations with important male photographers and intellectuals that helped to obscure and mystify their own careers.

For instance, only recently have Modotti and Lola Álvarez Bravo been discussed as artists in their own right, rather than as "assistants," "lovers," or "copies" of their famous partners Edward Weston and Manuel Álvarez Bravo, respectively. Similarly, and perhaps quite aware of the repercussions of openly declaring her relation to Franz Boas, Mariana Yampolsky was reluctant to discuss the issue until later in her career.[58] In contrast to her older counterparts, Graciela Iturbide has been able to capitalize on her relation to Manuel Álvarez Bravo. Iturbide was his student and assistant in the early 1970s. This experience propelled her career as a photographer and now she is internationally recognized, along with Manuel Álvarez Bravo, as one of the two best-known Mexican photographers.

However, in addition to the intricate factors that helped make their works and careers compelling, another equally complex issue plays a role in the attention given to their photographs, which is the pleasure derived from looking at images of the Other. Visual images captivate us, especially when they depict something we find strange. As Michael Taussig argues, "The spell photography weaves around us is multiplied in images of people from the colonial or non-European world who appear both like us and not like us."[59] Nonetheless, this pleasure is also culturally and historically bounded.

In Mexico, images of indigenous women circulate and are mostly consumed as romantic depictions of Mexican women that feminize ethnicity; in turn, these practices are inextricably connected with shifting discourses on indigenismo. In spite of the fact that this discursive process (indigenismo) is not static or univocal but rather a dialogical construction, discourses of indigenismo circulate within a visual economy that gives priority to certain (mis)representations and obscures others. Internationally, a varied group of collectors shows interest in these images, perhaps to reassure themselves that something survives from the ongoing devastation of colonialism and imperialism and to fulfill the pleasure provoked by looking at the Other. Locally, the way these images are consumed is not that different. As Cuauhtémoc Medina states while discussing Iturbide's work, "Like most middle-class people in Mexico [Iturbide] was a tourist in her own country" and her practice needs to be understood as an exploration of Otherness.[60]

Jiménez, however, attempts something very different. While the images of Jiménez are aesthetically lacking in comparison to the repertoire of Modotti, Álvarez Bravo, Yampolsky, and Iturbide, they are nevertheless significant in offering an alternative strategy for addressing the power relations inherent in the economy of the visual. Jiménez's practice interrupts this genealogy when she directs her camera onto a diverse ensemble of women demanding their rights to represent themselves. Nonetheless, the power and complex meanings of both visual archives (that of Jiménez and that of the Modotti-Álvarez Bravo-Yampolsky-Iturbide genealogy) can only be established by reading them together. Read side by side, they offer different perspectives as to how women have visualized themselves, the answers they have offered, and the ways in which they have contested the power relations inherent in the act of taking a photograph. Taken together, they help chart the politics of representation within a visual economy.

Archival Practices and the Excavation of Revolutionary Moments

In the summer of 1980 the recently established Consejo Mexicano de Fotografía (National Council of Mexican Photography, CMF) sponsored two exhibitions, a selection of photographs from the Casasola archive and a sample of the work of twelve Cuban photographers.[61] The Casasola section included ninety-six images taken in Mexico between 1900 and 1919, showing the contrasts between the urban poor and the middle classes enjoying the Porfirian lifestyle and also images of the high points of the revolutionary armed conflict. It was one of the first exhibitions showcasing the recent institutionalization of this archive. The Cuban selection consisted of 122 images depicting the triumph of the Cuban Revolution and the ways it had changed everyday life for Cubans.[62] These two exhibitions represent a high point in ongoing debates over the role of photography in Latin América; they also frame the history of Latin American photography within a progressive narrative that begins and ends with two triumphant revolutions. They endow photography with a particular mission, more so at a time when the president of CMF, Pedro Meyer, was in Nicaragua documenting the Sandinista Revolution.

Described as an exhibition of "Two Revolutionary Moments" by the Mexican art bulletin *Semana de las Bellas Artes*, they attest to the powerful role of photographs as historical documents.[63] On the one hand, they remind us of what kinds of histories have been foregrounded in the region and the active role that images play in this process. On the other hand, they express the ways photographs have shaped and influenced public opinion, since images of both revolutions circulated widely, becoming signposts of

Latin American identity. Moreover, the photographs of these two exhibitions point to a Latin American tradition of photojournalism and to the role photographers had in representing the realities of the region. Within this revolutionary landscape, the new wave feminist revolution that Ana Victoria Jiménez chose to document did not play a significant role, nor was her practice recognized as that of a photojournalist.

During the 1970s, in Latin America as elsewhere, debates over the role of photography revolved around its legitimization as an art form or as a tool for documenting reality. The search for a particular Latin American photographic aesthetic and methodology—a search that would ultimately recognize the work of Latin American photographers in international markets and would posit their way of seeing as different from the exoticizing gaze of the foreigner—was behind the establishment of the CMF and the first Latin American colloquium of photography, *Hecho en Latino América*, in 1978. Besides the establishment of CMF and the organization of the colloquium, during the 1970s the Mexican publishing house Siglo Veintiuno began to edit photo books that documented the realities of the region. Among the best-known and most influential were *Para verte mejor, América Latina*, with photos by Paolo Gasparini and text by Edmundo Desnoes, and Enrique Bostelman's *América: Un viaje a través de la injusticia*, published in 1972 and 1970 respectively.[64]

In Mexico, photojournalism and the photo-essay were established as photographic practices in the midst of the Mexican Revolution, and the creation of Agustín Víctor Casasola's archive played a crucial role in the development of these genres. Long before the War on Terror, the Mexican Revolution was one of the first armed conflicts in which leaders experimented with embedded photographers and cinematographers. Villa and Zapata had their own personal photographers, and Villa famously signed a contract with the U.S.-based Mutual Film Company giving it exclusive rights to film his battles. Hence images of Villa and Zapata, along with a cadre of revolutionary *caudillos*, began to circulate in diverse venues. Out of the armed conflict, photojournalism and the photo-essay emerged as genres that would support and represent the histories of twentieth-century

Mexico, both nationally and internationally. From then on photojournalism and photo-essays became some of the most useful resources to advertise the ideologies of those in power and to shape public opinion.

The visualization of the armed conflict and the wide circulation of images about it also collaborated with the development of a visual practice that would alter the role of the *letrado*, the masters of the written word, and the image makers who produced myths of tradition and power. As Olivier Debroise states, Agustín Víctor Casasola played a crucial role in institutionalizing the role of photography as objective evidence of history in twentieth-century Mexico.[65] In this sense, he became part of a new generation of letrados who put photography extensively at the service of the construction of knowledge and the wielding of power. From Casasola's work emerge two important practices that I would like to foreground. One is the practice of photojournalism or the photo-essay, which inaugurated a tradition of image making in Mexico that is closely linked with the production of certain histories endowing the photographic image with historic objectivity.[66] The other is the practice of building a visual archive closely linked to the emergence of visual letrados.

In 1911 Casasola established the first Association of Press Photography in Mexico and, along with all his family, soon began building a visual archive that today holds more than half a million images that "have become indissolubly integrated into Mexican patrimony."[67] Early on, the Casasolas began publishing bilingual graphic histories (*historias gráficas*) that in many ways shaped the field of historical production in Mexico. According to John Mraz, the main meta-text in *historias gráficas* is "the presentation of history as if it were the domain of Great Men."[68] Beginning in the 1940s, Gustavo Casasola, Agustín's son, reprinted his father's archive and continued to publish illustrated histories that were crucial in producing a graphic history of Mexico's past. A ten-volume edition printed by Gustavo in 1973 charts the history of Mexico from El Porfiriato through the first years of Echeverría's presidency.

In 1976 the Mexican state purchased the archive, currently housed in Pachuca, Hidalgo, at La Fototeca Nacional, thus creating the first archive dedicated to collecting visual material. This achievement also legitimized photographic practice and reassured many photographers that their work was of interest to the nation. It now houses more than thirty collections of diverse photographers who worked in Mexico.[69]

Mariana Yampolsky (discussed in the previous section) played a crucial role in negotiating the establishment of the Casasola archive, thus providing an interesting counterpoint to Jiménez's archival practice. Like Jiménez's interest in feminist archives, Yampolsky's involvement with the Casasola archive also poses questions to traditional gender conceptions that see the activities of the letrados as exclusively masculine territory. Nonetheless, while both women show an interest in the power of photographic images and their political and historical value, one works within an officially sanctioned framework, the other within a framework that is considered irrelevant. Further, while these two archives traversed different paths—that is, Casasola's archive is officially sanctioned at the time when Jiménez begins to construct hers—reading them concurrently not only reveals what kind of images were deemed valuable and why but also posits both Yampolsky and Jiménez as important visual letradas of their time, as women who understood and commanded the visual from two very different revolutionary perspectives.

Photojournalism, Images of Women, and the Ethics of Seeing

By the 1940s advances in visual technology had encouraged the professionalization of photojournalists but also broadened the ways knowledge was constructed and the ways power was wielded through the reproduction of photographs. The contestation over what kind of images circulated became a battlefield as the improvement of reproduction techniques encouraged the establishment of a wide range of illustrated magazines in Mexico City.[70] However, government control of the press and illustrated magazines was widely known. It included editorial censorship as well as ownership of paper production and distribution through the state-owned company PIPSA.[71] Moreover, picture editors and government censors were well aware of the instability of photographic meaning; wisely, they forced photographers to surrender their negatives to the press, thereby controlling not only the circulation of images but also the meaning of images.[72] In time, as Mraz and others have argued, these magazines became crucial resources through which the government and intellectuals developed, manipulated, discussed, and tried to shape a sense of *mexicanidad*.[73] For instance, in March 1952 President Ruiz Cortines publicly acknowledged the role of these magazines by praising them for their collaborations in "homogenizing the national consciousness."[74]

While up to 1968 most of the press and magazines followed the presidential mandate and a great number of reporters and photojournalist received *embutes* or *chayotes* (illicit payments, bribes or kickbacks) for their work, many photographers also published their photos and photo-essays independently or were granted certain freedoms due to their personal relations.[75] These more independent works did not follow the current presidential mandate and could be read as being critical.[76] Examples of this include the work of Los Hermanos Mayo, Nacho López, and Héctor García.[77] Following the tradition already established by the Casasolas, these photographers began to make images of the daily lives and struggles of Mexico City's residents. Their works were an important influence on the development of a new kind of photojournalism after 1968, and their careers serve as a means of reflecting on the complex web of desires and affiliations that have characterized the practice of Mexican photography.

Héctor García is mostly known for his photos of student, teacher, and worker demonstrations (1958 and 1968), although recently his depictions of urban life in Mexico City have become popular in gallery circles.[78] His shots of teachers and railroad workers were highly censored and were only published in marginal magazines. In contrast, his images of the student massacre of 1968 were, and continue to be, crucial in disseminating and denouncing details about the Tlatelolco events. Most famously, his photos illustrate Elena Poniatowska's *La Noche de Tlatelolco* (1975) and Carlos Monsiváis's *Días de guardar* (1971) along with articles written by Juan García Ponce and Carlos Fuentes in established cultural magazines such as *Siempre!* and *La Cultura en México*. Right after the massacre, he infamously accepted a post as President Echeverría's official photographer (1971–76). This is perhaps not that surprising considering the incestuous relation that the Mexican state has had with intellectuals and artists since the early 1920s and Echeverría's co-optation of intellectuals at the beginning of his mandate.

Despite his humble origins, García developed relations with important intellectuals, politicians, and artists from early on in his career. These networks facilitated, to some extent, the exhibition of his photographs as artworks in New York in 1971 and at the Museum of Modern Art in Mexico City in 1975. But perhaps the kind of photos that he took played a more significant role in crowning him as an important Mexican photographer.

His images depict the urban poor in 1950s Mexico City, which at the time had a critical intent. Images of Mexico City slums, street beggars, and inequality as experienced in everyday life in the urban landscape defied the efforts of the government to present Mexico as a developed nation. For instance, in *Cada quién su grito* (To each his cry) García refers to the traditional Cry of Dolores that inaugurates the celebrations of the Mexican Day of Independence to signal how social class differences were experienced on the Mexico City streets and how each social class celebrated differently and some, perhaps, had nothing to celebrate (fig. 37). As is well documented, during the presidencies of Miguel Alemán (1946–52) and Adolfo Ruíz Cortines (1952–58), Mexico pursued a project of industrialization with the hope of becoming a developed nation. The release of Luis Buñuel's *Los olvidados* (1950), which depicted an episode in the lives of a group of destitute children in Mexico City, represented a fierce critique of the government's project, and the cinematography of Gabriel Figueroa became an influence for documentary photographers, such as García and López. Most famously, García returned to the neighborhood of La Candelaría de los Patos, one of the most impoverished and most violent areas of Mexico City and the place where he grew up, to document the marginalized living conditions of its inhabitants. In *Celestina, Candelaria de Los Patos* an older woman confronts García's gaze with a defiant attitude, and in the background a young couple seem to be courting (fig. 38). While the assertive stance of the woman, who is dressed in indigenous garb, breaks with the dominant portrayal of passive indigenous women begging on the street, heads covered with a rebozo, the title of the image, *Celestina*, provides clues as to the nature of the woman's defiant pose. The name Celestina is used to refer to women who arrange courtships; therefore, in shooting this scene, García documents the role of older women as guardians of tradition and heteronormative relations. García also took intimate shots of the starlets of the golden age of Mexican cinema, like his well-known series on Gloria Mestre (fig. 39). As mentioned earlier, he also documented social uprisings and demonstrations that have been taken up as icons of mid-twentieth-century Mexico's struggle for social justice. Despite Garcia's critical intentions and the aesthetic and documentary value of his work, his images also circulate and are consumed in a manner that serves to fulfill other kinds of desires: the nostalgic lure of the 1950s, the conception of Mexico as a never-ending source of revolutionary and leftist generations in which women are used as tropes for class difference, and most obviously, the image of Mexico's quintessential destitute: an indigenous woman or child begging for money on a street corner. In his photograph *Isla de injusticia en la gran ciudad (Island of Injustice in the Big City)* (1975, not pictured here), a young girl sits alone on the concrete island dividing a busy street and begs for money, with no adult supervision. In contrast to the straight angle and constructed composition used in *Entre el progreso y el desarrollo (Between Progress and Development)* (fig. 40), García snapped *Island of Injustice* through the window of a passing car he occupied. The composition is less controlled but equally powerful in portraying how inequality is experienced differently in the urban landscape, and how such experience is increasingly mediated through the effects of urbanization and development. Currently his work is held at the Fundación María y Héctor García, started by the photographer María Sánchez de García (García's colleague and wife) in 2008, as well as in international collections.[79]

A contemporary of García's, Nacho López is considered by many a role model due to his "ethical way of seeing" and for developing a critical and pluralistic tradition of photographing the daily lives of Mexico

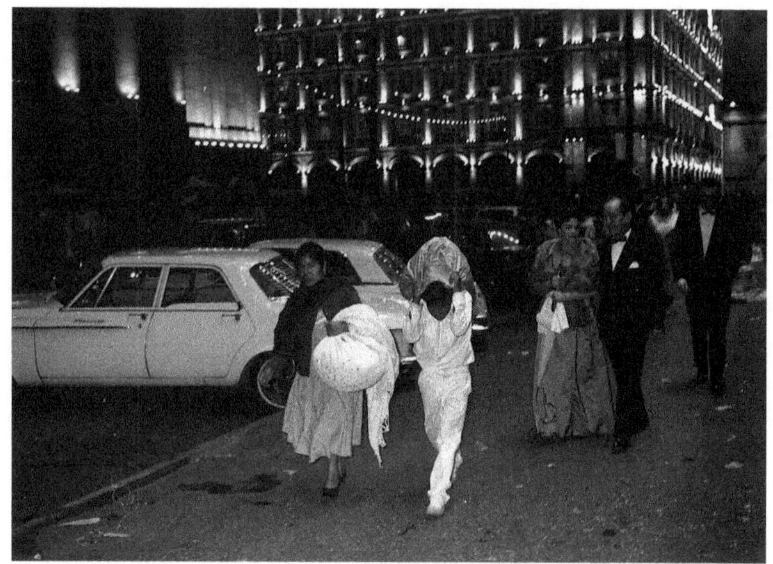

FIG. 37. *Cada quién su grito.* Photo © 1959 by Hector García. Fundación María y Hector García.

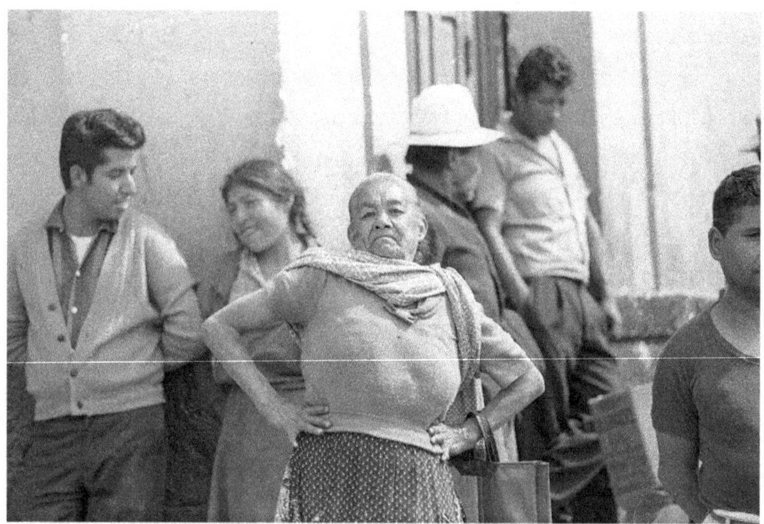

FIG. 38. *Celestina, Candelaría de Los Patos.* Photo © 1965 by Hector García. Fundación María y Hector García.

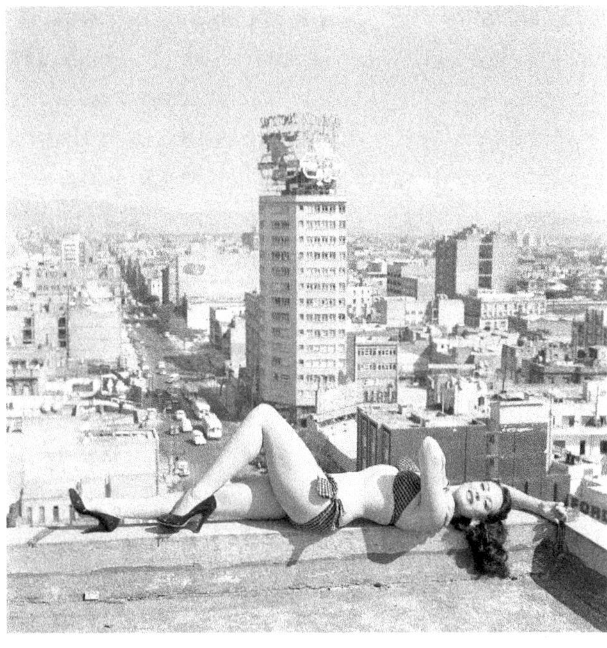

FIG. 39. *Gloria Mestre*. Photo © 1956 by Hector García. Fundación María y Hector García.

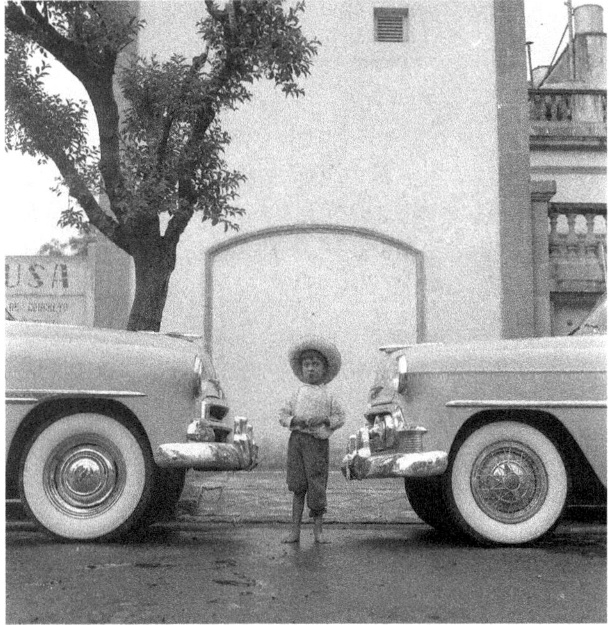

FIG. 40. *Entre el progreso y el desarrollo (Between Progress and Development)*. Photo © 1950 by Hector García. Fundación María y Hector García.

City dwellers. He is mostly known for his critical photo-essays about the urban poor and working classes of Mexico City published in illustrated magazines during the 1950s. According to Mraz, Nacho López was the first photographer to develop a theory of what became known in 1976 as the new photojournalism.[80] Less well known is his collaboration with INI, a relation that lasted for more than three decades and produced an archive of photographs and films of indigenous communities now accessible via the Comisión Nacional para el Desarrollo de los Pueblos Indígenas.[81] In the 1960s he was involved with a group of artists influenced by existentialist philosophy, collectively known as Nueva Presencia, who were interested in figuration as a way to develop an aesthetic that could speak to their time while reacting to the social realism of the Mexican Muralist School.[82] In the mid-1970s he began publishing critical essays on photography and teaching at universities (UNAM in Mexico City and Universidad Veracruzana in the state of Veracruz). As noted, in 1978 López participated in the first Latin American colloquium of photography, *Hecho en Latino América*. At the event he accused U.S. photographer Cornel Cappa of exoticizing Latin America's harsh realities through the publication of images in *Life* magazine. López contended that Cappa's images were nothing more than "a reflection of the uncommitted way of seeing of a foreigner."[83] Against this uncommitted way of seeing, López would write extensively—advocating for the development of a *conciencia óptica* (an optical conscience) and defending what he believed to be the true function of photography: "The function of photography, I fervently believe, is that which serves the vital struggles of the people and the affirmation of human dignity."[84]

That same year, in order to commemorate INI's thirtieth anniversary, López published a harsh critique of several renowned Mexican colleagues (Gabriel Figueroa, Luis Márquez, Guillermo Kahlo, Hugo Brehme, and Augustín Martínez) for having allowed themselves to continue their picturesque and exoticizing view that decontextualized indigenous communities.[85] "They allowed themselves to be carried away by the pictorial lyricisms produced by the images of Eisenstein and Tissé, and they search for particular contrasts to emphasize the harsh face of an Indian who has just finished taking a bath, as if suspended in time and oblivious to their intrusion."[86]

In the midst of the Latin American photographic effervescence of the late 1970s, López enunciated a critique that was already in the making; however, the distance between his theory and his photographic practice reveals the complexities of attempts at controlling the meaning of photographic images and the conundrums of the search for a more ethical way of seeing in a system that *a priori* establishes a power relation between the one who possesses the camera and the one who is possessed by it. This relation persists, to some extent, even if one subscribes to a politics of representation that advocates for self-representation (the Other representing itself). Rather than subscribing to the idea that the solution to the problem is to *not* represent the Other, I espouse the existence of diverse strategies that undermine and decenter the power relations that structure the production of knowledge by diverse actors at different historical moments, including, but not exclusively, self-representation. This is the value that I find in Ana Victoria Jiménez's archive. Reading her archive and practice alongside other practices allows for a wider understanding of the complex workings of the visual economy.

In 1950 López published a photo-essay in the magazine *Mañana* titled "Noche de Muertos," documenting the celebration of the Day of the Dead on the island of Janitzio in the state of Michoacan. Just as Oaxaca had been the fountain of Mexicanness and a well of iconographic images of Mexico that circulated internationally, by the mid-twentieth century the Day of the Dead celebration was becoming one of the most typical Mexican tourist attractions, and López's photo-essay played an important role in its institutionalization as a tourist destination.[87] After him, photographers such as Walter Reuter, Héctor García, and Luis Mayo flocked to Janitzio to produce photo-essays of the same celebration for illustrated magazines that the government would then use to promote the site as a tourist destination. In López's photo-essay women were portrayed as sorrowful mourners of their dead relatives. Indigenous women were depicted with downcast eyes, their faces half lit by the candlelight and their heads covered with *rebozos* (fig. 41).

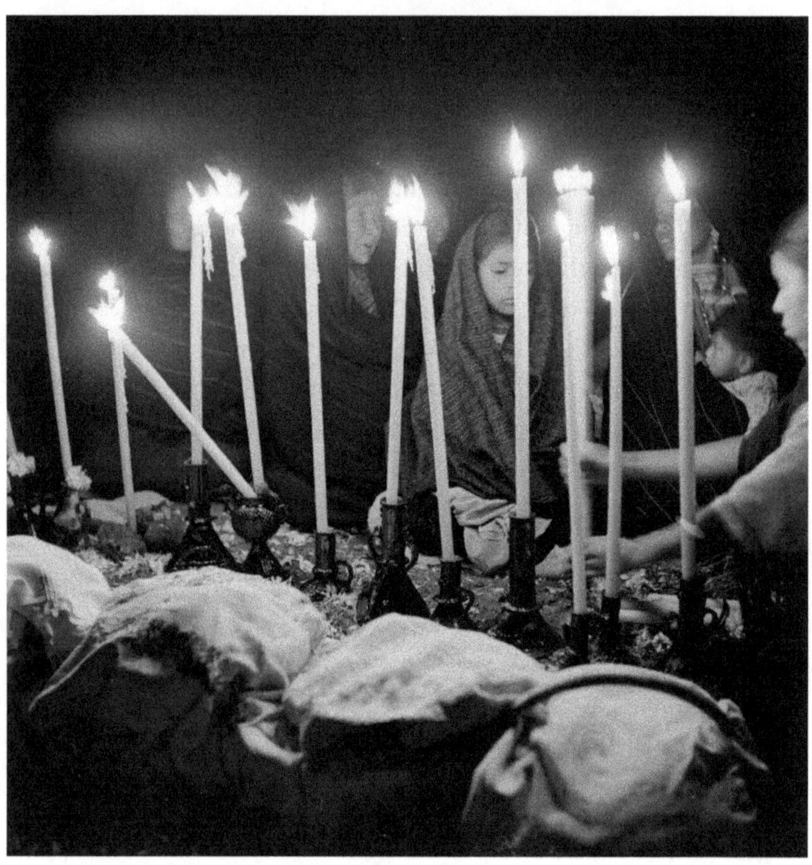

In the case of urban Mexico, López extended his representation of the female population to include images of upper-class women. In his photo-essay "Un día cualquiera en la vida de la ciudad" (1958), published in *Siempre!*, images of bourgeois women are juxtaposed with those of the lower classes to reflect and contrast how class disparity is lived in Mexico City. In the image including the caption *Iguales,* two overwhelmed women are captured while waiting in line at a supermarket (fig. 42). One woman is dressed in an apron and has braided brown hair; the other is taller with short blonde hair and wears a skirt and blouse. In this image, a commentary about how domestic chores have the capacity to erase class differences was present.[88] López's critical intentions were anchored by the photo's cutline: "Heavy and slim, ugly and beautiful, rich and poor, maids or employers, they are all the same at the market. They are the same as they look for the cheapest item of the best quality; they are the same when they pay and they are completely identical when they bargain, a practice that has disappeared in the so-called supermarkets."[89] The cutline, as Roland Barthes has observed, serves to fix the meaning of the image.[90]

In spite of this photo, which seems to propose a more complex critique—one that takes gender seriously as a category actively shaping the lives of Mexico City's inhabitants—the meta-narrative constructed by this photo-essay was a denunciation of class disparities as the source of all the ailments afflicting Mexican society. This was demonstrated in the spread where an image of two upper-class women having tea and smoking cigarettes is placed above an image that depicts two poor men drinking beer on the street. Here, middle-class women are used as symbols of class oppression (fig. 43).

From the work of García and López an image-making tradition emerged that was as critical as it was fraught. Its most important legacy was the treatment of the city as a crucial actor. Their images opened up the possibility of reading the city as a space of contestation where negotiations about class and gender were actively taking place. Nonetheless, on the whole, their depictions of urban women seem to be reduced to representational tropes that fall into the categories of the despotic bourgeoisie, the prostitute, or the oppressed victim. While García extended his gaze to the starlets of the Golden Era, López mostly stayed within the aesthetic of Luis Buñuel's *Los olvidados* (1950)—poor urban women as prostitutes or covered in *rebozos* playing the victim on a street corner or in court. On some occasions, López chose to represent women as sexual symbols, as in his iconic photo-essay *Cuando una mujer guapa parte plaza por madero* (1953) (fig. 44). Urban women were never presented as active members of society but rather as tropes for class difference and sexual desire and as matchmakers (as in the

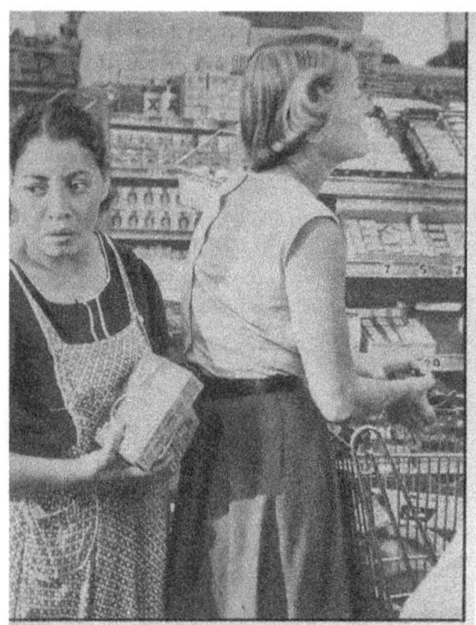

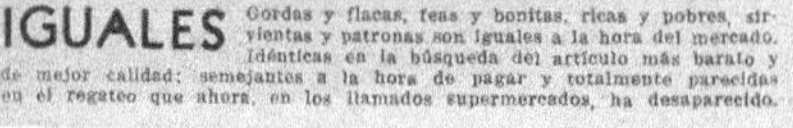

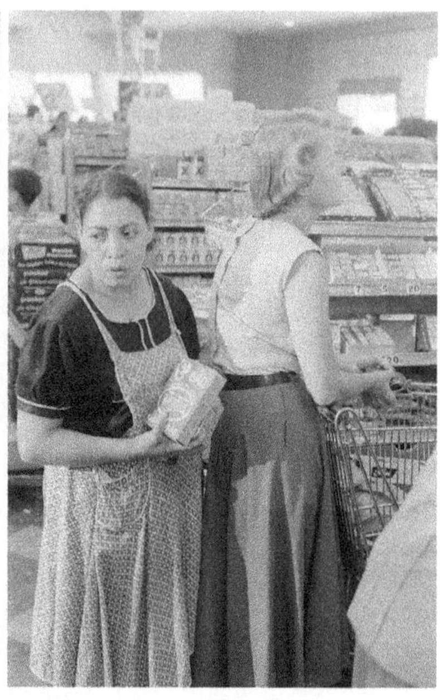

FIG. 42. (*Left*) "Un día cualquiera en la vida de la ciudad." Photo © 1958 by Nacho López, photo-essay in *Siempre! Presencia de México*, volume 188, July 3, 1958. Courtesy of *Revista Siempre! Presencia de México*. (*Right*) *Mujeres realizan compras en el supermercado*. Photo © ca. 1950 by Nacho López. 380228 CONCACULTA-INAH-SINAFO-Fototeca Nacional.

case of García's *Celestina*). In the case of indigenous women, both García and López were mostly unable to escape the picturesque yet "Othering" tradition that they fought against. They depicted indigenous women as victims—ciphers of the "crude realities of our countries." That fact notwithstanding, Garcia and López were able to produce aesthetically valuable works in a highly surveyed environment, and they have become models for many in subsequent generations of photojournalists.

New Photojournalism

In 1976 President Echeverría's takeover of one of the biggest national newspapers, *El Excelsior*, prompted various journalists to establish independent

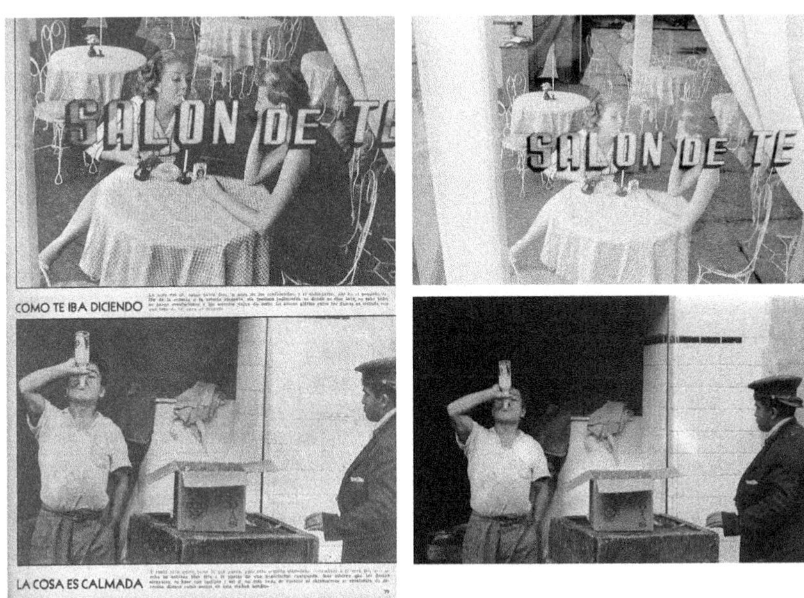

FIG. 43. (*Left*) "Un día cualquiera en la vida de la ciudad." Photo © by Nacho López, photo-essay in *Siempre! Presencia de México*, volume 188, July 3, 1958. Courtesy of *Revista Siempre! Presencia de México*. (*Right*) *Salón de té* (*top*), ca. 1950; *Hombres tomando cervezas* (*bottom*). Photo © ca. 1950s by Nacho López. 405767 and 405768 CONCACULTA-INAH-SINAFO-Fototeca Nacional.

media. These independent media outlets gave journalists more freedom and photojournalists more credit, giving rise to what Mraz and others labeled "new photojournalism."[91] Newspapers such as *Unomasuno* and *El Sol de México* began sending their own photojournalists to cover the armed conflicts in Guatemala, Nicaragua, and El Salvador rather than depending on international news agencies. Photojournalists were paid and given editorial independence and, most important, credit for their images.[92] For Mraz the characteristics of new photojournalism are its emphasis on representing daily life; the portrayal of *el pueblo* in a manner that avoids the picturesque, exotic, romantic, or condemning image-making traditions; an aesthetic emphasis on photography as a subjective rather than objective

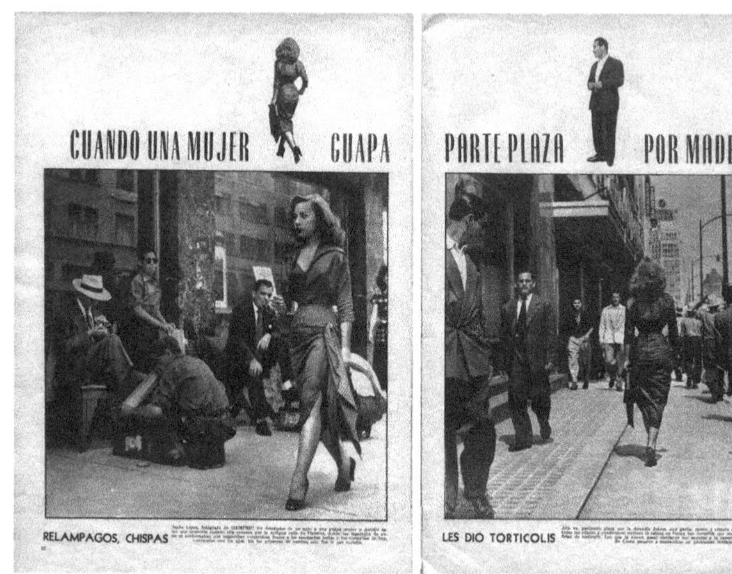

FIG. 44. *Cuando una mujer guapa parte plaza por madero*, photo-essay *in Siempre! Presencia de México*, Photos © 1953 by Nacho López. Courtesy of *Revista Siempre! Presencia de México*.

representation; a revaluation of a photograph's fundamental value as information independent from the text; and most important, the participation of women as photojournalists.[93]

Mraz's photojournalism studies are interesting for two reasons: first, his work in the fields of Mexican visual culture, photography, and photojournalism is highly recognized within both Spanish- and English-speaking academia, and second, because he credits women's participation as one characteristic of the new photojournalism. I would like to take issue with this second point, however, because it is something Mraz addresses differently in the Spanish and English editions of this text—and this difference helps us understand why Jiménez's practice has been mostly ignored.

In the Spanish edition, *La mirada inquieta: Nuevo fotoperiodismo mexicano, 1976–1996*, published in 1996, Mraz interviews several young and established photojournalists. He highlights the work of only one female photojournalist, Elsa Medina, who began this work in the mid-1980s for the newspaper *La Jornada*. For Mraz, a photo by Medina, *Hands in the Subway* (1988), serves to introduce the characteristics of new photojournalism. Medina's *Hands in the Subway* depicts a series of hands holding a post inside a subway car, with arms and bodies wrapped around a woman wearing a traditional rebozo who attentively looks at something outside the picture frame, unaware that she is being photographed (fig. 45).

> This image that shows . . . hands holding onto a subway post presents some of the elements that have defined the new Mexican photojournalism of the last twenty years. The focus on the daily life of the people is not picturesque, laudatory, condemnatory, or alarmist. Rather, by documenting the infrahumane conditions of the public transit, we see an implicit critique of the public administration of the country. There is also an aesthetic search that ignores the classic conventions of composition; in this case by making reference to the space outside the frame to insist that a photograph only isolates one slice of reality. . . . On the other hand, the photograph was taken by a woman. The participation of women in photojournalism of the last twenty years presents characteristics never seen before.[94]

Besides the portrayal of the subway as a new actor, this image does not seem to add anything new to the existing repertoire of images of life in Mexico City. While Mraz makes an example of this image because it is taken by woman, and this fact does give us an idea of women's participation in photojournalism (only one), Mraz's reading of this image is a continuation of tropes and traditions that closely follow those established by López and García. Moreover, Mraz does not account for ways in which this image could be contesting or speaking to normative gender constructions, which in my opinion would be an important aspect of any kind of image-making practice in post-1968 Mexico, whether done by women or men. By emphasizing the hands that are holding the metro rail, other readings of the image could be explored. We could interrogate the experience of riding a subway car as a space where gender and class boundaries are reconfigured.

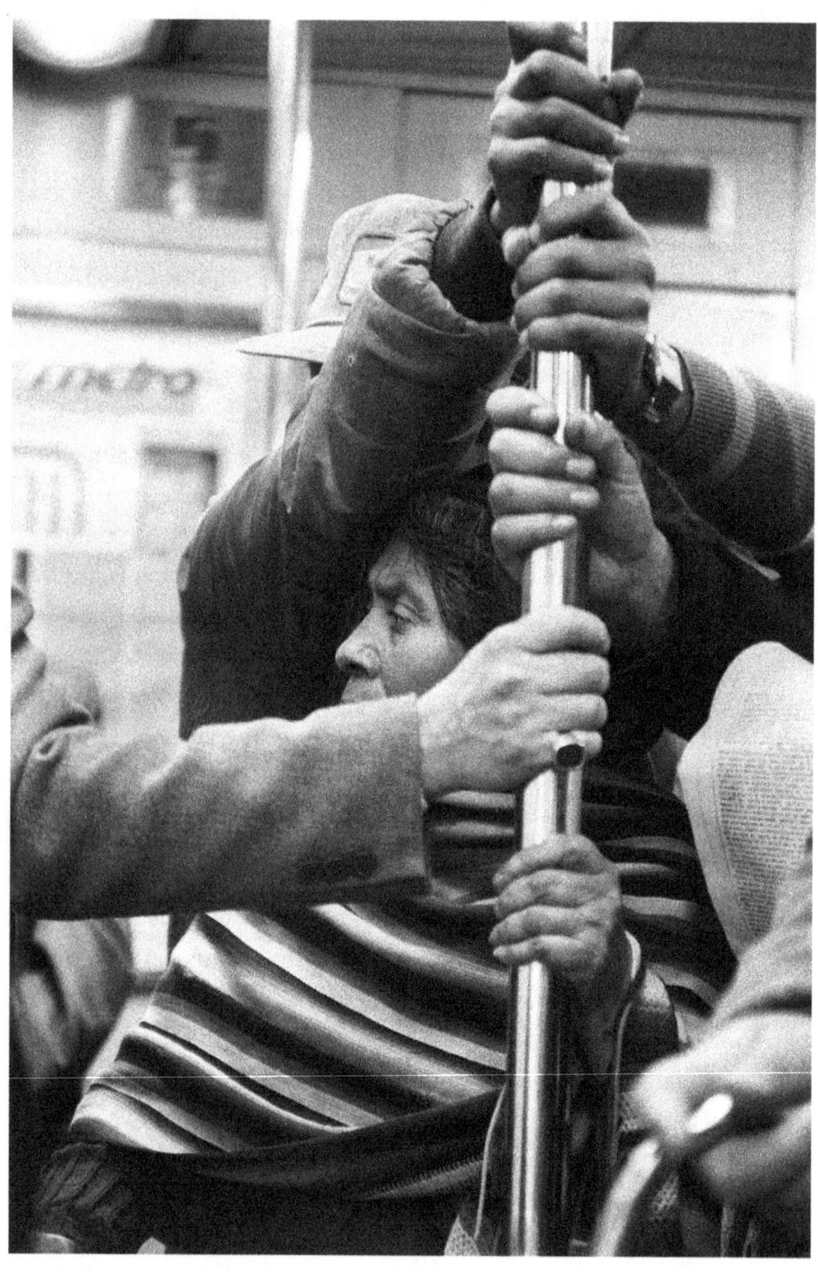

FIG. 45. *Hands in the Subway*. Photo © 1988 by Elsa Medina. Courtesy of the artist.

Mraz is more concerned with the fact that the woman depicted in the image is looking outside the frame and how that act in itself points to Medina's concern with a critique of the medium as a producer of objective reality (something that, indeed, was in vogue in the field of photography at the time).[95] Having said that, the fact that a woman wields the camera does not mean that a critical view of sexual difference is intended, since gender constructions (masculinity and femininity in this case, although of course there are others) are subject positions that can be cohabitated by all kinds of gendered bodies at different points in time. The issue here is the way that Mraz accounts for the participation of women as having a say in changing photojournalism in Mexico and that he includes only Medina in his analysis.

Ana Victoria Jiménez had begun taking photos of feminist demonstrations in 1971. Her images did appear in some newspapers and magazines, mostly without credit, as was customary.[96] While Mraz's study points to a complex set of issues that gave rise to what he labels new photojournalism, it is revealing that no mention is made of the legacy of the new feminist movement, not only in opening spaces for women's participation in photojournalism in the 1980s but in recognition of their work as image makers who, like Jiménez, covered an important revolutionary event independently, or of feminist academics who were criticizing the ways women were represented. While this may be the result of editorial decisions or, arguably, a lack of knowledge of Jiménez's practice, it also speaks to the ways dominant institutions that authorize artistic careers and that research the histories of Mexican new wave feminism have mostly ignored their legacies in cultural practices.

El Centro de la Imagen, the publisher of the Spanish edition of Mraz's book, was established in 1994 as part of the package of cultural reforms that consolidated the creation of the Mexican Council for Arts and Culture (CNCA) under the Carlos Salinas de Gortari administration. It grew out of the dissatisfaction that had provoked the demise of the by then disbanded CMF. Over the years, Centro de la Imagen has become an important research and publishing center dedicated to the promotion of photography and an important legitimizing institution for aspiring photographers. It seems fitting that in 1996 it would sponsor the publication of Mraz's book, which offers a positive and redeeming narrative of contemporary photojournalism at a time when many institutions and photojournalists needed to appear critical and unbiased. It was also a time when emphasis was being placed, once again, on the "indigenous question," now in the context of Zapatismo. This context may help explain Mraz's emphasis on the non-picturesque representation of the woman in the *rebozo* in Medina's image.

The English edition of this text is included in *Looking for Mexico: Modern Visual Culture and National Identity* (2009). It also focuses on Medina's image as an example of new photojournalism, but this time Mraz gives credit to the feminist movement as one of the elements that converged in the development of new photojournalism: "The feminist movement of the 1970s also contributed novel perspectives, as women such as Graciela Iturbide and Flor Garduño became internationally recognized photographers largely because of their imagery that portrayed women as the new national essence."[97]

This mention needs some clarification. Images portraying women as the national essence are not new in the visual archives of twentieth-century Mexico. Given this, one might imagine that the legacy of the feminist movement, instead, would be to contest "images of women" as the national essence. However, there are distinct and varied feminisms, and indeed the highly romanticized images of Garduño and Iturbide could be taken as representing one vision of feminism that romanticizes femaleness as the national élan, or as symbols of matriarchal politics, as noted earlier. But for Mraz, the legacy of the feminist movement seems to be that certain Mexican women photographers gained international recognition. The inclusion of a gendered critique of the production of images—that is, as a different perspective on the content of the images, whether produced by a man or a woman—is not within his purview.

Another interesting difference in the English version of Mraz's text is his reading of Medina's photograph. According to Mraz, Medina's image avoids folkloric and picturesque depictions, but in spite of this, he resorts to tropes such as the pyramid, the *rebozo*, and the baseball cap as signifiers of difference to describe the image for an English-speaking audience: "The photo encompasses Mexico in a jumbled pyramid of arms and bodies that form around a woman wearing a traditional *rebozo*—a metaphor for the Indian base of Mesoamerican civilization—while at the top a man's baseball cap attests to the pervasive U.S. presence in today's society."[98]

The use of these recognizable signifiers of difference (Mexican and Anglo-American) reveals the incapacity to escape "Othering" tropes that exoticize as much as facilitate consumption and understanding. These different readings of Medina's image by the same author—how women as photographers and the legacy of the feminist movement are portrayed for different audiences, by different publishers, at distinct historical moments—point to the mutability and instability of the meaning of photographs and to the changing parameters and power relations that are at play in the construction of knowledge. In this movement of re-readings, my focus on Jiménez and my intention to place her practice as an interruption of the narrative of new photojournalism is also a response to my particular historical moment.

The various actors I have briefly followed in this section produce one of the many networks and genealogies that had a say in defining what the fields of photography, photojournalism, and the photo-essay looked like in 1970s Mexico. The images that were valued were those that fit certain imaginings of the realities of Latin America and followed previous representational conventions. Most prominent were the ills of the poor in relation to a growing metropolis and faulty industrialization programs; the question of a more ethical way of representing the Other (who had the right to capture the Indian and how); and the framing of Latin America as the land of revolution (against imperial oppressors and foreign or national governments). Within this network, images of urban women actively demanding their rights were not within the purview of photographers, institutions, or academics who had the power to legitimize who counted as a photographer and what contents were critical, creative, and representative of Latin American photography.

Nonetheless, within this genealogy a trace of what I refer to as the visual letrada begins to emerge. This trace was present in photographers who were concerned with finding a personal, political, or ethical way of seeing. It was also present in image makers who understood the importance that images play in constructing personal and national projects: photographers who comprehended and commanded the visual from very different revolutionary perspectives—particularly those like López and García whose images opened up the possibility of reading the city as a space of contestation where negotiations about class and gender were actively taking place.

8

Feminist Collaborations in 1970s Mexico

In 1978 Mónica Mayer and Ana Victoria Jiménez found themselves collaborating with Cine-Mujer (1975–85), a women's collective dedicated to the production of films about social issues. Its establishment by Rosa Martha Fernández and Beatriz Mira, then students of film at Centro Universitario de Estudios Cinematográficos (CUEC), coincided with the emergence of feminist film around the world.[1] As I have discussed in chapters 2 and 3, Cine-Mujer's films were used to raise consciousness in different feminists gatherings and protests, including meetings involving women workers, campesinas, and community activists.[2] According to Esperanza Tuñon, these gatherings played a crucial role in introducing the question of gender to struggles previously understood solely in terms of class.[3]

However, the reception of the productions of Cine-Mujer in Mexico by both the commercial and independent film industries was not favorable. They gained recognition only in the mid-1980s when their films began to circulate internationally. According to Rosa Martha Fernández, *Cosas de mujeres* and *Rompiendo el silencio* were projected in Kenya at the Third UN Women's Conference held in Nairobi in 1985 and also in 1981 during the first international encounter of feminist cinema and video that took place in Holland. In 1984 the film *Amas de casa* (1984) was included in Karen Ranucci's compilation of independent Latin American film and video.[4]

In Mexico, despite Echeverría's reforms to the film industry and relaxed censorship, issues of sexuality, including rape and abortion, were still taboo topics for the majority of Mexicans.[5] Even more taboo was the realistic approach with which Cine-Mujer depicted female characters and bodies.

233

Although, as Charles Ramírez Berg argues, Mexican film production after 1968 began to witness the emergence of female characters that seem to contest and confront Mexican patriarchal schemas, the conventions of representation adopted by Cine-Mujer still contested this apparently new approach to female characters.[6] Likewise, the political commitment of those involved with Cine-Mujer was not in the purview of dominant social documentary schemas, nor did the avant-garde faction of independent Mexican cinema value its realistic approach.

In addition to disrupting norms in terms of content and cinematic and generic conventions by which women had previously been represented in film, Cine-Mujer also developed a team of women who tackled all aspects of the film industry, including production, content, and distribution. They developed their own mechanisms of distribution in collaboration with Universidad Nacional Autónoma de México and through the establishment of an independent distributor, ZAFRA.[7] Their films were shown through alternative networks of distribution and in non-commercial spaces, including women's collectives around the country, university forums, and informal gatherings.[8] In spite of scathing critiques from the established film community, several of their films were nominated for prizes and recognized by the Mexican film industry. *Cosas de mujeres* was nominated for an Ariel in the category of short film in 1978, and *Vicios en la cocina*, directed by Beatriz Mira, won an Ariel in the category of documentary that same year.[9]

Ana Victoria Jiménez collaborated on two films produced by Cine-Mujer and directed by Fernández: *Cosas de mujeres* (1975–78), which dealt with abortion, and *Rompiendo el silencio* (1979), which took on the issue of rape.[10] Jiménez provided Fernández with photos for both these films, and both Jiménez and Mónica Mayer collaborated with research for *Rompiendo el silencio*. Both are black-and-white 16 mm films that mixed strategies and conventions of fictional and documentary films. They featured interviews, statistical data, still photography, and a fictional narrative.

These two films are pivotal nodes that meaningfully connect the practices of the visual letradas discussed in this book. *Cosas de mujeres* and *Rompiendo el silencio* map out the ways in which gender and sexual violence against women are deeply embedded in, and in a dialogic relation to, the production of urban space. The creative connections these women produced through filmmaking not only questioned disciplinary boundaries and genres but provided an alternative model of production premised upon the importance of developing and keeping visual records of their political practices. Moreover, these two films, like Jiménez's photographs, speak to and function as records of the ways in which feminist demonstrations were politicizing the female body throughout the streets of Mexico City. Together, all these different media practices that turned to the streets of Mexico City during the 1970s—photography, film, street demonstrations, and video—transgressed dominant representations of the female body. In doing so they contravened normative divisions of public and private space and ultimately transformed the geographies of Mexico City as well as its regimes of media and visuality.

"¿Cosas de mujeres?": Breaking the Silence on "Women's Issues"

One of the chief preoccupations among feminist activists at this time was how to raise consciousness, and with this in mind, two points of contention demanded attention: first, how to intervene in the media, and second, how to develop links with working-class women's organizations. To this end in 1975 Rosa Martha Fernández and Beatriz Mira promoted the establishment of Cine-Mujer. In particular, Rosa Martha Fernández's militancy in the feminist movement shaped the direction of Cine-Mujer from 1975 to 1980 toward a preoccupation with unveiling the social mechanisms that oppressed women within the broader context of class struggle. In the words of Fernández, the purpose of the group was to work toward *contra-ideologización*, which she defines this way: "to show the political, economic and cultural interests that sustain the present conditions that women face."[11]

Fernández was already a university professor of psychology when she decided to study film after her experience with Cooperativa de Cine Marginal, an earlier film collective producing super-8 films that served as communication tools between various workers' unions across Mexico. In Cooperativa de Cine Marginal, Fernández worked as a camerawoman and was responsible for filming a nationwide protest by the female textile workers' union from Medalla de Oro, which marched from the city of Monterrey to Mexico City to demand better wages and job security.[12] Fernández had first become politically active after witnessing the 1968 movement in Paris as a psychology student. She was then introduced to feminist activism while studying television production in Japan in 1972. Upon her return to Mexico, and before establishing Cine-Mujer in 1975, she published several articles exposing and analyzing the sexist mechanisms of the country's advertising industry, and she participated in various small feminist consciousness-raising groups and became a militant of Mujeres en Acción Solidaria (MAS, 1971).

The first film produced by Cine-Mujer and directed by Fernández was *Cosas de mujeres* (42 min., dir. Rosa Martha Fernández, 1975–78). The film's title ironically refers to a phrase used to diminish the importance of an issue. Anything that was deemed to be a woman's issue was regarded as irrelevant for public discussion and not pertinent to broader social, cultural, and political fields. But the title also makes the personal political by revealing how various levels of government and civil society were implicated in the issue of abortion. The movie was screened as part of the activities of the campaigns in favor of the decriminalization of abortion that in 1976 had unified all the feminist collectives into establishing Coalición de Mujeres Feministas. *Cosas de mujeres* functioned as a didactic tool to promote discussions and raise awareness about the campaign.

The film is held together by means of a central fictional narrative that describes the experience of Paz, a nineteen-year-old sociology student, who is trying to obtain an abortion. The movie begins with Paz traversing the streets of Mexico City on public transit. At each stop a different woman boards the bus while Paz looks at them, reflecting on her own situation. The city is presented as an important character in the movie—not merely as context but also as an element to develop identification with potential viewers.

We are shown how the young student, having no one else to turn to, seeks help from a friend to find a doctor who will agree to perform an abortion. Meanwhile, the narrator reads two articles from the civic code that define abortion as a criminal act. The story of Paz unfolds as we listen to Janis Joplin's "Me and Bobby McGee." The story is interrupted by the testimony of an older woman, clearly from another social stratum, who narrates her experience with abortion and sexual abuse. Paz's story ends as we see her, accompanied by her friend, inside a taxi being driven to a hospital, already semi-unconscious, where she most likely dies.

The film continues in a hospital, where we see numerous women on the verge of giving birth or being treated for the effects of induced abortions. Women's bodies are carried through hospital hallways, inspected with speculums or medicated as we listen to doctors question them about the reasons for their conditions. The images of the hospital fade as we read some statistics on abortion; then we are shown a newspaper clipping in which Mario Moya Placencia, then secretary of government, declares that abortion is a "cruel and antisocial remedy." Right after that we are presented with an interview with Carmen Coto, a gynecologist. She talks about the number of Mexican women who are using contraceptive methods (8 percent), the diverse kinds of contraceptives that are available in Mexico, and their side effects. We hear the voice of a doctor demystifying the risks of inducing an abortion. He says that risks of mortality, which are two for every four women, would be reduced if abortions were performed legally and if women were cared for properly. While the doctor and Fernández discuss these issues, the viewer is presented with a series of still images of women's bodies in hospital gowns being examined with speculums and other kinds of vaginal apparatus (fig. 46). The film ends with a series of still images that show various groups of women demonstrating in favor of the decriminalization of abortion, including women from Italy, the United States, and Japan. The last shot is a still image taken by Ana Victoria Jiménez. In it we see Mexican feminists demonstrating outside the Chamber of Deputies in Mexico City in November 1977 as part of the campaigns for the decriminalization of abortion (fig. 47).

Still images, interviews, testimonies, and news clippings are some of the most frequently used visual strategies (or rhetorical tools) in a doc-

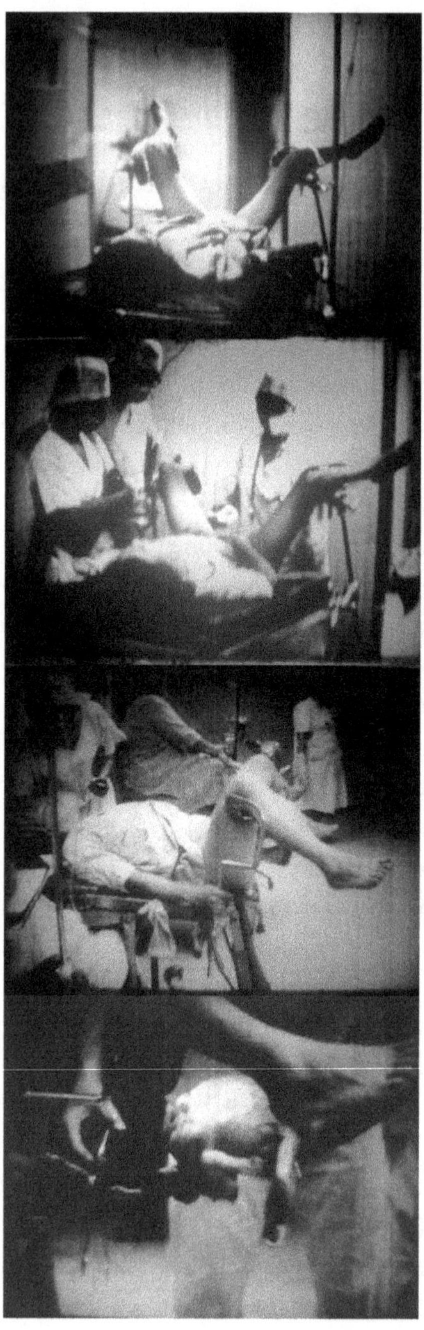

FIG. 46. *Cosas de mujeres* (still shots of hospital scenes). Photos © 1975–78 by Colectivo Cine-Mujer. Courtesy of Rosa Martha Fernández.

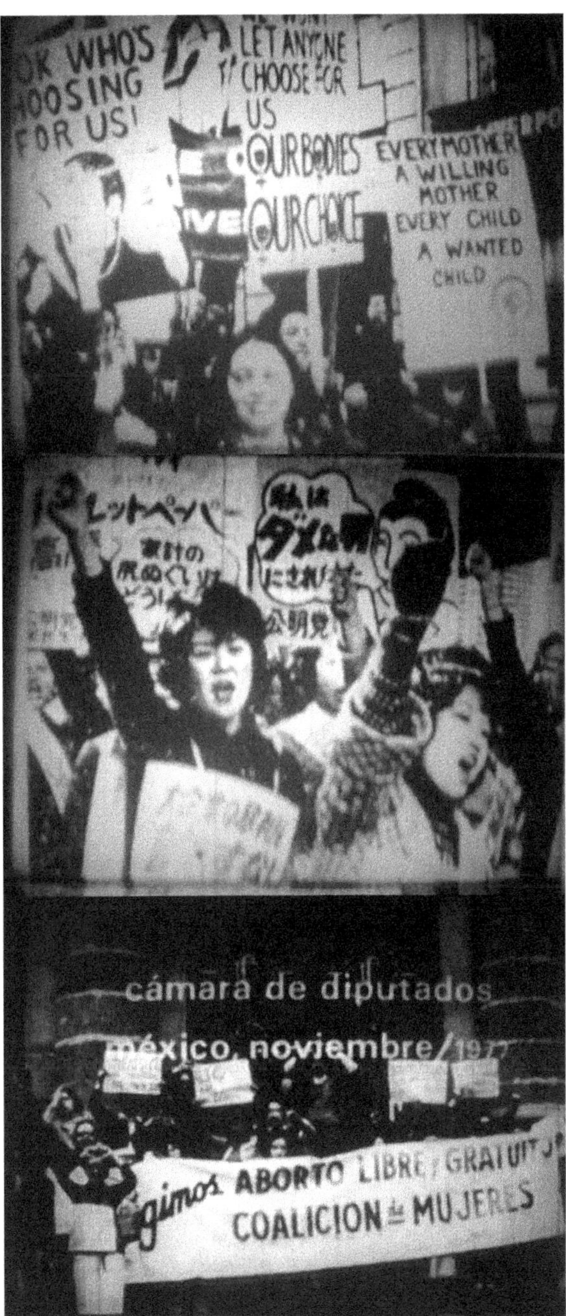

FIG. 47. *Cosas de mujeres* (still shots of demonstrations). Photos © 1975–78 by Colectivo Cine-Mujer. Courtesy of Rosa Martha Fernández.

umentary film. Edited together they produce a reality effect, a sense of credible connection with a real event, which legitimizes the documentary film as a "credible" source of knowledge compared to a fictional film.[13] Jiménez's image intervenes in the development of this reality effect at various levels. On one level, Jiménez's photograph contextualizes the Mexican feminist movement in the midst of a global fight for women's issues. Her image gives international relevance to the small group of Mexican women who dared to propose and demand reforms to laws pertaining to their bodies. In this manner, Jiménez's photographs begin to acquire political and historical weight through this film. As Andrea Noble argues: "For demonstrations to achieve an impact beyond the localized public spaces in which they take place, they depend on the presence of photographers and film crews to create a widely disseminated spectacle of protest. In short, their political agency is predicated in their ability to travel across media and space, thereby appealing to a broader national and international community of viewers."[14]

On another level, Jiménez's photos are used as evidence of the real, as indexes of reality. As Geoffrey Batchen and others have argued, the indexicality of photographs "is crucial to the process of memory work, as it operates in and through photographs. This is because the indexical sign, as a relic of past reality, takes us back to the scene of memory."[15] The still shots used at the end of this film are indexical signs that point to events of the past, in this case to previously held demonstrations. However, I argue that the images also work in the opposite direction; they serve to actualize the present. They work in the present not as mnemonic devices of the past but as images of the actual moment. Jiménez's image of the 1977 demonstration shown in the film was closely linked to events that were unfolding at the same time that the film was screened. As mentioned earlier, the film was shown at demonstrations and encounters as a way to raise consciousness: to demonstrate how many levels of society and lives were implicated in and affected by abortion. Viewers were presented with images of bodies being scrutinized at hospitals that they might be able to recognize; they saw images of newspaper clippings that they might have read alongside images of Mexico City streets where they perhaps walked. As they recognized the women in the photos, since perhaps they were the same ones screening the movie, such images served to provoke a sense of shared experience and to locate this film in the present.

In 1979 Fernández directed the movie *Rompiendo el silencio* (42 min.), which deals with the issue of rape. As in the previous film, Jiménez collaborated by providing still images. Throughout the film, interviews and statistical data on rape are woven together with three main testimonies—one by a rapist in jail, another by a young female worker, and a third by a married woman, the latter two having been raped. For this project Fernández interviewed people on the streets of Mexico City, questioning them about their perceptions of rape.[16] Filmed also in black-and-white, still images of the people interviewed are frozen in time as we listen to their responses in real time. Arguably, the stillness of the images makes the viewer more aware of the sound of the voices of those being interviewed. It allows the viewer time to scrutinize the faces, to identify them, thus adding a more dramatic tone to their responses.[17] As we listen to the responses of all kinds of city dwellers, the still images locate the issue of rape as a public theme open to discussion (which, as the title indicates, it wasn't). As in the previous film, Jiménez's photographs were crucial in the development of a reality effect, giving the documentary a sense of relevance in the present but also endowing it with credibility as a source of knowledge (fig. 48).

In both films—*Cosas de mujeres* and *Rompiendo el silencio*—the female body is open to public scrutiny. Vulnerable and grotesque, it is also shown as politically active in street demonstrations. The visual archive of female bodics that these films construct includes spread-legged female bodies being examined with speculums; bodies giving testimony of rape and sexual abuse; and bodies on the street demanding reproductive rights. This repertoire of representations of female bodies stands in stark contrast to those depicted in both mainstream and independent film at the time. While certain commercial films that began to circulate in Mexico during the 1970s seemed to break with some of the more traditional stereotypes

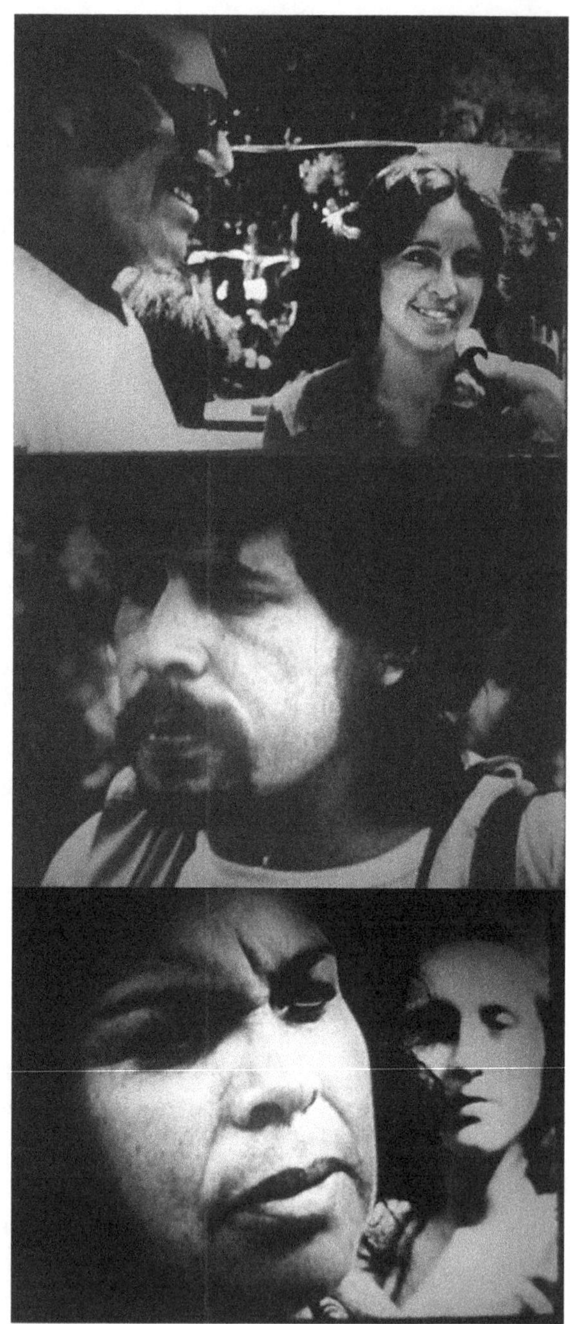

FIG. 48. *Rompiendo el silencio*. Photos © 1979 by Colectivo Cine-Mujer. Courtesy of Rosa Martha Fernández.

of the Golden Era of Mexican cinema and offer new roles to which women could aspire, these films were mostly directed by men and still read as cautionary tales of the perils of women's liberation.[18] As Ramírez Berg argues, there was a shift from the virginal self-sacrificing mother and fallen-woman archetypes toward the archetype of a mad woman who sacrifices her sanity in search of career independence and sexual freedom.[19]

In terms of the independent film movement produced in super-8 film, Cine-Mujer's approach also represented a different engagement in production, content, and political commitment. After Fernández established Cine-Mujer, Cooperativa de Cine Marginal continued to produce films on workers' strikes and union mobilizations. On some occasions women were represented as politically active, but mostly they appeared as background bodies in the context of a broader workers' struggle.[20]

Representation of female bodies and characters in the independent movies produced as part of the super-8 movement followed, to some extent, the changes that Ramírez Berg alludes to but were perhaps bolder in their depictions of the female nude. In the experimental film *La segunda primera matriz* (15 min., dir. Alfredo Gurrola, 1972) close-up images of doctors extracting a baby from a female body as she is giving birth are shown as part of a fragmented narrative that includes nude male and female characters traversing a forest. In *Materia nupcial* (20 min., dir. Alfredo Robert, 1974) a male and female couple is filmed while having sexual intercourse.[21] These two representative examples of non-militant super-8 productions provide a distinct repertoire of images of the female body. However, these representations are mediated by the male director's existential search. The female body in these films is used as a metaphor of origin or as a site to overcome male sexual fears. Indeed, the independent super-8 film movement was predominantly male.[22]

In contrast to these films, Cine-Mujer films show a vulnerable, abused but nonetheless politically active female body that turns to the city, the space shaping the structures that oppressed her, as the stage from which to demand her right to claim the personal as political. These movies break with the silencing mechanisms that relegate issues of sexual violence to the private domain. More than cautionary tales, they were meant to inspire women to deconstruct their own living conditions by resorting to realist strategies to promote a sense of self-identification with their potential viewers.

Critique, Reception, and Mechanisms of Exclusion

For many members of Cine-Mujer each film they produced was a learning process, the results of which were not always well received. Fernández recalls that her movies were severely criticized because they would not fit within the strict boundaries of either fiction or documentary. Their reception was enmeshed in the political debates that divided the two existing film schools in Mexico City and larger discussions about the political commitments of documentary films versus the capitalist interests that backed up fiction films. Fernández explains:

> At CUEC everyone produced documentaries; fictional films were seen as something reactionary. On the other hand, the people from CCC would tell me that making documentaries was a thing of the poor. In this situation, it was inconceivable that the two genres would mix. Nonetheless, the documentary provided me with the veracity that I needed because the objective was to raise consciousness; however, in most of the cases it didn't provided me with enough material to prove through visual means the whole situation I wanted to portray.[23]

In contrast to these views, Jorge Ayala Blanco, a film critic, locates the problems of Cine-Mujer's films in their formal and ideological weaknesses. In a scathing assessment of Cine-Mujer's early films, written in the mid-1980s, he argues that they were gratuitously denigrating and tasteless, "*desabridos y gratuitamente denigratorios*," and further, that this lack of aesthetic quality provoked the demise of feminist cinema in Mexico: "Feminist film in Mexico disappeared as quickly as it emerged. Despite its rambunctious and critical demands, the movement gave birth to a scared and feeble little mouse."[24]

Ayala Blanco makes reference to the situation of feminist film by the mid-1980s. when many film students were no longer interested in producing feminist militant films. Rather, these younger filmmakers supported the idea of a feminine film, one that dealt with personal issues, but that didn't declare itself feminist in an a priori manner.[25] Later members of Cine-Mujer, such as María Novaro, also indicted the early films directed by Fernández: "Her feminist discourse was intensely mystified and very radicalized. I never liked her themes. The movies on abortion and rape were awful."[26]

At play in such indictments of Cine-Mujer's earlier productions are also larger debates that have obscured the legacies of feminist documentaries in favor of feminist avant-garde film internationally. While neither practice officially exists as an established genre of filmmaking in Mexico, Alexandra Juhasz raises interesting points on diverse feminist mechanisms that have excluded 1970s feminist realist documentaries from the history of feminist filmmaking. Juhasz points out that one of those mechanisms was enacted by British, French, and American feminist film theorists, who shifted their focus from realism toward feminist avant-garde film, which they saw as a powerful means of feminist critique.[27] However, this focus resulted in the marginalization of documentaries. In contrast, Juhasz argues that "realist images of women discussing their lived experience constitute an important strategy with which to initiate a challenge to the depiction of reality."[28] Interestingly, to back up her arguments, Juhasz proposes to look at the "theoretically sophisticated approach of directors of Latin American Third Cinema" like Fernando Birri.[29] Birri defended his reality-based approach to filming political movements as a powerful strategy of criticism: "By testifying critically to this reality, to this sub-reality, to this misery, cinema refuses it. It rejects it. It denounces, it judges, it criticizes and deconstructs it."[30] Indeed, social documentary production in Latin America approached reality as a form of deconstruction and on many occasions fused fiction and documentary.[31] Yet new wave feminist demands were not considered part of the realities of Latin American countries until the mid-1980s. Birri's defense of realism as a strategy for deconstruction is effective for the recovery of 1970s U.S. feminist realist documentary; but, from a Latin American perspective, such a focus on reality and misery took place without the concomitant inclusion of feminist demands for reproductive rights and criminalization of violence as part of a valid and real political movement. These early productions of Cine-Mujer were caught up in various structures of exclusion that have obscured its legacies.

Legacies and Networks

Despite these critical views, Cine-Mujer was a relevant endeavor. At a time when many other cultural producers were searching for alternative forms of production and distribution, as well as ways to reach other non-specialized audiences, Cine-Mujer can be seen as another attempt to achieve these goals. For Jiménez, her experience in Cine-Mujer represented one of the many avenues through which feminist militants addressed difficult issues like abortion and rape. She told me that the collective and interdisciplinary approach of Cine-Mujer provided these women with a space of experimentation, particularly as "we did not have manuals or precedents on how to address the issues of rape and abortion in Mexico. We had been exposed to many European films that circulated at the time and which indeed served as inspiration, but the fact was that each of us came from a different background and each brought different ideas to the project."[32]

Moreover, for Jiménez the experiences with Cine-Mujer augmented her awareness of the importance that her images had as historical and political tools. Her participation in the two films discussed provided her with another perspective on the social and political uses of photography. As the films were projected in diverse venues, Jiménez's photos gave relevance to the movement beyond Mexico City. Through her participation in Cine-Mujer, Jiménez met Mónica Mayer, who also helped with the production of *Rompiendo el silencio*.

For Mayer, her participation in Cine-Mujer was a valuable learning experience that confirmed her interest in feminist militancy through the arts. She related to me her experience as akin to other revolutionary moments, such as the Russian Revolution or the first years of Mexican Muralism, when an interdisciplinary and collective approach to art making was linked to a revolutionary goal: "I think [Cine-Mujer] was akin to those revolutionary movements in which the collaborations between artists, historians, and the society in general share a commitment for a cause such as the early years of the Mexican Movement or the Russian Revolution and that there's a sense that the work means something."[33]

Cine-Mujer also provided her with an opportunity to experience first-hand the social mechanisms of sexual discrimination against women.

> In the late 1970s I interviewed the police department doctor who examined women who had been raped. I was meeting him as part of the research for the film *Rompiendo el silencio* (*Breaking the Silence*), by Rosa Martha Fernández, during my brief participation in the first film collective Cine-Mujer. I listened to the doctor as, without even blinking an eye, he said that it was impossible to penetrate a women against her will, even though his most recent case had been that of a seventy-year-old women who had been knocked out. The man was unable to see how absurd and discriminatory his approach was.[34]

Cine-Mujer expanded Mayer's sphere of militancy into broader social fields. For instance, through her research experience for *Rompiendo el silencio* she learned about Cecilia, a young single mother who was repeatedly abused since "she had nothing to lose" until she committed murder in self-defense as a way out of abuse.[35] Mayer and other members of Cine-Mujer took on Cecilia's legal case.

Influences between the two generations of visual letradas did not work in only one direction—from the oldest to the youngest or from Fernández and Jiménez to Weiss and Mayer. As seen in part 2, Mayer influenced and supported Jiménez's participation in feminist art groups such as Tlacuilas y Retrateras. Similarly, but perhaps not so directly, Pola Weiss informed Fernández's current practice as a videodance producer.

In 1980 Fernández left Cine-Mujer and volunteered with the Sandinistas in Nicaragua, where she produced television programs for women and children and directed movies until her return to México in 1984.[36] Years later, as director of TV UNAM (1989–94), she negotiated the establishment of a screening venue in honor of Pola Weiss, and she also negotiated the initial transfer of Weiss's videos at TV UNAM.[37] Throughout the 1990s Fernández continued with her documentary and didactical approach toward audiovisual media. She produced a television series entitled *Prisma universidad* (1985–97) on student organizations at UNAM and documentary films such as *Casa dividida* (1988), which addressed a phase of Che Guevara's life.[38] She also adopted video as her medium of choice and began experimenting with videodance, a video art genre that Pola Weiss introduced to Mexico in 1977, as described in the next chapter.[39]

As director of TV UNAM she supported the production of several videodance projects. When I interviewed her at her home in Mexico City she was finishing the production of *Entre paredes de agua* (30 min, dir. Fernández, 2010). *Entre paredes de agua* is a highly sophisticated videodance project, most of it shot underwater. It took four years to produce and makes use of computer animation software as well as video visual effects like chroma-key, the use of a green screen to layer different scenes. As our conversation came to an end she told me that her future plans are to continue experimenting with video art and videodance. As she told me this, I couldn't stop thinking about the ways in which Pola Weiss's work is present in Fernández's approach to video.

Cine-Mujer represents another model that was open to the participation of women in cinema and audiovisual media in general. Growing out of independent Latin American and Mexican practices of politically committed film, the audiovisual productions of the filmmakers of this collective politicized the female body and, by doing so, broke with conventional forms of representation to propose an alternative approach to film production. The early films of Cine-Mujer interrogated the ways in which visual images created and reproduced dominant power relations.

9

POLArizing the Archive

Among the visual letradas I follow in this work, Pola Weiss (1947–90) is the only one who did not self-identify as a feminist. However, like Rosa Martha Fernández, Mónica Mayer, and Ana Victoria Jiménez, she was interested in exploring feminine subjectivity and the living conditions of urban Mexican women through visual media. Like Mayer and Fernández, Weiss pursued a career as a visual artist on her own terms. Convinced of its potential as an artistic medium, Weiss used video to explore and experiment with a wide variety of disciplines—dance, music, poetry, live performance, and moving images. Also like Mayer's and Fernández's work in performance and film, Weiss's experiments with television broadcasting and video contested established disciplinary divisions and traditions of visual representation.

Video also provided Weiss with a platform from which to explore herself, adopting video as an extension of her own body. From 1977 to 1989 she developed a series of works in which she established an embodied relationship with the video camera that complicated the representation and the reading of her body as well as the relationship between artist and spectator (subject and object of representation). In this way Weiss's audiovisual experiments articulate what Beauchesne and Santos have labeled a utopian impulse.[1] Weiss's utopian impulse was motivated by a desire to transform and challenge what counted as female experience, intellectual and artistic inquiry, and dominant class and racial hierarchies. Some of her experiments with video point to the development of an alternative audiovisual space in which dreams of a better world could come to fruition.

Like other artists experimenting with video at the time, Weiss used the video camera as a confidante with which to share her most intimate secrets and the video monitor as a mirror. Writing in 1976, art critic Rosalind Krauss concluded that this prevalent use of the camera and the monitor as tools to investigate the self pointed to narcissism as the condition that defined video art as a genre in the 1970s.[2] While a narcissistic impulse is present in Weiss's video productions and the construction of her artistic persona, I focus instead on the ways in which her "narcissism" led to alternative understandings of female subjectivity and women's experience while contesting hegemonic regimes of representation.

At times Weiss transformed her camera, which she referred to as her *escuincla* (daughter, in Náhuatl), into an eye or a limb as she danced with it in her hand, filming her movements. During these live *videodanzas*, the interplay of projections and reflections from monitors and mirrors fractured the spatial and durational sequence of her performances. At the same time, such reflections and projections blurred the boundaries between spectator, artist, and object of representation. Like other artists at the time, Weiss adopted the camera as a prosthetic to explore and push the limits of bodily experiences. Moreover, in conceiving each of her videos as an *alumbramiento* (an act of giving birth), Weiss transformed her creative process into an act of copulation with her *escuincla*, something akin to what Donna Haraway would later label cyborg sex.[3]

In 1985 Donna Haraway's manifesto famously presented the cyborg, as a hybrid model of feminine subjectivity that defied any kind of fixed definition of what counted as female experience, and as a critique of the exclusionary practices of white heterosexual feminist discourses. In her manifesto Haraway refers to cyborg sex as "couplings between organism and machine, each conceived as coded devices, in an intimacy and with a power that was not generated in the history of sexuality."[4] Weiss's incestuous act of copulation with her *escuincla* resulted in productive experimentation that radically altered what counted as female experience. Indeed, Weiss's experiments led her to a particular kind of self-fashioning that integrated video technology as an extension of herself. Much like Haraway's use of the cyborg as a model to explain the diversity of women's experiences, Weiss invented her own categories to explain her practice and self, which constantly overflowed existing frameworks. Through the creation of playful neologisms like *extraPola*, *interPola*, POLA*roid*, *Venusina*, *teleasta*, and *videa*, which she used to describe herself and her practice, Weiss crafted an out-of-the-ordinary artistic persona that avoided any kind of fixed definition, thus challenging and exploding established meanings of what counted as women's experience in 1970s Mexico. Through her embodied approach to video technology, Weiss proposed an alternative model of a visual letrada that not only questioned the art establishment by embracing interdisciplinarity but also explored different corporeal sensibilities and new relations between self and technology. She championed video as a valid form of intellectual inquiry and a medium that conceived embodied subjects. Weiss's blurring of the object and subject of representation went beyond breaking with the construction of women as the object of the male gaze. Through her combined use of sound, music, voice, visual effects, images, and movement, Weiss exploits what media theorist Laura U. Marks would later label "haptic visuality" to demonstrate that the way we see and relate to screen images is neither disembodied nor void of desire.[5]

In her study of intercultural cinema—*The Skin of Film: Intercultural Cinema and the Senses*—produced from an experience of exile or the diaspora in the late 1980s and 1990s, Marks proposed a model of haptic visuality to oppose an optic visuality based on a Cartesian and disembodied model of perception that excludes desire. Marks argues that haptic visuality is a synesthetic visual encounter with a screen image involving touch, smell, and desire. Feminist art historian Amelia Jones follows Marks to explore how artworks produced in the post-1960s period explored televisual images (video, film, television) to convey embodied subjects in a manner that evoked haptic opticality rather than following the object-subject construction reversal that Laura Mulvey proposed in the early 1970s.[6] As I will discuss, Weiss's conception of video, as presented in her writings, interviews, and videos, is more in line with Marks's and Jones's approaches than with a mere reversal of object and subject of representation. Weiss's video work and exaggerated use of metaphor, allegory, and performance overflow any kind of binary construction of perception. Like Weiss, artists such as Carolee Schneemann, Joan Jonas, Sonia Andrade, Leticia Parente, and Shigeko Kubota, to name a few, began challenging the ways in which the female body was represented by blurring the boundaries between the subject and the object of representation through the use of video, installation, and performance, and above all by proposing a messier and more embodied model of perception. In particular, Japanese-born and U.S.-based Shigeko Kubota (b. 1937) would be an important motivation for and influence on Weiss's video production.

While some scholars have discussed Weiss's approaches to video as being "queer *avant la letter*," my purpose is to study Weiss as a significant producer and theorist who proposed her own categories to understand her practice and the potential of video and television broadcasting, rather than appropriating Weiss as a representative of subsequent discourses and interests.[7] Weiss's videos were part of a meaningful dialogue with an international group of artists who, in the 1960s, began to interrogate and develop distinct corporeal sensibilities mediated through audiovisual technologies. This increased interest in the body responded to emerging practices brought about by technological advances like the proliferation of televisual images of unknown bodies in live and recorded time that inundated the once private realm of living rooms in many urban centers around the world.

In her local context, Weiss's video production broke with several conventions of representation that radically transformed Mexican visual and media regimes, but her practice also gave continuity to ways of seeing and conventions of representation established through film and photography decades earlier. Her practice was deeply embedded in and committed to the local context. Weiss championed image making as a valid form of intellectual inquiry and understood the potential of audiovisual information for educational and political purposes in a way that aligned her to approaches of documentary filmmakers in Latin America. Some of her work explored issues of poverty and unequal gender, racial, and class relations, as they were experienced on the streets of Mexico City. In some of her best-known videos her body is used as an allegory of the city. By inscribing her personal experience in relation to the urban landscape through video, Weiss, like the other visual letradas discussed, points to the city as a crucial space for the negotiation and production of gendered subjectivities and regimes of knowledge. In doing so, her work speaks to the battle of representation (visual and in formal politics) that was taking place on the streets of Mexico City throughout the decade and to transformations in the sphere of action of the letrados. On several occasions she traveled to small communities to videotape and document traditional dances and performances.[8] These documentary approaches to video making followed a well-established anthropological way of seeing—an objectifying gaze underscored by an unequal distance between the object and the subject of the gaze. However, she attempted to break with this established way of seeing by making use of the self-reflexive potential and new capacities afforded by video to activate and awaken the spectator.

One of the ways that Weiss attempted to break with an objectifying way of seeing was by trying to break with what Yvonne Spielmann and others have called the media border—the separation between real experience and the reality structured by a medium.[9] She did so by using visual effects, incorporating feedback, using multiple cameras, experimenting with sound and music, and by "extraPOLAting" (making the viewer see images), "interPOLAting" (interrupting the viewer to disrupt the narrative), and "POLArizing" (inviting viewers to reflect on what they saw).[10]

Weiss's diverse engagements with video represent an important link within a network of image makers that meaningfully connects the previous generation of visual letradas, including Ana Victoria Jiménez and Rosa Martha Fernández, and the following generation of image makers who would adopt video as a medium of choice. Much like Mayer's, Weiss's body of work anticipates an interest in the potentialities of new media technologies in relation to performance and archival traditions that would become prevalent in the decades to follow.

Although her practice radically transformed Mexican regimes of media and visuality, Weiss's work has not been significantly incorporated into the histories of media, art, and feminism. Some monographs of her work exist, but not a thorough study that aims to link her practices to a genealogy of visual letradas, both national and transnational.[11] This is due, in part, to entrenched misogynistic practices that have historically obscured the legacies of women in the arts.[12] In the case of Weiss, such silencing mechanisms were exacerbated by several factors that have to do with the skepticism toward video as an artistic genre and Weiss's unconventional personality and practice that abjured any kind of definition. Rumors of Weiss videotaping her suicide (May 6, 1999), in combination with anecdotes of her eccentric personality and the lack of interest from the art establishment to understand video as an art form, contributed to the development of a marginal cultish following that, in part, distracted from her achievements as a visual letrada.

Another crucial aspect that until recently hindered a meaningful discussion of Weiss's work is the lack of support for keeping and maintaining her personal archive and work. The stories behind the bequest of her personal papers and the limited access to her video work underscore and set the limits of this chapter.

In 1998 one of Weiss's students, Edna Torres-Ramos, donated Weiss's work to TV UNAM. Ramos received Weiss's material from Fernando Mangino, Weiss's partner at the time of her death. Torre-Ramos then catalogued the material, consisting of thirty-eight videos and several stock images, to write her bachelor's thesis titled "El video arte en México: el caso de Pola Weiss." From 1998 until 2012, when Weiss's archive was donated to ARKEHIA, the center of documentation of the Museo Universitario de Arte Contemporáneo (MUAC), some of her videos circulated surreptitiously among circles of artists within Mexico. Internationally, a couple of her videos were distributed through the Netherlands Media Art Institute.[13] Currently many of her videos are available on YouTube.

In the context of a renewed interest in rescuing artists' archives and the attention the exhibition *La era de la discrepancia* brought to the work of Mexican artists working in the 1970s, Edna Torres-Ramos obtained funding in 2011 from Fondo Nacional para la Cultura y las Artes (FONCA) to curate and restore Weiss's archive.[14] Between 2009 and 2011, when I was researching this project, I was able to see thirty-eight of Pola Weiss's videos held at ARKEHIA. The videos were on loan from TV UNAM and held as part of the archive for the exhibition *La era de la discrepancia*. The video footage I saw does not represent Weiss's complete body of work. The initial donation to TV UNAM included various versions of the same videos as well as many video stock images. It is possible that different versions of the same video exist. I was also able to consult other material held at the Museum of Modern Art in Mexico City, including catalogues, posters, and invitations for Weiss's shows. At Biblioteca de las Artes, Hemeroteca Nacional, and the Faculty of Political Science and Communications at UNAM, I was able to consult Weiss's thesis and some newspaper interviews. Conversations with Rosa Martha Fernández, Sarah Minter, Mónica Mayer, Maris Bustamante, and Eli Bartra also helped in reconstructing parts of Weiss's legacy. While recognizing Weiss as a video pioneer, all of them directed our conversations toward Weiss's difficult personality and tragic death. These conversations confirmed the ways in which the myth and stigma surrounding Weiss have limited the recognition of her achievements.

Pola Weiss and the History of Video Art

Historically the emergence of new technologies has prompted artistic experimentation. Video and television broadcasting were not exceptions. The terms are often used interchangeably to refer to audiovisual images viewed through a television monitor. Beginning in the 1960s, visual artists collaborated in blurring this distinction as they began to experiment with both technologies as a way to explore and transform their image-making and broadcasting capacities. As is well known, in 1964 the Korean artist Nam June Paik and the Japanese artist Shuya Abe began to experiment with the handheld video camera (Sony Portapak). Some years earlier, in 1954, the German artist Wolf Vostell also used television monitors as part of his art installations. Soon afterward, Paik and Vostell joined George Maciunas in Fluxus, an international art movement, which promoted the experimentation across media and disciplines and derided the aspirations of bourgeois taste.[15] These artists, along with Bruce Nauman, Chris Burden, and Vito Acconci, are known as the "pioneers" of video art and the protagonists of a history that emanates from the dominant centers of the art world through a male-based perspective.[16] Yet another important milestone in the history of video was Jean Luc Godard's use of a video camera to record images of the student demonstration in Paris in 1968. In Canada the Vancouver-based collective Intermedia, established in 1968, was the first of its kind to begin discussing the ways in which television was changing art production via the theories of Marshall McLuhan.[17] Outside these networks of Western male art, Brazilian artists, for instance, began to experiment with video in the late 1960s, and by the mid-1970s a group of artists, including Sonia Andrade, Letícia Parente, and Regina Silveria, was already working in the medium.[18]

With time, video's affordability and ease of use prompted more intimate interactions and the establishment of independent networks of distribution, in turn providing new ways to produce and relate to audiovisual images. All these abilities made video the medium of choice for many grassroots movements, including feminist collectives.[19] Many feminist artists in the 1970s were attracted to video because of "its lack of history, its immediacy and less commodifiable nature."[20] Many felt empowered by the newness of video, as they thought it would enable them to achieve a place as art producers. At the time, video as an artistic medium did not have the male historical focus of other media.

Simultaneously videos began circulating in festivals, galleries and museums, and through marginal video collectives. By the mid-1970s these spaces began to distribute and archive experimental video. International exhibitions and video festivals held in Toronto (1974), Philadelphia (1975), and London (1976) were crucial to the process of institutionalizing video as an art form within the gallery system.[21] In such exhibitions video was still idealized as a means to democratize television broadcasting. However, this ideal soon vanished, as galleries and museums—mostly in Canada, the United States, and Western Europe—began to develop spaces to exhibit video art, and in the process produced genres, subgenres, and even disciplinary categories to distinguish between performative, documentary, and experimental video. In the process video was transformed into a medium, as Yvonne Spielmann puts it: "a specific media language and semiotic system that established an aesthetic vocabulary specific to the video-graphic capacities of electronic signal processing."[22] Part of this new vocabulary included an emphasis on video recording capacities that allowed artists to document their works.

Video provided artists with a more affordable and immediate means to record performances. Soon the documentation of the performance would gain equal—or greater—value than the event itself. The record, rather than the actual performance, became the marketable and collectable art piece, leading to the incorporation of video art as a marketable art commodity. Simultaneously, video increased the possibilities for keeping records of all kinds of events and of building more affordable personal audiovisual archives. As Douglas Rosenberg argued, conceptual artists' emphasis on the record anticipated what Jacques Derrida would label our contemporary archival fever, a displacement of experience that privileges playback over liveliness.[23]

In the early 1970s video was still an expensive technology in Mexico. Feminist and grassroots collectives resorted to super-8 and 16-mm film rather than video to produce independent media.[24] Artists interested in experimenting with video had to have links with the broadcasting industry. Both private and state broadcasting companies were open to experimenting with the newly available video technology and eagerly opened their doors to new generations of media professionals—including women. As mentioned earlier, Pola Weiss began to collaborate with both state and private television in 1974, and soon she declared herself to be a *teleasta*—a producer of televisual images. It was not only broadcasting companies that were interested in video; several efforts to introduce the emergent medium of video to young generations of artists were organized in Mexico City.

In 1973 Video Art nueva estética visual, an exhibition held at MAM and sponsored by the U.S. embassy, introduced the vanguard of U.S.-based video artists and experimental television to Mexican audiences.[25] Among those artists were Woody and Steina Vasulka, owners of New York City's The Kitchen, one of the first and best-known independent video art distribution spaces.[26] The exhibit also included the work of William and Louise Etra and Stephen Beck, all of whom were involved in the design of machines that could produce and distort audio and visual signals without the need for a camera.[27] While there are no records of the influence of such an exhibit on Pola Weiss's career development, it is possible that through this exhibit she was introduced to the potential of image distortions and effects—such as chroma-keys, solarization, and audio/image interchangeability as well as experiments with choreography and sound.

By the early 1970s Weiss, like other artists of her generation, was already interested in exploring video as an alternative to commercial television broadcasting. In the early stages of her career she used the neologism *videa* to explain her practice as a person who has visual ideas or who thinks visually.[28] At a moment when Mexican male intellectuals and politicians debated the content of television programming and the management of broadcasting, Weiss advocated for video as a tool to explore audiovisual production as a valid form of intellectual activity. She championed the potential of video to develop an alternative to commercial television programming. But Weiss also imbued video and television with a utopian potential that could give rise to what she called the "cosmic man," new sensorial beings in touch with their feelings.[29] In other words, Weiss believed that video was able to convey how our experiences are embodied. She conceived of video as a translator of our deepest feelings and memories: "Because of its technical characteristics, video is an excellent translator of our memory. It provides us with a way to access what happens inside ourselves, in our minds, and with our sensations."[30]

Pola Weiss also believed in the twin potential of video as a recording device and as a tool to develop generations of audiovisual producers and users. In an interview in 1982 Weiss commented on the future of video, on her belief that people would own personal video libraries, and that people could become the product of their audiovisual experiences: "I think that in the future, each person will be able to record his or her own experiences according to his/her own capacities. By doing so, they will discover that many people identify themselves with their messages. Currently, tape recorders, photographs and, lately, Betamax equipment are being used as recording devices. So if in the past people owned libraries of books, in the future they will own videotape libraries."[31]

Weiss's enthusiasm for the potential of video to engender an infinite number of producers is in stark contrast to Jacques Derrida's fear of the annihilation of memory due to an overabundance of documentation and record producers.[32] Weiss also celebrates the possibility that video could give people ways of communicating with each other in a more meaningful manner. Most important, Weiss's approach to video as a form of self-knowledge speaks to an archival impulse. Weiss, like the other three visual letradas I have discussed, expanded the notion of an archive by using video as a medium to keep a record of her life, her feelings, and her thoughts and desires. Her experiments with video form an archive of sorts that consists of audiovisual records of how daily experiences are inscribed onto the female body. Her work is an attempt to build an archive of embodied perceptions and sensations through screen images.

Throughout her career Weiss produced scripts and documentaries for television and private clients in combination with more experimental video and performance work.[33] Some records indicate that part of her archival footage contains video spots for Carlos Salinas de Gortari and Luis Donaldo Colosio's presidential campaign.[34] Other sources indicate that in 1983 she participated in the production of an experimental television program called *Videocosmos* for Channel 9 in Mexico City.[35] Meanwhile, she continued to produce work experimenting with dance, sound, music, and poetry. At times these different approaches to video making were indistinguishable in her work. At other times she made clear attempts to construct a vocabulary to understand different approaches and uses of video and television broadcasting through different neologisms, like self-portraits, *videodanza* (dance performances), and *artVEing* (video interviews). Mainly, she aimed to produce experimental programming for television through her company artTV —a studio she funded with difficulty and through her own means.[36]

In one of her last interviews, she affirmed that more than anything else, she was a *teleasta*—a producer of televisual images. Video art was her other voice and her other self; "*antes que nada soy teleasta, el videoarte es mi otra voz, mi otra mirada mi otro yo,*" Weiss stated.[37] Thus Weiss confirmed that while she was interested in video art, she was equally interested in producing televisual images for a broader audience, while also signaling her refusal to be classified in any established discipline or association.

V Is for Video and Vagina: The Exchanges of Pola Weiss and Shigeko Kubota

In 1975, as Weiss was finishing her bachelor's thesis on the uses of video as an alternative medium to commercial television broadcasting, Weiss met and interviewed Japanese-born and U.S.-based video artist Shigeko Kubota. The meeting with Kubota marked an important transformation in Weiss's approach to video. It confirmed that her search for an experimental approach was of interest in other places. After the meeting with Kubota, Weiss began to conceptualize some of her work as video art, while still keeping her commitment to being a *teleasta.*

In examining Kubota's life and career, certain parallels with Weiss's career and approach to video emerge. However, in narrating her exchanges with Kubota, rather than placing Weiss in a derivative position in relation to those artists who produce work from hegemonic centers of the art world, my purpose is to shed light on parallel networks of exchange and production. My aim is to locate Weiss as a meaningful producer and theorist who proposed her own categories to understand not only her practice but also the potential of video and television broadcasting emerging from Mexico.

As we shall see, Weiss and Kubota developed an embodied relation with video that empowered their positions as female video producers. Much like other artists in the early 1970s, they were both attracted to video because of its lack of history, which afforded many feminist-minded artists a clean slate from which to launch their careers without the burden of an existing male tradition or established categories and genres. Both Weiss and Kubota were deeply invested in developing categories to understand their media explorations. While using video's intermedial capacities to mix and fuse a wide range of practices and conventions of representation, they also transformed traditional female forms of expression. For instance, following their interest in using video as a tool for self-knowledge, they both championed video as a medium akin to diary writing, what Kubota labeled *videodiary*.[38] They both produced videos to record important events in their lives, like the deaths of their respective fathers and their travel experiences in search of their past and their ancestors. Kubota's father died in 1974, and she incorporated her experience of attending his funeral into *Broken Diary* (1969–75). Weiss explored her own story in *Autovideoato* (1979) where we see Weiss telling her story from behind a body silhouette created with visual effects, given the appearance that she is telling her story from within her own body (fig. 49). She also traveled to Strasburg in Alsace, France, to search for her grandparents and produced a video of the experience in *Videorigen de Weiss* (1984). According to some sources, in 1989 she attempted to bring the camera to the funeral of her father, Leopoldo Weiss. In using video to transform the female experience of diary writing, they transgressed traditional gendered conceptions of technology as male and diary writing as female.[39] They also explored and blurred conceptions of what was considered a record of an event and what constituted a work of art. In doing so, they established audiovisual discourses, frameworks, and practices that were in dialogue with other experimental approaches and that would characterize genres in feminist media production decades later.[40]

While Kubota is considered one of the female pioneers of video art, her artistic career, like that of many other female artists, has been overshadowed by that of her partner, Nam June Paik. Nonetheless, among feminist art scholars Kubota is widely regarded for her performance *Vagina Painting* (1965), in which she attached a brush to her underwear and painted the floor with red ink.[41] She is also one of the few women officially recognized as a member of Fluxus and credited as a pioneer who experimented with and coined the terms video installation and video sculpture.[42]

Kubota began to use the video camera as early as 1969 to videotape important events in her life, like her travels through Europe, Japan, and the

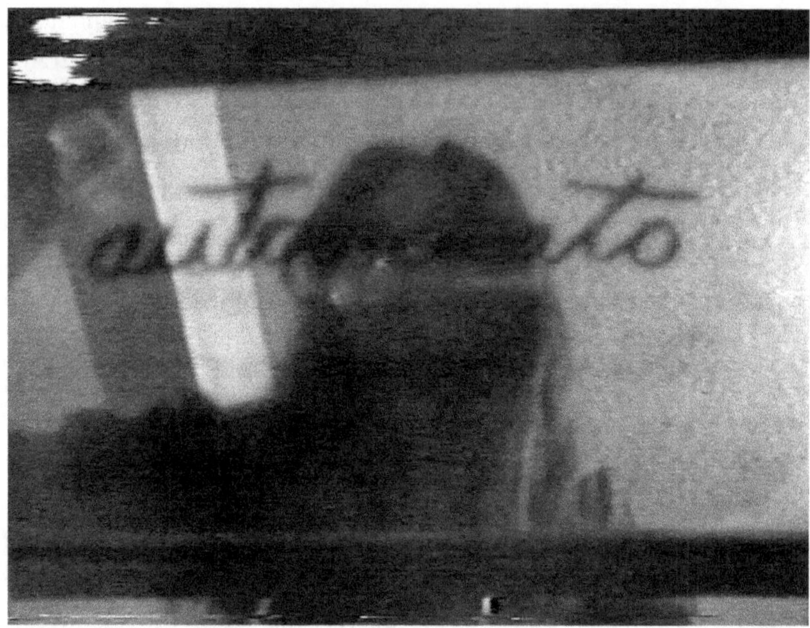

FIG. 49. *Autovideoato*. © 1979 by Pola Weiss. Fondo Pola Weiss, Catalogación Edna Torres-Ramos, Centro de Documentación ARKEHIA, Museo Universitario Arte Contemporáneo, UNAM.

United States. About the difficulties of working with early video equipment, Kubota stated: "When I began taking my video diary, the video equipment had just been invented and was very large and heavy. Besides, its battery was even heavier. Since I was carrying around this equipment on my back, I totally hurt my back and hips."[43]

The exertion required to carry the large, heavy video equipment caused Kubota to have a miscarriage, an experience she shared with Weiss and one that would be the subject of one of Weiss's most emotionally charged videos, *Mi corazón* (1986, 10 min.).[44] Both Kubota and Weiss developed embodied relations with their cameras. Each of these women saw her camera as an extension of her body and a prosthetic for a mother-daughter relation but also as a substitute for a sexual partner and a means to claim self-sufficiency. In a poem that accompanied Kubota's video installation

Behind the Video Door (1969–76), which incorporated parts of Kubota's personal and professional life, she stated: "I travel alone with my Portapak on my back, as Vietnamese women do with their babies. I like video, because it is heavy. Portapak and I traveled over Europe, Navajo land, and Japan without male accompany. Portapak tears down my shoulder, backbone and waist. I feel like a Soviet woman, working on the Siberian Railway."[45]

In July 1975 when Weiss interviewed Kubota in Mexico City, Kubota was acting as the curator of Anthology Films Archives (1974–85), a center for the preservation and study of independent, experimental, and avant-garde film established in New York City in 1969.[46] A month prior to her arrival to Mexico, Kubota exhibited *VideoPoem* (1975) at The Kitchen in New York City. *VideoPoem* consisted of a small monitor inserted inside a zippered cloth bag that Kubota had sewn. The monitor showed a video with images of Kubota's face peaking through the zipper of the bag. The piece was dedicated to Kubota's previous husband, avant-garde Japanese musician Kosugi. The poem accompanying the installation reveals the empowered and embodied relation Kubota developed with video.

Video is Vengeance of Vagina
Video is Victory of Vagina
Video is Venereal Disease of Intellectuals
Video is a Vacant Apartment
Video is Vacation of Art
Viva Video . . .[47]

According to Mary Jane Jacob, Kubota's claim for video as vengeance of the vagina emphasizes video "as a medium empowering women and enabling them to achieve a place in Western art that many felt could not be made through the more traditional male-dominated disciplines of painting and sculpture."[48] In *VideoPoem* Kubota quite literally re-creates the icon of the *vagina dentata*, which represents the male fear of female genitalia. With the artist as the focus of the video, Kubota's *VideoPoem* announced how video, as a new medium, could finally bring justice to the forgotten female artist. But *VideoPoem* also signals Kubota's embodied relation with video. Her body was able to speak and to be seen through a monitor that represented her vagina—the inside and the outside of her body were blurred. Moreover, the video was an extension of her body that brought her into being. Like Kubota, Weiss would resort to the vagina as a metaphor to explain her relation with video.

Weiss interviewed Kubota at Weiss's home studio in Mexico City on July 17, 1975 (fig. 50). The video recording of the interview demonstrates that Weiss was deeply aware of Kubota's life and career and also shows Weiss's particular interests in exploring and contesting the limits and possibilities of video and television broadcasting.[49] With an audience present, Kubota and Weiss spoke about different approaches to video making (video art and video installation) and about Kubota's experience as a female artist in Japan and New York. However, beyond disseminating Kubota's experiences, Weiss used the interview to present her own views about video and television broadcasting to a Mexican audience. Kubota was there to affirm Weiss as a valid visual letrada.

The exchange between Kubota and Weiss begins with a conversation on the differences between video art and video installation. Next Weiss asks Kubota if she has experienced gender discrimination in New York or if gender equity exists. Interestingly, Weiss prefaces this question by stating that Kubota is the wife of Nam June Paik. As we listen, the camera focuses on the face of an unidentified male in the audience. During the interview Weiss constantly interrupts the conversation to ask the audience if the recording of the interview is playing live on the monitors she located in the back of the studio (as the background of the interview). She asks someone (an assistant, perhaps) to distort the image so that the intended viewers think their television is not working properly. Then the camera focuses on Weiss, who talks to the viewer (not the live audience, but the intended viewer of the recorded interview) and explains that video art consists of distorting images (the clear image that the television decodes and presents to the viewer). Video art, she continues, consists of creating feedback, image distortions, and color alterations by playing with brilliance and contrast. After an intermission the camera focuses on Kubota, who

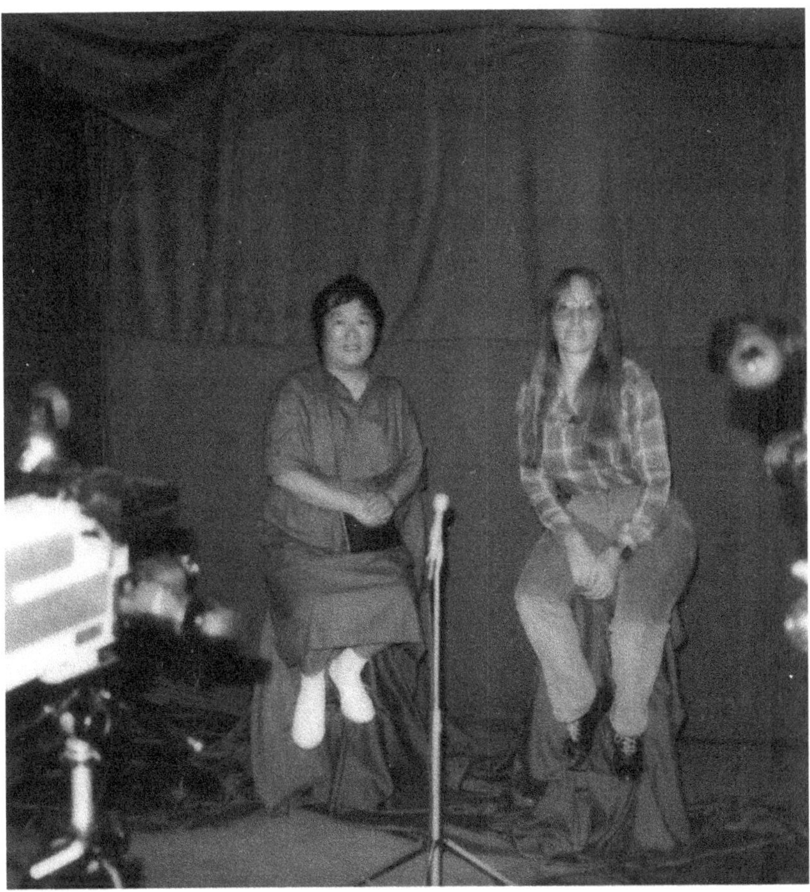

FIG. 50. (*Left to right*) Shigeko Kubota and Pola Weiss in *Weiss and Kubota interview*, 1975. Fondo Pola Weiss, Catalogación Edna Torres-Ramos, Centro de Documentación ARKEHIA, Museo Universitario Arte Contemporáneo, UNAM.

sits on a chair. The interview ends with a blurred and distorted image of Kubota smiling.

After this meeting Weiss traveled to New York City in the summer of 1977 to learn more about video art in the United States, where she met Kubota at her studio. The two artists remained in touch and exchanged correspondence about Kubota's visit to Mexico in 1977 (fig. 51). Weiss speaks of her trip to the United States as a revelation in contrast to what she had witnessed earlier through her travels in Europe: "In Europe they showed me theater plays and documentaries made for television, and I thought to myself, this is not what I am looking for. After, I went to New York, and there I found video art, and to my surprise, what I found was exactly what I was teaching my students at a video workshop in the Faculty of Social Sciences."[50]

After Weiss returned from her trip to New York City she began producing videos and promoting video art as an artistic genre more openly. In 1977 Weiss participated in the organization of the "IX Encuentro Internacional, I Encuentro Nacional de Videoarte," held at the Museo de Arte Carrillo Gil. Weiss and Miguel Ehrenberg were the only Mexican artists included in the 1977 show, along with many Canadian, European, U.S.-based, Chilean, and Argentinian video artists. Weiss presented one of her first experimental videos, *Flor cósmica* (1977, 15 min.) (fig. 52). Like Kubota, Weiss resorted to iconic references to female genitalia to express her approach to video making. In *Flor cósmica* Weiss used the flower as a symbol of her identity.[51] The video is a playful experiment with visual distortions and sound to the rhythm of Chick Corea's "Return Forever." In the video a sequence of shapes morph into each other, transforming into images of highly contrasted and fluorescent flower shapes that combine with text to spell the name of Pola Weiss.

A year later, and more in line with Kubota's more radical stance, Weiss referenced the vagina as a machine of video production. In a graphic manifesto that accompanied the exhibition of her videos *Mujer-ciudad-mujer* (1977) and *Somos mujeres* (1977) at the 1978 February Biennial at the Museum of Modern Art in Mexico City, Weiss claimed the vagina as the site of video production through word play and image collage. In this graphic manifesto she declared her self-sufficiency and independence as a video producer.

The focal point of Weiss's graphic manifesto is the phrase: "*Yo rubricaba poemas en su cuerpo, en su vagina eyaculaba imagines*" (I inscribed poems in her body, and in her vagina I ejaculated images) (fig. 53). Without the support of the images, it would be unclear who the "*yo*" (I) identifies and who is performing the action of inscribing poems. On the first page we

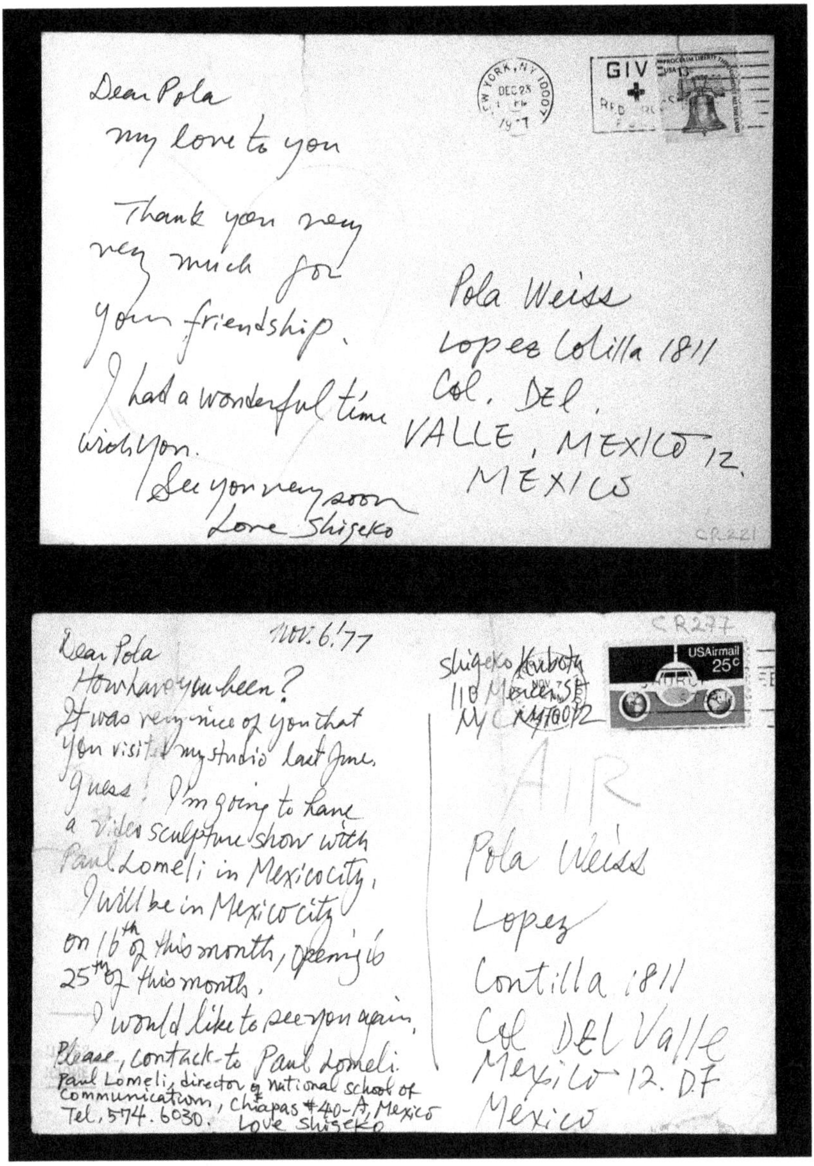

FIG. 51. Weiss and Kubota correspondence, 1977. Fondo Pola Weiss, Catalogación Edna Torres-Ramos, Centro de Documentación ARKEHIA, Museo Universitario Arte Contemporáneo, UNAM.

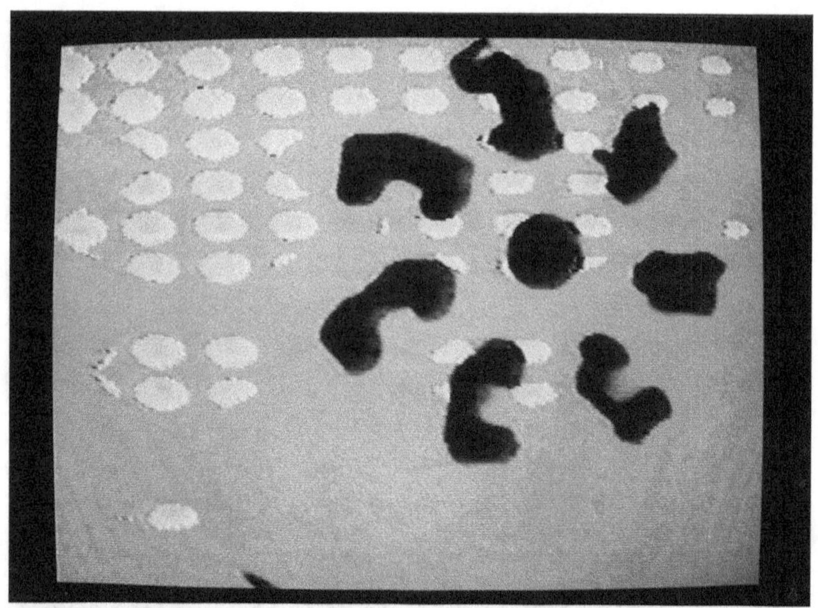

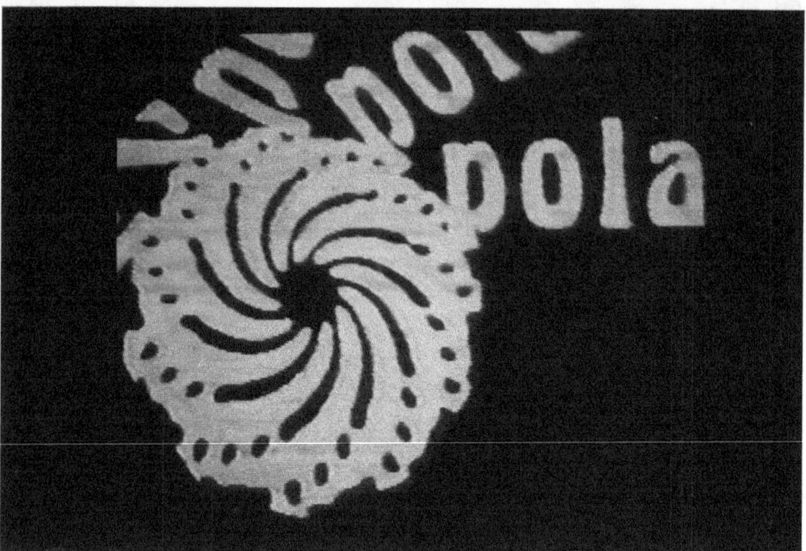

FIG. 52. *Flor cósmica.* © 1977 by Pola Weiss. Fondo Pola Weiss, Catalogación Edna Torres-Ramos. Centro de Documentación ARKEHIA, Museo Universitario Arte Contemporáneo, UNAM.

see the outline of a woman (clearly Weiss) carrying a camera, videotaping the silhouette of another women (Weiss as well), who stands with her legs open; the poem comes from her vagina. Below, on the floor, another camera films the letters coming from the vagina. The camera, the vagina, the text and the mouth of the women's silhouette are highlighted in red, emphasizing them as sites of enunciation. The camera is filming the vagina, the site of women's production from which the voice of the artist emerges as text.

Weiss is the artist, the object, and the subject of the gaze in this visual poem. She claims complete authorship for both the inspirations (the poems) and the creative production (ejaculation of images). The following page is an image of Weiss carrying a television monitor with the logo of her company, artTV, with a printed typographical composition that reads: "*ciudad-mujer-analogía-ciudad*" (city, woman, analogy, city) (fig. 54).

This last page serves to frame both the videos Weiss included in the exhibition. Both videos are meditations on the relation between feminine bodies and the urban landscape. In *Ciudad-mujer-ciudad* Weiss uses the female body as an allegory of the city and urban decay in a manner that breaks with conventional representations of the female nude. According to Jorge Carrasco, the video was censored on commercial television because it showed a female nude.[52] The body of Vivianne Blackmore, the model, is seen from the front; her breasts are exposed, and she is performing undulating movements (fig. 3, in introduction).

As Mónica Mayer recalled years later: "I was surprised by the fact that [*Ciudad-mujer-ciudad*] showed a real woman, with scars and cellulite. It made me laugh to see her breasts bouncing to the sound of the bells, and I was surprised to see the frontal shots of her pubic area. It was a female body seen by a woman."[53]

As discussed in the introduction, in *Somos mujeres* Weiss records how poor indigenous women begging on the streets respond to her intrusive camera by attempting to throw things back at her to stop her from filming them. The inclusion of the women's responses speaks to Weiss's overall interest in breaking the media border and *interpOLAting* (interpellating)

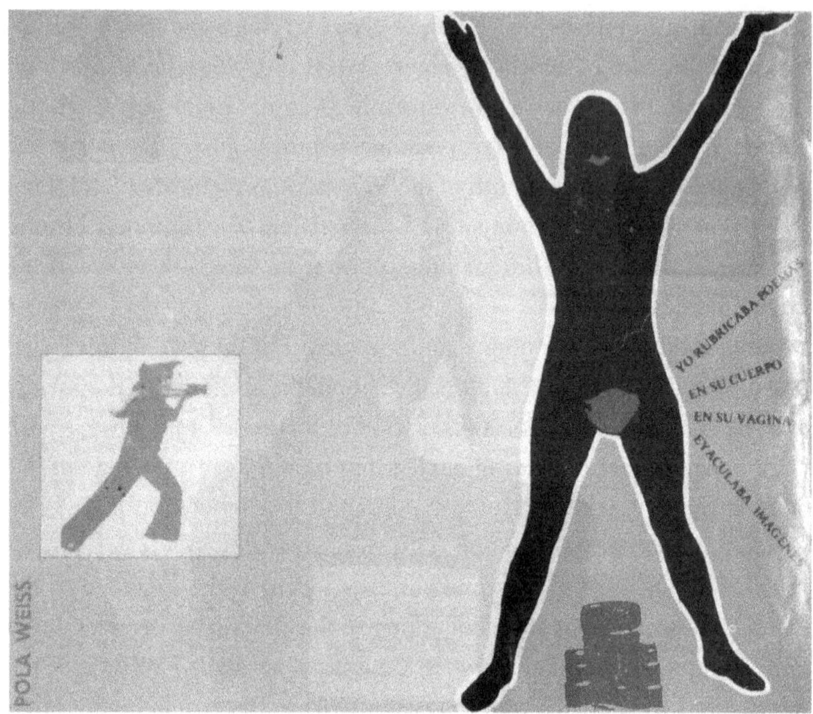

FIG. 53. *Salón 77–78 Bienal de Febrero Nuevas Tendencias* (*front page*). Instituto Nacional de Bellas Artes, México. © 1978 by Pola Weiss. Fondo Pola Weiss, Catalogación Edna Torres-Ramos, Centro de Documentación ARKEHIA, Museo Universitario Arte Contemporáneo, UNAM.

the viewer, something that was already present in Kubota's interview and that would become a constant in her work (fig. 2, in introduction).[54]

These three works—the videos and the graphic manifesto—contain elements that Weiss would continue to explore and that would become prevalent in her approach to video making: first, an interest in being both the object and the subject of the gaze; second, the use of video to blur the distinction between the private and the public—the images that come from her vagina and her dance performances; third, the use of words as an element of a visual sequence; and fourth, the use of the female body as an allegory of the city. This focus on the relationship between the city and

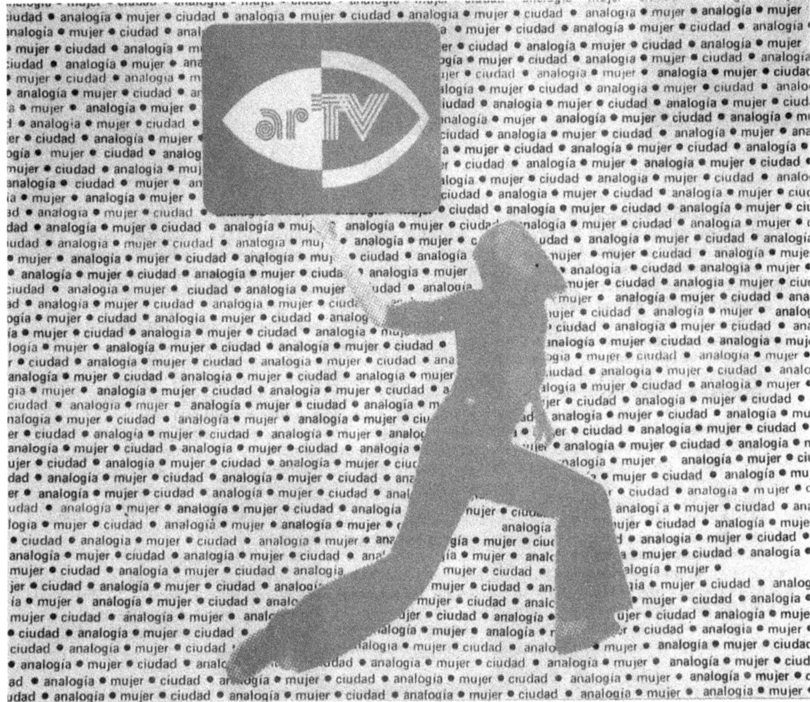

FIG. 54. *Salón 77–78 Bienal de Febrero Nuevas Tendencias* (*back page*). Instituto Nacional de Bellas Artes, México. © 1978 by Pola Weiss. Fondo Pola Weiss, Catalogación Edna Torres-Ramos, Centro de Documentación ARKEHIA, Museo Universitario Arte Contemporáneo, UNAM.

the female body connects Weiss with the work of the other visual *letradas* I have examined and to crucial transformations in the spheres of action of the *letrados*.

Besides their shared interest in developing categories for understanding self-knowledge and their embodied approach to video, Kubota and Weiss also shared an interest in producing videos in direct reference to dominant male icons in the history of art. In *Marcel Duchamp's Grave* (1975), Kubota visits Duchamp's grave in Rouen, France, as a meditation on death and as homage to Duchamp.[55] In *Video Chess* (1975) Kubota merges an image of herself with an image of Duchamp, while superimposing an image of Paik

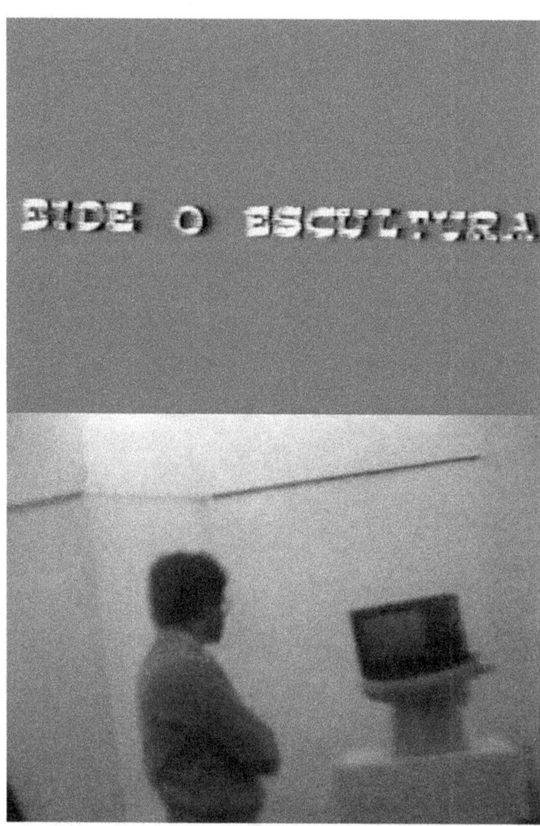

FIG. 55. *Video insta-lación: Bidé o escultura.* © 1980 by Pola Weiss. Catalogación Edna Torres-Ramos, Centro de Documentación ARKEHIA, Museo Universitario Arte Contemporáneo, UNAM.

into Edouard Manet's *Le Déjeuner sur L'Herbe,* thus reversing the tradition of the depicting the female nude.[56] Weiss, in a more satirical and irreverent manner, presented a video installation at Chapultepec Gallery in Mexico City entitled *Video instalación: Bidé o escultura* (1980) (fig. 55).[57]

The installation makes reference to Duchamp's *Fountain* (1917), in which the artist famously signed a urinal with the pseudonym Richard Mutt and claimed it as art. In *Bidé o escultura* Weiss appropriates and feminizes the Dadaist act of naming an everyday life object as art by placing a television monitor playing a video of a stream of water on top of a bidet. During the exhibition, she interviewed the audience and asked them if they knew what a bidet was.[58] Most of them did not know that it was a porcelain object that

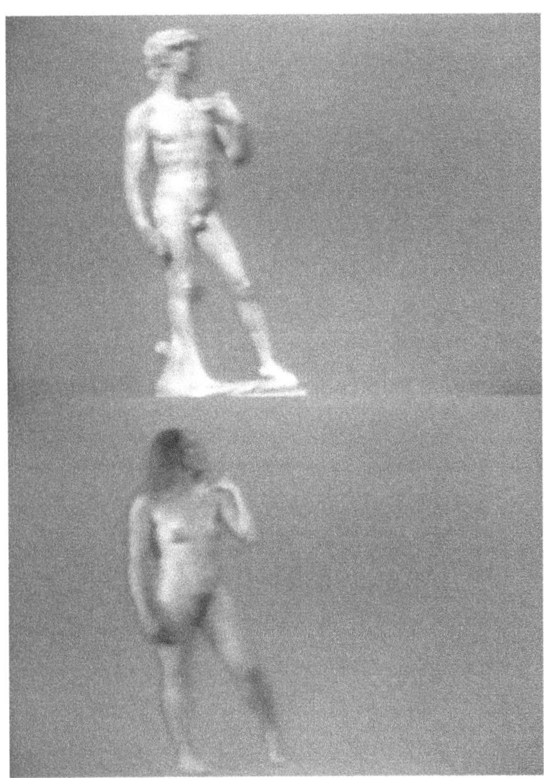

FIG. 56. *David.* © 1983 by Pola Weiss. Catalogación Edna Torres-Ramos, Centro de Documentación ARKEHIA, Museo Universitario Arte Contemporáneo, UNAM.

was mostly used by women to wash their genitalia. In *David* (1983, 11 min.), a video filmed in Yugoslavia, Weiss is seen throwing stones at a replica of Michelangelo's sculpture; she then intermixes images of her body taking the place of the sculpture through video effects (fig. 56).[59] In the video installation *Bidé o escultura* Weiss takes the place of the male artist, while in *David* she claims her place as the object of the gaze. In both cases Weiss explores her position as a woman making videos about female bodies and is guided by a desire to see and to be seen. Her approach is not a simple reversal of the objectifying male gaze; she understands that there is power in the act of being seen.

Both Weiss and Kubota feminized video making through wordplay and allegory. In the process they contested and explored normative definitions of female experiences and ways of seeing and perceiving. Video allowed them to make sense of and reconcile contrasting and competing female experiences and desires, leading toward a reconfiguration of their own female subjectivity. For Weiss, video was a tool of empowerment and self-knowledge but also a tool to seduce viewers.

Videodanza and Recognition

The video exhibitions organized in Mexico City, first in 1973 and then in 1977, locate the capital city as a node within this early international network of art video history.[60] However, in spite of this initial interest in video art, art critics in Mexico did not recognize video as an art form until the 1990s. As in most of the Latin American region, video in Mexico was more openly used as a medium of communication for independent and artistic projects, grassroots organizations, and government-funded productions in the mid-1980s, when it became more affordable. For instance, according to Felipe Ehrenberg—an artist who experimented with video technology at a time when some television stations were open to inviting artists to experiment with their video equipment—no one understood the value of such work as art.[61] In spite of this situation, Weiss did receive government support for some of her productions. Her participation in the dance festival as part of the 1979 Venice Biennale, in which she performed *Videodanza, viva videodanza,* was funded through a government grant (Fondo Nacional Para Actividades Sociales, FONAPAS).[62] Weiss's work also received media attention; however, most of this attention emphasized the lack of support and recognition she received, speculating about the depression that may have caused her suicide in 1990.[63] The myth of the unrecognized and misunderstood artist negated a deeper engagement with her work. In media interviews Weiss complained about the lack of support and recognition she suffered in Mexico, in comparison to the attention videos and performances received abroad.[64] In 1987, as a member of the jury at the IV International Festival of Video and Film in Rio de Janeiro, she declared: "In Mexico, nothing like this exists. This is why even though all my video production is made in Mexico, I am only recognized as a video artist abroad."[65]

During 1979 Weiss produced more than ten videos. In addition to the Venice Biennial, her work was shown in Caracas, Athens, Paris, Kansas City, and New York City.[66] Most of the videos experimented with what she would label *videodanza* but also fused an interest with a documentary tradition. Weiss's experiments with videodance locate her as a pioneer in the development of a practice that has only recently been recognized in Mexico.[67]

Some of these videos were shot in the Mexican states of Oaxaca, Puebla, and Mexico. In these videos Weiss used a second camera that she labeled the objective camera, while her camera work was credited as the subjective camera. In most of these productions the cameras show Weiss dancing from different angles. The objective camera takes the place of an audience, while the subjective camera is an extension of Weiss's body. Weiss worked with both cameras and visual effects to break the media border and add a self-reflexive intentionality to her work. About her use of effects, she said:

> Even though they add a formal element, visual effects are really important for my work because they make the viewer reflect on what they are seeing. I send a message and then, all of a sudden, I use a visual effect. The rupture that the effect causes gives the viewer the opportunity to think about what he/she saw, assimilate it, and then follow with what is next. As I've told you before, video is a great opportunity to mobilize and awaken your curiosity.[68]

Weiss also used effects to provoke a sensorial reaction in her intended viewer. She believed that content and form should go hand in hand to produce an embodied response in the viewer: "When I began to play with shapes, I mixed black-and-white inputs to create shapes that suddenly brought up old sensations that made me want to shout, to cry: they gave me goose bumps. Then I reflected on this and realized that form is an integral part of content. And that if the form was given or determined by technique, it became indispensable to work both—form and content—so that my videos could reach other people."[69]

Weiss experimented with various techniques to create effects. She adopted a hands-on approach to overcome the lack of available technology. In a recent interview, Fernando Mangino recalled how Weiss produced visual effects: "She was interested in taking things out of the norm; she created visual effects by videotaping shiny things such as crystal balls or Christmas decorations out of focus. She then fed those images through a monitor and a video camera, creating an infinite feedback loop."[70]

Sound is also an important aspect of Weiss's body of work. Her work incorporates ambient sounds, her voice, and music. Weiss's voice is mainly heard in her *autovideoatos* and interviews. In her *videodanzas* she relies more on music. Federico Luna, a musician and composer, and Weiss's sister, Kitzia Weiss, also a composer, collaborated with Weiss on numerous occasions. Weiss's approach to video signaled that sound and visual regimes needed to be understood and perceived as a whole.

In *Cuilapan de Guerrero* (1979, 6 min.), Weiss dances at the entrance of an old hacienda in the state of Oaxaca to the rhythm of music composed by her sister Kitzia Weiss. In *Papalotl* (1979, 3 min.), Weiss introduces herself, her *escuincla*, and her practice as art for television, in English. Then she is seen dancing on the streets wearing a yellow dress. To distinguish between the objective and subjective, she uses a visual effect that distorts the image as if it were seen through a transparent sphere to frame the *escuincla* view. *Papalotl* was shown on Channel 10 in New York City. In *Cuetzalan y yo* (1979, 8 min.), Weiss captures a procession in the town of Cuetzalan. In the video Weiss talks about her impressions and experiences as we see a collage of images showing the pyramid located near the town and a scene of the procession through the town's streets. She attempts to break the media border using graphic effects. Her face breaks the border of the screen as she appears through a small peephole (fig. 57), telling the viewer how she felt as she witnessed the procession: "I felt as if I was one of them," Weiss says.[71] This image fades and morphs into a scene of Papantla dancers (*voladores de Papantla*) approaching the camera and giving Weiss a flute. The video ends with images of Papantla dancers performing their traditional flying dance intermixed with images of Weiss's body as if she

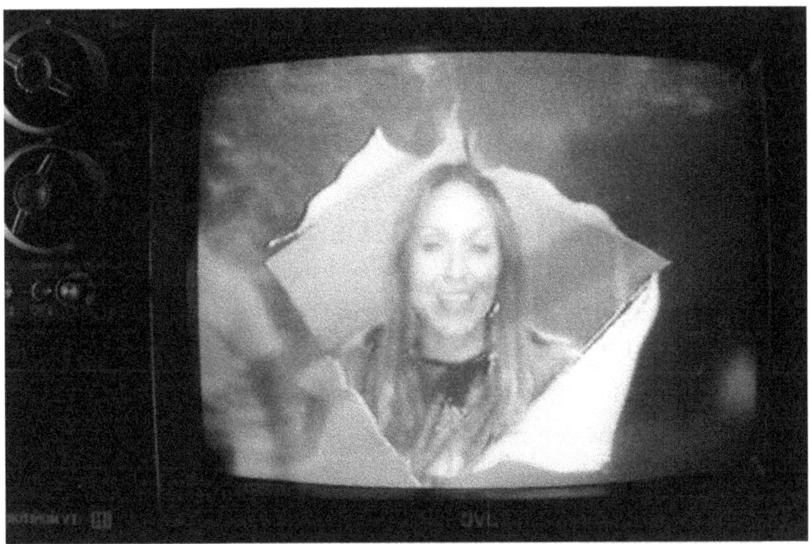

FIG. 57. *Cuetzalan y yo.* © 1979 by Pola Weiss. Catalogación Edna Torres-Ramos, Centro de Documentación ARKEHIA, Museo Universitario Arte Contemporáneo, UNAM.

were flying along with them, created through the use of chroma-key effects. As in *David* (1983), in which Weiss uses video to create an imaginary space in which she can realize her fantasy of taking the place of the male body, in *Cuetzalan y yo* Weiss creates an imaginary space in which her desire to integrate herself with others can finally be sated.

Video provided Weiss with an alternate space in which a utopian project abolishing class, ethnic, gender, and racial divisions could be realized—according to her own desires. Because a utopia must by definition be idealistic, Weiss's attempts to break the media border and interpellate the viewer at times became patronizing and idealistic experiments that could easily be placed within an anthropological way of seeing. Nonetheless, her playful approach and attempts to integrate herself as part of the representation did provide an alternative approach to the dilemmas of seeing and representing the Other. Some unfinished work I was able to see seems to indicate that she attempted to follow this line of exploration further.[72]

Pola *la Venusina*

While Weiss was enthusiastic about video's potential to enable a wide number of users and producers, she also believed that viewers were unable to see that potential on their own. On the occasion of her solo exhibition at Galería Chapultepec in Mexico City in 1983, *La Venusina renace y reforma*, Weiss conceptualized herself as a kind of female audiovisual messiah, bringing viewers out of their darkness and showing them how to see. In so doing, Weiss claimed to be an extraterrestrial love-goddess, a *Venusina*, who would guide viewers from a place without images into a better world where light would bring them into being. She offered to guide viewers out from under the control of commercial television and into a state of reflection and introspection.

> She extraPOLAtes [you, the viewer], she extracts you from darkness, a place where no images exist; she brings you out into the light and as you see the light you are born. She extraPOLAtes [you] with her eye, she extracts you from darkness with her camera, and she gives you birth [and you see the light] through a monitor.
> But she also interPOLAtes you: She places herself between you and the camera; she interrupts your old habits of seeing; she interrupts; she makes an intermission in the continuity of the universe. Like a comet, her light keeps shining to illuminate what is coming: the video of the future.
> She POLArizes you: she makes you focus your attention, your intention, through her videos as she modifies the light rays through reflection.[73]

Weiss had first put those theories into practice a few years earlier when she enacted the role of audiovisual messiah in *Videodanza a dos tiempos* (1980), a videodance performance that took place in the public plaza outside the Auditorio Nacional in Mexico City (fig. 58). With her heavy camera on her shoulders, she danced as she traversed the bodies of the spectators, who watched her move through mirrors. The camera filmed the reflections of the public and her movements, while monitors played back her movements

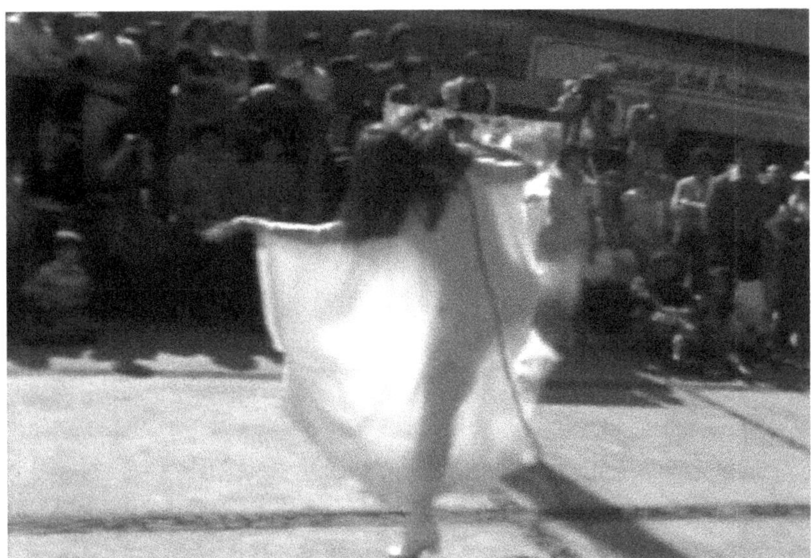

FIG. 58. *Videodanza a dos tiempos.* © 1980 by Pola Weiss. Catalogación Edna Torres-Ramos, Centro de Documentación ARKEHIA, Museo Universitario Arte Contemporáneo, UNAM.

in real time. Reflections and projections of movements were in constant feedback, thus blurring of the divide between the object and the subject of representation, or in Weiss's terms, *extraPOLAting* (making the viewer see images), *interPOLAting* (interrupting the viewer to disrupt the narrative), and *POLArizing* (inviting viewers to reflect on what they saw). Underneath the wordplay and exaggerated metaphor, it is clear Weiss understood that the separation the screen produced between object and subject was not real. Her live experiments with dance, music, and video could also be read as didactic demonstrations of the ways we experience the world through representations. For Weiss, this process was always messy and embodied, rather than separated.

Weiss's attempts at extraPOLAting, interPOLAting, and POLArizing the viewer extended beyond her experimental work. Like other visual letradas, she resorted to humor in her efforts to break the media border and claim her place as rightful heir to a genealogy of Mexican artists. She appropriated masculine cultural symbols of the Mexican Revolution, by stating that she was "La Nieta del Ahuizote," the female grandchild of *El hijo del Ahuizote* (1903), the satirical periodical opposing the Porfirio Díaz regime (1876–1911), directed by Ricardo Flores Magón. At another performance, at the Museo del Chopo in Mexico City, she playfully adapted the title of a popular song by Francisco Gabilondo Soler ("Cri Cri"), which talks about a kid's fascination for all the memorabilia that her grandmother keeps inside her wardrobe: "*Toma el llavero abuelita y enséñame tu ropero*" (Grandmother, take the keys and show me your wardrobe). For her performance Weiss changed the title to "*Toma el video abuelita y enséñame tu ropero*" (Grandmother, take the video and show me your wardrobe). In the first case Weiss claims an oppositional voice akin to that of revolutionary leader Ricardo Flores Magón, and in the latter case she positions video as the archival technology that would allow us to view and record our past. That is, we no longer need the keys to our grandmother's wardrobe—we just need to give her a video camera to record and access our memories.

In a series of documentaries she produced for TV UNAM Weiss used irreverent visual allegories as a surreptitious mode of critique. In *Freud-hombre* (1978, 12 min.) she re-creates the life of the psychoanalyst Sigmund Freud through images that fade in and out against a backdrop of pink fluorescent effects and psychedelic spirals.[74] The final sequence of the video shows a series of images of nude female bodies taken from famous paintings combined with live video shots, while the voice of the narrator explains the relation between the patient and the psychoanalyst (fig. 59). Weiss implies that the patient takes the position of the object of the gaze—a nude, reclining female body—while the psychoanalyst is mainly fulfilling his voyeuristic desires.

In *Sol o águila* (1980, 27 min.), images of the Teotihuacán ruins, the Mayan Calendar, and popular renditions of the Aztecs are fused with shots of poor people walking on the streets of Mexico City; at the same time, an image of a Mexican peso spins up into the air.[75] The viewer is left to guess whether the coin flip will come out heads (*sol*) or tails (*águila*). The choice

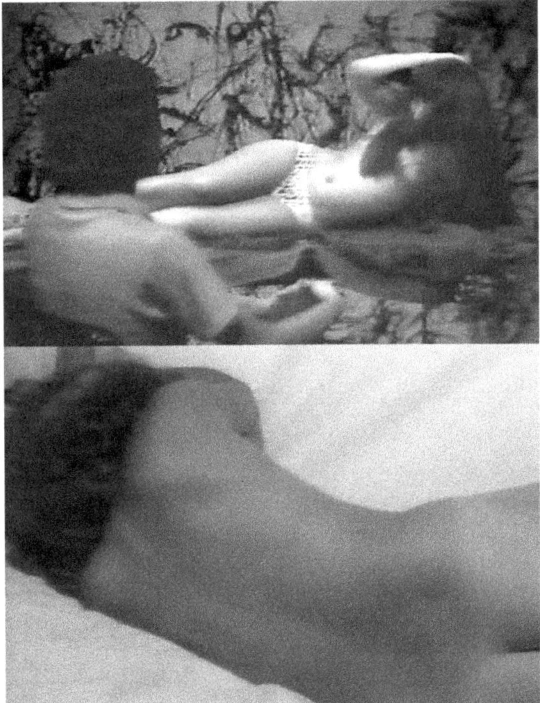

FIG. 59. *Freud-hombre.* © 1979 by Pola Weiss. Catalogación Edna Torres-Ramos, Centro de Documentación ARKEHIA, Museo Universitario Arte Contemporáneo, UNAM.

is between the living indigenous migrants begging on the streets of Mexico City or a mythical pre-Hispanic past: this is sarcastic commentary on government leaders' use of Mexico's indigenous past and present for their own means and interests (fig. 60). In *Las tazas de interés* (1983, 6 min.), porcelain teacups swirl and move up and down the screen; this visual allegory for the fluctuation of interest rates provides sarcastic commentary on Mexico's preparations to embrace a neoliberal economic model to escape the economic stagnation of the early 1980s.[76]

El Salto 1 and 2 (1982, 13 min.) is perhaps the most representative video in this series, as it is the only video in which Weiss literarily addresses feminist political concerns (fig. 61).[77] The video was supposed to be a documentary about the life and thinking of Karl Marx; however, Weiss's interpretation of Marx turns into a commentary on how visual thinking and art could

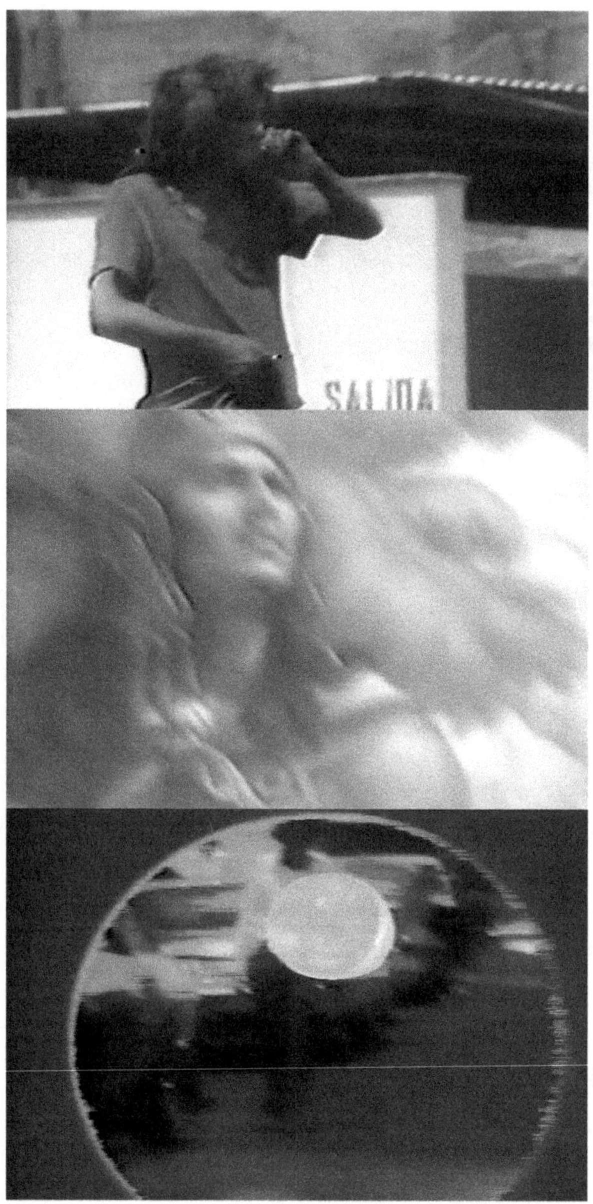

FIG. 60. *Sol o águila.* © 1980 by Pola Weiss. Catalogación Edna Torres-Ramos, Centro de Documentación ARKEHIA, Museo Universitario Arte Contemporáneo, UNAM.

lead to the emancipation of women. According to some sources, the video was not well received at UNAM.[78] The video fuses and layers a series of historical images depicting many women performing different kinds of activities as well as objects that are identified as feminine—including a woman's jewelry box. The sequence ends by fading into images of women demanding suffrage rights on the streets. Marx appears as a still image with a mouth that moves like a puppet over a series of vocal arrangements, stating that: "Marx, Capital, Labor, Marx, Class Struggle . . . The force of women, power of change is in your hands; women can change if they can tell what they see; women work with their minds."[79]

The final image sequence is a profile of a woman in whose head a video screen opens—like a window into her mind—in which we see a hand writing the word *arte* (art), an image of Weiss at her desk, and most significant, an image of the cover of *Fem*, the feminist magazine that Alaíde Foppa and Margarita García Flores established in Mexico City in 1976. Weiss was never associated with the feminist movement in Mexico, but this video shows that while she was perhaps not a militant, Weiss did have a very particular feminist sensibility that crucially informed her role as a visual *letrada*. Her video camera was the tool of labor and her capital. Other examples in her series of documentaries show that Weiss was searching for an audiovisual vocabulary and a style of narration that was playfully fragmented and tactile so that she could reach potential audiences and show them how to see differently.[80]

Mi ojo es mi co-ra-zón: The Return to the City as Allegory of the Female Body

In the aftermath of the 1985 earthquake that destroyed parts of Mexico City, and coinciding with the increased affordability of video equipment, a number of independent projects and production houses emerged throughout Mexico.[81] Different approaches to and uses of video began to emerge. In 1986, a year after the earthquake, Weiss revisited the approach to the city as an allegory of the female body that she had established with *Somos mujeres* and *Ciudad-mujer-ciudad*. In Weiss's best-known video, *Mi corazón* (1986,

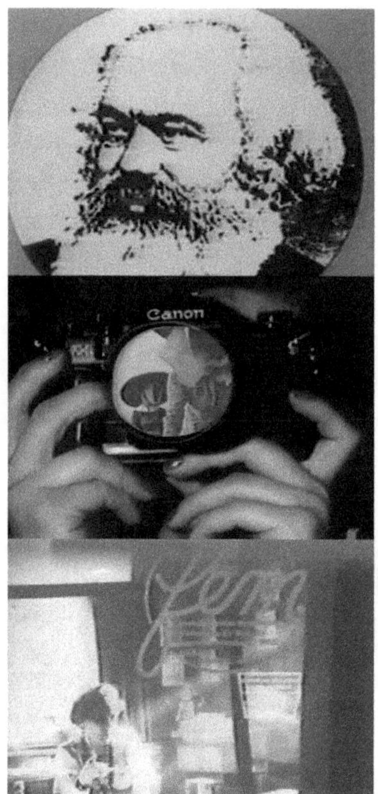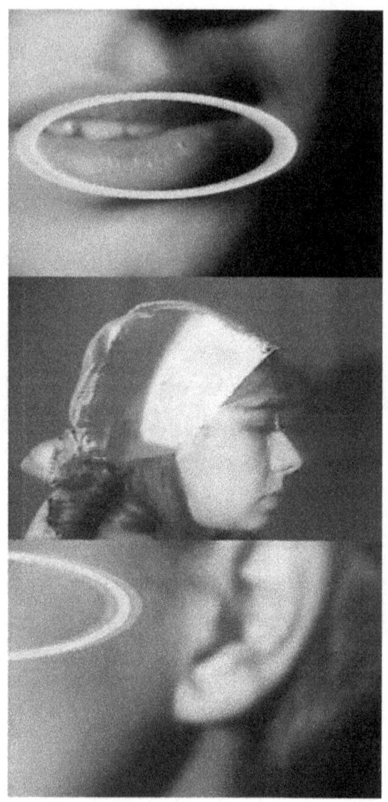

FIG. 61. *El Salto I y II*. © 1983 by Pola Weiss. Catalogación Edna Torres-Ramos, Centro de Documentación ARKEHIA, Museo Universitario Arte Contemporáneo, UNAM.

10 min.), she uses the destruction of the city as an allegory of her abortion.[82] In the video we see her body bleeding as images of destruction and chaos after the earthquake fade in and out. As Weiss dances to the beating of a heart, a collage of images of the rescue effort after the earthquake blends with hospital images and photos of her childhood. Mexico City is broken, and so is she (fig. 62).

The video begins with a series of close-ups of Weiss's mouth, each image with one syllable of the phrase *mi co-ra-zón* layered on top of it. Each image is accompanied by Weiss's voice uttering the syllable that is written on the

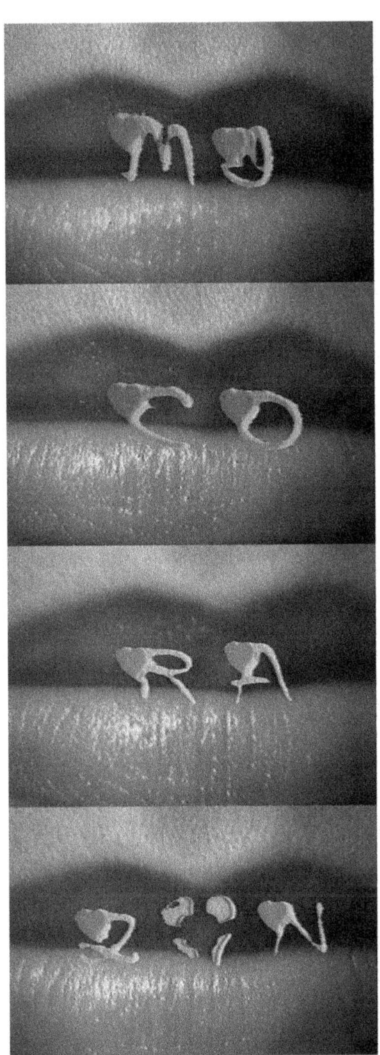 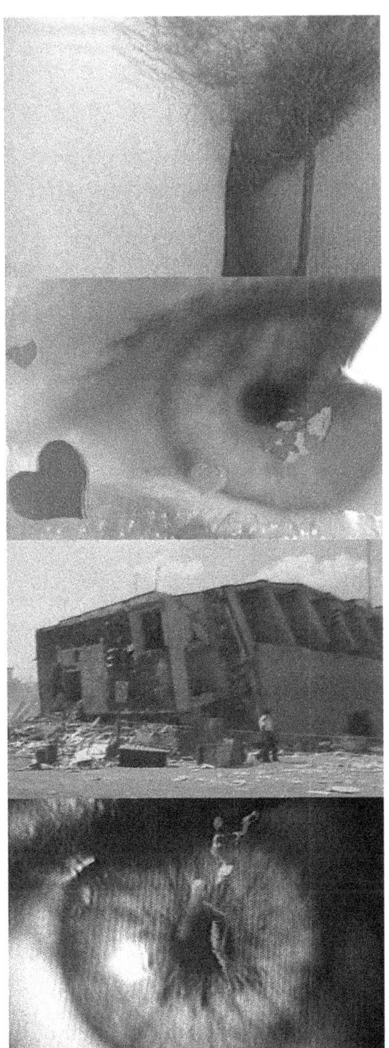

FIG. 62. *Mi ojo es mi corazón.* © 1986 by Pola Weiss. Catalogación Edna Torres-Ramos, Centro de Documentación ARKEHIA, Museo Universitario Arte Contemporáneo, UNAM.

screen, layered on top of the mouth that enunciates the sounds. We hear her voice and we see her mouth: the sound is not disembodied. Her voice continues: "*Mi ojo es mi co-ra-zón* (My eye is my heart).[83] For Weiss, there is no difference between the inside and the outside—what she sees and what she feels. Weiss blends her body with the camera.

Weiss's eye is a camera. Images of the city and her body fuse into each other. She is part of the city and the city is part of her. If the city is turned inside out, so is she. As Rita Eder proposes, Weiss's production creates an archive of images that suggests an interest in self-representation and interrupting and creating different visual signals and ways of decoding them: the relation between voice and place, and eye and heart; the city as an allegory of the body; the body as self-knowledge; the camera as mirror.[84] But *Mi corazón* also links the private with the public—Weiss's abortion with the earthquake—in a manner that speaks of an interest in producing a record of an important event. In developing a narrative out of fragments of images of her childhood, her abortion, and the city in ruins, she inscribes her history in relation to an urban landscape that is also the seat of government: the place from which hegemonic discourses and ways of being and seeing are dictated. *Mi corazón* is also a visual archive of a city in ruins: a record of a moment that has been narrated as a watershed period in the history of Mexican civil society.[85] Weiss's work, like that of Jiménez, Fernández, and Mayer, functions as an archive for an alternative narration of the development of a civil society, a narrative that considers the importance of a feminist sensibility engaged in the production of historical records through an emphasis on female self-representation (both visually and politically). In *Mi corazón* Weiss turns a recurrent feminist art strategy—using her sexualized female body against a hegemony of masculine ways of seeing—into one that challenges what counts as history and who counts as a historian by assuming herself as the object and the subject of representation and as an allegory of the city. This focus on the relation between the body and the city connects all the visual letradas I discuss and points to the transformations in the gendering and spheres of action of the letrado tradition that gave rise to alternative regimes of media and visuality. These regimes placed the city as a crucial actor in producing and reproducing gendered subjectivities prompting a reconfiguration of the cultural geographies of Mexico City. By championing video production as a valid form of knowledge production and using the female body as an allegory of the city, Weiss contests the masculine hold of the letrados in producing myths of tradition and power. Here Weiss no longer writes the city but visualizes it as a feminized space—that is, as a place where diverse female subjectivities are co-constructed and reproduced, not as passive subjects but rather as agents of their own representation.

Transnational Networks, Forms of Erasure, and Other Video Visual Letradas

Other approaches to video making and transnational and local networks of production began to develop as Weiss was producing *Mi corazón*. Some aimed to develop independent means of communication, while others were more interested in institutionalizing video as an art practice. For instance, Francis García and members of Redes Cine y Video continued with the tradition established by Cooperativa de Cine Marginal and other earlier super-8 film collectives interested in producing alternative networks of information.[86] They independently produced and distributed videos documenting the demands and fights of worker and student unions in the 1980s.[87] Meanwhile, Rafael Corkidi became instrumental in establishing a program of Video Biennials and promoting video as an artistic practice.[88] Also in the mid-1980s, Sarah Minter, Gregorio Rocha, and Andrea Di Castro began to produce video work that would garner international attention.

Sarah Minter (1953–2016) is of particular relevance, since her practice represents the generation of visual letradas that came after Pola Weiss and continued to explore the relation between the urban landscape and the construction of embodied subjectivities. After working as a graphic designer and a super-8 filmmaker, Minter began producing videos in 1982 and taught video production at La Esmeralda in Mexico City.[89] Like Weiss, Minter acquired her video equipment independently through her own means and connections.[90] Between 1985 and 1986 she produced *Nadie es inocente*, a

56-minute video that fused a fictional narrative with a documentary about a punk gang, Los Mierdas Punks, from Neza, an underprivileged sector of Mexico City also known as Nezahualcóyotl. At a time when punk music in public spaces was heavily policed and Neza was the site of constant gang confrontations, Minter befriended Los Mierdas Punk and followed them through their sojourns, fights, heartbreaks, and arrests.[91] The experience with Los Mierdas Punk deeply marked Minter's initial overt political approach to video making that followed an earlier established documentary/fiction tradition espoused by Cine-Mujer. Minter also developed a more experimental body of video work, but when I interviewed her in 2010, she had returned to her documentary roots. She was finishing *Nadie es inocente 20 años después* (2010–11), in which she traces what happened with Los Mierdas Punk over twenty years.[92] While at first *Nadie es inocente* was not well received because of the harsh realities it presented, it was shown at several international festivals, including Havana Film Festival.

Parallel to these developments, in 1980, Martha Colmenares, Álvaro Vásquez, Fernando Hernández Mata, and Inocencio Mena established the Zapotec video collective K-Chon Video Cine Zapoteca. All from the Zapotec region of Oaxaca, these artists had migrated to Mexico City in the early 1970s to study for different careers and had returned to their communities in the late 1970s.[93] The K-Chon collective's use of video stemmed from an interest in producing newsletters and photomurals to disseminate information about community and assembly meetings throughout the Chinantec and Zapotec regions of Oaxaca.[94] The K-Chon collective, and especially Colmenares's participation, is of interest because the group not only represents another way of seeing but also exemplifies other independent networks of production, anticipating several government-funded programs that would promote the use of video as tool of indigenous self-representation.[95] As seasonal migrants in the United States, K-Chon members acquired their video equipment with wages earned as farm workers in California. By 1987 the Institute of Indigenous Affairs (INI) began to organize and sponsor video workshops in indigenous communities through a program called Transferencia de Medios Audiovisuales a Comunidades

Indígenas (TMA), as part of its aim to pluralize entrenched indigenista practices, by teaching and giving indigenous communities access to newly available technology. Like the institutionalization of video art, programs to promote the production of video in indigenous communities became formally established in the 1990s.[96] Through networks of migration, the videos of the members of the K-Chon collective became known among other migrant communities in California, which also began to support video production in their own regions in Mexico.[97]

In the 1980, New York journalist Karen Ranucci put together a video compilation of Latin American media that included video productions by the K-Chon collective, Sarah Minter, and Cine-Mujer.[98] This compilation is interesting on two levels. First, it points to both the local and transnational networks that gave rise to Mexican media in 1970s and 1980s. Art, video, film, and photography could no longer be framed through a nationalistic perspective; cosmopolitan, migrant, and political networks of production and exchange broke with such national bounds. Second, as one of the first compilations of Latin American independent media, Ranucci's compilation set a particular standard for what would be considered political and independent media in Latin America for an international audience. Minter's work *Video Road* (1985), shot on super-8 film and transferred to video, is a collage of images of a road trip through Mexico. *Amas de casa* (1984), from Cine-Mujer, is a testimonial video of the experiences of a group of housewives evicted by their landlords.[99] *Nuestro tequio* (1984), by the K-Chon collective, documents community work (*tequio*) in the Zapotec community of Yalalag (the same community shot by Lola Álvarez Bravo in the 1940s). In Ranucci's words, "The video depicts hundreds of Zapotecs coming together from the surrounding villages to put on a new roof for a building that took more than three years to construct."[100] These works were all part of the collection. Absent from the compilation of Mexican independent media are Weiss's experimental videos and media theories. Also absent are the earlier works of Cine-Mujer (1976–79) that focus on abortion and rape. While these exclusions could be coincidental, this selection developed a narrative of women making media in Mexico that erased Pola Weiss from the trajectory. It denied her approach to video as "Latin American" or "political."

By weaving together the practices and relations of all these women, my aim is to break the silencing mechanisms producing compilations of Latin American history that bind artistic production to a projection of desires and that fail to examine diverse feminist sensibilities and networks of exchange and production. In broad strokes, the events and networks Weiss laid out through her video practice were fragments within a set of histories that would set in motion a new generation of visual letradas, from indigenous video producers such as Teófila Palafox to internationally known Mexican video artists like Ximena Cuevas.

Pola Weiss's practice not only broke with dominant ways of seeing and representing the female body but also championed video production and television broadcasting as media that could develop an awareness of embodied forms of perception and knowledge. With precarious means, she developed a body of work loaded with a complex feminist sensibility that allowed for an existential search and political engagement. As a pioneer, she was able to foresee the future uses of audiovisual technology. Her eccentric approach was, at times, idealistic, but it represented a political engagement that anticipated relations between technology and the self. In particular, Weiss's use of the body as an allegory of the city speaks to the battle of representation (visual and in formal politics) that was taking place throughout the streets of Mexico City. Her approach alludes to the importance that the capital city has had in forging myths of tradition and power, previously the exclusive territory of the letrados. Weiss turns this tradition around. The city is no longer written by the letrado, or visualized by the letrado (García and López); the city is a female body and the site of Weiss's personal experiences. By visualizing the connection between her personal experience and the urban landscape, Weiss's practice points to the transformations that I have been arguing for throughout this book: the feminization of the cultural geographies of Mexico City and the concomitant emergence of new regimes of media and visuality.

Conclusion
NEW AND EMERGENT VISUAL LETRADAS

The emergence of the visual letradas mapped in this book suggests new ways of thinking about the role of feminisms in developing new regimes of media and visuality as well as in transforming existing ones in post-1968 Mexico. In contrast to the closed disciplinary focus and national parameters that have characterized the twentieth-century Mexican historiography of feminisms, media, art, and women's history, this book emphasizes the interconnections between these fields; it does so by focusing on three main categories—the city, the archive, and the media—all previously conceived as masculine territories in which letrados mediated and produced myths of power, tradition, and knowledge. By bringing an interdisciplinary, local, and transnational lens to bear on these categories and by showing how visual letradas appropriated them as key spheres of action, this project narrates how normative representations of the female body (visually and in formal politics) were contested throughout Mexico City and how, in turn, such challenges affected and effected politics.

Much as it was for those letrados featured in the work of Angel Rama, the city (both physical and imagined) was the site of mediation, contestation, and articulation for the visual letradas I have discussed. Indeed, all the visual letradas considered here lived in Mexico City and understood that in Mexico during the 1970s, the fight for representation and the struggle for meaning occurred and were articulated against and within "the place where hegemonic meaning is established and from which it is dissemi-nated."[1] Ana Victoria Jiménez, Rosa Martha Fernández, Mónica Mayer, Pola

Weiss, and all the activists who participated in feminist demonstrations made Mexico City their battleground.

The centralized cultural and political structure of Mexico, as well as its "apparent stability" (compared to other Latin American countries), made Mexico City a privileged world capital for many in the 1970s and well into the 1980s, when a neoliberal economic model was implemented and a democratic transition of power was planned. Such restructurings would set in motion a process of decentralization and privatization that would give more power to media conglomerates and private corporations and would open up more avenues of expression and action for women and other marginalized sectors of the population in other regions of the country—a process that took shape in the 1970s and in which feminist activists played a crucial role.

By the mid-1980s many militants of the early 1970s feminist collectives developed links with urban and rural popular and women's organizations as well with grassroots organizations, which grew into a trend of feminism labeled as *feminismo popular* (popular feminism). This transformation was motivated by a number of factors that produced important changes in the geographies of Mexico City during this decade. One of these was the political reform enacted in 1979 by President José López Portillo (1976–82). Despite well-documented corruption and embezzlement scandals, it was at this time that the existence of opposition parties in Mexican political practice, however flawed, came to be formalized. This reform would be crucial for many feminist groups and for many women who would gain access to political posts in opposition parties.

The emergence of a wider mobilization of women also set in motion a process of institutionalization and professionalization. On the one hand, this process set autonomous feminists against popular feminists, while on the other hand, it marked the entrance of 1970s activists into formal politics and the establishment of women's studies and gender studies in academia. Important avenues for political action became available to women in Mexico as a result of these processes. However, while studies of the formal political achievements of new wave feminisms have been undertaken, and the careers of several activists have been explored, the role of creative forms of expression across disciplines and through diverse performative practices in changing the terms of civic engagement, politics, and regimes of media and visuality have, for the most part, been ignored.

López Portillo's administration also ushered the Mexican economy into a period of severe financial crisis that would prompt a change in policy toward neoliberal economics under the administration of President Miguel de la Madrid (1982–88). Visual artists were not immune to the crisis, and many collectives dissolved as artists shed the ideals of collectivism to establish individual careers and participate in newly established private art markets or to earn a living through other means. During López Portillo's tenure the private sector, both national and transnational, was encouraged to participate in the arts. This encouragement gave a boost to the Mexican art market and led to the inclusion of many Mexican artists in international markets. Televisa became a major protagonist of this process when it financed the construction of the Museo de Arte Rufino Tamayo (1981) and opened the Cultural Center for the Arts, both in Mexico City (1987). During the 1980s several self-declared feminist art collectives were established and disbanded in Mexico City, including Jiménez's Tlacuilas y Retrateras (1983–84) and Mayer's Polvo de Gallina Negra (1983–93). While the Museo de Arte Carillo Gil (established in 1974), a museum supported by private and state funding, did support several exhibitions of feminist art, the work was generally met with harsh criticism and was not active in the art market. By the 1990s a new generation of artists began to establish collectives and alternative spaces. The politics that drove the 1970s and early 1980s collectives—including feminism—were then shed for an interest in participating in the global languages of contemporary art, effectively erasing the histories of this earlier period. These new generations of artists were supported by the Consejo Nacional para la Cultura y las Artes (CONACULTA, 1988) and Fondo Nacional para la Cultura y las Artes (FONCA, 1989), two state intuitions President Carlos Salinas de Gortari (1988–94) established to foster and protect cultural production as part of his decentralization and privatization measures in the cultural sector. In conjunction with national and international corporate funding, CONACULTA and FONCA fostered the introduction of these generations of young Mexican artists into the international market to promote and update the image of Mexican culture as the country prepared to sign the North American Free Trade Agreement (NAFTA, 1992). Artists such as Gabriel Orozco (b. Jalapa, Veracruz, 1962), Miguel Calderón (b. Mexico City, 1971), and Francis Alÿs (b. Belgium, 1951) have been discussed as ambassadors of this process, which was backed by a generation of curators eager to ease the burden of the nationalistic framework through which Mexican art had traditionally been consumed both nationally and internationally.[2] This process entailed an effective disavowal of the experimental practices of Mexican artists working in the 1970s.

By the late 1990s scholars all over the world began to revise the histories of conceptual art to incorporate artists from previously marginalized regions as meaningful players, including Latin American artists working in the 1970s.[3] By the end of the first decade of the twenty-first century two revisionist projects in Mexico had already attempted to historicize the role of Mexican artists working in the 1970s as part of a global history of conceptual art.[4] In particular the curators of the exhibition *La era de la discrepancia: Arte y cultura visual en México, 1968–1997* approached this revision through the interdisciplinary framework of visual culture rather than art. In doing so, they hoped to dismantle the limitations of art historical analysis that classifies cultural forms according to "high and low" categories or according to discipline based on media specificity (photography, painting, film, sculpture). However, the narrative of *La era de la discrepancia* is premised upon the boundaries between media specialization and artist prestige; the practices of visual letradas and new wave feminisms, key for visual studies, are, as a result, mostly disregarded. As I have shown, feminist scholars and artists have engaged in a global interrogation of visuality and representation since the 1960s, providing a crucial framework of analysis for visual culture. My contribution to this current reframing is to insist that the practices of visual letradas working in Mexico City were theoretical engagements in and of themselves that critically interrogated established regimes of media and visuality in post-1968 Mexico. Visual letradas showed how gender and sexual differences were inscribed in a diverse range of cultural forms by positioning visuality and performativity as key forms of political representation.

In this context, studying the creative practices of a group of diversely minded feminist artists and activists based in Mexico City, and the local and transnational networks they forged, contributes to a more nuanced understanding of the legacies of feminisms in the histories of post-1968 Mexico in at least three ways. First, it confirms the existence of a diverse range of feminist demands beyond politics as formally defined. Second, it locates the practices of Mexican feminist-minded artists within a wider political geography of feminist artists, activists, and theorists interested in unveiling the ways in which visual representations create and reproduce patriarchal power relations within their production, distribution, and reception. And last, it shows how the advent of audiovisual technologies opened avenues of expression to a diverse spectrum of women and, in turn, how these women played an important role in transforming fields of power and knowledge previously deemed masculine territories.

In the summer of 2000, several months before Vicente Fox became Mexico's president, and signaling the temporary end of the PRI's seventy-one-year rule, a new generation of media-savvy visual letradas rekindled the battle for female representation in the streets of Mexico City. These visual letradas continued to propose that a transition to democracy should include women's right to return the gaze; that is, to represent themselves across media and by means of many practices. Between July and August 2000, a series of billboards surreptitiously appeared in ten of the busiest intersections in Mexico City. The billboards attacked El Palacio de Hierro, one of the oldest department stores in the city, for its *Soy totalmente palacio* (I am totally Palacio) ad campaign, which sexualized, racialized, and promoted consumerism among Mexican women.[5] Lorena Wolffer (b. Mexico City, 1971), an artist and cultural activist, was behind the counter ad campaign.[6]

In this, Wolffer was responding to Ana María Olabuenaga (b. Mexico City, 1960), the creative director of the advertising firm Teran TBWA, responsible for designing and launching the internationally recognized ad campaign, *Soy totalmente palacio*. Olabuenaga's objective was to enhance the image of El Palacio de Hierro among Mexican female consumers and position the store above Liverpool, its main competitor.[7] The most popular media format in the *Soy totalmente palacio* campaign was a series of billboards with witty slogans accompanied by images of thin, tall, white or light-skinned women in luxurious landscapes, positioning El Palacio de Hierro's products as an integral part of Mexican women's lifestyles, desires, and attitudes as Mexico became an economic partner of the United States and Canada:

> Because a psychoanalyst would never understand the curative power of a dress.
>
> Because only a good wife avoids going shopping often.
>
> There are two things that a woman can't avoid: crying and buying shoes.
>
> Every day there are fewer princes, but fortunately there are more Palacios.
>
> The curious thing is that what a housewife loves are the stores.[8]

Following the strategy of many female lifestyle magazines, *Soy totalmente palacio* appropriated and twisted feminist aspirations for an independent and professional lifestyle. Their campaign constructs an image of a woman no longer interested in attracting a man or being a good housewife: it posits consumerism, beauty, and luxury as forms of female empowerment. That this elitist, racist lifestyle, unattainable for the majority of the Mexican population, was promoted throughout Mexico City was perhaps not surprising. Since the beginnings of the print industry, advertising campaigns have produced lifestyle aspirations that target women, and as many have argued, these ads offer insight into changes in gender relations, attitudes, and aspirations as well as competing political and economic interests.[9] However, what is of importance here is to map out the emergent generation of visual letradas who continue to fight the war for representation and articulate the battle through the same spheres of action used by the visual letradas of the 1970s.

Despite major attempts at dismantling its symbolic standing, Mexico City is still one of the most important sites for the articulation and contestation of meaning at a national level. Indeed, in October 1996, when a masked and traditionally dressed Comandante Ramona of the Ejército Zapatista de Liberación Nacional (EZLN) finally reached *el Zócalo* to participate in the National Indigenous Forum and famously declared "*Nunca más un México sin nosotros*"[10] (Never again a Mexico without us), she most likely encountered a city plastered with *Soy totalmente palacio* billboards that denied both her presence in the city and her lifestyle. However, Ramona's performance at *el Zócalo* made visible another kind of visual letrada who, like Olabuenaga and Wolffer, was also the product of Mexico's democratic transition. The visibility of this visual letrada was also enabled by transformations that led to the process of democratization, including the feminization of several spheres of action previously deemed masculine territories through the active participation of an earlier generation of visual letradas in these fields.

Wolffer's 2000 counter ad campaign, *Soy totalmente de hierro*, used the same media strategy designed by Olabuenaga, but her model was a medium-built, dark-skinned woman not placed in a luxurious setting. Wolffer located her model in a quotidian urban setting and framed her image with witty slogans that, according to the artist, directly responded to the ways in which Olabuenaga's campaign manipulated the female body and reinscribed stereotypes of femaleness:[11]

> Not a single advertisement campaign is capable of silencing my voice.
>
> The problem is that you think that my body belongs to you.
>
> The curious thing is that you think that you can control my image.
>
> Who teaches you how to be a woman? [12]

With close affinities to Mayer's *El tendedero*, one of the billboards produced by Wolffer speaks to everyday street encounters that sexualize female bodies through touch or innuendo. It shows a defiant woman with arms crossed in the foreground framed by the slogan "*Este es mi palacio y soy totalmente de hierro*" (This is my palace and I am made of steel), while a group of men approaches the woman from behind. Indeed, much like Mayer's *El tendedero*, Jiménez's photographs, Fernández's movies, Weiss's videos, and the feminist demonstrations discussed in this project, Wolffer, Olabuenaga, and Comandante Ramona use the streets of Mexico City and the female body as the sites in which to fight for political representation and specific constructions of femininity. All use different media and practices that construct audio, visual, and embodied archives of different female experiences and subjectivities to do so. Wolffer, Olabuenaga, and Comandante Ramona make use of regimes of media and visuality that have been opened up through a long process of transformation in historically constituted fields of power and knowledge. Beginning with Jiménez's *madrinas*, these fields have changed and will keep doing so as new modes of female experience continue to be explored through the city and the archive, across regimes of media and visuality.

NOTES

INTRODUCTION

1. Out of the fifty-nine artists participating in the show, thirty-three were based or born in Mexico and the rest were from other parts of the world. Magali Lara, Mónica Mayer, Pola Weiss, Silvia Naranjo, and Jesúsa Rodríguez were the only women included in the show. See Museo de Arte Moderno, *Salon 77, Bienal de Febrero: Nuevas Tendencias*.
2. Spieker, *The Big Archive*, 1, 24.
3. Eichhorn, *The Archival Turn in Feminism*.
4. I use the term new wave feminisms (*feminismo de la nueva ola*) to refer to 1970s feminisms because this is the term used by Ana Victoria Jiménez. However, it should be noted that the use of the waves metaphor to distinguish ideological differences and phases of activity and inactivity to explain different historical periods within the histories of feminism has been under scrutiny by numerous scholars. For debates on the use of the term in Mexico see Bartra et al., *Feminismo en México, ayer y hoy*.
5. Foucault, *The Birth of Biopolitics*, and for a definition of visuality see Mirzoeff, *The Right to Look*.
6. These shifts are described in García Canclini, *Hybrid Cultures*, and Franco, *The Decline and Fall of the Lettered City*, although neither specifically points to the emergence of new feminism as being a factor that influenced such shifts.
7. Rama, *The Lettered City*.
8. González Echevarría, *Myth and Archive*, 46.
9. Monsiváis, "Foreword: When Gender Can't Be Seen amid the Symbols," 4.
10. Burns, *Into the Archive*, 3.
11. Gruzinski and MacLean, *Images at War*; Adelman, "Latin American Longue Durées," 223–37; Rappaport and Cummins, *Beyond the Lettered City*.
12. Richard, *Masculine/Feminine*, 21–28.

13. Lefebvre, *The Production of Space*; Kofman and Lebas, *Writing on Cities*.

14. Besides Nelly Richard, I am drawing primarily from the work of Grosz, *Space, Time, and Perversion*; Massey, *Space, Place, and Gender*; Butler, *Gender Trouble*; and de Lauretis, *Technologies of Gender*. For other studies that rely on the concept of embodiment to discuss the work of contemporary artists who use new media and performance, see Jones, *Self/Image*; and Schneider, *The Explicit Body in Performance*.

15. Lindón, "Diálogo con Néstor García Canclini," 89–99.

16. Appadurai defines mediascapes as "image-centered, narrative based accounts of strips of reality." Appadurai, *Modernity at Large*, 34–36.

17. In the catalogue of the exhibition other mentions of feminist art in Mexico include a list of artists who participated in an exhibition held as part of "El Primer Simposio Mexicano-Centroamericano de Investigaciones sobre la Mujer," held at the Mexican Institute of Fine Arts in Mexico City on November 7–30, 1977, and an invitation to the art exhibit of Mexican women artists held in Berlin in 1981. Other Latin American artists who produced work in the region included in the exhibition were Sonia Andrade, Iole de Freitas, and Lygia Clark from Brazil; Marta Minujín from Argentina; and Cecilia Vicuña and Catalina Parra from Chile; see Butler and Mark, *WACK!: Art and the Feminist Revolution*, 473, 488. Since then *el tendedero* has been reinstalled in different venues and on numerous occasions to raise awareness about violence against women—most prominently in 2016 at Mónica Mayer's individual retrospective at MUAC, *Mónica Mayer: Sí tiene dudas . . . pregunte: Una exposición retrocolectiva*—and in 2017 it was featured in *Radical Women: Latin American Art, 1960–1985* at the Hammer Museum in Los Angeles.

18. Cosío Villegas, *El estilo personal de gobernar*; Schmidt, *The Deterioration of the Mexican Presidency*; Agustín, *Tragicomedia mexicana no. 2*; Sánchez Susarrey, *El debate político e intelectual en México*.

19. The exhibition *La era de la discrepancia* curated by Debroise and Medina in 2006 spearheaded this trend. Some of the work that came out with reference to Los Grupos includes Decker, *Los Grupos and the Art of Intervention*; and Murillo and García de Germenos, *Grupo Proceso Pentágono*.

20. Some exceptions to this trend at the time of research include García, Millán, and Pech, *Cartografías del feminismo mexicano*, and Gutiérrez Castañeda, *Feminismo en México*.

21. In the summer of 2009 many artists and academics gathered to discuss the condition of artists' archives in Mexico through a series of roundtable panels organized as part of the exhibition of *Arte (no es) Vida. Acciones por artistas de las*

Américas 1960–2000 at Museo Carillo Gil, July 3–August 13, 2009. See "Archivos del Arte Acción en México y sus vinculos en America Latina," http://revista.escaner.cl/node/1481, accessed September 16, 2009; Mónica Mayer, Maris Bustamante, Victor Muñoz, and Felipe Ehrenberg, interviews with author.

22. The UNMM was established in 1964 to unite a wide range of women's organizations mostly affiliated with the Communist Party. Reyes Castellanos and Jiménez, *Sembradoras de futuros*, 111–65. It should also be noted that the Mexican Communist Party had long played an important role in mobilizing women. For a history of PCM and its role in mobilizing women see Olcott, *Revolutionary Women in Postrevolutionary Mexico*.

23. Ana Victoria Jiménez, interview by the author, México, August 2, 2010; August 2, 2011; and telephone conversation on July 22, 2013.

24. See "Mujeres ¿y que más?: Reactivando el archivo de Ana Victoria Jiménez," http://archivoavj.com, accessed April 5, 2011.

25. Rosa Martha Fernández, interview by the author, México, September 21, 2010; David Arriaga, interview by the author, México, September 19, 2010.

26. In October 2012 a more comprehensive archive of Pola Weiss was opened to the public at ARKEHIA, the documentation center at the Museo Universitario de Arte Contemporáneo (MUAC). In 2014 Aline Hernández, Benjamin Murphy, and Edna Torres curated an exhibition in the same institution to honor the transfer of Weiss's archive to ARKEHIA. Edna Torres, electronic correspondence, November 29, 2012; Hernández and Torres Ramos, *Pola Weiss*.

27. Weiss, "*Diseño para una unidad de producción de material didactico en video tape*"; Torres Ramos, *El video arte en México*.

28. At the time I was conducting this research, only thirty-eight videos were catalogued for public viewing.

29. Weiss, *Ciudad-mujer-ciudad* (1978).

30. See Echeverría's first government report on September 1, 1971, http://www.biblioteca.tv/artman2/publish/1971_84/Primer_Informe_de_Gobierno_delpresidente_Luis_Ech_1209.shtml, accessed September 9, 2017. For a history of water management in Mexico see Wolf, *Watering the Revolution*.

31. Mónica Mayer, interview by the author, México, September 5, 2009, and July 23, 2010.

32. See "Mujeres ¿y que más?: Reactivando el archivo de Ana Victoria Jiménez"; Karen Cordero Reiman, interview by the author, México, September 3, 2010; Mónica Mayer, interview by the author, México, September 5, 2009, and July 23, 2010; and Ana Victoria Jiménez, interview by the author, México, August 2, 2010; August 2, 2011; and telephone conversation on July 22, 2013.

33. See Schmidt, *The Deterioration of the Mexican Presidency*; and Agustín, *Tragicomedia mexicana no. 2*.

34. Aguayo, *La Charola*; Doyle, "The Mexico Project"; Magdaleno Cárdenas, "Documentos sobre la Policía"; Padilla and Walker, "Spy Reports."

35. In 2002 after a long debate involving many interested parties, the Vicente Fox administration transferred the archives of Dirección Federal de Seguridad and Dirección General de Investigaciones Políticas y Sociales to the Archivo General de la Nación (hereafter DFS, DGIPS, and AGN) as part of the development of a new law regarding the freedom of information, La Ley de Transparencia y Acceso a la Información (LTAI). For more information on LTAI, see Padilla and Walker, "Spy Reports."

36. At the time I consulted them, the files of the DGIPS and feminist activism were located at Archivo General de La Nación, Galería 2.

37. Casanova and Konzevik, *Luces sobre México*.

38. Mónica Mayer, interview by the author, México, September 5, 2009, and July 23, 2010; Maris Bustamante, interview by the author, México, August 10, 2010; Victor Muñoz, interview by the author, México, September 25, 2009; and Felipe Ehrenberg, electronic communication with the author, April 13, 2011.

39. For a discussion and critique of UNESCO's proposals for preserving intangible practices, see Taylor, *The Archive and the Repertoire*, 22–25.

40. Foster, "An Archival Impulse," 22; Merewether, *The Archive*; Enwezor, *Archive Fever*.

41. Stoler uses this term to refer to the process of re-conceptualization of archives that began to take prominence in academic circles in response to the work of Michel Foucault and Jacques Derrida. See Stoler, "Colonial Archives," 83–100.

42. Stoler, *Along the Archival Grain*; Spivak, "The Rani of Sirmur," 247–72; Burton, *Dwelling in the Archive*; Cvetkovich, *An Archive of Feelings*.

43. Taylor, *The Archive and the Repertoire*; Schneider, "Archive Performance Remains," 100–108.

44. Arondekar, *For the Record*, 2.

45. Stoler, "Colonial Archives."

46. Schneider, "Archive Performance Remains"; Muñoz, "Ephemera as Evidence," 5–16.

47. Jones, "'Presence in Absentia,'" 11–18.

48. See for example Zapata Galindo, "Feminist Movements in Mexico"; Lamas, *Feminismo: Transmisiones y retransmisiones*; Tuñon Pablos, *Mujeres en escena*; Bartra et al., *Feminismo en México, ayer y hoy*; and Lau Jaiven and Damián, *Un fantasma recorre el siglo*.

49. See for example Fernández, "La mujer Mexicana y la conciencia de la opresión."

50. La Revuelta was a feminist collective established by Bertha Hiriart, Eli Bartra, María Brumm, Chela Cervantes, Bea Faith, Lucero González, Dominque Guillement, and Ángeles Necoechea. At first they began to publish their own bulletin and later on they published a column called *El Traspatio* in the newspaper *Uno Más Uno*. See Bartra et al., *La Revuelta*; and Eli Bartra, interview by the author, México, July 29, 2011, and January 2, 2013.

51. *Fem* was established with the purpose of developing an alternative to the commercial women's magazines, such as *Cosmopolitan*, *Vanidades*, and *Kena*, which promoted consumerism and culture for the stay-home mom who always looks beautiful and ready for her husband. See Quintero, "Prensa feminista," 203–31.

52. I am referring at the seminal work by Berger, *Ways of Seeing*; Mulvey, "Visual Pleasure and Narrative Cinema," 6–18; and Nochlin, "Why Haven't There Been No Great Women Artists?"

53. For an overview of this process see Jones, *The Feminism and Visual Culture Reader*, 1–9.

1. THE OFFICIAL CITY

1. Oscar Chávez and José de La Vega, "Junio de 75," popular song. All translations are mine unless otherwise stated.

2. For more on the IWY and NGO forum, see *International Women's Year World Conference Documents* (Brok NY: UNIFO Microfiche Edition Publishers, 1975); and Olcott, "Cold War Conflicts and Cheap Cabaret," 733–54.

3. For instance, records of a system of surveillance focused on women activists and organizers in the 1960s begin in 1965, a year after the Unión Nacional de Mujeres Mexicanas was established. AGN, DGIPS, Caja 1634-B, November 1, 1965–March 2, 1979; Caja 1634-B-011, March 20–November 23, 1981; Caja 1634-B-009, June 12, 1978–February 12, 1981; and Caja 1697-C, February 1, 1977–February 7, 1981. For more information on social repression in the second half of twentieth century see Trevizo, *Rural Protest and the Making of Democracy*; Calderón and Cedillo, *Challenging Authoritarism in Mexico*; and for the histories of the secret services in Mexico see Aguayo, *La Charola*.

4. Alan Knight uses this phrase to explain how "Mexicans" endorsed the democratic and reformist goals of the 1910 Revolution, but they took a cynical view of *políticos* whose policies contradicted those goals. See Knight, "The Revolution Is Dead," 18–21.

5. González de Bustamante, *"Muy buenas noches."*

6. According to the same report the number of households in 1970 amounted to 9.9 million. González de Bustamante, *"Muy buenas noches,"* 181–82.

7. Soto Laveaga, "'Let's Become Fewer,'" 19–33.

8. See "Resolution 181 Actions Taken by the Conference, Women and Media," in *International Women's Year World Conference Documents*, 32–36.

9. While the popularity of Latin American protest songs during those years cannot be attributed to Echeverría's anti-imperialistic stand, many have argued for the ways in which Echeverría's embrace of the Latin American protest folk song worked to support his policies; however, like any other cultural expression, it also worked to counter them. See Zolov, *Refried Elvis*; and AGN, Luis Echeverría Álvarez (hereafter LEA), Caja 571, exp. 111, "Universidad del Tercer Mundo."

10. Olcott, "Cold War Conflicts and Cheap Cabaret."

11. Lau Jaiven, *La nueva ola*; Lau Jaiven and Damián, *Un fantasma recorre el siglo*.

12. Lamas, *Feminismo: Transmisiones y retransmisiones*, 17.

13. Lau Jaiven, *La nueva ola*, 143; Ramos Escandón, "Women's Movements, Feminism, and Mexican Politics," 199–221; Reyes Castellanos and Jiménez, *Sembradoras de futuros*.

14. Zapata Galindo, *Feminist Movements in Mexico*, 16–17; Ramos Escandón, "Women's Movements, Feminism, and Mexican Politics," 207; Lamas, *Feminismo: Transmisiones y retransmisiones*, 16.

15. Elvira Sánchez Navarro, "Liberación Femenina en el Senado," *Crucero*, September 20, 1974, AGN, DGIPS Caja 1634-B, November 1, 1965–March 2, 1979, exp.7, F.S. 867; various articles in *Siempre!*, num. 114, October 30, 1974.

16. Lau Jaiven, *La nueva ola*, 112.

17. Lamas, *Feminismo: Transmisiones y retransmisiones*.

18. Melchor Ocampo's epistle has been read out loud and printed in the civil matrimony contract since 1859 as part of the reforms led by President Benito Juárez. In 1974 several feminist collectives demanded the removal of Melchor Ocampo's letter from the civil matrimony contract. Since then every March 8, discussions of its removal arise in the context of women's day celebration. In 2007 the Mexican Senate began to ask state governors to remove the poem from the civil matrimony contract. See Ana Lau Jaiven, *La nueva ola*, 108; Miguel Angel de Alba, "Las Feministas Pediran a LEA que se suprima la epístola de Melchor Ocampo," *El Heraldo de Mexico*, June 3, 1975, AGN, DGIPS, Caja 1634-B, November 1, 1965–March 2, 1979, exp.7, F.S. 867, 186; and for current debates see "Pide Senado a estos sustituir epístola de Melchor Ocampo," *El Universal*, May 2, 2007; and "Se eliminará la epistola de Melchor Ocampo del DF," *La Jornada*, March 7, 2013.

19. Melchor Ocampo, *Epístola de Melchor Ocampo*, 1859.

20. Melchor Ocampo, *Epístola*.

21. Melchor Ocampo, *Epístola*.

22. The reforms were passed by Congress on December 31, 1974. "Constitución Política de los Estados Unidos Mexicanos," *Diario Oficial de la Federación*, Capitulo 1 de los Derechos Humanos y sus Garantías.

23. See "La iniciativa es un primer paso a la emancipación femenina: Proponene importantes medidas complementarias," *El Dia*, September 26, 1974.

24. Lamas, *Feminismo: transmisiones y retransmisiones*, 16; "Por una maternidad libre y gratuita" (flyer), AGN, DGIPS, Caja 1634-B, November 1, 1965–March 2, 1979, exp. 7, F.S. 867.

25. Beginning with the UN's 1965 International Conference on Population and Development in Belgrade, population growth is considered as a global problem and population control programs are encouraged. Guevara Villaseñor, "Las políticas públicas de salud," 374–99.

26. Guevara Villaseñor, "Las políticas públicas de salud."

27. Soto Laveaga notes that earlier campaign emphasis on women "Señora, usted decide si sale embarazada" (1976) was changed to "Family Planning: It's a couple's" by 1978. See "Let's Become Fewer," 25.

28. "According to information supplied by the Instituto Mexicano del Seguro Social, of the 2.6 million women of a certain fertile age who had sought treatment by the end of 1974, a total of 521,007 had accepted a form of family planning. Of these, 60% were using intrauterine devices, 25% were using oral contraceptives, 14% were using spermicidals, and 1% had surgery," cited in Soto Laveaga, "Let's Become Fewer," 23.

29. Ramírez Berg, "Women's Images I and II," 55–97.

30. Barbosa Sánchez, *Arte feminista*, 32–35.

31. Art exhibitions extolling women's creativity were organized all over the country in the context of IWY. See "Arte en la Provincia," *Excelsior*, June 21, 1975.

32. *La mujer como creadora y tema de arte* was shown at the Museum of Modern Art in June 1975. In this exhibit thirty-six men participated along with renowned Mexican women artists from various generations with work that depicted women as on object of representation. In August the show *Pintoras y escultoras en México* was held at *El Poliforum Siqueiros* and included forty-six female artists. Mónica Mayer, interview by the author, México, September 5, 2009, and July 23, 2010.

33. Barbosa, *Arte feminista*, 31.

34. Barbosa, *Arte feminista*.

35. *Artes Visuales* was a bilingual art magazine (English and Spanish) published in Mexico City by the Museum of Modern Art from 1973 to 1981 under the direction of Fernando Gamboa and Carla Stellweg. This magazine was the most important art publication of its time and played a crucial role in introducing international art movements and critics to Mexico City. Museo de Arte Moderno, *Artes Visuales. Una seleccion facsimilar: En homenaje a Fernando Gamboa* (Mexico: CONACULTA, Museo de Arte Moderno, 2010); and "Mujeres /Arte/ Femineidad," *Artes Visuales*, no. 9, Spring 1976.

36. "Mujeres /Arte/ Femineidad."

37. "Mujeres /Arte/ Femineidad," 18.

38. "Mujeres /Arte/ Femineidad," 15.

39. "Mujeres /Arte/ Femineidad," 21–25.

40. "Mujeres /Arte/ Femineidad," 21–22.

41. "Mujeres /Arte/ Femineidad," 21–22.

42. See "Zora entrevista a Judy Chicago y Arlene Raven," *Artes Visuales*, no. 9, Spring 1976, 25–29; Lucy Lippard, "¿Porque separar el arte femenino?," 31–36; Charlotte Moser, "El mundo interior y exterior del movimiento artistico femenino," *Artes Visuales*, no. 9, 37–42. For more on the Women's Art Building see http://womansbuilding.org/, accessed May 12, 2011.

43. Acevedo, "Nuestro sueño"; Lau Jaiven, *La nueva ola*; Barbosa Sánchez, *Arte feminista*.

44. Lau Jaiven, *La nueva ola*, 76–80.

45. Carla Stellweg, *Artes Visuales*, no. 9, 2.

46. Maria Eugenia Vargas de Stavenhagen, *Artes Visuales*, no. 9, 6–7.

47. See French and Bliss, *Gender, Sexuality, and Power in Latin America since Independence*, 7–8.

48. For a discussion on the state of Mexican feminist criticism in the arts, see Cordero Reiman and Sáenz, *Critica feminista*, 5–16. Barbosa Sánchez, *Arte feminista*; Villegas, *La imagen femenina en artistas mexicanas contemporáneas*; García S., *M-D1: Desbordamientos de una periferia femenina*; Mayer, *Rosa Chillante*.

49. Frérot, *El mercado del arte en México, 1950–1976*.

50. Frérot, *El mercado del arte en México, 1950–1976*, 83.

51. As students of La Esmeralda or San Carlos (the two main art schools in Mexico City, the former belonging to the Secretariat of Education, SEP, and the latter to the National University, UNAM), many students had organized the production of graphics for demonstrations and taught other students on the use of reproduction technologies such as photocopies, mimeographs,

and stencils in order to facilitate the dissemination and production of information about the movement. This was a collective experience of production that would later influence their desire to form artists' groups. Victor Muñoz, interview by the author, México, September 25, 2009.

52. Fondo "Grupo de los Setentas," Centro Nacional de Investigación, Documentación e Información de Artes Plásticas (CENIDIAP); Álvaro Vázquez Mantecón, *Fondo de Los Grupos a los individuos, 26 de Junio al 15 de Septiembre, 1985*, Biblioteca del Museo de Arte Carrillo Gil, video recordings; Cristina Híjar, *Siete grupos de artistas visuales de los setenta*; Gallo, "The Mexican Pentagon."

53. Mónica Mayer, interview by the author, México, September 5, 2009, and July 23, 2010.

54. Several of the collectives that belonged to the Los Grupos movement had exhibitions in state art venues, including the gallery José María Velasco, located in Tepito, and the Palacio de Bellas Artes. The other institutional venue that supported this emerging generation of artists in the 1970s was UNAM. Helen Escobedo was the curator of the Museo Universitario de Arte Contemporáneo (MUAC) and through this venue provided exhibition spaces for Los Grupos as well as international exhibitions of conceptual art. Guillermina Guadarrama, interview with author, México, September 1, 2009; and Guadarrama and Martínez "Una galería de arte en Tepito."

55. Alberto Híjar, interview by the author, México, September 4, 2009.

56. The Syndicate of Technical Workers, Painters, and Sculptors was part of the wealth of workers' movements that emerged at the end of the official armed conflict in Mexico in the 1920s. The best known legacy of this group of artists was the magazine *El Machete*. Members of this syndicate included David Alfaro Siqueiros, Fermin Revueltas, José Clemente Orozco, Diego Rivera, Germán Cueto, and Carlos Merida, among many others. See Híjar, *Frentes, coaliciones y talleres*.

2. THE MEDIA CITY

Epigraph: Maris Bustamante and Mónica Mayer, *Madre por un día*, 1987 VHS, Mónica Mayer's personal archive.

1. Miró Vázquez, *La televisión y el poder político en México*, 66.

2. The best known criticism of the interference of the state in cultural affairs is Paz, *El ogro filantrópico*. For other debates see Carlos Monisváis, Héctor Aguilar Camín, and José Joaquín Blanco, "INBA, nada te debo INBA, nada te temo (notas sobre el estado y la política cultural)," *La cultura en México*

suplemento de Siempre!, no. 691, May 7, 1975, vii–ix; and "Sobre el Consejo Nacional de las Artes," no. 691, May 7, 1975, xvi.

3. See José Montaño Oseguera, "Desastroza invasion de nuestros hogares," *El Universal*, November 29, 1971, AGN, DGIPS, Caja 1339-A, "Radio y Television."

4. Juan Cervera, "La TV y el Estado y el Estado y la TV," *Ovaciones*, January 11, 1972, AGN, DGIPS, Caja 1339-B, "Información General de los Estados."

5. For a review on the role of INBA, see Luis Spota, "Picaporte," *El Heraldo de México*, January 2, 1972; Paco Ignacio Taibo, "La Television y el Estado," *El Universal*, January 22, 1972, and "La televisión imaginada," *El Universal*, January 29, 1972, AGN, DGIPS, Caja 1339-B, "Información General de los Estados"; and Fernández and Paxman, *El Tigre*, 147.

6. Fernández and Paxman, *El Tigre*, 79, 142.

7. In the 1950s not one female reporter had generated news content. In contrast, of the nine reporters who filed reports on September 15, 1970, at least four were women. González de Bustamante, *"Muy buenas noches,"* 200.

8. For more on these reforms see "Integró la Cámara de Diputados una Comisón Especial para revisar la Ley Federal Vigente de Radio y Television," *Ovaciones*, July 18, 1972; "La TV debe llegar a los pobres aunque no tengan capacidad de compra: SCT," *El Sol de México*, July 13, 1972, AGN, DGIPS, Caja 1604-B, 1982, exp. 6–8; Mejía Barquera "Television y política."

9. Francisco Aguirre Jiménez was in the media business from 1946 with his family of several radio stations, Grupo Radio Centro. In 1968 he established Canal 13 and broadcast the fourth presidential address of Diaz Ordaz. For a history of Canal 13, see de la Lama and de la Lama, *El Canal 13*.

10. De la Lama and de la Lama, *El Canal 13*.

11. Canal 13 and Televisa entered a battle for the production of cultural programming, a process chronicled by García Canclini through the example of the non-televised interview between Jorge Luis Borges and Octavio Paz in 1978. See García Canclini, *Hybrid Cultures*, 101; and de la Lama and de la Lama, *El Canal 13*.

12. De la Lama and de la Lama, *El Canal 13*, 5–6.

13. González de Bustamante, *"Muy buenas noches,"* 200.

14. De la Lama and de la Lama, *El Canal 13*, 5–6.

15. See Ehrick, "Radio Transvestism," 18–36; and Gitelman, *Always Already New*.

16. For Gitelman, media are less points of "epistemic rupture than they are socially embedded sites for the ongoing negotiation of meaning." Gitelman, *Always Already New*, 6, 26.

17. For discussion on radio as embodied, see Ehrick, "Radio Transvestism"; and for a discussion on the disembodied qualities of voice, see Silverman, *The Acoustic Mirror*.

18. In 1979 the school of medicine at UNAM hosted the IV World Congress of Sexology, and de la Lama was invited by a group of doctors to direct a program on sexology. The programs *Sex 7* and *Sex o No Sex* began to air on channel 1. See Roberto Rueda Monreal, "Entrevista con Marta de la Lama: Una pionera del periodismo televisivo y política feminist," *Revista Replicante*, Seccion Apuntes y Notas, January 2012, http://revistareplicante.com, accessed January 15, 2013.

19. In 1987 Mónica Mayer and her two children were guests of *A Brazo Partido* to promote the performative action *Madres!* by Polvo de Gallina Negra; a couple of months afterward Mayer produced a live performance in the same show and proposed a video sketch, *Un año de Madres: Las madres también aman*, for de la Lama's program on sexuality *Sex 7*, see "Polvo de Gallina Negra Curriculm Vitae," in Mónica Mayer personal archive.

20. Mónica Mayer and Ana Victoria Jiménez participated in Patricia Berumen's show "De 3 en 3" in 1987 and 1989. "Polvo de Gallina Negra Curriculm Vitae," in Mónica Mayer personal archive.

21. According to Sara Lovera, reporters working for Telesistema Mexicano and Televicentro who regularly appeared in Jacobo Zabludousky's news program, including Rosa María Campos, Marcela Mendoza, and Rita Ganen, followed official discourse against feminism. Lovera, "Feminismo y medios de comunicación," 529.

22. Maris Bustamante and Monica Mayer, *Madre por un día*, 1987 VHS, Mónica Mayer personal archive.

23. Bustamante and Mayer, *Madre por un día*.

24. Mónica Mayer, interview by the author, México, September 5, 2009, and July 23, 2010.

25. Mónica Mayer, interview by the author, México, September 5, 2009, and July 23, 2010.

26. Before Bustamante and Mayer's intervention on television, the Chilean-born Alejandro Jodorowsky used television as an art medium in the 1960s. He presented his *arte efímero* in a filming of Juan López Moctezuma's show in which he played and destroyed a piano. Maris Bustamante, interview by the author, México, August 10, 2010; Barbosa Sánchez, *Arte feminista*, 69.

27. For more on the introduction of video technology to Mexico, see Picazo Sánchez, *Una década de video en México*.

28. Weiss worked as a screen writer for Televisa's programs "Debate ante la Imagen" and "La Grapa," which aired in 1972 and 1974 respectively, and in 1972 she worked for Canal 13. Pola Weiss, "Los Extrapola, se interpola Weiss (performance y videos)," in *ExtraPOLAción*, exhibition brochure (Ciudad de México: Galería Chapultepec, July 1981). Pola Weiss, Carpeta Documental, Museo de Arte Moderno; Mendiola et al., "El ritual amoroso de la bruja electrica"; Torres Ramos, *El video arte en México*.

29. Weiss, "Diseño para una unidad de producción de material didáctico en video tape," 10.

30. Naranjo and Reyes, *El condicionamiento mental a través de las imágenes*.

31. See Museo de Arte Moderno, *Video Cinta de Vanguardia, VideoArt: Estética Visual*, exhibition catalogue.

32. Hickey, "Notas sobre el video subterranero."

33. Juan Acha, "El arte del video tape encontra de la t.v.," in *Diaroma Cultural de Excelsior* (n.d.), document no. 000059, Fondo *Márgenes Conceptuales, La era de la discrepancia*; ARKEHIA, MUAC.

34. Fernández and Paxman, *El Tigre*, 197.

35. Weiss, *La TV TE VE*.

36. Garibay Mora, "El video arte."

37. Sandra Shaul, "Video arte, Museo de Arte Alvar y Carmen T. Carrillo Gil, Mexico DF," *Artes Visuales*, no. 17, March–May 1978.

38. See Mendiola et al., "El ritual amoroso de la bruja electrica"; Carrasco, "Pola Weiss: La cineasta olvidada."

39. For a review of Latin American cinema see Martin, *New Latin American Cinema*.

40. Roberto Echeverría, cited in Mraz, *Looking for Mexico*, 206.

41. The Cineteca consisted of two film theaters, an exhibition space, a library, and bookstore as well as specialized storage for film archiving and preservation. In 1982 the building and almost 99 percent of the film archive were destroyed due to a fire. See Magadalena Acosta, "Dos décadas del incendio en la Cineteca," *La Jornada*, March 23, 2002.

42. Mraz, *Looking for Mexico*, 206.

43. For a review of Mexican films produced from 1973 to 1985, see Ayala Blanco's *La condición del cine mexicano*.

44. For more on independent cinema or Nuevo Cine in Mexico see Méndez, "Hacia un cine político"; Vázquez Mantecón, "Contracultura e ideología en los inicios del cine mexicanos en super-8"; Millán, *Derivas de un cine en femenino*. For a review of the films produced from 1973 to 1985 in Mexico see

Ayala Blanco, *La condición del cine mexicano*, and Ramírez Berg, *Cinema of Solitude*.

45. A particular focus of concern was the film production workers' union (Sindicato de Trabajadores de la Producción Cinematiográfica, stpc), which was in charge of Estudios Churubusco and the production of long features. Millán, *Derivas de un cine en femenino*.

46. Méndez, "Hacia un cine político."

47. In fact one of the emergent groups had launched a manifesto entitled *Ocho milimetros contra ocho millones* to critique the 8-million-peso production of *Zapata* (dir. Felipe Cazals, 1970) financed by Echeverría. Vázquez Mantecón, "Contracultura e ideología en los inicios del cine mexicanos en super-8."

48. For the reception of "third cinema" and *"cine imperfecto"* in Mexico, see Méndez, "Hacia un cine político," and Martin, *New Latin American Cinema*.

49. Other politically inclined film collectives were Taller de Cine Octubre and Grupo Testimonio. Millán, *Derivas de un cine en femenino*, 112.

50. Méndez, "Hacia un cine político."

51. See Marta Acevedo, Marta Lamas, and Ana Luisa Ligurí, "México: Una bolsita de cal por las que van de arena"; Rosa Martha Fernández, interview by the author, México, September 21, 2010.

52. Rosa Martha Fernández, interview by the author, México, September 21, 2010.

53. Rosa Martha Fernández, interview by the author, México, September 21, 2010.

54. A whole generation of women filmmakers collaborated in Cine-Mujer, including, for example, María Novaro and Sonia Fritz, who moved to Puerto Rico to produce feminist films in the late 1980s. See Sonia Fritz's testimony in her "Annemarie Maier, Cine Mujer"; and Rashkin, *Women Filmmakers in Mexico*.

55. Millán, *Derivas de un cine en femenino*, 115; Rosa Martha Fernández, interview by the author, México, September 21, 2010.

56. Millán, *Derivas de un cine en femenino*, 115.

57. For more on Fernández Violante and Matilide Landeta, see Ayala Blanco, *La condicion del cine mexicano*; Rashkin, *Women Filmmakers in Mexico*; and Millán, *Derivas de un cine en femenino*; for a work that traces a break in the dual role of mother/prostitute in 1970s Mexican film see Ramírez Berg, *Cinema of Solitude*.

58. Millán, *Derivas de un cine en femenino*, 113.

59. Lau Jaiven, *La nueva ola*, 108.

60. Abelardo Villegas, "El tutuelaje masculino: La protesta feminista," *Excelsior*, June 23, 1975, 7-A.

61. Rosa Martha Fernández, interview by the author, México, September 21, 2010.

62. Fernández, "La mujer mexicana y la conciencia de la opresión."

63. Fernández, "La mujer mexicana y la conciencia de la opresión."

64. Rosa Martha Fernández, interview by the author, México, September 21, 2010.

65. Jorge Ibargüengoitia, "El dia de la invasión: La mujer liberada." *Excelsior,* June 24, 1975, 7-A.

3. THE EMBODIED CITY

1. Ana Victoria Jiménez, interview by the author, México, August 2, 2010; August 2, 2011; and telephone conversation on July 22, 2013; Rosa Martha Fernández, interview by the author, México, September 21, 2010.

2. Acevedo, "Nuestro sueño."

3. Acevedo, "Lo volvería a elegir," 4–15.

4. For a detailed discussion on the relation of the establishment of Mother's Day celebration and 1920s feminism, see Acevedo, "10 de Mayo . . . ," and Carlos Martínez Asad in Acevedo and Lamas, *40 Años de feminismo en México.*

5. Feminists' leagues began to emerge in the states of Yucatán and Tabasco during the first decades of the twentieth century. In Yucatán the governments of Salvador Alvarado (1915–18) and Felipe Carillo Puerto (1922–24) opened up spaces for the discussion of women's emancipation. In 1916 a group of feminists organized the First Feminist Congress, and in its aftermath several feminist organizations (*ligas feministas*) were established. In 1922 a manual of sexual education written by an American feminist nurse, Margaret Sanger, began to circulate through Yucatán's print media and schools, as part of a program of sexual education, causing the outrage of many conservative sectors of the population. The discussion reached the federal level and was widely discussed at a national level in the newspaper *Excelsior.* Acevedo, "10 de Mayo . . ."

6. In response to Margaret Sanger's bulletin, critics referred to "propaganda grotesca."

7. Acevedo, "Lo volvería a elegir."

8. Lau Jaiven, *La nueva ola,* 76–100; Ávila G. "Maternidad Elegida," 247; Ana Victoria Jiménez, interview by the author, México, August 2, 2010; August 2, 2011; and telephone conversation on July 22, 2013.

9. There are different accounts of the date of this event, as happening in June 1971 or June 1972. Father's Day is celebrated in Mexico on the third Sunday of the month of June, hence according to Ana Victoria Jiménez, in 1971 the meeting at Insurgentes Avenue took place two weeks after the Corpus Christi Massacre. See Ana Victoria Jiménez, interview by the author, México, August 2, 2010; August 2, 2011; and telephone conversation on July 22, 2013.

10. The literature on embodied citizenship is extensive, and the term is used interchangeably with cultural citizenship. For studies on public performances,

filmmaking, and spontaneous forms of violence as claims to embodied citizenship, see Goldstein, *The Spectacular City*; Marsh, *Brazilian Women's Filmmaking*; and Klein, "Spectacular Citizenship," 102–12. For a study on diverse public-performance practices and how the modern city is implicated in producing forms of civic engagement, see Prakash and Kruse, *The Spaces of the Modern City*.

11. Grosz, *Space, Time, and Perversion*, 104.

12. For debates about the naming of 1970s feminism, see Bartra, "Tres decádas de neofeminismo en México," 45–81.

13. Antonieta Rascón, "Feminismo de los años 70," in Acevedo and Lamas, *40 años de feminismo*.

14. See Acevedo, Lamas, and Ligurí, "México: Una bolsita de cal por dos de las que van de arena," 111–48; González Alvarado, "El espíritu de una época," 65–15; and MAS (Dulce Maria Pascual, Rocio Peraza, Antonieta Rascón and Rosalinda Tovar), "Un punto de vista sobre las reformas a los articulos 4 y 5 de la constitución: Hacia la dualidad," *Siempre!*, no. 1114, October 30, 1974, v–ix; "Hoy de las 10:35 a las 13:25 horas, con una audiencia de 200 mujeres se llevó acabo el Segundo día de audiencias públicas, en el salon de actos de la gran commission," AGN, DGIPS, Caja 1634-B, November 1, 1965–March 2, 1979, exp. 7, F.S. 867, 176–80.

15. See MAS, "Un punto de vista," and "Hoy de las 10:35 a las 13:25 horas."

16. Here I am drawing from Michael Warner's and Lisa Gitelman's ideas on how publics and media co-evolve. See Warner, *Publics and Counterpublics*, and Gitelman, *Always Already New*.

17. Lovera, "Feminismo y medios de comunicación."

18. Most famous were the performances of Las Leonas, a group of musicians lead by Marta Lamas. Amparo Ochoa also performed in various feminist events. Ana Victoria Jiménez, interview by the author, México, August 2, 2010; August 2, 2011; and telephone conversation on July 22, 2013.

19. Movimiento de Liberación de la Mujer, "Protesta 10 de Mayo" (flyer), AGN, DGIPS, Caja 1634-B, November 1, 1965–March 2, 1979, exp. 7, F.S. 867, 203.

20. "Las Liberadas se burlan de la madre abnegada ante el Monumento a la Madre," *El Universal*, May 10, 1976, AGN, DGIPS, Caja 1634-B, November 1, 1965–March 2, 1979, exp. 8, 207–8.

21. "Las Liberadas se burlan de la madre abnegada ante el Monumento a la Madre."

22. There are several accounts of how the Italian song arrived in Mexico and when it was performed for the first time. According to Marta Lamas and Dora Cardaci, the song was first performed on March 8, 1975, at a feminist event

organized by MLM in Casa del Lago. According to photographs taken by Ana Victoria Jiménez and published in a book by Eli Bartra, the staging at Casa del Lago took place in 1976. They all agree that the song and the play were performed several times at diverse gatherings. Mexican feminists borrowed the concept of *maternidad voluntaria* (roughly translated as a freedom to decide the terms on which to become a mother) from the Italian feminist movement. Eli Bartra, interview by the author, México, July 29, 2011, and January 2, 2013.
23. Lamas and Cardaci, "Dossier: El feminismo en Italia," 29–33.
24. Coalición de Mujeres Feministas was established in October 1976 by the initiative of three ex-militants of MLM, Lourdes Arizpe, Mireya Toto, and Yan María Castro, then members of Movimiento Feminista Mexicano (MFM). They were joined by members of MNM including Esperanza Brito and Anilú Elías; members of Colectivo La Revuelta including Eli Bartra, María Brumm, Chela Cervantes, Bea Faith, Lucero González, Dominique Guillemet, Berta Hiriart, and Ángeles Necoechea; and members of Lesbos, the first lesbian collective. See González Alvarado, "El espíritu de una época," and Lau Jaiven, *La nueva ola*. For more on the campaigns and their demands see Lamas, *Política y reproduccion. Aborto*.
25. "Se inicio hoy a las 9:30 horas en el auditorio de Recursos Minerales, la segunda Jornadad Nacional sobre el Aborto, conducida por Rosa Martha Fernández, September 24, 1977," AGN, DGIPS, Caja 1634-B, November 1, 1965–March 2, 1979, exp. 7, F.S. 867, 220.
26. "40 militantes del MNM por medio de pancartas hoy solicitaron frente a la camara de Diputados que se legisle sobre el aborto," AGN, DGIPS, Caja 1634-B, November 1, 1965–March 2, 1979, exp. 7, F.S. 867, 222.
27. Lesbos was the first feminist collective established in Mexico City. It actively participated in the 1978 feminist demonstrations against Miss Universe. However, lesbian involvement with 1970s feminist activists in Mexico can be traced to the establishment of MAS, in which Nancy Cárdenas, a lesbian activist and theater director, participated. For a state report that details the collaboration of Lesbos in feminist demonstrations see "Coalición de Mujeres Feministas, tiene programado para el próximo 9 de Julio en las afueras de la Secretaria de Turismo a fin de protestar por la *celebración* del certamen Miss Universo," AGN, DGIPS, Caja 1634-B, November 1, 1965–March 2, 1979, exp. 7, F.S. 867, 264–65. For contradictions within the feminist movement regarding the relationship to the lesbian movement, see Mongrovejo's, "Sexual Preference, the Ugly Duckling of Feminist Demands," and *Un amor que se atrevió a decir su nombre*.
28. See Morgan, *Sisterhood Is Powerful*.

29. Nigro, "Inventions and Transgressions," 135–58; Lau Jaiven, "Emergencia y trascendencia del neofeminismo," 158; Larson and Vargas, *Latin American Women Dramatists*; Flores, *The Drama of Gender*; Rizk, *Posmodernismo y teatro en América Latina*.

30. Taylor and Villegas, *Negotiating Performance*.

31. This was not only a perception that Mexican feminists were influenced by various feminist communities. See, for example, the influence of the Italian feminist movement in the crafting of the proposal for the law of volunteer motherhood: Lamas and Cardaci, "Dossier: El feminismo en Italia."

32. "Sin incidents aproximadamente 100 activistas de 5 organizaciones feministas, hoy efectuaron un mitin en la explanada del auditorio nacional en protesta por la realizacion del evento Señorita México," AGN, DGIPS, Caja 1634-B, November 1, 1965–March 2, 1979, exp. 7, F.S. 867, 246–49.

33. "Sin incidents aproximadamente 100 activistas de 5 organizaciones feministas."

34. "Miss Universo o la obligación de ser Bellas" (flyer), AGN, DGIPS, Caja 1634-B, November 1, 1965–March 2, 1979, exp. 7, F.S. 867, 16.

35. See López, "Ethnicizing the Nation," 29–65; Zavala, "De santa a india bonita,"149–88.

36. It is interesting to note how "gringa" here becomes a signifier for the U.S. imperialist interest in the region, a discourse that was mobilized by many actors as way to defend "national" interests or attack private investment, as in the case of antagonisms between the state and Televisa. As I have discussed previously, it was also used to discredit the existence of Latin American feminists who would focus their demands on issues of sexuality. "Sin incidents aproximadamente 100 activistas de 5 organizaciones feministas."

37. "Señorita México 1978, Comite Organizador," AGN, DGIPS, Caja 1634-B, November 1, 1965–March 2, 1979, exp. 7, F.S. 867, 250–52.

38. "Violencia en Guerrero" and "Miss Universo o la obligacion de ser bellas," AGN, DGIPS, Caja 1634-B, November 1, 1965–March 2, 1979, exp. 7, F.S. 867, 14, 16.

39. On pain and trauma see Scarry, "The Difficulty of Imagining Other Persons," 282, cited in Klein, "Spectacular Citizenship," 102–24. For more on performing trauma see Taylor "'You Are Here,'" 149–69.

40. "La Coalición de Mujeres Feministas, tiene programado un mitin para el proximo 9 de Julio en las afueras de la Secretaría de Turismo a fin de protestar por la celebración del certamen Miss Universo," AGN, DGIPS, Caja 1634-B, November 1, 1965–March 2, 1979, exp. 7, F.S. 867, 264–67.

41. "La Coalición de Mujeres Feministas se dedica a elaborar pancartas y propaganda que utilizara el 9 de Junio proximo durante el concurso Miss

Universo," AGN, DGIPS, Caja 1634-B, November 1, 1965–March 2, 1979, exp. 7, F.S. 867, 1–5.

42. El Auditorio Nacional, explanada, "La Coalición de Mujeres Feministas efectuo un mitin en defense de ese sexo," AGN, DGIPS, Caja 1634-B, November 1, 1965–March 2, 1979, exp. 7, F.S. 867, 19–22.

43. El Auditorio Nacional, explanada, "La Coalición de Mujeres Feministas."

44. Portilla, *Fenomenología del relajo*, cited in Broyles-González, *El Teatro Campesino*, 25–29.

45. In the 1960s Teatro Campesino originated in California as the theatrical branch of the United Farm Workers Association, and it is closely related to the career of Luis Valdez, an important activist of the Chicano movement and also a playwright and filmmaker. Broyles-González's study aims at understanding the role of women within Teatro Campesino in order to narrate a different history of the movement that does not center on Valdez's career. Broyles-González, *El Teatro Campesino*.

46. The bibliography on *Madres de la Plaza de Mayo* is extensive. For a study that frames their practices through the concept of *relajo* see Klein, "Spectacular Citizenship."

47. Pensado, *Political Violence and Student Culture in Mexico*.

48. Pensado, *Political Violence and Student Culture in Mexico*, 95–96.

49. Pensado, *Political Violence and Student Culture in Mexico*, 94.

50. Members of FMTC included Grupo MIRA, Grupo SUMA, Grupo TIP, Taller Cine Octubre, Grupo TAI, Grupo Proceso Pentagono, Grupo Germinal, and El Taco de la Perra Brava, among many others. See "Declaración del Frente Mexicano de Grupos Trabajadores de la Cultura," February 5, 1978, in *Fondo Los Grupos: Carpeta Frente de Los Trabajadores de la Cultura FMTC*, Mexico DF: CENIDIAP.

51. See "Cartel Convocatoria America en la Mira," in *Fondo Los Grupos*.

52. For more on CLETA, see http://www.cleta.org/, accessed January 28, 2013.

53. González Alvarado, "El espíritu de una de época."

54. Report of the meeting organized by FNALIDM held on March 31, 1979, outside the Chamber of Deputies, AGN, DGIPS, Caja 1634-B, November 1, 1965–March 2, 1979, exp. 9, 92–96.

55. For more on Los Estridentistas and Los Hartos, see Híjar, *Frentes, coaliciones y talleres*.

56. Lamas and Cardaci, "Dossier: El feminismo en Italia"; Eli Bartra, interview by the author, México, July 29, 2011, and January 2, 2013; and AGN, DGIPS, Caja 1634-B, November 1, 1965–March 2, 1979, exp. 9, 126.

57. "Informe Marcha Mitin Hemicilo a Juárez, 9 Septiembre, 1980," agn, dgips, Caja 1339-a, exp. 36, 1–57.

58. Taylor, "'You Are Here,'" 154.

59. Mónica Mayer, interview by the author, México, September 5, 2009, and July 23, 2010.

60. For more on Chicago's *Dinner Party* see http://www.brooklynmuseum.org /eascfa/dinner_party/home.php, accessed April 20, 2011.

61. For more info on Suzanne Lacy's *International Dinner Party,* see http://www .suzannelacy.com/1980sdinner_international.htm, accessed April 20, 2011.

62. Mayer, *Traducciones: Un diálogo internacional de mujeres artistas,* 1979, in Mayer, personal archive.

63. Mónica Mayer, interview by the author, México, September 5, 2009, and July 23, 2010.

64. Mayer, *Traducciones: Un diálogo internacional de mujeres artistas.*

65. Mónica Mayer, interview by the author, México, September 5, 2009, and July 23, 2010.

66. For the more on the history of the plaque see Lamas, "Cuerpo y política"; and Lamas, *Política y reproducción. Aborto,* 190.

4. AWAKENINGS OF ANA VICTORIA JIMÉNEZ

1. Cortázar, "Conservación de los recuerdos," in Cortázar, *Cuentos completos,* 2.

2. For studies that characterize new wave feminisms as the project of an exclusive group of university-educated women, see Lau Jaiven, *La nueva ola*; Zapata Galindo, "Feminist Movements in Mexico"; Lamas, *Feminismo: Transmisiones y retransmisiones*; and Bartra et al., *Feminismo en México, ayer y hoy.* For a study that links new wave feminisms with popular movements see Sánchez Olvera, *El feminismo méxicano ante el movimiento urbano popular.*

3. James, *Doña María's Story.*

4. James, *Doña María's Story,* 134.

5. James, *Doña María's Story,* 134.

6. James, *Doña María's Story,* 139.

7. James, *Doña María's Story,* 139.

8. Reyes Castellanos and Jiménez, *Sembradoras de futuros,* 171.

9. Foster, "An Archival Impulse," 3–4.

10. For a history of tgp, see Híjar, *Frentes, coaliciones y talleres.*

11. See Quintero, "Prensa feminista," 203–31.

12. James, *Doña María's Story,* 162.

13. James, *Doña María's Story,* 165–66.

14. See Olcott, "'Take Off That Streetwalker's Dress,'" 36–59.

15. Ana Victoria Jiménez, interview by the author, México, August 2, 2010; August 2, 2011; and telephone conversation on July 22, 2013.

16. As is also commonly known, the writings of seventeenth-century Sor Juana Inés de La Cruz that advocate women's right to education and the end of a sexual double standard are taken by many to be the first feminist writings in Mexico. Others go as far as tracing a concern with a sexual double standard in a series of poems written in Náhuatl dating back to pre-Cuauhtemic times. See Macías, *Against All Odds*.

17. Macías, *Against All Odds*; Sánchez Olvera, *El feminismo mexicano*.

18. Ana Victoria Jiménez, interview by the author, México, August 2, 2010; August 2, 2011; and telephone conversation on July 22, 2013.

19. The exhibition was held from September 12 to 21, 1978 at La Galeria Contraste, and other participants included Rosalba Huerta, Magali Lara, Yolanda Andrade, Mónica Mayer, Esperanza Balderas, Mayra Nuñez, Ana Victoria Jiménez, Concepción Lozada, Hilda Rodríguez, Jackie, and Carolina Paniagua. Mayer, "De la vida y el arte como feminista," 403.

20. In 1983 Ana Victoría Jiménez, Consuelo Almeda, Karen Cordero, Lorena Loaiza, Patricia Torres, and Elizabeth Valenzuela established the feminist art collective Tlacuilas y Retrateras. See "Tlacuilas y Retrateras," 41–44.

21. De Chungara and fellow activist Marisa de Los Andes were appalled when they arrived at the tribune and found a group of U.S. activists defending prostitution and lesbianism. There are diverse versions of the confrontations between the Latin American and U.S. activists, mainly Betty Friedan. For an in-depth analysis, see Olcott, "Cold War Conflicts and Cheap Cabaret"; and Barrios de Chungara and Viezzer, *Let Me Speak!*

22. Ana Victoria Jiménez, interview by the author, México, August 2, 2010; August 2, 2011; and telephone conversation on July 22, 2013.

23. Olcott, "Cold War Conflicts and Cheap Cabaret," 748.

24. Olcott, "Cold War Conflicts and Cheap Cabaret," 748–49.

25. Olcott, "Cold War Conflicts and Cheap Cabaret," 748–49.

26. *El Universal*, June 24, 1975, 1, cited in Olcott, "Cold War Conflicts and Cheap Cabaret," 743.

27. Olcott, "Cold War Conflicts and Cheap Cabaret," 742.

28. González Alvarado, "El espíritu de una de época," 95.

29. Burton, *Dwelling in the Archive*, 20–25.

30. Rolnik, "Furor de Archivo."

31. Some of these exhibitions include *Donna: Avanguardia femminista negli anni '70* (Rome, 2010); *re.act.feminism—performance art of the 1960s and 1970s today* (2009–8); *The F Word* (Vancouver, 2008); *Global Feminisms* (London and New York, 2007); *WACK! Art and the Feminist Revolution* (Los Angeles, 2007); *Cyberfem: Feminisms on the Electronic Landscape* (Spain, 2007).

32. Huyssen, *Twilight Memories*, 15.

33. Espinoza Vera, "Recuperación de la memoria."

34. Ehrenberg's papers are housed in different venues. Some went to Stanford University Special Collections, some are held at the Museo Universitario de Arte Contemporáneo (MUAC) at UNAM, some are held by his son Matthias Ehrenberg in Xico, Veracruz, and a portion containing only documents about his practices in England is held by the Tate Modern in London. See "Breve explicación de cómo nació y creció mi archivo," *Ojo Avisor*, August 13, 2008, http://ehrenberg.ojoavizor.arts-history.mx/entrada.php?id=326; and Kam, "Archives as Art," 5–16.

35. Wood, *Conceptual Art*, 6, cited in Kam, "Archives as Art," 10.

36. Foster, "An Archival Impulse," 4–6.

37. Mónica Mayer, "Archivos de arte y arte sobre archivos," April 24, 2006, http://www.la-pala.com/articulos/item/152–archivos-de-arte-y-arte-sobre-archivos.html, accessed April 29, 2011.

38. Mónica Mayer, interview by the author, México, September 5, 2009, and July 23, 2010.

39. Cited in Kam, "Archives as Art," 10.

40. Mayer, "Archivos de arte y arte sobre archivos."

41. Mónica Mayer, "Documentar o no documentar," *El Universal*, October 10, 1992, 4.

42. For a discussion on the privatization of culture in Mexico see my MA thesis, Aceves-Sepúlveda, "Art and Possibility." For a historical review of the legislation on cultural patrimony in Mexico and numerous debates surrounding this issue, see Amador Tello, "Cronología del Patrimonio Nacional," 635–47.

43. Mónica Mayer, interview by the author, September 5, 2009, and July 23, 2010.

44. See Mayer and Cordero, "Mujeres ¿y que más? Reactivando el Archivo de Ana Victoria Jiménez."

45. Ana Victoria Jiménez, interview by the author, México, August 2, 2010; August 2, 2011; and telephone conversation on July 22, 2013.

46. Appadurai, *The Social Life of Things*.

5. SECRET DOCUMENTS AND FEMINIST PRACTICES

1. According to the Mexican Human Rights Commission, this is the number of complaints that were received and investigated. The official report acknowledges that this number is probably not the total amount of the disappeared, indicating that the number could be larger. See "Informe especial sobre las quejas en materia de desapariciones forzaas ocurridas en la decada de los 70 y prinicpios de los 80," in Comision Nacional de los Derechos Humanos, México, http://www.cndh.org.mx/Informes_Especiales, accessed June 2012.

2. For a history of the polemics around transferring these archives, see Aguayo, *La Charola*; Doyle, "The Mexico Project"; Padilla and Walker, "Spy Reports."

3. AGN, DGIPS, Caja 1491-B; Caja 1634-B, November 1, 1965–March 2, 1979; Caja 1697-C; Caja 1602-B; Caja 1692-B.

4. AGN, DGIPS, Caja 1634-B, November 1, 1965–March 2, 1979, exp. 7, 1965–81.

5. AGN, DGIPS, Caja 1634-B, November 1, 1965–March 2, 1979, exp. 8, 189–93.

6. "Se inicio hoy a las 9:30 horas en el auditorio de Recursos Minerales, la segunda Jornadad Nacional sobre el Aborto, conducida por Rosa Martha Fernández," September 24, 1977, AGN, DGIPS, Caja 1634-B, November 1, 1965–March 2, 1979, exp. 7, F.S. 867, 220

7. Up to 1952 when the two agencies merged, DFS agents reported directly to the president and DGIPS agents reported to the Ministry of Interior. Aguayo, *La Charola*, 62.

8. "La Asociación Mexicana de Mujeres Jefas de Empresa, A.C. apoya incondicionalmente las reformas económicas del presidente Echeverría," January 12, 1973, AGN, DGIPS, Caja 1634-B November 1, 1965–March 2, 1979, exp. 8, 220, and exp. 8, 109; "Yo Mujer en Mexico Creo," an open letter supporting the democratic reforms adopted by President Echeverría and his fourth presidential address to the nation, signed by three female senators, fifteen female deputies, nine government employees, and eleven women's organizations.

9. Aguayo, *La Charola*, 250.

10. Aguayo, *La Charola*, 94.

11. Walker, "Spying at the Drycleaners," 52–61.

12. Derrida, *Archive Fever*, 10–12.

13. Stoler, *Along the Archival Grain*, 27.

14. Reading archives "along or against the grain" refers to seminal studies by Gayatri Chakravorty Spivak and Ana Laura Stoler. See Spivak, "The Rani of Sirmur," and Stoler, *Along the Archival Grain*. For creative ways in which women's voices are represented in a wide range of archives, see Chaudhuri et al., *Contesting the Archives*.

15. Most studies that use DFS and DGIPS declassified documents as sources concentrate on histories of workers, peasants, students, and guerrilla movements. Slowly some of these studies are incorporating indigenous movements and other actors such as doctors or the middle classes. See, for example, Padilla and Walker, "Spy Reports."

16. Mónica Mayer, interview by the author, México, September 5, 2009, and July 23, 2010. Eli Bartra, interview by the author, México, July 29, 2011, and January 2, 2013.

17. "La Policia actúa: Aprhensiones a granel," *Novedades*, April 15, 1965, in Jiménez's archive; Ana Victoria Jiménez, interview by the author, México, August 2, 2010; August 2, 2011; and telephone conversation on July 22, 2013.

18. Trouillot, *Silencing the Past*, 106.

19. "Sin incidents, aproximadamente 100 activistas de 5 organizaciones feministas, hoy efectuaron un mitin en la explanada del auditorio nacional, de protesta por la realizacion del evento señorita Mexico," May 28, 1978, AGN, DGIPS, Caja1634-B, November 1, 1965–March 2, 1979, exp. 8, 246–48.

20. Warner, "Publics and Counterpublics (abbreviated version)," 413–25.

21. "En el Auditorio Nacional Explanada la coalicion de mujeres feministas efectuo un mitin en defensa de ese sexo," July 17, 1978, AGN, DGIPS, Caja 1634-B, November 1, 1965–March 2, 1979, exp. 7, F.S. 867, 19–22.

22. "Mitin contra los concursos de belleza, frente al Auditorio Nacional," *El Día*, May 29, 1978, AGN, DGIPS, Caja 1634-B, November 1, 1965–March 2, 1979, exp. 8, 258.

23. Noble, *Photography and Memory in Mexico*, 117.

24. Noble, *Photography and Memory in Mexico*, 117.

25. Piccato, "Comments: How to Build a Perspective on the Recent Past," 91–102.

26. "La Coalición de Mujeres en una reunión de temas que les atañen," May 31, 1978, AGN, DGIPS, Caja 1634-B, November 1, 1965–March 2, 1979, exp. 8, 259.

27. "Antecendentes y objetivos de la Coalicion de Mujeres Feminstas que encabezan Juana Armanda, Anilu Elias y la Dra, Edna Brostein," June 5, 1978, AGN, DGIPS, Caja 1634-B, November 1, 1965–March 2, 1979, exp. 8, 271.

28. On critical assessments on the Federal Law of Archives, see "Impide Ley de Archivos hacer uso discrecional de documentos: IFAI," *El Informador*, December 11, 2011; and Nora Rodríguez Aceves, "Ya es gananacia tener una ley de archivos: Entrevista con Ramón Aguilera, director general de la escuela Mexicana de Archivos," *Siempre! Presencia en Mexico*, March 2, 2012, http://www.siempre.com.mx/2012/03/ya-es-ganancia-tener-una-ley-de-archivos/, accessed June 12, 2012.

29. See Ley Federal de Archivos, http://www.diputados.gob.mx/LeyesBiblio/ref/lfa
    /LFA_orig_23ene12.pdf, accessed June 12, 2012.

30. Padilla and Walker, "In the Archives: History and Politics," in Padilla and Walker,
    "Spy Reports," 5.

31. For recent debates on access to DFS files, see Andrew Paxman, "Crisis at Mexico's
    National Archives," https://andrewpaxman.wordpress.com/2015/04/12/crisis
    -at-mexicos-national-archive/, accessed September 25, 2015; Fabiola Martínez,
    "Canceló gobernación accesso directo a los Archivos de la Guerra Sucia," *La
    Jornada*, Wednesday 11, 2015; Alonso Urrutia, "El Archivo General de la Nación
    permitirá el acceso a expedientes de la extinta DFS," *La Jornada*, May 26, 2016.
    For a review of the responses by Mexican historians, see Históricas, Comité
    Mexicano de Ciencias, 2017, "Ley General de Archivos," htttps://cmch.colmex
    .mx/ley-general, accessed September 25, 2017.

6. PERFORMING FEMINIST ART

1. Cordero Reiman and Sáenz, *Crítica feminista*, 6.

2. Maris Bustamante, interview by the author, México, August 10, 2010.

3. Mayer, "De la vida y el arte como feminista," 401–13; and Lara, "La memoria es
   como una piedra pulida," 415–20.

4. Butler, "Art and Feminism: An Ideology of Shifting Criteria," in *WACK!*, 15.

5. Mayer, *Rosa Chillante*, 30–41.

6. *Fem* 9, no. 33 (April–May 1984).

7. T.M., "Presentation," *Fem* 9, no. 33 (April–May 1984): 2.

8. Bartra, "El movimiento feminista en México y su vínculo con la academia," 214–32.

9. Zapata Galindo, "Feminist Movements in Mexico," 19.

10. Besides Tibol in the 1980s, Leonor Cortina edited a catalogue of women painters
    in the nineteenth century in which several established art critics collaborated.
    See Tibol, "Mujer en el Arte Mexicano del siglo XIX," 4–6; and Cortina, *Pintoras
    mexicanas del siglo XIX* [catalogue].

11. Eder, "Las mujeres artistas en México," 7–11.

12. Also, one has to remember that at this time the iconic work of Frida Kahlo was
    gaining international recognition, and some of these readings approach her
    work from a feminist perspective. The biography published by Hayden Herrera
    in 1983 played a crucial role in popularizing her work. See Herrera, *Frida: A
    Biography of Frida Kahlo*.

13. Ocharán, "La mujer en la gráfica mexicana," 20–21; Hiriart, "Cine de mujeres,"
    39–40.

14. Mayer, "Propuesta para un arte feminista," 12–15.

15. Other collective practices in the 1980s included those of Magali Lara, Rowena Morales, and writer Carmen Boullosa. Lara, "La memoria es como una piedra púlida," 415–20.

16. Herminia Dosal participated briefly with Mayer and Bustamante. See Barbosa Sánchez, *Arte feminista*; and Mayer, *Rosa Chillante*.

17. Barbosa Sánchez, *Arte feminista*, 138–39.

18. Barbosa Sánchez, *Arte feminista*, 138–39.

19. "Tlacuilas y Retrateras," 41–44.

20. For the work of Hervé Fisher see http://www.hervefischer.net/, accessed May 20, 2011. Guerrilla Girls is an anonymous group of "women" established in 1985 in response to the Museum of Modern Art's exhibition "An International Survey of Recent Painting and Sculpture" that showcased 169 artists; out of those 169, only 17 were women. See Guerrilla Girls, *Confessions of the Guerrilla Girls*. The Peruvian Teresa Burga experimented with sociological and conceptual strategies from the late 1960s. In the 1980s she published an interdisciplinary study on the conditions of Peruvian women alongside Marie-France Cathelat. Cathelat and Burga, *Perfil de la mujer peruana*.

21. Other activities of Tlacuilas and Retrateras included their participation at a demonstration against rape organized by Red Nacional de Mujeres at el Hemiciclo a Juárez on October 7, 1983. The group made several signs and banners for the demonstration. Later they participated in Polvo de Gallina Negra's performance *Las mujeres artistas o se solicita esposa* held at La Biblioteca Mexico. Mayer's personal archive.

22. Raquel García Peguero, "En la Academia de San Carlos, Entre olanes, tules y pastels se inauguró *La fiesta de quince años*," *El Día*, August 30, 1984, in Jiménez's archive.

23. Peguero, "En la Academia de San Carlos."

24. Other performances included "Por Isabel," a performance by María Guerra, Eloy Tarciso, and Robin Luccini; and a performance by Patricia Torres and Elizabeth Valenzuela. Peguero, "En la Academia de San Carlos"; Barbosa Sánchez, *Arte feminista*, 103–6.

25. *La fiesta de quince años*, invitation in Jiménez's archive.

26. "Juego de la sirena tratando de romper el círculo sin fin versión de Ana Victoria Jiménez," in Jiménez's archive; Ana Victoria Jiménez, interview by the author, México, August 2, 2010; August 2, 2011; and telephone conversation on July 22, 2013.

27. The game was set up inside a vitrine and hence no real participatory experience existed.

28. Peguero, "En la Academia de San Carlos."

29. Among the artists who decided not to show were Arnold Belkin and José Luis Cuevas. "Damas y Caballeros, madrinas y Raquel Tibol en *La fiesta de quince años*," in Mayer's personal archive.

30. "Damas y Caballeros, madrinas."

31. Mayer and Jiménez, along with Karen Cordero and Maris Bustamante, appeared on a TV show hosted by Paty Berumen to expose their views about and the objectives of feminist art. Mayer, interview by the author, México, September 5, 2009, and July 23, 2010.

32. In conversation with Araceli Barbosa, Jiménez acknowledges how many feminist activists didn't understand what the feminist art collectives were trying to do. In fact, she argues that Mayer began to advertise her feminist art workshop at La Coalicion de Mujeres Feministas and, disappointingly, no one showed up. See Barbosa Sánchez, *Arte feminista*, 157.

33. Saide Sesín, "Nube de hielo seco, escalinatas y telas vaporosas en el agasajo de los intelectuales as los 15 años," *Uno Más Uno*, August, 30, 1984; "La Fiesta de Quince Años: Muestra de 40 artistas," *Excelsior*, August 26, 1984; "Dice Arnold Belkin que no es galán," *Uno Más Uno*, September 4, 1984; and Peguero "En la Academia de San Carlos."

34. Magali Lara, interview by the author, México, August 28, 2010.

35. Bio Arte disbanded in 1983, and Polvo de Gallina Negra disbanded in 1993. Barbosa Sánchez, *Arte feminista*.

7. INTERRUPTING PHOTOGRAPHIC TRADITIONS

1. See Mandoki, "Boom y trasfondo ideológico de la fotografía en México," 41–42; Franco et al., *Fernell Franco*; and Debroise and Fuentes Rojas, *Fuga mexicana*, 18.

2. For different ways of addressing these uneven power relations, see Azoulay's *The Civil Contract of Photography*, 85–86; Poole, *Vision, Race, and Modernity*; Smith, *Photography on the Color Line*; and Edwards, "Thinking Photography Beyond the Visual?" 31–48.

3. Poole, *Vision, Race, and Modernity*; Smith, *Photography on the Color Line*.

4. Smith, *Photography on the Color Line*, 3.

5. Gabara, *Errant Modernism*, 2.

6. Benjamin, "The Work of Art in the Age of Mechanical Reproduction," 217–52.

7. See Gabara, *Errant Modernism*; Mraz, *Looking for Mexico*; Tejada, *National Camera*; Gallo, *Mexican Modernity*; Folgarait, *Seeing Mexico Photographed*; and Segre, *Intersected Identities*.

8. Mraz, *Looking for Mexico*, 5.

9. Knight, "Racism, Revolution and *Indigenismo.*"

10. On indigenismo and the importance of anthropology in developing such discourses from the 1920s through the 1970s see Warman, *De eso que llaman antropología mexicana*. For critical studies on indigenismo and anthropology see Lomnitz-Adler, *Deep Mexico, Silent Mexico*; and Dawson, *Indian and Nation in Revolutionary Mexico*.

11. See Monsiváis, "Travelers in Mexico," 48–72.

12. On how these symbols relate to the *costumbrista* and came to be regarded as representatives of *mexicanidad*, see Pérez Salas, *Costumbrismo y litografía en México*; and Pérez Montfort, "Indigenismo, hispanismo y panamericanismo en la cultura popular Mexicana de 1920 a 1940." On the history of this tradition in relation to notions of race and vision see Poole, "An Image of 'Our Indian,'" 37–82.

13. See López, "Ethnicizing the Nation," 29–64; Hershfield, *Imagining la Chica Moderna*, 128–55.

14. Segre, *Intersected Identities*, 177.

15. Ramos Escandón, "Women's Movements, Feminism, and Mexican Politics," 199–205.

16. Gabara, *Errant Modernisms*, 150–52.

17. For a discussion of these performances see Rubenstein, *Bad Language*; Rubenstein "The War on Las Pelonas," 57–80; and Sluis, "Bataclanismo! Or, How Female Deco Bodies Transformed Postrevolutionary Mexico City," 469–99. For an analysis of how members of Los Contemporaneos, Estridentistas, and the government wrote pieces attacking women's unruly behavior see Gabara, *Errant Modernism*, 145–94.

18. Rubenstein, *Bad Language*, 46; Hershfield, *Imagining la Chica Moderna*, 128–55.

19. Rubenstein, *Bad Language*, 46.

20. Rubenstein, *Bad Language*, 46.

21. Tuñon, "Femininity, Indigenismo, and Nation," 95.

22. Salvador Novo, "El arte de la fotografía," *Contemporaneos* 9 (1931): 165–72, cited in Gabara, *Errant Modernism*, 152–53.

23. As multiple copies of one image could be produced from one negative, photographic images were able to circulate in various places at the same time (i.e., newspapers, illustrated magazines, and art galleries) and could be part of different clubs, organizations, or artistic institutions, locating photography in the "sphere of the legitimizable." Bourdieu, *Photography: A Middle-Brow Art*, 73–99.

24. Noble, *Tina Modotti*, 59–86.

25. Gabara, *Errant Modernism*, 152.

26. Debroise and Fuentes Rojas, *Fuga mexicana*, 38.

27. Novo, "El arte de la fotografía."

28. See Rubenstein, *Bad Language*; and Hershfield, *Imagining la Chica Moderna*.

29. See Muñoz, *"We speak for ourselves,"* 8.

30. Graciela Iturbide's *Those Who Live in the Sand* looks at the daily existence of the Seri inhabitants of Punta Chueca in Baja California. Nacho López's *Los pueblos de bruma y de sol* explores the Mixe area in the state of Oaxaca. Pablo Ortiz Monasterio looks at the Huave fisherman in the Juchitán district of the state of Oaxaca. Mariana Yampolsky's *La casa de la tierra* documents the lives of Nahuas, Otomis, Tarascos, Amuzgos, Zapotecas, Chinantecos, and Tepehuanos. A text by Elena Poniatowska accompanies her book. The four books were published as a collection of audiovisual ethnographic archives directed by INI-FONAPAS as part of the Olin Yoliztli program between 1976 and 1981, financed by Carmén Romano de López Portillo.

31. See Lamas, "Fragmentos de una autocritica," and Perez, "La lucha por el placer," 71–82.

32. Ludec, "La Boletina de Morelia: Órgano informativo de la Red Nacional de Mujeres, 1982–1985," 89–113.

33. Gutierrez Castañeda, *Feminismo en Mexico*.

34. Getty Museum, *The Goat's Dance: Photographs by Graciela Iturbide*, http://www.getty.edu/art/exhibitions/iturbide/, accessed June 10, 2012.

35. Roberto Tejada discusses the *Our Lady of the Iguanas* audio podcast in Getty Museum, *The Goat's Dance*.

36. Iturbide was not the only artist Toledo invited to Juchitán. Interesting counterpoints to Iturbide's images are photographs by Lourdes Grobet depicting Juchitecas participating in street demonstrations.

37. Stephen, "The Creation and Re-Creation of Ethnicity," 17–37. For a review of a wide variety of artistic renditions of COCEI, see "Signs of Belonging and Exclusion," in McCaughan, *Art and Social Movements*, 57–100.

38. The only other exhibition of a Mexican photographer organized at the Getty was *Manuel Álvarez Bravo: Optical Parables* in 2011. The introduction to Iturbide's catalogue that accompanies this exhibition makes a point out of this and builds on the relation that Iturbide had with Manuel Álvarez Bravo. Iturbide and Keller, *Juchitán*, vi.

39. Iturbide and Kelller, *Juchitán*, vi.

40. Cited in Iturbide and Keller, *Juchitán*, 1.

41. Poniatowska, *Luz y luna, las lunitas,* 77–95, cited in Iturbide and Keller, *Juchitán,* 7.
42. Stephen, "The Creation and Re-Creation of Ethnicity," 25.
43. Stephen, "The Creation and Re-creation of Ethnicity," 25; Rubin, *Decentering the Regime,* 232.
44. Iturbide and Keller, *Juchitán,* 7.
45. For other communities, the image became a powerful sign of women's emancipation as "la medusa de Juchitán," Lynell George, "Day of the Iguanas," *Smithsonian Magazine,* September 2008, http://www.smithsonianmag.com /arts-culture/indelible-iguana-200809.html, accessed April 10, 2012.
46. See, for example, Noble's *Tina Modotti;* Ferrer's *Lola Alvarez Bravo;* Folgarait's *Seeing Mexico Photographed;* and Segre's *Intersected Identities.*
47. For instance, Mariana Figarella argues that Modotti's interest in the region has to be read in the context of her feminist and communist militancy. Figarella, *Edward Weston y Tina Modotti en México.*
48. For a critical assessment of the matriarchal practices in the isthmus of Tehuantepec see Taylor, "Malinche and Matriarchal Utopia," 815–40; and Stephen, "The Creation and Re-Creation of Ethnicity."
49. Segre, *Intersected Identities,* 177.
50. Ferrer, *Lola Alvarez Bravo.* 51.
51. Segre, *Intersected Identities,* 177.
52. See interview with Lola Álvarez Bravo in Pacheco, *La luz de México,* 58–73.
53. See Mraz, *Nacho López;* Segre, *Intersected Identities,* 174–75.
54. Debroise and Fuentes Rojas, *Fuga mexicana,* 117; Segre, *Intersected Identities,* 158.
55. Segre, *Intersected Identities,* 174–75.
56. Tyler, "Post-Modern Ethnography," 126.
57. Ferrer, "Una Mirada Apacionada," 56; Poniatowska, *La raíz y el camino,* 6.
58. Franz Boas was her uncle. See Reyes Palma and Monsiváis, *El México de Mariana Yampolsky,* 11.
59. Taussig, *Mimesis and Alterity,* 188, cited in Poole, *Vision, Race, and Modernity,* 17.
60. Medina, *Graciela Iturbide,* 8.
61. The National Council of Mexican Photography was established in 1977 by a group of Mexican photographers with the objective of promoting the work of Latin American photographers and organizing workshops, exhibitions, and conferences about photography. Its president was Pedro Meyer; vice presidents were Anibal Angulo and Lázaro Blanco; Julieta Giménez Cacho was secretary; Enrique Bostelman was treasurer; and José Luis Neyra was curator. See "Documento de Formación," in *Consejo Nacional de la Fotografía,*

Fondos de la Bibiloteca de las Artes, Ciudad de México (ba); and Angelina Camargo, "La Casa de la Fotografía se inaugurará hoy, con obras de Mexicanos y Cubanos," *Excelsior*, July 8, 1980, 12–c.

62. The Cuban selection included images by Alberto Korda, Rául Corrales, Mario García Joya ("Mayito"), E. Haya ("Marucha"), Ramón Grandal, and Rogelio López.

63. "Dos momentos revolucionarios," *Semana de las Bellas Artes* 136, July 9, 1980, Fondo Consejo Mexicano de Fotografía, in Fondos especiales Biblioteca de las Artes. Previous attempts to join the photographic histories of both revolutions had been made in 1963 by the Cuban periodical *Revolución* with the exhibitions "História Gráfica de la Revolución Mexicana del Archivo Casasola" and "La Exposición Cubana Diez Años de Revolución." See Joya, "Relación entre la realidad y estilos de la fotografía en America Latina," 11–18; and Camargo, "La Casa de la Fotografía."

64. See Consejo Mexicano de Fotografía, *Hecho en Latino América*.

65. Debroise and Fuentes Rojas, *Fuga mexicana*, 15–16.

66. For a counter-reading of Casasola's images that includes a gendered perspective, see Noble, "Gender in the Archive," 136–64.

67. Mraz, *Looking for Mexico*, 66.

68. Mraz, *Looking for Mexico*, 5.

69. See http://www.sinafo.inah.gob.mx/fototeca/fototeca.html, accessed May 28, 2011.

70. Magazines such as *Hoy, Rotofoto, Mañana*, and *Siempre!* were the most widely known. In all of them, presidential activity dominated the scene, and the work of photojournalists was censored regularly. Mraz, *Looking for Mexico*, 153–200.

71. Rubenstein, *Bad Language*, 17; Mraz and Arnal, *La mirada inquieta*, 18.

72. Barthes and Heath, *Image, Music, Text*, 32–50.

73. For instance, in 1951 the magazine *Hoy* covered a series of conferences organized at UNAM where famous intellectuals, including Samuel Ramos, Leopoldo Zea, Emilio Uranga, and Juan José Arreola, among others, centered on discussing "What are Mexico and *lo mexicano*?"; see Rosa Castro, "Qué es y cómo es lo mexicano?" *Hoy*, April 14, 1951, 36–39, cited in Mraz, *Looking for Mexico*, 158.

74. See "*Hoy* interroga a Ruiz Cortines," *Hoy*, March 1, 1952, 38–39, cited in Mraz, *Looking for Mexico*, 158.

75. Mraz, *Looking for Mexico*, 153–200.

76. Mraz, *Looking for Mexico*, 153–200.

77. On Héctor García see Carrillo et al., *Héctor García*, Fundación María y Hector García website, http://fundacionmariayhectorgarcia.com, accessed March 2, 2012; for Nacho López and Los Heramos Mayo see Mraz, *Looking for Mexico*, 185–92.

78. Carrillo et al., *Héctor García*.

79. See Erika Montaño Garfias, "Nace la fundación María y Héctor García con un millón de negativos," *La Jornada*, March 28, 2008; Rivera, *Pata de Perro*; and the foundation's website at https://www.fundacionmariayhectorgarcia.com/.

80. Mraz, *Nacho López*, 11.

81. This body of work is now kept at La Fototeca Nacho López and accessed via the website of the Comision Nacional para el Desarrollo de los Pueblos Indigenas, http://www.cdi.gob.mx/, accessed March 5, 2012.

82. Goldman, *Contemporary Mexican Painting in a Time of Change*.

83. Cornel Cappa's presentation "Social Photography: Testimony or Cliché" was one of the most contested panels of the colloquium. See Consejo Mexicano de Fotografía, *Hecho en Latino América*.

84. Nacho López, in Consejo Mexicano de Fotografía, *Hecho en Latino América: Memorias del Primer Coloquio de Fotografía*, 41; Mraz, *Nacho López*, 175; and Erica Segre, *Intersected Identities*, 174–75.

85. Mraz, *Nacho López*, 70.

86. Nacho López, "El Indio en la fotografía," *Mexico Indigena*, número especial de aniversario, INI 30 años después (December 1978): 330, cited in Mraz, *Nacho López*, 70.

87. The popularization of the Day of the Dead celebration was showcased extensively in the government-sponsored magazine *Mexican Folkways*. See Zaragoza, "The Selling of Mexico: Tourism and the State," 91–115.

88. For a discussion of López's *Un día cualquiera en la vida de la ciudad* see Mraz, *Nacho López*, 187–97.

89. Cited in Mraz, *Nacho López*, 195.

90. Barthes, "Rhetoric of the Image," in *Image, Music, Text*, 32–50.

91. Mraz and Arnal, *La mirada inquieta*, 23–24.

92. Mraz, *Nacho López*, 23–24.

93. Mraz and Arnal, *La mirada inquieta*, 23–24.

94. Mraz and Arnal, *La miradad inquieta*, 16.

95. By the mid-1970s many photographers engaged with a critique of the medium as a way to address the power relations implicit in the act of taking a photograph and most importantly as an attempt to interrupt the ways in which photographic images had been used to construct ideologies of objective reality. See Solomon-Godeau, *Photography at the Dock*.

96. Her images appeared in *Siempre!*, *Revista de Revistas*, *La Jornada*, and *Fem*. Ana Victoria Jiménez, interview by the author, México, August 2, 2010; August 2, 2011; and telephone conversation on July 22, 2013.

97. Mraz, *Looking for Mexico*, 215.

98. Mraz, *Looking for Mexico*, 217.

8. FEMINIST COLLABORATIONS IN 1970S MEXICO

1. Other members of Cine-Mujer included Ellen Camus, María del Carmen Lara, Carolina Fernández, Sonia Fritz, Lilian Liberman, Beatriz Mira, Angeles Necochea, Laura Rosseti, Guadalupe Sánchez, Eugenia María Tamés, Pilar Calvo, Sibillie Hayem, Amalia Attolini, and María Novaro. See Rashkin, *Women Filmmakers in Mexico*, 249–51.

2. In 1981 they released the documentary *Es primera vez* (dir. Beatriz Mira) about a gathering of women's organizations that took place in Mexico City in 1980 involving women workers, *campesinas*, and community activists. Other movies by Cine-Mujer include *La vida toda* (1978, dir. Carolina Fernández); *Yayaltecas* (1984, dir. Sonia Fritz); *Vicios en la cocina* (1978, dir. Beatriz Mira); *Vida de Ángel* (1981) and *Amas de casa* (1984), both directed by Angeles Necoechea; *Amor pinche amor* (1981) and *No es por gusto* (1981) codirected by María Eugenia Tamés and Mari Carmen de Lara. Rashkin, *Women Filmmakers in Mexico*, 249–51.

3. Tuñon Pablos, *Mujeres en escena*.

4. Rosa Martha Fernández, interview by the author, México, September 21, 2010; Ranucci, "On the Trail of Independent Video," 193–208.

5. Ramírez Berg, *Cinema of Solitude*, 6–7.

6. Ramírez Berg, *Cinema of Solitude*, 72.

7. Millán, *Derivas de un cine en femenino*, 115.

8. "Se inicio hoy a las 9:30 horas en el auditorio de Recursos Minerales, la segunda Jornadad Nacional sobre el Aborto, conducida por Rosa Martha Fernández," September 24, 1977, AGN, DGIPS, Caja 1634-B, November 1, 1965–March 2, 1979, exp. 7, F.S. 867, 220.

9. Millán, *Derivas de un cine en femenino*, 114–17.

10. *Cosas de mujeres* (Mexico City: Cine Mujer, 1978); and *Rompiendo el silencio* (Mexico City: UNAM and Cine-Mujer, 1979). Films consulted in Fernández personal archive.

11. Cited in Ana María Amado, "Entrevista al Cine-Mujer," *Imágenes*, July 1980, 12–19.

12. Rosa Martha Fernández, interview by the author, México, September 21, 2010.

13. However, precisely how the connection with the real is constructed and, moreover, the possibility of actually developing a connection with the real, has been theorized and debated intensely. For a review of major debates see Bruzzi, *New Documentary*.

14. Noble, "Family Photography and the Global Drama of Human Rights," 71.

15. Cited in Hughes and Noble, *Phototextualities*, 5.

16. Questions included: Do you think that a woman who has been raped loses her value? Do you think that rape is a violent and forceful act or does a woman provoke it (by wearing revealing clothes or a flirting attitude)? What kinds of men are more prone to become rapists (poor, rich, unemployed, etc.)? What kinds of women are most commonly raped (poor, rich, etc.)? Why do men rape women? Do you think that men's sexual appetite gives them the right to rape women?

17. Reading these images as an index of the voices of the interviewed is not as straightforward. The photos were taken because at the time the director did not have access to a camera that could record such interviews in real time on the streets; hence, the possibility exists that the voice does not match the face. Rosa Martha Fernández, interview by the author, México, September 21, 2010.

18. See Ramírez Berg, *Cinema of Solitude*, 55–96.

19. This shift toward insanity is present in Jaime Humberto Hermosillo's trilogy *La verdadera vocación de Magadalena* (1971), *Naufragio* (1977), and *María de mi corazón* (1979). Another interesting example that breaks with the self-sacrificing mother is Sara García's role as a murderer in *Mecánica nacional* (dir. Mauricio Wallerstein, 1971). Ramírez Berg, *Cinema of Solitude*, 55–96.

20. The only film produced by Cooperativa that focuses on women workers' struggles was the one from Medalla de Oro in which Fernández participated as a camera woman. However, according to Fernández, she never saw the final version of this movie, and she is not sure that it exists. The films of Cooperativa de Cine Marginal that I was able to consult at Filmoteca UNAM did not portray women and consisted of various *Comunicados*. They included *Comunicado 1 Insurgencia Obrera* (n.d.) on Rafael Galvan and Demetrio Vallejo; *Los Soplones y Los Judas* (n.d.) on worker mobilization in Irapuato, Guanajuato; *Comunicado 3 Por la Demo* on workers' mobilization in Torreon, Coahuila; and *Huelga Nissan Mexicana* (1973, dir. Alejo Pichardo). Cooperativa de Cine Marginal's approach to film as an alternative means of communication between different workers' unions throughout the country was continued by Redes Cine y Video in the mid-1980s. All films were consulted at Filmoteca UNAM in September 2010.

21. Filmoteca UNAM, *Superocheros: Antología del super 8 en méxico* (1970–86), DVD (Mexico: Filmoteca de la UNAM, 2007).

22. As part of the exhibition *La era de la discrepancia* Álvaro Vázquez Mantecón edited a DVD collection of the most representative super-8 films produced between 1970 and 1986. Of the thirteen films included, only two are directed by women: *Arena* (5:48 min., dir. Silvia Gruener, 1986); and *Popurrí* (21 min. dir. Maris Bustamante and Rubén Valencia, 1978–80).

23. Rosa Martha Fernández, interview by the author, México, September 21, 2010.

24. Further, Ayala Blanco describes Cine-Mujer as the personal project of Fernández, whose purpose was to secure free volunteer work and to produce her films. Ayala Blanco, *La condición del cine mexicano*, 447–62.

25. Millán, "Vocaciones: Cine y video mexicano hecho por mujeres," 417.

26. María Novaro is one of the most recognized Mexican film directors due to the success of her film *Danzón* (1991). She joined Cine-Mujer after Fernández had left. She worked on the films *Es primera vez* (1981) and *Vida de Ángel* (1981). She had a previous history as militant of the left, and with this background she had difficulty with women's groups since she saw them as a petit-bourgeoisie endeavor. She defines her films as a personal search; as such, her feminine condition comes through, but she rejects feminism as a political stance. Millán, "Vocaciones: Cine y video mexicano hecho por mujeres," 426.

27. In the article Juhasz also discusses how this exclusion emanating from the academic world has led to the loss of many of these kinds of documentaries. See Juhasz, "They say we were trying to show reality," 136–71.

28. Juhasz, "They say we were trying to show reality," 158.

29. Juhasz, "They say we were trying to show reality," 167.

30. Juhasz, "They say we were trying to show reality," 167.

31. For a review of genres and categories of social documentary in Latin America see Burton, *Social Documentary in Latin America.*

32. Ana Victoria Jiménez, interview by the author, México, August 2, 2010; August 2, 2011; and telephone conversation on July 22, 2013.

33. Mónica Mayer, interview by the author, México, September 5, 2009, and July 23, 2010.

34. Mayer, "Video a la Mexicana: De sexo-s, amor y humor."

35. Mónica Mayer, interview by the author, México, September 5, 2009, and July 23, 2010.

36. Rosa Martha Fernández, interview by the author, México, September 21, 2010.

37. Rosa Martha Fernández, interview by the author, México, September 21, 2010.

38. *Prisma universidad* (Mexico: TV UNAM, 1985–97); *Casa dividida* (Mexico: TV UNAM, 1985–97). Rosa Martha Fernández, interview by the author, México, September 21, 2010.

39. Fernández's experiments with videodance include *Danza picnic* (Mexico City: TV UNAM, 2002) and *Entre paredes de agua* (Mexico: IMCINE, Canal 22, 2010).

9. POLARIZING THE ARCHIVE

1. Beauchesne and Santos, *Utopian Impulse in Latin America*, 1–26.

2. Krauss, "Video: The Aesthetics of Narcissism," 50–64.

3. Haraway, "The Cyborg Manifesto," 291–324.

4. Haraway, "The Cyborg Manifesto," 291.

5. Marks, *The Skin of Film*.

6. Jones, *Self/Image*.

7. See Mayer, "Video a la mexicana: De sexo-s, amor y humor."

8. Some of these works include *St. Cruz Tepepexpan* (n.d.), filmed in the state of Mexico; *Cuilapan de Guerrero* and *Los Muertos en Etla* (1979), filmed in Oaxaca (1979); and *Papalotl* (1979) and *Cuetzalan y yo* (1979), filmed in the state of Puebla.

9. Spielmann, "Video: From Technology to Medium," 54–69.

10. Weiss, "Antología de videos y performance."

11. Pech, *Fantasmas en tránsito*; Debroise, *La era de la discrepancia*; Mayer, "Video a la mexicana: De sexo-s, amor y humor"; Fernández Medellín, *Mujeres a tráves del video*; Torres Ramos, *El videoarte en Mexico: El caso de Pola Weiss*; Hernández Miranda, *Pola Weiss: Pionera del videoarte en México*. Recognition of Weiss's work in the form of screenings and posthumous exhibitions includes Pola Weiss *Panóramica*, Museo Rufino Tamayo, February 1–April 30, 2005; "Puntos Ciegos en la Historia del Arte," VIII Simposio de Teoría de Arte Contemporáneo, February 4–6, 2010, MUAC, Mexico City; *Homenaje minimo a Pola Weiss*, directed by Victor Blanco (Mexico City: TV UNAM, 1990); and *Forjadores del video*, directed by Rafeal Corkidi (1990).

12. Cordero Reiman and Sáenz, "Introduction," *Crítica feminista*, 6.

13. See LIMA (media arts foundation), previously the Netherlands Media Art Institute, http://catalogue.nimk.nl/site/?page=%2Fsite%2Fartist.php%3Fid%3D3730, accessed November 29, 2012.

14. Electronic communication with Edna Torres Ramos.

15. For more on Fluxus, see Newman and Bird, *Rewriting Conceptual Art*, 6.

16. Meigh-Andrews, *A History of Video Art*.

17. Roy, "Corporeal Returns"; http://intermedia.vancouverartinthesixties.com
/1968/default, accessed July 5, 2012.

18. For Brazilian video art, see Machado, "Video Art: The Brazilian Adventure,"
225–31.

19. For the uses of video by French feminist collectives see Dougherty, "Stories
from a Generation," 8–11; and Jean, "Disobedient Video in France in the
1970s," 5–16. For alternative histories of video activism in the United States,
see Drew, "The Collective Camcorder in Art and Activism," 95–114.

20. Meigh-Andrews, *A History of Video Art*, 9.

21. Some of these centers of distribution were established in New York (The
Kitchen, 1960), in Toronto (A-Space, 1971 and Art Metropole, 1974), and in
Vancouver (Intermedia, 1967). See Meigh-Andrews, *A History of Video Art*;
and Roy, "Corporeal Returns."

22. Spielmann, "Video: From Technology to Medium," 54.

23. Rosenberg, *Screendance*, 26.

24. Grassroots collectives adopted video more widely in the 1980s, when the
equipment became more affordable. Aufdeheide, "Grassroots Video in Latin
America"; Lesage, "Women Make Media," 315–50.

25. Museo de Arte Moderno, *Video Cinta de Vanguardia*.

26. Museo de Arte Moderno, *Video Cinta de Vanguardia*.

27. At the time, most of these machines were called video synthesizers, but as
Spielmann notes, there was much incoherence in naming apparatus at this
experimental time, as no proper protocols or distinctions were put in place.
Spielman distinguishes between video synthesizers, image processors, and
scan processors. Spielmann, "Video: From Technology to Medium."

28. Fernández Medellín, *Mujeres a tráves del video*, 21.

29. Garibay Mora, "Pola Weiss y el video arte."

30. Garibay Mora, "Pola Weiss y el video arte."

31. Garibay Mora, "Pola Weiss y el video arte."

32. Derrida, *Archive Fever*, 11.

33. Fernández Medellín, *Mujeres a tráves del video*, 17; Mendiola et al., "El ritual
amoroso de la bruja electrica."

34. Fernández Medellín, *Mujeres a tráves del video*, 17.

35. Mendiola et al., "El ritual amoroso de la bruja electrica."

36. Weiss complained about her lack of resources and how she had to work
as a professor at UNAM and write articles to support her productions. See
Hernandez and Torres Ramos, *Pola Weiss: La TV TV. TV Sees You*; Carrasco,
"Pola Weiss: ccineasta olvidada."

37. *Forjadores del Video.*

38. Yoshimoto, *Into Performance*, 186.

39. Ann-Sargent Wooster, "Shigeko Kubota: I Travel Alone," *High Performance,* Winter 1991, 28.

40. Earlier, several experimental filmmakers had produced films focusing entirely on female vaginas, as exploratory exercises conducted in small consciousness-raising groups. See, for example, *Near the Big Chakra* (17 min., 1971); and for later interpretations of feminist self-explorations, see Juhasz, "Our Auto-Bodies, Ourselves."

41. While numerous anthologies of feminist art credit Kubota's *Vagina Painting* performance as an iconic piece in the history of feminist art, Midori Yoshimoto reviews the ways in which Western feminist scholars have interpreted Kubota's performance and offers an alternative interpretation of the performance that invokes particular Japanese cultural traditions, including reference to geishas' performative and seduction practices. Yoshimoto, *Into Performance*, 79–180.

42. Yoshimoto, *Into Performance.*

43. Jonathan Price, "Shigeko Kubota and the Video of Wipe, Flash, Crash," *Woman Artists Newsletter* 2, no. 6 (1976): 4, cited in Yoshimoto, *Into Performance*, 189. Yoshimoto, *Into Performance*, 186.

44. Weiss, *Mi corazón* (1986).

45. Roth, "The Voice of Shigeko Kubota," Catalogue, 74.

46. I could not find information on the purpose of Kubota's travel to Mexico City, but she was in Mexico in November (see fig. 51). It is interesting that it roughly coincides with the UN's International Women's Year Celebration in Mexico City.

47. Shigeko Kubota, invitation card to the exhibition *VideoPoem* at The Kitchen, New York, June 7, 1975; Kubota file, Anthology Film Archives, cited in Yoshimoto, *Into Performance*, 233.

48. Jacob, *Shigeko Kubota*, 8.

49. Pola Weiss, "Entrevista a Shigeko Kubota," 1975, 3 min., sound, cited in Fernández Medellín, *Mujeres a tráves del video*, 16–17.

50. Garibay Mora, "El video arte."

51. Weiss, *Flor cósmica* (1977).

52. Carrasco, "Pola Weiss: La cineasta olvidada."

53. Mayer, "Video a la mexicana: De sexo-s, amor y humor."

54. Weiss, "Entrevista a Shigeko Kubota," cited in Fernández Medellín, *Mujeres a tráves del video*, 16–17.

55. After this initial engagement, Kubota continued to pay homage to Duchamp in *Duchampiana: Nude Descending a Staircase* (1975–91) and *Duchampian Door* (1976–77). Yoshimoto, *Into Performance*, 190.

56. Jacob, *Shigeko Kubota*, 6.

57. *Pola Weiss, Re-Conocimiento*, dir. Edna Torres (2012), http://vimeo.com /48597997, accessed July 15, 2013.

58. Fernando Mangino, in *Pola Weiss, Re-Conocimiento*.

59. Weiss, *David* (1983).

60. Juan Acha, "El arte del video tape encontra de la t.v.," in *Diaroma Cultural de Excelsior* (n.d.), document no. 000059, Fondo "Márgenes conceptuales, La era de la discrepancia," ARKEHIA, MUAC.

61. "Mexico Participa en un evento de TV," *Excelsior*, Seccion Radio y TV, 1978, Fondo "Felipe Eherenberg," ARKEHIA, MUAC.

62. As part of her experience in Venice she recorded interviews with other festival participants; however, records of such interviews were not kept, arguably because of the lack of interest in this work. Torres Ramos, *El video arte en Mexico*, 62.

63. Mendiola et al., "El ritual amoroso de la bruja electrica"; Fernandez Medellin, *Mujeres a tráves del video*.

64. Garibay Mora, "El video arte"; Garibay Mora, "Pola Weiss y el video arte."

65. Rivera, "Pola Weiss, pionera del videoarte en Mexico, denuncia al video clip."

66. Weiss, "Antología de videos y performance."

67. Rosenberg, *Screendance*; Lachino and Benhumea, *Videodanza*.

68. Garibay Mora, "Pola Weiss y el video arte."

69. Garibay Mora, "Pola Weiss y el video arte."

70. Mangino in *Pola Weiss, Re-Conocimiento*.

71. Weiss, *Cuetzalan y yo* (1979).

72. In *Santa Cruz Tepexpan*, Weiss's camera follows the town's people in a procession that culminates with a typical dance on top of a mountain. *Los Muertos en Etla, Oaxaca* shows images of children playing in a graveyard. In *Inertia*, aerial images of Mexico City are intermixed with images of pre-Hispanic ruins. *Santa Cruz Tepexpan* (1979); *Los Muertos en Etla* (1979); *Inertia* (1989).

73. Weiss, "Antología de videos y performance."

74. Weiss, *Freud-hombre* (1978).

75. Weiss, *Sol ó águila* (1980).

76. Weiss, *Las tasas de interés* (1983).

77. Weiss, *El salto* (1982).

78. This video has been read as a critique of Marxism and was not welcomed in UNAM's intellectual circles. Mendiola et al., "El ritual amoroso de la bruja electrica."

79. Weiss, *El salto* (1982).

80. Weiss, *Videopus* (1980).

81. Zapett, "Video arte en México."

82. Weiss, *Mi corazón* (1986).

83. This piece could be a direct reference to Carolee Schneemann's *Body Eye* (1963), in which the artist merged her own body with the material of her performance. The possibility that Weiss could have known about Schneemann's works is not farfetched since Schneemann collaborated with Kubota and with Mexican artist Felipe Ehrenberg for his *Beau Geste Press* project. Ehrenberg, who also befriended Pola Weiss, lived in Mexico in the early 1970s after his temporary exile in London and experimented with video and conceptual arts. For Schneemann's work, see Jones, *Self/Image*, 172–73; and Felipe Ehrenberg, electronic communication with the author, April 13, 2011.

84. Eder, "El Cuerpo y el espejo: Ansiedades en la autorepresentación," 52–64.

85. Monsiváis, *Entrada libre*.

86. In 1986 Rafael Corkidi, Miguel Baéz, Adriana Portillo, Francis García, and members of Redes, Cine y Video organized one of the first festivals of video film at the Agora Library in Mexico City. See *Forjadores del Video*; and Zapett, "Video arte en Mexico."

87. *Forjadores del Video*.

88. *Primera Bienal de Video México 1990, September 4–10, 1990* (Mexico City: CONACULTA, UNAM, 1990); Zapett, "Video arte en Mexico."

89. Sarah Minter, interview by the author, México, August 10, 2010.

90. Sarah Minter, interview by the author, México, August 10, 2010.

91. *Nadie es inocente*, directed by Sarah Minter (1986).

92. Sarah Minter, interview by the author, México, August 10, 2010.

93. Wortham, *Indigenous Media*.

94. Wortham, *Indigenous Media*, 112.

95. For a history of INI's media transference programs, see Wortham, *Indigenous Media*, 60–89.

96. Ranucci, "On the Trail of Independent Video," 193–208; Minter, "A vuelo de pájaro, el video en México."

97. Wortham, *Indigenous Media*, 112.

98. Through this collection, entitled "Democracy in Communication," Ranucci introduced Latin American contemporary independent media to the United States. See Ranucci, "On the Trail of Independent Video," 193–208.

99. Ranucci, "On the Trail of Independent Video," 193–208.

100. Ranucci, "On the Trail of Independent Video," 193–208.

CONCLUSION

1. Franco, *The Decline and Fall of the Lettered City*, 266.

2. Stallabrass, *Art Incorporated*, 108.

3. See Camnitzer et al., *Global Conceptualism*; "Conceptualismos del Sur," http://conceptual.inexistente.net/, accessed April 15, 2009.

4. Debroise, *La era de la discrepancia*; Museo del Barrio, Cullen, and Bustamante, *Arte [No Es] Vida*.

5. El Palacio de Hierro was developed by J. Tron and Company in 1888. Its first department store opened in 1891 in a five-story iron and steel building (hence its name) located at the corner of present-day 5 de Febrero and Venustiano Carranza streets in downtown Mexico City. Since then it has grown to be one of the biggest department stores, with establishments all over the country. See Samperio Díaz and Vázquez Salcedo, *Análisis de la representación de la mujer*.

6. Wolffer's billboards were exhibited from July 1 to August 30, 2000, at Tlalpan and Eje 6 Sur; Periférico Canal de Garay and Eje 6 Sur; San Antonio Abad, Plaza Santa Cruz; Insurgentes and Avenida del Imán; Insurgentes and Copilco; Insurgentes and Quintana Roo; Avenida Santa Teresa, Pedregal del Lago; Río Churubusco and Calle 17; Periférico Sur and Zacatépetl; and Viaducto and Tránsito, in México City. See Lorena Wolffer's website, http://www.lorenawolffer.net/00home.html, accessed March 10, 2014; "Campaña de Olabuenaga: Wolffer reucurre a la estrategía critica," *La Jornada*, July 31, 2000.

7. Marketing analyses at the time pointed out that El Palacio de Hierro had a 25 percent market share, in contrast to Liverpool's 30 percent. See "Fabrica de Ideas que 'Son Totalmente Palacio,'" *Al Diseño* 44 (September 1999): 2–7; Samperio Díaz and Vázquez, *Análisis de la representación de la mujer*.

8. Agencia Terán TBWA, *Campaña institucional "Soy Totalmente Palacio,"* 2003, cited in Samperio Díaz and Vázquez, *Análisis de la representación de la mujer*.

9. Rubenstein, *Bad Language*; Hershfield, *Imagining la Chica Moderna*.

10. See http://www.latinamericanstudies.org/ezln/cronologia.htm, accessed March 15, 2014.

11. Lorena Wolffer's website, http://www.lorenawolffer.net/00home.html, accessed March 10, 2014.

12. Lorena Wolffer's website, http://www.lorenawolffer.net/00home.html, accessed March 10, 2014.

BIBLIOGRAPHY

ARCHIVAL AND LIBRARY COLLECTIONS

Archivo General de la Nación (AGN), México.

Biblioteca Central, Universidad Nacional Autónoma de México (UNAM), México.

Biblioteca Daniel Cosío Villegas, Colegio de México, México.

Biblioteca de las Artes del Centro Nacional de las Artes, México.

Biblioteca Justino Fernández, Instituto de Investigaciones Estéticas, UNAM, México.

Centro de Documentación ARKEHIA, Museo Universitario de Arte Contemporáneo, México.

Centro Nacional de Investigación, Documentación e Información de Artes Plásticas (CENIDIAP) del Instituto Nacional de Bellas Artes (INBA), México.

Filmoteca, UNAM, México.

Fondo de la Secretaría de Educación Pública del Instituto de Bellas Artes, México.

Fondo Los Grupos, Carpeta Frente de Los Trabajadores de la Cultura *FMTC*, CENIDIAP, México.

Hemeroteca Nacional, UNAM, México.

Ana Victoria Jiménez, personal archive, México.

Mónica Mayer, personal archive, México.

Museo de Arte Carrillo Gil, México.

Museo de Arte Moderno, México.

Polvo de Gállina Negra archive, México.

Promotora Fernando Gamboa, México.

Stanford University Libraries, Special Collections, Stanford, California.

SECONDARY SOURCES

Acevedo, Marta. "10 de Mayo . . ." In *Feminismo en México: Revisión histórico-crítica del siglo que termina*, edited by G. Gutiérrez Castañeda, 39–51. México: UNAM, Programa Universitario de Estudios de Género, 2002.

———. "Lo volvería a elegir." *Debate Feminista* 786 (October 1995): 4–15.

———. "Nuestro sueño esta en escarpado lugar (crónica de un miércoles santo entre las mujeres) Woman's Liberation, San Francisco." *Siempre!*, September 30, 1970.

Acevedo, Marta, and Marta Lamas. *40 años de feminismo en México, conferencia del feminismo en México,* May 4, 2011, México, audio recordings, http://seminariodefeminismonuestroamericano.blogspot.com/2011/05/audios-40-anos-de-feminismo-en-mexico.html, accessed June 18, 2011.

Acevedo, Marta, Marta Lamas, and Ana Luisa Ligurí. "México: Una bolsita de cal por las que van de arena." In *Fem: 10 Años de periodismo feminista,* 111–48. México DF: Planeta, 1988.

Aceves-Sepúlveda, Gabriela. "Art and Possibility: From Nationalism to Neoliberalism. The Cultural Interventions of Banamex and Televisa." MA thesis, University of British Columbia, 2007.

Adelman, Jeremy. "Latin American Longues Durées." *Latin American Research Review* 39, no. 1 (2004): 223–37.

Aguayo, Sergio. *La Charola: Una historia de los servicios de inteligencia en México.* México DF: Grijalbo, 2001.

Agustín, José. *Tragicomedia mexicana no. 2: La vida en México de 1970–1980.* México: Planeta, 2007.

———. *La contracultura en México: La historia y el significado de los rebeldes sin causa, los jipitecas, los punks y las bandas.* México: Grijalbo, 1996.

Alvarez, Sonia E., Evelina Dagnino, and Arturo Escobar, eds. *Cultures of Politics/Politics of Cultures: Re-Visioning Latin American Social Movements.* Boulder CO: Westview Press, 1998.

Alvarez, Sonia E., and Arturo Escobar, eds. *The Making of Social Movements in Latin America: Identity, Strategy, and Democracy.* Boulder CO: Westview Press, 1992.

Amad, Paula. *Counter-Archive: Film, the Everyday, and Albert Kahn's Archives de la Planète.* New York: Columbia University Press, 2010.

Amado, Ana María. "Entrevista al Colectivo Cine-Mujer," *Imágenes,* July 1980, 12–19.

Amador Tello, Judith. "Cronología del Patrimonio Nacional." In *Mexico su apuesta por la cultura: El Siglo XX testimonio del presente,* 635–47. Mexico DF: Grijalbo, 2003.

Appadurai, Arjun. *Modernity at Large: Cultural Dimensions of Globalization.* Minneapolis: University of Minnesota Press, 1996.

———. *The Social Life of Things: Commodities in Cultural Perspective.* Cambridge: Cambridge University Press, 1986.

Arondekar, Anjali. *For the Record: On Sexuality and the Colonial Archive in India.* Durham NC: Duke University Press, 2009.

Aufdeheide, Patricia. "Grassroots Video in Latin America." In *The Social Documentary in Latin America*, edited by Julianne Burton, 315–50. Pittsburgh: University of Pittsburgh Press, 1990.

Ávila G., Alba Elena. "Maternidad Elegida: Recuerdos, ficciones y olvidos del movimiento feminist." In *Cartografías del feminismo Mexicano, 1970–2000*, edited by Nora Nínive García, Márgara Millán, and Cynthia Pech, 247. México: Universidad Autónoma de la Ciudad de México, 2007.

Aviña, Alex. "Insurgent Guerrero: Genaro Vázquez, Lucio Cabañas and the Guerrilla Challenge to the Postrevolutionary Mexican State, 1960–1968." PhD diss., University of Southern California, 2009.

Ayala Blanco, Jorge. *La condición del cine mexicano*. México: Editorial Posadas, 1986.

Azoulay, Ariella. *The Civil Contract of Photography*. New York: Zone Books, 2008.

Baigorri, Laura, ed. *Video en Latino America: Una historia crítica*. Madrid: Aecid, 2008.

Balsamo, Anne. *Technologies of the Gendered Body: Reading Cyborg Women*. Durham NC: Duke University Press, 1995.

Barbosa Sánchez, Araceli. *Arte feminista en los ochenta en México: Una perspectiva de género*. México DF: Casa Juan Pablos, 2008.

Barrios de Chungara, Domitila, and Moema Viezzer. *Let Me Speak!* New York: Monthly Review Press, 1978.

Barthes, Roland. *Camera Lucida: Reflections on Photography*. New York: Hill and Wang, 1987.

Barthes, Roland, and Stephen Heath. *Image, Music, Text*. New York: Hill and Wang, 1997.

Bartra, Armando, Alejandra Moreno Toscano, and Elisa Ramírez Castañeda. *De fotógrafos y de indios*. México DF: Ediciones Tecolote, 2000.

Bartra, Eli, ed. *Crafting Gender: Women and Folk Art in Latin America and the Caribbean*. Durham NC: Duke University Press, 2003.

———. "El movimiento feminista en México y su vínculo con la academia." *Revista de Estudios de Género. La ventana* (Diciembre 1999), 214–31, http://www.redalyc.org/articulo.oa?id=88411129009, accessed April 24. 2011.

———. *Museo Vivo: La creatividad femenina*. México DF: Casa Abierta al Tiempo, 2008.

———. "Tres décadas de neofeminismo en México." In *Feminismo en México, ayer y hoy*, edited by Eli Bartra et al., 45–81. México: Universidad Autónoma Metropolitana, 2000.

Bartra, Eli, et al. *La Revuelta: Reflexiones, testimonios y reportajes de mujeres en México*. México: Martín Casillas, 1983.

Bartra, Eli, Anna Maria Fernández Poncela, Ana Lau Jaiven, and Ángeles Mastretta. *Feminismo en México, ayer y hoy*. México DF: Universidad Autónoma Metropolitana, 2000.

Beauchesne, Kim, and Alessandra Santos, eds. *The Utopian Impulse in Latin America*. New York: Palgrave Macmillan, 2011.

Beezley, William H., Cheryl E. Martin, and William E. French, eds. *Rituals of Rule, Rituals of Resistance: Public Celebrations and Popular Culture in Mexico*. Wilmington DE: SR Books, 1994.

Bell, David, and Barbara M. Kennedy, eds. *The Cybercultures Reader*. New York: Routledge, 2001.

Benjamin, Walter. "The Work of Art in the Age of Mechanical Reproduction." In *Illuminations*, by Walter Benjamin. New York: Schocken Books, 2007.

Berger, John. *Ways of Seeing*. London: Penguin Books, 1972.

Blancarte, Roberto. *Cultura e identidad nacional*. México: Fondo de Cultura Económica, 1994.

Bolaño, Roberto. "Los Detectives Salvajes." *Narrativas Hispánicas*, 256. Barcelona: Editorial Anagrama, 1998.

Bolter, Jay David, and Richard Grusin. *Remediation: Understanding New Media*. Cambridge MA: MIT Press, 2000.

Bourdieu, Pierre. *Photography: A Middle-Brow Art*. Stanford CA.: Stanford University Press, 1990.

Bradley, Mark, and Patrice Petro. *Truth Claims: Representation and Human Rights*. New Brunswick NJ: Rutgers University Press, 2002.

Brah, Avtar, Mary J. Hickman, and Mairtin Mac an Ghaill, eds. *Global Futures: Migration, Environment, and Globalization*. New York: St. Martin's Press, 1999.

Bronfman, Alejandra, and Andrew Grant Wood. *Media, Sound, and Culture in Latin America and the Caribbean*. Pittsburgh: University of Pittsburgh Press, 2012.

Broyles-González, Yolanda. *El Teatro Campesino: Theater in the Chicano Movement*. Austin: University of Texas Press, 1994.

Bruzzi, Stella. *New Documentary: A Critical Introduction*. London: Routledge, 2000.

Burns, Kathryn. *Into the Archive: Writing and Power in Colonial Peru*. Durham NC: Duke University Press, 2010.

Burton, Antoinette M. *Archive Stories: Facts, Fictions, and the Writing of History*. Durham NC: Duke University Press, 2006.

———. *Dwelling in the Archive: Women Writing House, Home, and History in Late Colonial India*. New York: Oxford University Press, 2003.

Burton, Julianne, ed. *The Social Documentary in Latin America*. Pittsburgh: University of Pittsburgh Press, 1990.

Butler, Cornelia H., and Lisa Gabrielle Mark, eds. *WACK!: Art and the Feminist Revolution*. Los Angeles: Museum of Contemporary Art, 2007.

Butler, Judith. *Gender Trouble: Feminism and the Subversion of Identity*. New York: Routledge, 1990.

———. *Undoing Gender*. New York: Routledge, 2004.

Calderón, Fernando, and Adela Cedillo, eds. *Challenging Authoritarianism in Mexico: Revolutionary Struggles and the Dirty War, 1964–1982*. New York: Routledge, 2012.

Camnitzer, Luis, Jane Farver, Rachel Weiss, and László Beke. *Global Conceptualism: Points of Origin, 1950s–1980s*. New York: Queens Museum of Art, 1999.

Carrasco, Jorge V. "Pola Weiss: La cineasta olvidada." *Etcétera: Política y Cultura*, http://www.etcetera.com.mx/2000/399/jcv399.html, accessed June 10, 2011.

Casanova, Rosa, and Adriana Konzevik. *Luces sobre México: Cátalogo selectivo de la Fototeca Nacional del INAH*. México: CNCA–INAH–Editorial RM, 2006.

Castellanos, Alejandro, and Cecilia Hidalgo. *Revelación, revuelta y ficción: Hecho en Latino America*. México: Centro Nacional de las Artes, Centro de la Imagén, 2007.

Carrillo, Alfonso Morales, Pablo Ortiz Monasterio, and Paulina Lavista. *Héctor García*. Madrid: Turner, 2004.

Cathelat, Marie-France, and Teresa Burga. *Perfil de la mujer peruana (1980–1981)*. Perú: Fondo del Libro Industrial del Perú, 1981.

Chaudhuri, Nupur, Sherry J. Katz, and Mary Elizabeth Perry, eds. *Contesting the Archives: Finding Women in the Sources*. Urbana: University of Illinois Press, 2010.

Clifford, James, and George E. Marcus, eds. *Writing Culture: The Poetics and Politics of Ethnography*. Berkeley: University of California Press, 1986.

Cohen-Cruz, Jan, ed. *Radical Street Performance: An International Anthology*. London: Routledge, 1998.

Consejo Mexicano de Fotografía. *Hecho en Latino América: Memorias del primer coloquio Latino Americano de fotografía*. Ciudad de México: Consejo Mexicano de Fotografía, 1978.

Cordero Reiman, Karen, and Inda Sáenz, eds. *Critica feminista en la teoría e historia del arte*. México: Universidad Iberoamericana, 2007.

Cordero Reiman, Karen, Andrea Giunta, Amelia G. Jones, Pablo Helguera, Sol Henaro, Erin L. McCutchcon, Griselda Pollock, Mónica Mayer and María Laura Rosa. *Mónica Mayer: Sí tiene dudas . . . pregunte: Una exposición retrocolectiva*. México DF: Museo Universitario Arte Contemporáneo, UNAM, 2016.

Cortázar, Julio. *Cuentos completos, 2*. Buenos Aires: Punto de Lectura, 2007.

Cortina, Leonor. *Pintoras mexicanas del siglo XIX* [catalogue]. México: Museo de San Carlos INBA, 1985.

Cosas de mujeres, DVD, directed by Rosa Martha Fernández. México: Colectivo Cine Mujer, 1978.

Cosío Villegas, Daniel. *El estilo personal de gobernar*. México: Cuadernos Joaquín Mortiz, 1974.

Cvetkovich, Ann. *An Archive of Feelings: Trauma, Sexuality, and Lesbian Public Cultures*. Durham NC: Duke University Press, 2003.

Danbolt, Mathias, Jane Rowley, and Louise Wolthers, eds. *Lost and Found: Queerying the Archive*. Copenhagen: Nikolaj Copenhagen Contemporary Art Center, 2009.

Davalos, Karen Mary. *Yolanda López*. Minneapolis: University of Minnesota Press, 2009.

Davis, Diane E. *Urban Leviathan: Mexico in the Twentieth Century*. Philadelphia: Temple University Press, 1994.

Davis, Natalie Zemon. *Fiction in the Archives: Pardon Tales and Their Tellers in Sixteenth-Century France*. Stanford CA: Stanford University Press, 1987.

Dawson, Alexander S. *Indian and Nation in Revolutionary Mexico*. Tucson: University of Arizona Press, 2004.

Debroise, Olivier. *La era de la discrepancia: arte y cultura visual en México, 1968–1997*. México: UNAM, 2006.

Debroise, Olivier, and Elizabeth Fuentes Rojas. *Fuga mexicana: Un recorrido por la fotografía en México*. México DF: Consejo Nacional para la Cultura y las Artes, 1994.

Decker, Arden. *Los Grupos and the Art of Intervention in 1960s and 1970s Mexico*, PhD diss., City University of New York, 2015.

De la Dehesa, Rafael. *Queering Public Space in Mexico and Brazil: Sexual Rights Movements and Emerging Democracies*. Durham NC: Duke University Press, 2010.

De la Lama, Marta, and Felipe de la Lama. *El Canal 13: Vida, pasión y obra. Apuntes para la historia de la televisión publica en México*. México: Editorial Porrua, 2001.

De Lauretis, Teresa. *Technologies of Gender: Essays on Theory, Film, and Fiction*. Bloomington: Indiana University Press, 1987.

Derrida, Jacques. *Archive Fever: A Freudian Impression*. Chicago: University of Chicago Press, 1996.

Dorfman, Ariel, and Armand Mattelart. *Para leer el Pato Donald*. México: Siglo Veintiuno Editores, 1973.

Dougherty, Cecilia. "Stories from a Generation: Early Video at the L.A. Woman's Building." *Afterimage* 26, no. 1 (July–August 1998): 8–11.

Doyle, Katy. "The Mexico Project," http: www.gwu.edu/nsarchiv/mexico, accessed January 9, 2009.

Drew, Jesse. "The Collective Camcorder in Art and Activism." In *Collectivism after Modernism: The Art of Social Imagination after 1945*, edited by Black Stimson and Gregory Sholette, 95–114. Minneapolis: University of Minnesota Press, 2007.

Eder, Rita. "Las mujeres artistas en México." *Anales de Investigaciones Estéticas de la UNAM* vol. XIII, tomo 2, núm. 50 (1982): 251–60.

———, "El Cuerpo y el espejo: Ansiedades en la autorepresentación." Paper presented at *Puntos Ciegos—Blind Spots*. Memorias del Simposio Internacional de Teoría sobre Arte Contemporáneo (SITAC) VIII, 52–64. Patronato de Arte Contemporáneo A.C. (PAC), 2011.

Edwards, Elizabeth. "Thinking Photography Beyond the Visual?" In *Photography: Theoretical Snapshots*, edited by J. J. Long, Andrea Noble, and Edward Welch, 31–48. London: Routledge, 2009.

Ehrenberg, Felipe. *Felipe Ehrenberg. [Manchuria Vision Periférica]*. México: Editora Diamantina, 2007.

Ehrick, Christine. "Radio Transvestism and the Gendered Soundscape in Buenos Aires, 1930–1940s." In *Media, Sound and Culture in Latin America and the Caribbean*, edited by Alejandra Bronfman and Andrew Grant Wood, 18–36. Pittsburgh: University of Pittsburgh Press, 2012.

Eichhorn, Kate. *The Archival Turn in Feminism: Outrage in Order*. Philadelphia: Temple University Press, 2013.

Enwezor, Okwui. *Archive Fever: Uses of the Document in Contemporary Art*. New York: International Center for Photography, Steidl, 2007.

Espinoza, Cesar, and Aracelí Zuñiga. *La perra brava: Arte, crisis y políticas culturales*. México DF: UNAM-STUNAM, 2002.

Espinoza Vera, Cesar Horacio. "Recuperación de la memoria: Los Archivos de Arte Exposición en México de Arte ≠ Vida. Acciones por artistas de las Américas, 1960–2000," *Escaner Cultural*, August 3, 2009, http://revista.escaner.cl/node/1481, accessed August 9, 2009.

Evans, Jessica, and Stuart Hall, eds. *Visual Culture: The Reader*. London: SAGE Publications, 1999.

Fajardo-Hill, Cecilia, Andrea Giunta, and Rodrigo Alonso. *Radical Women: Latin American Art, 1960–1985*. Los Angeles: Hammer Museum, 2017.

Figarella, Mariana. *Edward Weston y Tina Modotti en México*. México: UNAM, Instituto de Investigaciones Estéticas, 2002.

Fem: 10 Años de periodismo feminista. México DF: Planeta, 1988.

Femenías, María Luisa, and Amy Oliver. *Feminist Philosophy in Latin America and Spain*. Amsterdam: Rodopi, 2007.

Fernández-Aceves, María Teresa. "Imagined Communities: Women's History and the History of Gender in Mexico." *Journal of Women's History* 19, no. 1 (Spring 2007): 200–5.

Fernández-Aceves, María Teresa, Susie Porter, and Carmen Ramos Escandón. *Orden social e identidad de género. México Siglo XIX y XX*. Guadalajara: UdeG, CIESAS, 2006.

Fernández, Claudia, and Andrew Paxman. *El Tigre: Emilio Azcarraga y su imperio Televisa*. México: Grijalbo, 2000.

Fernández, Rosa Martha. "La mujer mexicana y la conciencia de la opresión." In *La Cultura en México, Siempre!* July–September 1972, x–xi.

Fernández Christlieb, Fátima. *Los medios de difusión masiva en México*. México: J. Pablos, 1982.

Fernández Medellín, Marcela. "Mujeres a tráves del video: intimidad y subversion." MA thesis, UNAM, 2005.

Ferrer, Elizabeth. "Una Mirada Apacionada." In *Mariana Yampolsky: Imagen, memoria/Image-Memory*, edited by Elizabeth Ferrer, Elena Poniatowska, and Francisco Reyes Palma, 56. Mexico: Centro de la Imagen, 1999.

Ferrer, Elizabeth, and Lola Alvarez Bravo. *Lola Alvarez Bravo*. New York: Aperture, 2006.

Flores, Yolanda. *The Drama of Gender: Feminist Theater by Women of the Americas*. New York: Peter Lang, 2000.

Florescano, Enrique. *El patrimonio nacional de México*. México: Consejo Nacional para la Cultura y las Artes, 1997.

Folgarait, Leonard. *Seeing Mexico Photographed: The Work of Horne, Casasola, Modotti, and Álvarez Bravo*. New Haven: Yale University Press, 2008.

Forgues, Roland. *Mujer, creación y problemas de identidad en América Latina*. Mérida, Venezuela: Universidad de los Andes, Consejo de Publicaciones, 1999.

Forjadores del Video, VHS, directed by Rafael Corkidi. México: Cineteca Nacional, 1990.

Foster, Hal. "An Archival Impulse." *October* 110 (Autumn 2004): 3–22.

Foucault, Michel. *The Archeology of Knowledge*. London: Routledge, 1989.

———. *The Birth of Biopolitics: Lectures at the College de France, 1978–79*, ed. Michel Senellart, trans. Graham Burchell. New York: Picador, 2010.

Franco, Fernell, Sagrario Berti, María Iovino, and Graciela Iturbide. *Fernell Franco: Amarrados (Bound)*. New York: Americas Society, 2009.

Franco, Jean. *Critical Passions. Selected Essays*. Durham NC: Duke University Press, 1999.

———. *The Decline and Fall of the Lettered City: Latin America in the Cold War*. Cambridge MA: Harvard University Press, 2002.

———. *Plotting Women: Gender and Representation in Mexico*. New York: Columbia University Press, 1989.

French, William E., and Katherine Elaine Bliss, eds. *Gender, Sexuality, and Power in Latin America since Independence*. Lanham MD: Rowman and Littlefield Publishers, 2006.

Frérot, Christine. *El mercado del arte en México, 1950–1976*. México: INBA, 1995.

Fritz, Sonia. "Annemarie Maier, Cine Mujer: Individualismo y Colectividad." In *Lo personal es político: Feminismo y documental*, 100–32. España, Gobierno de Navarra: Instituto Navarro de las Artes Audiovisuales y la Cinematografía, 2011.

Fuoss, Kirk. *Striking Performances/Performing Strikes*. Jackson MS: University Press of Mississippi, 1997.

Fusco, Coco. *Corpus Delecti: Performance Art of the Americas*. London: Routledge, 2000.

Gabara, Esther. *Errant Modernism: The Ethos of Photography in Mexico and Brazil*. Durham NC: Duke University Press, 2008.

Gallo, Rubén. "The Mexican Pentagon: Adventures in Collectivism during the 1970s." In *Collectivism after Modernism*, edited by Blake Stimson and Gregory Sholette, 165–92. Minneapolis: University of Minnesota Press, 2007.

———. *Mexican Modernity: The Avant-Garde and the Technological Revolution*. Cambridge MA: MIT Press, 2005.

García, Héctor. *Héctor García*. Madrid: Turner, 2004.

García, Nora Nínive, Márgara Millán, and Cynthia Pech. *Cartografías del feminismo mexicano, 1970–2000*. México: Universidad Autónoma de la Ciudad de México, 2007.

García Canclini, Néstor. *Hybrid Cultures: Strategies for Entering and Leaving Modernity*. Minneapolis: University of Minnesota Press, 2005.

———. *Imaginarios Urbanos*. Buenos Aires: Eudeba, 1997.

García Gossio, María Ileana. *Mujeres y sociedad en el México contemporáneo: Nombrar lo inombrable*. México: H. Cámara de Diputados, LIX Legislatura, Tecnológico de Monterrey, 2004.

García Krinsky, Emma Cecilia, Eli Bartra, Carmen Boullosa, Blanca Ruiz, and María Elena Blanco. *Mujeres detrás de la lente: 100 Años de creación fotográfica en México 1910–2010*. México DF: Dirección General de Publicaciones del Consejo Nacional para la Cultura y las Artes, 2012.

García Marquez, Gabriel, et al. *Grupo Processo Pentágono/Grupo Suma/Grupo Tetraedro/Taller de Arte e Ideología X Bienal de Paris*. México: INBA, 1977.

García S., Laura. *M D1: Desbordamientos de una periferia femenina*. México DF: Sociedad Dokins para las Nuevas Prácticas Artísticas, 2008.

Garduño, Ana. *El poder del coleccionismo de arte: Alvar Carrillo Gil*. México DF: UNAM, 2009.

Garibay Mora, Juan. "Pola Weiss y el video arte" (parte 2), *Excelsior*, August 17, 1982, C–1.

———. "El video arte, superación de la caja idiota para los seres cuyo pensamiento es visual." *Excelsior*, August 14, 1982, E–1.

Gitelman, Lisa. *Always Already New: Media, History, and the Data of Culture.* Cambridge MA: MIT Press, 2006.

Giunta, Andrea. "Feminist Disruptions in Mexican Art, 1975–1987." *Artelogie V: Arte y género: mujeres creadoras en América Latina,* http://cral.in2p3.fr/artelogie/spip.php article271, accessed September 30, 2013.

Glanz, Margo. *Onda y escritura en México: Jóvenes de 20 a 33.* México: Siglo Veintiuno Editores, 1971.

Goldman, Shifra M. *Contemporary Mexican Painting in a Time of Change.* Austin: University of Texas Press, 1981.

———. *Dimensions of the Americas: Art and Social Change in Latin America and the United States.* Chicago: University of Chicago Press, 1994.

Goldstein, Daniel M. *The Spectacular City: Violence and Performance in Urban Bolivia.* Durham NC: Duke University Press, 2004.

González Alvarado, Rocio. "El espíritu de una época." In *Cartografías del feminismo Mexicano, 1970–2000,* edited by Nora Nínive García, Márgara Millán, and Cynthia Pech, 65–115. México: Universidad Autónoma de la Ciudad de México, 2007.

González de Bustamante, Celeste. *"Muy buenas noches": Mexico, Television, and the Cold War.* Lincoln: University of Nebraska Press, 2013.

González Echevarría, Roberto. *Myth and Archive: A Theory of Latin American Narrative.* Cambridge: Cambridge University Press, 1990.

Goodman, Lizbeth. *Contemporary Feminist Theater: To Each Her Own.* New York and London: Routledge, 1993.

Graham, Richard, ed. *The Idea of Race in Latin America, 1870–1940.* Austin: University of Texas Press, 1990.

Grosz, Elizabeth A. *Space, Time, and Perversion: Essays on the Politics of Bodies.* New York: Routledge, 1995.

Gruzinski, Serge, and Heather MacLean. *Images at War: Mexico from Columbus to Blade Runner (1492–2019).* Durham NC: Duke University Press, 2001.

Guadarrama, Guillermina, and Carlos Martínez. "Una galería de arte en Tepito." In *Abrevian Videos,* vol. 1. Mexico City: CENIDIAP, INBA, 2007.

Guerrilla Girls. *Confessions of the Guerrilla Girls.* New York: Harper Perennial, 1995.

Gutierrez Castañeda, G., ed. *Feminismo en México: Visión histórico-crítica del siglo que termina.* México: UNAM, Programa Universitario de Estudios de Género, 2002.

Guevara Villaseñor, Elsa S. "Las políticas públicas de salud." In *Feminismo en México: Revisión histórico-crítica del siglo que termina,* edited by G. Gutierrez Castañeda, 374–99. México: UNAM, Programa Universitario de Estudios de Género, 2002.

Gutiérrez Castañeda, G. ed. *Feminismo en México: Revisión histórico-crítica del siglo que termina*. México: UNAM, Programa Universitario de Estudios de Género, 2002.

Haraway, Donna J. "A Cyborg Manifesto: Science, Technology, and Socialist-Feminism in the Late Twentieth Century." In *The Cybercultures Reader*, edited by D. Haraway, D. Bell, and B. M. Kennedy, 291–324. New York: Routledge, 2000.

Henaro, Sol. *No Grupo: Un zangoloteo al corsé artístico*. México DF: Museo de Arte Moderno, 2011.

Hernández, A., B. Murphy, and E. Torres-Ramos. *Pola Weiss: La TV. TV Sees You*. México: Museo Universitario de Arte Contemporáneo, 2014.

Hernández Miranda, Dante. *Pola Weiss: Pionera del videoarte en México*. Orizaba, Ver.: Comunidad Morelos, 2000.

Herrera, Hayden. *Frida: A Biography of Frida Kahlo*. New York: Harper and Row, 1983.

Hershfield, Joanne. *Imagining la Chica Moderna: Women, National and Visual Cultures in Mexico 1917–1940*. Durham NC: Duke University Press, 2008.

Hesse, Carla Alison, and Robert Post, eds. *Human Rights in Political Transitions: Gettysburg to Bosnia*. New York: Zone Books, 1999.

Hickey, Neil. "Notas sobre el video subterraneo." In *Video Cinta de Vanguardia, VideoArt: Estética Visual*, exhibition catalogue. México: Galeria de Exposiciones Temporales del Museo de Arte Moderno de Chapultepec, INBA and U.S. Embassy, 1973.

Híjar, Alberto. *Frentes, coaliciones y talleres: Grupos visuales en México en el siglo XX*. México DF: Casa Juan Pablos, Centro Cultural, 2007.

Híjar, Cristina. *Siete grupos de artistas visuales de los setenta*. México DF: Casa Abierta al Tiempo, Universidad Autónoma Metropolitana, Unidad Xochimilco, División de Ciencias y Artes para el Diseño, 2008.

Hiriart, Bertha. "Cine de mujeres." *Fem* 9, no. 33 (April–May 1984): 39–40.

Hirsch, Marianne. *Family Frames: Photography, Narrative, and Postmemory*. Cambridge MA: Harvard University Press, 1997.

Homenaje mínimo a Pola Weiss, VHS, directed by Victor Blanco. México: TV UNAM, 1990.

Hughes, Alex, and Andrea Noble. *Phototextualities: Intersections of Photography and Narrative*. Albuquerque: University of New Mexico Press, 2003.

Huyssen, Andreas. *Twilight Memories: Marking Time in a Culture of Amnesia*. New York: Routledge, 1995.

International Women's Year World Conference Documents. Brok NY: UNIFO Microfiche Edition Publishers, 1975.

Iturbide, Graciela, and Judith Keller. *Juchitán*. Los Angeles: Getty Publications, J. Paul Getty Museum, 2007.

Jacob, Mary Jane. *Shigeko Kubota: Video Sculpture*. New York: American Museum of the Moving Image, 1991.

James, Daniel. *Doña María's Story: Life History, Memory, and Political Identity*. Durham NC: Duke University Press, 2000.

Jaquette, Jane S., ed. *The Women's Movement in Latin America: Participation and Democracy*. Boulder Co: Westview Press, 1994.

Jean, Stéphanie. "Disobedient Video in France in the 1970s: Video Production by Women's Collectives." *Afterall: A Journal of Art, Context, and Enquiry*, issue 27 (Summer 2011): 5–16.

Jones, Amelia. *Self/Image: Technology, Representation, and the Contemporary Subject*. London: Routledge, 2006.

——— . "'Presence in Absentia': Experiencing Performance as Documentation." In *Art Journal* 56, no. 4 (Winter 1997): 11–18.

Jones, Amelia, ed. *The Feminism and Visual Culture Reader*. London: Routledge, 2010.

Joseph, Gilbert M., Anne Rubenstein, and Eric Zolov, eds. *Fragments of a Golden Age: The Politics of Culture in Mexico since 1940*. Durham NC: Duke University Press, 2001.

Joya, Mario García. "Relación entre la realidad y estilos de la fotografía en America Latina." In *Hecho en Latino América: Memorias del primer coloquio latino americano de fotografía*, by Consejo Mexicano de Fotografía, 11–18. Ciudad de México: Consejo Mexicano de Fotografía, 1978.

Juhasz, Alexandra. "Our Auto-Bodies, Ourselves: Representing Real Women in Feminist Video." *Afterimage* 21, no. 7 (February 1994): 10–14.

——— . "They say we were trying to show reality—all I wanted to show is my video: The Politics of Realist Feminist Documentary." In *Lo personal es político: Feminismo y documental*, 136–71. España, Gobierno de Navarra: Instituto Navarro de las Artes Audiovisuales y la Cinematografía, 2011.

Kam, Vanessa D. "Archives as Art: The Accumulations of Felipe Ehrenberg and Lynn Hershman Lesson." *Imprint* 26, no.1 (Winter 2008): 5–16.

Kendall, Richard, and Griselda Pollock. *Dealing with Degas: Representations of Women and the Politics of Vision*. New York: Universe, 1992.

Kiddle, Amelia M., and María L. O. Muñoz, eds. *Populism in Twentieth-Century Mexico: The Presidencies of Lázaro Cárdenas and Luis Echeverría*. Tucson: University of Arizona Press, 2010.

Klein, Emily. "Spectacular Citizenship: Staging Latina Resistance through Urban Performances of Pain." *Frontiers: Journal of Women's Studies* 32, no. 1 (2011): 102–12.

Knight, Alan. "Racism, Revolution and *Indigenismo*." In *The Idea of Race in Latin America, 1870–1940*, 71–114, edited by Richard Graham. Austin: University of Texas Press, 1990.

———. "The Revolution Is Dead: *Viva la Revolución*." *LASA Forum* 41, no. 4 (Fall 2010): 18–21.

Kofman, Eleonore, and Elizabeth Lebas, eds. *Writing on Cities: Henri Lefebvre*. Oxford: Blackwell Publishers, 1999.

Krauss, Rosalind. "Video: The Aesthetics of Narcissism." *October* 1 (Spring 1976): 50–64.

Lachino, Hayde, and Nayeli Benhumea. *Videodanza, de la escena a la pantalla*. México: UNAM, 2012.

Lamas, Marta. "Cuerpo y política: La batalla por despenalizar el aborto." In *Un fantasma que recorre el siglo*, edited by Lau Jaiven and Espinoza Damian, 183–212. México: Universidad Autónoma Metropolitana, 2011.

———. *Feminismo: transmisiones y retransmisiones*. México: Taurus, 2006.

———. "El Feminismo Mexicano y la lucha por el aborto." *Politica y Cultura* 1 (Otoño, 1992): 9–22.

———. "Fragmentos de una autocritica." In *Feminismo en México: Revisión histórico-crítica del siglo que termina*, edited by Griselda Gutiérrez Castañeda, 71–79. Mexico City: UNAM, Programa Universitario de Estudios de Genero, 2002.

———. *Miradas feministas sobre las mexicanas del siglo XX*. México DF: Fondo de Cultura Económica, 2007.

———. *Politica y reproducción. Aborto: La frontera del derecho a decidir*. México: Plaza y Janés, 2001.

Lamas, Marta, and Dora Cardaci. "Dossier: El feminismo en Italia," *Debate Feminista* 1, no. 2 (1990): 29–33.

Lara, Magali. "La memoria es como una piedra pulida." In *Critica feminista en la teoría e historia del arte*, edited by Karen Cordero Reinman and Inda Sáenz, 415–20. México: Universidad Iberoamericana, 2007.

Larson, Catherine, and Margarita Vargas, eds. *Latin American Women Dramatists: Theater, Texts, and Theories*. Bloomington: Indiana University Press, 1998.

Lau Jaiven, Ana. "Emergencia y trascendencia del neofeminismo." In *Un fantasma recorre el siglo: Luchas feministas en México 1910–2010*, edited by Ana Lau Jaiven and Gisela Espinosa Damián, 158. México: Universidad Autónoma Metropolitana, 2011.

———. *La nueva ola del feminismo en México: Conciencia y acción de lucha de las mujeres*. México DF: Fascículos Planeta, 1987.

Lau Jaiven, Ana, and Gisela Espinosa Damián, eds. *Un fantasma recorre el Siglo: Luchas feministas en México 1910–2010*. México: Universidad Autónoma Metropolitana, 2011.

Lefebvre, Henri. *The Production of Space*. Oxford: Blackwell, 1991.

Lesage, Julia. "Women Make Media: Three Modes of Production." In *The Social Documentary in Latin America*, edited by Julianne Burton, 315–50. Pittsburgh: University of Pittsburgh Press, 1990.

Levitas, Ruth. *The Concept of Utopia*. Syracuse NY: Syracuse University Press, 1990.

Lindón, Alicia. "Diálogo con Néstor García Canclini ¿Qué son los imaginarios y cómo actúan en la ciudad?" *Revista Eure* XXXIII, no. 99 (2007): 89–99.

Lippard, Lucy. *Mixed Blessings: New Art in a Multicultural America*. New York: Pantheon, 1990.

Liquois, Dominique. *De los grupos a los individuos: Artistas plásticos de los grupos metropolitanos*. México: Museo Carrillo Gil–INBA, 1985.

Lomnitz-Adler, Claudio. *Deep Mexico, Silent Mexico: An Anthropology of Nationalism*. Minneapolis: University of Minnesota Press, 2001.

Long, J. J., Andrea Noble, and Edward Welch, eds. *Photography: Theoretical Snapshots*. London: Routledge, 2009.

López, Ana M. "Towards a 'Third' and 'Imperfect' Cinema: A Theoretical and Historical Study of Filmmaking in Latin America. Thesis." PhD diss., University of Iowa, 1986.

López, Rick A. *Crafting Mexico. Intellectuals, Artisans, and the State after the Revolution*. Durham NC: Duke University Press, 2010.

———. "Ethnicizing the Nation. The India Bonita Contest of 1921." In *Crafting Mexico: Intellectuals, Artisans, and the State after the Revolution*, 29–65. Durham: Duke University Press, 2010.

Lovera, Sara. "Feminismo y medios de comunicación." In *Un fantasma recorre el siglo: Luchas feministas en México 1910–2010*, edited by Ana Lau Jaiven and Gisela Espinosa Damián, 529. México: Universidad Autónoma Metropolitana, 2011.

Ludec, Nathalie. "La Boletina de Morelia: Órgano informativo de la Red Nacional de Mujeres 1982–1985." *Comunicacion y Sociedad* (Universidad de Guadalajara), no. 5 (Enero–Junio 2006): 89–113.

Mabire, Bernardo. *Políticas culturales y educativas del Estado Mexicano, 1970 a 1997*. México: El Colegio de México, Centro de Estudios Internacionales, 2003.

Macías, Anna. *Against All Odds: The Feminist Movement in Mexico to 1940*. Westport CT: Greenwood Press, 1982.

Macías-González, Víctor M., and Anne Rubenstein, eds. *Masculinity and Sexuality in Modern Mexico*. Albuquerque: University of New Mexico Press, 2012.

Machado, Arlindo. "Video Art: The Brazilian Adventure." *Leonardo* 29, no. 3 (1996): 225–31.

Magdaleno Cárdenas, María de los Ángeles. "Documentos sobre la Policía." *Históricas: Boletín de Instituto de Investigaciones Históricas* 77 (September–December 2006): 34–45.

Mandoki, Katya. "Boom y trasfondo ideológico de la fotografía en México." In *Aspectos de la fotografía en México, vol. 1*, edited by Rogelio Villareal, 41–42. México: Federación Editorial Mexicana, 1981.

Marks, Laura U. *The Skin of Film: Intercultural Cinema, Embodiment, and the Senses*. Durham NC: Duke University Press, 2000.

Marsh, Leslie L. *Brazilian Women's Filmmaking: From Dictatorship to Democracy*. Urbana: University of Illinois Press, 2013

Martin, Michael T., ed. *New Latin American Cinema*, vol. 1: *Theory, Practices and Transcontinental Articulations*. Detroit MI: Wayne State University Press, 1997.

Massey, Doreen. *Space, Place, and Gender*. Minneapolis: University of Minnesota Press, 1994.

Massolo, Alejandra. *Por amor y coraje: Mujeres en movimientos urbanos de la ciudad de México*. México DF: Colegio de México, Programa Interdisciplinario de Estudios de la Mujer, 1992.

Mayer, Mónica. "De la vida y el arte como feminista." In *Critica feminista en la teoría e historia del arte*, edited by Karen Cordero Reinman and Inda Sáenz, 403. México: Universidad Iberoamericana, 2007.

———. "Propuesta para un arte feminista," *Fem* 9, no. 33 (April–May 1984): 12–15

———. *Rosa Chillante: Mujeres y performance en México*. México: CONACULTA-FONCA, 2004.

———. *Traducciones: Un diálogo internacional de mujeres artistas*. In Mayer, personal archive, self-published, 1979.

———. "Video a la mexicana: De sexo-s, amor y humor." In *Exposiciones: Contraseñas, nuevas representaciones sobre la femineidad*. Araba, Territorio Basco: Centro Cultural Montehermoso, 2010, http://www.montehermoso.net/pagina.php?id_p=351, accessed July 25, 2013.

Mayer, Mónica, and Karen Cordero. "Mujeres ¿y que más? Reactivando el archivo de Ana Victoria Jiméncz," http://archivoavj.com, accessed April 5, 2011.

Mayer, Sophie, and Elena Oroz. *Lo personal es politico. Feminismo y documental: Una compilación de ensayos sobre documental y feminismo (The personal is political: Feminism and documentary: A compilation of essays on documentary and feminism)*. Pamplona: Gobierno de Navarra, 2011.

McCaughan, Edward J. *Art and Social Movements: Cultural Politics in Mexico and Aztlán*. Durham NC: Duke University Press, 2012.

Medina, Cuauhtémoc. *Graciela Iturbide*. London: Phaidon Press, 2001.

Meigh-Andrews, Chris. *A History of Video Art: The Development of Form and Function*. Oxford: Berg, 2006.

Mejía Barquera, Fernando. *La industria de la radio y la televisión y la política del estado mexicano*. México DF: Fundación Manuel Buendía, 1989.

———. "Television y política." In *Apuntes hacia la historia de la television en México*. México DF: Fundación Manuel Buendía, 1989.

Méndez, José Carlos. "Hacia un cine político: La cooperativa de cine marginal." *La Cultura en México, Siempre!*, July 19, 1972, ix–xiii.

Mendiola, Salvador, Hortensia Moreno, et al. "El ritual amoroso de la bruja eléctrica (1947–1990)." Museo de las Mujeres, 1999, http://www.museodemujeres.com /matriz/biblioteca/020_polaWeiss.html, accessed May 10, 2012.Merewether, Charles. *The Archive*. London: Whitechapel, 2006.

Millán, Márgara. *Derivas de un cine en femenino*. México DF: M. A. Porrúa, 1999.

———. "Vocaciones: Cine y video mexicano hecho por mujeres." In *Miradas feministas sobre las mexicanas del siglo XX*, edited by Marta Lamas, 417. México DF: Fondo de Cultura Económica, 2007.

Minter, Sarah. "A vuelo de pájaro, el video en México: Sus inicios y contextos." In *Video en Latino America: Una historia crítica*, edited by Laura Baigorri, 159–67. Madrid: Aecid, 2008.

Miró Vázquez, Juan José. *La televisión y el poder político en México*. México: Diana, 1997.

Mirzoeff, Nicholas. *An Introduction to Visual Culture*. London: Routledge, 1999.

———. *The Right to Look: A Counterhistory of Visuality*. Durham NC: Duke University Press, 2011.

Moi, Toril. *French Feminist Thought: A Reader*. Oxford: Blackwell, 1987.

Mongrovejo, Norma. "Sexual Preference, the Ugly Duckling of Feminist Demands: The Lesbian Movement in Mexico." In *Female Desires: Same-Sex Relations and Transgender Practices across Cultures*, edited by E. Blackwood and S. Wieringa, 308–36. New York: Columbia University Press, 1999.

———. *Un amor que se atrevió a decir su nombre: La lucha de las lesbianas y su relación con los movimientos homosexual y feminista en América Latina*. Mexico: UNAM, 1998.

Monroy Nasr, Rebeca. *Ases de la cámara: Textos sobre fotografía mexicana*. México: Instituto Nacional de Antropología e Historia, 2010.

Monsiváis, Carlos. *Entrada libre: Crónicas de la sociedad que se organiza*. México: Ediciones Era, 1987.

———. "Foreword: When Gender Can't Be Seen amid the Symbols." In *Sex in Revolution: Gender Politics, and Power in Modern Mexico*, edited by Jocelyn

Olcott, Mary K. Vaughan, and Gabriela Cano. Durham NC: Duke University Press, 2007.

———. "Travelers in Mexico: A Brief Anthology of Selected Myths." *Diogenes* 32, no. 125 (1984): 48–72.

Morgan, Robin. *Sisterhood Is Powerful: An Anthology of Writings from the Women's Liberation Movement*. New York: Random House, 1970.

Mraz, John. *Looking for Mexico: Modern Visual Culture and National Identity*. Durham NC: Duke University Press, 2009.

———. *Nacho López y el fotoperiodismo de los años cincuenta*. México: Oceano-CONACULTA, 1999.

Mraz, John, and Ariel Arnal. *La mirada inquieta. Nuevo fotoperiodismo mexicano: 1976–1996*. México: Centro de la Imagen, 1996.

Mulvey, Laura, "Visual Pleasure and Narrative Cinema." *Screen* 16, no. 3 (Autumn 1975): 6–18.

Muñoz, J. E. "Ephemera as Evidence: Introductory Notes to Queer Acts." *Women and Performance* 8, no. 2 (1996): 5–16.

Muñoz, María L. *"We speak for ourselves": The First National Congress of Indigenous Peoples and the Politics of Indigenismo in Mexico, 1968–1982*. PhD diss., University of Arizona, 2009.

Murillo, Julio García, and Pilar García de Germenos. *Grupo Proceso Pentágono: Politics of the Intervention 1969–1976*. Mexico: Museo Universitario de Arte Contemporáneo, UNAM, 2015.

Museo de Arte Moderno, *Salon 77, Bienal de Febrero: Nuevas Tendencias*. México DF: INBA, 1978.

———. *Video Cinta de Vanguardia, VideoArt: Estética Visual*, exhibition catalogue. México: Galeria de Exposiciones Temporales del Museo de Arte Moderno de Chapultepec, INBA and U.S. Embassy, 1973.

Museo del Barrio (New York), Deborah Cullen, and Maris Bustamante. *Arte [No Es] Vida: Actions by Artists of the Americas 1960–2000*. New York: El Museo del Barrio, 2008.

Nadie es inocente, DVD, directed by Sarah Minter, 1986.

Naranjo, Silvia, and Humberto Reyes. "El condicionamiento mental a través de las imágenes." Bachelor's thesis, UNAM, December, 1977.

Near the Big Chakra, directed by Ann Severson (aka Alice Anne Parker). USA, 1971.

Newman, Amy. *Changing: Art Forum 1962–1974*. New York: Soho Press, 2000

Newman, Michael, and Jon Bird. *Rewriting Conceptual Art*. London, UK: Reaktion Books, 1999.

Nigro, Katherine F. "Inventions and Transgressions: A Fractured Narrative on Feminist Theater." In *Negotiating Performance: Gender and Sexuality in Latin/o America*, edited by Diana Taylor and Juan Villegas, 135–58. Durham NC: Duke University Press, 1994.

Noble, Andrea. "Family Photography and the Global Drama of Human Rights." In *Photography: Theoretical Snapshots*, edited by J. J. Long, Andrea Noble, and Edward Welch, 71. London: Routledge, 2009.

———. "Gender in the Archive: Maria Zavala and the Drama of (Not) Looking." In *Phototextualities: Intersections of Photography and Narrative*, edited by Alex Hughes and Andrea Noble, 136–64. Albuquerque: University of New Mexico Press, 2003.

———. *Photography and Memory in Mexico: Icons of Revolution*. Manchester: Manchester University Press, 2010.

———. *Tina Modotti: Image, Texture, Photography*. Albuquerque: University of New Mexico Press, 2000.

Nochlin, Linda. "Why Haven't There Been No Great Women Artists?" *Art News* 69, no. 9 (January 1971): 22.

Noordegraaf, Julia, Cosetta G. Saba, Barbara Le Maître, and Vinzenz Hediger, eds. *Preserving and Exhibiting Media Art: Challenges and Perspectives*. Amsterdam: Amsterdam University Press, 2013.

Noriega, Chon A. *Visible Nations: Latin American Cinema and Video*. Minneapolis: University of Minnesota Press, 2000.

Ocharán, Leticia. "La mujer en la gráfica mexicana." *Fem* 9, no. 33 (April–May 1984): 20–21.

Olcott, Jocelyn. "Cold War Conflicts and Cheap Cabaret: Sexual Politics at the 1975 United Nations International Women's Year Conference." *Gender and History* 22, no. 3 (November 2010): 733–54.

———. *Revolutionary Women in Postrevolutionary Mexico*. Durham NC: Duke University Press, 2006.

———. "'Take Off That Streetwalker's Dress': Concha Michel and the Cultural Politics of Gender in Postrevolutionary Mexico." *Journal of Women's History* 21, no. 3 (Fall 2009): 36–59.

Olcott, Jocelyn, Mary K. Vaughan, and Gabriela Cano, eds. *Sex in Revolution: Gender, Politics, and Power in Modern Mexico*. Durham NC: Duke University Press, 2006.

Pacheco, Cristina. *La luz de México: Entrevistas con pintores y fotógrafos*. México DF: Fondo de Cultura Economica, 1988.

Padilla, Tanalis, and Louise E. Walker, eds. "Spy Reports: Content, Methodology, and Historiography in Mexico's Secret Police Archive." *Journal of Iberian and Latin American Research* 19, no. 1 (July 2013): 1–103.

Paz, Octavio. *El ogro filantrópico: Historia y política, 1971–1978*. México: Joaquín Mortiz Editores, 1979.

Pech, Cynthia. *Fantasmas en tránsito: Prácticas discursivas de videastas mexicanas*. México: Universidad Autónoma de la Ciudad de México, 2009.

Pensado, Jaime M. "Political Violence and Student Culture in Mexico: The Consolidation of Porrismo during the 1950s and 1960s." PhD thesis, University of Chicago, 2008.

———. *Rebel Mexico: Student Unrest and Authoritarian Political Culture during the Long Sixties*. Stanford: Stanford University Press, 2013.

Perez, Careaga. "La lucha por el placer." In *Feminismo en México: Revisión histórico-crítica del siglo que termina*, edited by G. Gutierrez Castañeda, 71–82. México: UNAM, Programa Universitario de Estudios de Género, 2002.

Pérez Montfort, Ricardo. *Estampas de nacionalismo popular mexicano: Ensayos sobre cultura popular y nacionalismo*. México: CIESAS, 1994.

———. "Indigenismo, hispanismo y panamericanismo en la cultura popular Mexicana de 1920 a 1940." In *Cultura e identidad nacional*, edited by Roberto Blancarte, 343–83. Mexico City: Fondo de Cultura Económica, 1994.

Pérez Salas, María Esther. *Costumbrismo y litografía en México: Un nuevo modo de ver*. México: UNAM, Instituto de Investigaciones Estéticas, 2005.

Piccato, Pablo. *City of Suspects: Crime in México, 1900–1931*. Durham NC: Duke University Press, 2001.

———. "Comments: How to Build a Perspective on the Recent Past." *Journal of Iberian Research* 19, no. 1 (July 2013): 91–102.

Picazo Sánchez, Leticia. *Una década de video en México: Dependencia extranjera y monopolios nacionales*. México: Editorial Trillas, 1991.

Pola Weiss, Re-Conocimiento. Digital video, directed by Edna Torres, screenplay by Roberto Galicia Casas. México: CominTV, 2012.

Pollock, Griselda. *Encounters in the Virtual Feminist Museum: Time, Space, and the Archive*. London: Routledge, 2007.

———. "Unexpected Turns: The Aesthetic, the Pathetic, and the Adversarial in the Long Durée of Art's Histories." *Journal of Art Historiography*, no. 7 (2012): 1–32.

Ponce, Armando. *México, su apuesta por la cultura: El siglo XX, testimonios desde el presente*. México DF: Editorial Grijalbo, 2003.

Poniatowska, Elena. *La raíz y el camino: Mariana Yampolsky*. México DF: Fondo de Cultura Económica, 1985.

———. *Luz y luna, las lunitas*. México DF: Editorial Era, 1994.

Poniatowska, Elena, and Pablo Ortiz. "Monasterio." In *Juchitán de las mujeres*. México: Ediciones Toledo, 1989.

Poole, Deborah. "An Image of 'Our Indian': Type Photographs and Racial Sentiments in Oaxaca, 1920–1940." *Hispanic American Historical Review* 84, no. 1 (February 2004): 37–82.

———. *Vision, Race, and Modernity: A Visual Economy of the Andean Image World*. Princeton: Princeton University Press, 1997.

Portilla, Jorge. *Fenomenología del relajo*. México: Ediciones Era, 1966.

Prakash, Gyan, and Kevin M. Kruse, eds. *The Spaces of the Modern City: Imaginaries, Politics, and Everyday Life*. Princeton: Princeton University Press, 2008.

Quintero, Genoveva Flores. "Prensa feminista: 30 años de batallas por el espacio público." In *Mujeres y sociedad en el México contemporáneo: Nombrar lo inombrable*, edited by María Ileana García Gossio, 203–31. México DF: H. Cámara de Diputados, LIX legislatura, Tecnológico de Monterrey, 2004.

Rama, Angel. *The Lettered City*. Durham NC: Duke University Press, 1996.

Ramírez Berg, Charles. *Cinema of Solitude: A Critical Study of Mexican Film, 1967–1983*. Austin: University of Texas Press, 1992.

———. "Women's Images I and II." In *Cinema of Solitude: A Critical Study of Mexican Film, 1967–1983*, 55–97. Austin: University of Texas Press, 1992.

Ramos Escandón, Carmen. "Women's Movements, Feminism, and Mexican Politics." In *The Women's Movement in Latin America: Participation Democracy*, edited by Jane S. Jaquette, 199–221. Boulder CO: Westview Press, 1994.

Ranucci, Karen. "On the Trail of Independent Video." In *The Social Documentary in Latin America*, edited by Julianne Burton, 193–208. Pittsburgh: University of Pittsburgh Press, 1990.

Rappaport, Joanne, and Tom Cummins. *Beyond the Lettered City: Indigenous Literacies in the Andes*. Durham NC: Duke University Press, 2012

Rashkin, Elissa J. *The Stridentist Movement in Mexico: The Avant-Garde and Cultural Change in the 1920s*. Lanham MD: Lexington Books, 2009.

———. *Women Filmmakers in Mexico: The Country of Which We Dream*. Austin: University of Texas Press, 2001.

Reyes Castellanos, Francisca, and Ana Victoria Jiménez. *Sembradoras de futuros: Memoria de la Unión Nacional de Mujeres Mexicanas*. México: UNMM, 2000.

Reyes Palma, Francisco, and Carlos Monsiváis. *El México de Mariana Yampolsky: Rito y regocijos*. México: Fundación Cultural Mariana Yampolsky, 2005.

Richard, Nelly. *Masculine/Feminine: Practices of Difference(s)*. Durham NC: Duke University Press, 2004.

Rivera, Hector. "Pola Weiss, pionera del videoarte en México, denuncia al video clip." *Revista Proceso*, no. 578, November 30, 1987, 44–45.

Rivera, Norma Inés. *Pata de perro: Biografia de Héctor García*. México: CONACULTA, 2007.

Rizk, Beatriz J. *Posmodernismo y teatro en América Latina: Teorías y prácticas en el umbral del siglo XXI*. Madrid: Iberoamericana, 2001.

Rolnik, Suely. "Furor de Archivo." *Estudios Visuales: Ensayo, teoría y crítica de la cultura visual y el arte contemporáneo*, no. 7, 2010, http://www.estudiosvisuales .net/revista/, accessed April 24, 2011.

Rompiendo el Silencio, DVD, directed by Rosa Martha Fernández. México: UNAM and Colectivo Cine-Mujer, 1979.

Rosenberg, Douglas. *Screendance: Inscribing the Ephemeral Image*. Oxford: Oxford University Press, 2012.

Roth, Moira. "The Voice of Shigeko Kubota: A Fusion of Art and Life, Asia and America." In *Shigeko Kubota. Video Sculpture*, edited by Mary Jane Jacob, Catalogue, 74. New York: American Museum of the Moving Image, 1991.

Roy, Marina. "Corporeal Returns: Feminism and Phenomenology in Vancouver Video and Performance 1968–1983." *Canadian Art* (Toronto), Summer 2001.

Rubenstein, Anne. *Bad Language, Naked Ladies, and Other Threats to the Nation: A Political History of Comic Books in Mexico*. Durham NC: Duke University Press, 1998.

———. "The War on Las Pelonas: Modern Women and Their Enemies, Mexico City, 1924." In *Sex in Revolution: Gender, Politics and Power in Modern Mexico*, edited by Mary Kay Vaughan et al., 57–80. Durham NC: Duke University Press, 2007.

Rubin, Jeffrey W. *Decentering the Regime: Ethnicity, Radicalism, and Democracy in Juchitán, México*. Durham NC: Duke University Press, 1997.

Samperio Díaz, Jessica, and María de Pilar Vázquez Salcedo. "Análisis de la representación de la mujer en los medios impresos de la campaña de El Palacio de Hierro." Bachelor's thesis, Universidad de las Américas Puebla, 2004.

Sánchez Olvera, Alma Rosa. *El feminismo méxicano ante el movimiento urbano popular: Dos expresiones de lucha de género (1970–1980)*. México: Plaza y Valdés, 2002.

Sánchez Susarrey, Jaime. *El debate político e intelectual en México*. México: Grijalbo, 1993.

Scarry, Elaine. "The Difficulty of Imagining Other Persons." In *Human Rights in Political Transition: Gettysburg to Bosnia*, edited by Carla Hesse and Robert Post, 282. New York: Zone Books, 1999.

Schmidt, Samuel. *Democracia Mexicana. La reforma política de López Portillo: Un nuevo discurso?* México DF: UNAM, Facultad de Ciencias Políticas y Sociales, Centro de Estudios Latinoamericanos, 1981.

———. *The Deterioration of the Mexican Presidency: The Years of Luis Echeverría.* Tucson: University of Arizona Press, 1991.

Schneider, Rebecca. "Archive Performance Remains." *Performance Research* 6, no. 2 (2001): 100–8.

———. *The Explicit Body in Performance.* London: Routledge, 1997.

———. *Performing Remains: Art and War in Times of Theatrical Reenactment.* Abingdon, UK: Routledge, 2011.

Scott, Joan Wallach. *Género e historia.* México: Fondo de Cultura Económica, 2008.

Segre, Erica. *Intersected Identities: Strategies of Visualisation in Nineteenth- and Twentieth-Century Mexican Culture.* New York: Berghahn Books, 2007.

Sierra, Sonia. "Pola Weiss, la madre del videoarte mexicano." *El Universal*, Friday, September 7, 2012.

Silverman, Kaja. *The Acoustic Mirror: The Female Voice in Psychoanalysis and Cinema.* Bloomington: Indiana University Press, 1988.

Sluis, Ageeth. "Bataclanismo! Or, How Female Deco Bodies Transformed Postrevolutionary México." *Americas* 66, no. 4 (April 2010): 469–99.

Smith, Shawn Michelle. *Photography on the Color Line: W. E. B. DuBois, Race, and Visual Culture.* Durham NC: Duke University Press, 2004.

Solomon-Godeau, Abigail. *Photography at the Dock: Essays on Photographic History, Institutions, and Practices.* Minneapolis: University of Minnesota Press, 1994.

Soto Laveaga, Gabriela. *Jungle Laboratories: Mexican Peasants, National Projects, and the Making of the Pill.* Durham NC: Duke University Press, 2009.

———. "'Let's Become Fewer': Soap Operas, the Pill and Population Campaigns, 1976–1986." *Sexuality Research and Social Policy Journal* 4, no. 3 (September 2007): 19–33.

Spieker, Sven. *The Big Archive: Art from Bureaucracy.* Cambridge MA: MIT Press, 2008.

Spielmann, Yvonne. *Video: The Reflexive Medium.* Cambridge MA: MIT Press, 2008.

———. "Video: From Technology to Medium." *Art Journal* 65, no. 3 (Fall 2006): 54–69.

Spivak, Gayatri Chakravorty. "The Rani of Sirmur: An Essay in Reading the Archives." *History and Theory* 24, no. 3 (1985): 247–72.

Stallabrass, Julian. *Art Incorporated: The Story of Contemporary Art.* Oxford: Oxford University Press, 2004.

Steele, Cynthia. *Politics, Gender, and the Mexican Novel, 1968–1988.* Austin: University of Texas Press, 1992.

Stephen, Lynn. "The Creation and Re-Creation of Ethnicity: Lessons from the Zapotec and Mixtec of Oaxaca." *Latin American Perspectives* 23, no. 2 (1996): 17–37.

Stimson, Blake, and Gregory Sholette, eds. *Collectivism after Modernism: The Art of Social Imagination after 1945.* Minneapolis: University of Minnesota Press, 2007.

Stites Mor, Jessica. *Transition Cinema: Political Filmmaking and the Argentine Left Since 1968.* Pittsburgh: University of Pittsburgh Press, 2012.

Stoler, Ann Laura. *Along the Archival Grain: Epistemic Anxieties and Colonial Common Sense.* Princeton: Princeton University Press, 2009

———. "Colonial Archives and the Art of Governance: On the Content in the Form." In *Refiguring the Archive,* edited by Carolyn Hamilton et al., 83–100. Cape Town, South Africa: David Phillip, 2002.

Superocheros: Antologia del Super 8 en México (1970–1986), DVD. México: Filmoteca de la UNAM, 2007.

Tapia López, Hilda. "Manifestación de Mujeres en Pro de Que Se Legalice el Aborto," *El Día,* May 11, 1979.

Taussig, Michael. *Mimesis and Alterity.* New York: Routledge, 1993.

Taylor, Diana. *The Archive and the Repertoire: Performing Cultural Memory in the Americas.* Durham NC: Duke University Press, 2003.

———. *Disappearing Acts: Spectacles of Gender and Nationalism in Argentina's "Dirty War."* Durham NC: Duke University Press, 1997.

———. "'You Are Here': The DNA of Performance." *TDR: The Drama Review* 46, no.1 (2002): 149–69.

Taylor, Diana, and Juan Villegas, eds. *Negotiating Performance: Gender and Sexuality in Latin/o America.* Durham NC: Duke University Press, 1994.

Taylor, Analisa. "Malinche and Matriarchal Utopia: Gendered Visions of Indigeneity in Mexico." *Signs: Journal of Women in Culture and Society* 31, no. 3 (Spring 2006): 815–40.

Tejada, Roberto. *National Camera: Photography and Mexico's Image Environment.* Minneapolis: University of Minnesota Press, 2009.

Tibol, Raquel. "Mujer en el arte mexicano del siglo XIX," *Fem* 9, no. 33 (April–May 1984): 4–6.

"Tlacuilas y Retrateras," *Fem* 9, no. 33 (April–May 1984): 41–44.

Torres-Ramos, Edna. "El video arte en México: El caso de Pola Weiss." Bachelor's thesis, UNAM, 1997.

Tovar Ramírez, Aurora. *Mil quinientas mujeres en nuestra conciencia colectiva: Catálogo biográfico de mujeres de México.* México: Documentación y Estudio de Mujeres, 1966.

Trejo Delarbe, Raúl. *Televisa, Quinto Poder.* México: Claves Latinoamericanas, 1985.

Trevizo, Dolores. *Rural Protest and the Making of Democracy in Mexico, 1968–2000.* University Park: Pennsylvania State University Press, 2011.

Trouillot, Michel-Rolph. *Silencing the Past: Power and the Production of History.* Boston MA: Beacon Press, 1995.

Tuñon, Julia. "Femininity, Indigenismo, and Nation: Film Representation by Emilio 'El Indio' Fernández." In *Sex in Revolution: Gender, Politics, and Power in Modern Mexico*, edited by Mary Kay Vaughan et al., 95. Durham NC: Duke University Press, 2007.

Tuñón Pablos, Esperanza. *Mujeres que se organizan: El Frente Unico Pro Derechos de la Mujer, 1935–1938.* México: UNAM, 1992.

———. *Mujeres en escena: De la tramoya al protagonismo (1982–1994).* México DF: PUEG, 1997.

Tyler, Stephen A. "Post-Modern Ethnography: From Document of the Occult to Occult Document." In *Writing Culture: The Poetics and Politics of Ethnography*, edited by James Clifford and George Marcus, 126. Berkeley: University of California Press, 1986.

Uribarri, Gabriel A. *Tiempo de Echeverría.* México: Martín Casillas Editores, 1985.

Urrutía, Elena, coord. *Estudios sobre las mujeres y las relaciones de género en México: Aportes desde diversas disciplinas* (colloquium, September 21, 1998). México: El Colegio de México, 2002.

Vázquez Mantecón, Álvaro. "Contracultura e ideología en los inicios del cine mexicanos en super-8." In *Superocheros: Antologia del Super 8 en México (1970–1986)*. Mexico: Filmoteca de la UNAM, 2007.

Vergara, Erandy. "Electronic Traces: Archeological Perspectives of Media Art in Mexico." *Arceee. Revue en Ligne: Arts Mediatiques & Cyberculture*, http://archee .qc.ca/ar.php?page=article&no=430, accessed July 4, 2013.

Villareal, Rogelio M. *Aspectos de la fotografía en México, vol. 1.* México: Federación Editorial Mexicana, 1981.

Villegas, M. Gladys. *La imagen femenina en artistas mexicanas contemporáneas: Una perspectiva no androcéntrica.* Xalapa, Ver.: Universidad Veracruzana, 2006.

Villela, Samuel, and Sara Castrejón Reza. *Sara Castrejón: Fotógrafa de la Revolución.* México: Instituto Nacional de Antropología e Historia, 2010.

Walker, Louise E. "Spying at the Drycleaners: Anonymous Gossip in 1973 Mexico City." *Journal of Iberian and Latin American Research* 19, no. 1 (July 2013): 52–61.

Warman, Arturo. *De eso que llaman antropología mexicana.* México DF: Editorial Nuestro Tiempo, 1970.

Warner, Michael. *Publics and Counterpublics.* Cambridge MA: MIT Press, 2002.

———. "Publics and Counterpublics (abbreviated version)." *Quarterly Journal of Speech* 88, no. 4 (September 2002): 413–25.

Weiss, Pola. "Antología de videos y performance." Tríptico—Invitación. Galería Chapultepec, México, 1982. Fondo "Pola Weiss," ARKEHIA, MUAC.

———. "Diseño para una unidad de producción de material didáctico en video tape." Bachelor's thesis, UNAM, 1975.

———. "*La* TV TE VE," *Artes Visuales*, no. 17, March–May 1978.

Weiss, Pola, director. *artveing.* VHS, n. 3. México: artTV, 1982–83.

———. *Autovideoato,* VHS, n. 2. México: artTV, 1979.

———. *Autovideoato 2,* VHS, n. 3. México: artTV, 1982.

———. *El Avion,* VHS, n. 5. México: artTV, 1983.

———. *Ciudad-mujer-ciudad,* VHS, n. 1. México City: artTV, 1978.

———. *Cuetzalan y yo.* México City: artTV, 1979.

———. *Cuilapan de Guerrero,* VHS, n. 1. México: artTV, 1979.

———. *David,* VHS, n. 5. Mexico City: artTV, 1983.

———. *El eclipse,* VHS, n. 3. México: artTV, 1982.

———. *El salto,* VHS, n. 3. Mexico City: artTV, 1982.

———. *Exogeo,* VHS, n. 3. México: artTV, 1981.

———. *Flor cósmica,* VHS, n. 1. Mexico City: artTV, 1977.

———. *Freud-hombre,* VHS, n. 1. Mexico City: artTV and Series Pensamiento Analítico Actual, TV UNAM, 1978.

———. *Inertia,* VHS, n. 4. Mexico City: artTV, 1985, 1989.

———. *Merlin,* VHS, n. 4. México: artTV, 1985.

———. *Los Muertos en Etla,* VHS, n. 1. Mexico City: artTV, 1979.

———. *Mi corazón,* VHS, n. 4. México: artTV, 1986.

———. *Navideo,* VHS, n. 3. México: artTV, 1982.

———. *Papalotl,* VHS, n. 2. México: artTV, 1979.

———. *Romulado García,* VHS, n. 4. México: artTV, 1985.

———. *Santa Cruz Tepexpan,* VHS, n. 1. Mexico City: artTV, 1979.

———. *Sol ó aguila,* VHS, n. 2. Mexico City: artTV, 1980.

———. *Las tasas de interés, El salto,* VHS, n. 3. Mexico City: artTV, 1983.

———. *Todavía Estamos,* VHS, n. 2. México: artTV, 1979.

———. *Toti Amiga,* VHS, n. 3. México: artTV, 1983.

———. *Videodanza,* VHS, n. 2. México: artTV, 1979.

———. *Videoorigen de Weiss,* VHS, n. 4. México: artTV, 1983.

———. *Videopus,* VHS, n. 4. México: artTV, 1980, 1982.

———. *Wegee,* VHS, n. 4. México: artTV, 1985.

Williams, Raymond. *Keywords: A Vocabulary of Culture and Society*. New York: Oxford University Press, 1983.

Wolf, Mikael D. *Watering the Revolution: An Environmental and Technological History of Agrarian Reform in Mexico*. Durham NC: Duke University Press, 2017.

Wood, David M. J. "Film and the Archive: Nation, Heritage, Resistance." *Cosmos and History: The Journal of Natural and Social Philosophy* 6, no. 2 (2010): 162–74.

Wood, Paul. *Conceptual Art*. New York: Delano Greenidge, 2002.

Wortham, Erica Cusi. *Indigenous Media in Mexico: Culture, Community, and the State*. Durham NC: Duke University Press, 2013.

[Yampolsky, Mariana], Elizabeth Ferrer, Elena Poniatowska, and Francisco Reyes Palma, eds. *Mariana Yampolsky: Imagen, memoria/Image-Memory*. México: Centro de la Imagen, 1999.

Yoshimoto, Midori. *Into Performance: Japanese Women Artists in New York*. New York: Rutgers University Press, 2005.

Zapata Galindo, Martha. "Feminist Movements in Mexico: From Consciousness-Raising Groups to Transnational Networks." In *Feminist Philosophy in Latin America and Spain*. Amsterdam: Rodopi, 2007.

Zapett, Adriana. "Video arte en México." *Discurso Visual*, April–June 2003, http://discursovisual.net/1aepoca/dvweb07/index.html.

Zaragoza, Alex. "The Selling of Mexico: Tourism and the State, 1929–1952." In *Fragments of a Golden Age: The Politics of Culture in Mexico since 1940*, edited by Gilbert M. Joseph et al., 91–115. Durham NC: Duke University Press, 2001.

Zavala, Adriana. "De santa a india bonita: Género, raza y modernidad en la Ciudad de México, 1921." In *Orden social e identidad de género, México siglo XIX y XX*, edited by Maria Teresa Fernández Aceves, Susie Porter, and Carmen Ramos Escandón, 149–88. Guadalajara: UdeG, CIESAS, 2006.

Zolov, Eric. "Expanding Our Conceptual Horizons: The Shift from an Old to a New Left in Latin America." *A Contracorriente* 5, no. 2 (Winter 2008): 47–73.

———. *Refried Elvis: The Rise of the Mexican Counterculture*. Berkeley: University of California Press, 1999.

Zúñiga, Araceli, and César Espinosa. *La perra brava*. México: Sindicato de Trabajadores de la UNAM, 2002.

downtown Mexico City, 177; view
of television, 57
Butler, Cornelia, 169

Calderón, Felipe, 165
Calderón, Miguel, 294
"Campamento 2 de Octubre" (wom-
en's group), 112
Canal 13: all-women news program,
61–62; coverage of IWY celebration,
78; cultural and educational pro-
grams, 61; location of, 61; national
coverage, 108–9; participation of
feminist activists at, 72; programs
on women's issues, 63, 78, 109;
women employed at, 62, 68
Canoa (film), 73–74, 75
Cappa, Cornel, 220
Cardaci, Dora, 313n22
Cárdenas, Lázaro, 130
Cárdenas, Nancy, 84, 137, 314n27
Carillo Gil Museum, 168
Carrasco, Jorge, 269
Carreto, Estela, 150
Carrington, Leonora, 50
Casa de la Mujer (project), 93
Casasola, Agustín Víctor, 20, 213
Casasola's archive, 190, 211, 212, 214
Castillo Ledón, Amalia de, 115, *116*,
130, 131
Castro, Yan María, 314n24
Cazals, Felipe, 73
Centro de Capacitación Cinematográ-
fica, El (CCC), 73
*Centro Libre de Experimentacion
Teatral y Artística* (CLETA), 110, *111*
Centro Universitario de Estudios Cin-
ematográficos, El (CUEC), 74, 76

Cervantes, Chela, 314n24
Chapa, Esther, 130
Chávez, Carlos, 60
Chávez, Oscar, 33–34, 35, 41, 55
Chicago, Judy, 51, 115
China Poblana dressing style, 194
Chungara de Barrios, Domitila, 136–
37, 318n21; *Let Me Speak!* testimony, 136
Cihuatl (feminist publication), 80, 100
Cine-Mujer. *See* Colectivo Cine-
Mujer
Cineteca Nacional, 73, 310n41
citizenship, concept of embodied, 89
city: as allegory, 283; definition of, 9;
exploration of, 291
Coalición de Mujeres Feministas
(CMF): basic rights demand, 200;
campaign for decriminalization of
abortion, 99–100; demonstrations
organized by, 100–101, 103–4, 106,
108, 112–13, *114*; establishment of,
99, 200, 324n24; feminization of
masculine concepts by, 106; liberal
feminist ideology of, 44; *Miss Revolución* proposal, 106; performances
of, 198, *199*
Coalition of Workers, Peasants and
Students of the Isthmus, 202
Colectivo Bio-Arte (feminist art collective), 174
Colectivo Cine-Mujer (feminist art
collective): Cecilia's legal case and,
247; establishment of, 13, 76, 81, 233,
235; legacies of, 246, 248; members
of, 330n1; politics in the art of,
81–82

López, Nacho (*continued*)
representation of women, 222, 223–24; reputation, 217, 220; teaching career, 220; theory of new photojournalism, 220; "Un día cualquiera en la vida de la ciudad" (photoessay), 222–23, 224, 225
López, Rogelio, 328n62
López Moctezuma, Juan, 309n26
López Portillo, José, 46, 162, 292, 293
López Portillo de Tamayo, Marta, 150
Luna, Federico, 276

Machete, El (magazine), 307n56
Maciunas, George, 255
Madre por un día (Mother for a day) television project, 28, 64–66
Madrid, Miguel de la, 293
Manet, Edouard, 272
Mangino, Fernando, 254, 276
Marks, Laura U., 251
Materia nupcial (film), 243
Mattelart, Armand, 59
Mayer, Lila Lucido de, 112, 113, 115, *116, 155,* 173
Mayer, Mónica: appearance on television, 63, 64, 65, 66–67, 68, 81, 309n19; on archival practices, 144; art workshops of, 173; Cecilia's legal case and, 247; Colectivo Cine-Mujer and, 13, 17, 29, 233, 234, 246–47; creation of Jiménez's archive, 17–18, 139, 143, 146; education, 16, 49; *El tendedero* (The Clothesline), 1, 3, 297–98; exploration of sexual desires, 168–69, *170;* feminist activism of, 16–17, 113, 157, 291; influence of, 5, 27; interview with, 12;

¡Madres! project, 67; performances of, 177; Pinto Mi Raya project, 142, 143; on Pola Weiss's video, 269; Polvo de Gallina Negra and, 174; publications of, 173; on television, 57; *Traducciones* project, 115, 117, *117;* view of feminist art, 48, 173, 176
Mayo, Luis, 221
McLuhan, Marshall, 71, 256
media: conference on future of, 71; development of new regimes of, 5, 120–21; independent outlets, 224–25; international transformation of, 121; and production of knowledge, 5
mediascapes, concept of, 9
media studies, 63, 291
Medina, Cuauhtémoc, 146, 210
Medina, Elsa, 227, *228,* 231
Memora Project, 146
Mena, Inocencio, 288
Méndez, Leopoldo, 129
Mexican Communist Party, 110
Mexican Council for Arts and Culture (CNCA), 229
Mexican dressing styles, 193–94
Mexican lesbian manifesto, 137
Mexican muralism, 167
Mexican National Archives, 163–64
Mexican Revolution, 8, 212
Mexico: anthropological expeditions, 193; arts and craft, 35, 52, 54; Civic Code, 93; constitutional reform, 46, 55, 151; democratic reforms in, 18–19, 35; economic crisis, 172; Federal Law of Archives, 164–65; first feminist congress in, 194; gender inequalities in society, 43; intellectual sector, 5–6; Labor Laws,

Vázquez Mantecón, Álvaro, 332n22

Velasco, Raúl, 59

video: as alternative to television broadcasting, 258; as archival practice, 257, 258–59; in indigenous communities, production of, 289

video art: emergence of, 70, 255–56; in exhibitions and festivals, 70–71, 256–57; feminist movement and, 256; lack of recognition of, 274; narcissism in, 250; pioneers of, 256; potentials of, 72; vs. video installation, 264

Video art nueva estética visual (exhibition), 71, 257–58

Videocosmos (TV program), 259

videodance, genre of, 250

video technology, 60, 69, 70, 72–73, 334n27

Villagarcía, Rocío, 100

Villagrán, José, 85

visual letradas: development of, 6, 8–9, 232, 291; effect on regimes of media and visuality, 294–95; new generation of, 295, 296–97; outline of, 11–18; as political subjects, 23, 24; studies of, 7

Vostell, Wolf, 255

WACK! Art and the Feminist Revolution (exhibition), 11, 300n17

Walker, Louise, 151

Warhol, Andy, 140

Warner, Michael, 154

Weiss, Kitzia, 276

Weiss, Leopoldo, 261

Weiss, Pola: artistic practices of, 30; bachelor's thesis, 260; career, 249, 250, 257, 259, 280; creation of playful neologisms, 251; embodied relation with video technology, 249–50, 260; exchanges with Shigeko Kubota, 260, 263, 264–66, *265*, *267*; exhibitions, 274, 275, 278; experiments with video technology, 15–16, 69–70, 72, 73; exploration of self, 249, 286; feminist activism, 291–92; government support of, 274; graphic manifesto of, 266, 269; influence of, 5, 27; legacies of, 253–54, 255; as love-goddess *Venusina*, 278; myth about suicide of, 254, 274; participation in *IX Encuentro internacional de video*, 71–72, 266; performance at the Museo del Chopo, 280; personal archive, 254–55, 301n26; political activism, 8, 30; on potential of video, 258–59; promotion of video art by, 266; recognition of, 255, 274; representation of female bodies by, 290; reputation, 253–54; *Salón 77–78 Bienal de Febrero Nuevas Tendencias*, 270, *271*; as screen writer, 310n28; television production company of, 70; trip to Europe, 69; trip to the U.S., 266; use of video in television broadcasting, 81, 258; on vagina, 266; video production practices, 16, 252, 259–60, 270–71, 273–74, 277, 278–80, 336n72

Weiss's films, videos, and performances: *Autovideoato* (video), 261, *262*; *Ciudad-mujer-ciudad* (video), 14, 15, *17*, 269, 283; *Cuetzalan y yo* (video), 276–77, *277*; *Cuilapan de Guerrero* (video), 276; *David* (video), 273, *273*, 277; *El Salto 1 and*

Murder and Counterrevolution in Mexico: The Eyewitness Account of German Ambassador Paul von Hintze, 1912–1914
Edited and with an introduction by Friedrich E. Schuler

Deco Body, Deco City: Female Spectacle and Modernity in Mexico City, 1900–1939
Ageeth Sluis

Pistoleros and Popular Movements: The Politics of State Formation in Postrevolutionary Oaxaca
Benjamin T. Smith

Alcohol and Nationhood in Nineteenth-Century Mexico
Deborah Toner

Death Is All around Us: Corpses, Chaos, and Public Health in Porfirian Mexico City
Jonathan M. Weber

To order or obtain more information on these or other University of Nebraska Press titles, visit nebraskapress.unl.edu.

CPSIA information can be obtained
at www.ICGtesting.com
Printed in the USA
LVHW041622270219
608947LV00001B/87